V&R

Novum Testamentum et Orbis Antiquus

Series Archaeologica 9

Ancient Magdala Excavations Series (AMES) 1

Bruno Callegher

Coins and Economy in Magdala/Taricheae

With a Foreword by Rosario Pierri OFM
and a Contribution by Arianna D'Ottone

In collaboration with the Studium Biblicum Franciscanum (SBF) of Jerusalem

Vandenhoeck & Ruprecht

Bibliographic information published by the Deutsche Nationalbibliothek:
The Deutsche Nationalbibliothek lists this publication in the Deutsche Nationalbibliographie; detailed bibliographic data available online: https://dnb.de.

Typesetting by SchwabScantechnik, Göttingen
Printed and bound by ⊕ Hubert & Co, Göttingen
Printed in the EU

Vandenhoeck & Ruprecht Verlage | www.vandenhoeck-ruprecht-verlage.com

ISSN 1420-4622
ISBN 978-3-525-50193-1

Table of Contents

Foreword

The first stone has been laid. The Custody of the Holy Land has long awaited the publication of the results of the latest excavation campaigns in Magdala, if only for the considerable economic commitment undertaken over the years to finance them. The importance of the site for archaeologists engaged in research at or around the shores of Lake Tiberias is significant. The good news that we can finally draw from the data offered by the coins found in Magdala will certainly be welcomed by the academic community with great enthusiasm.

This volume by Prof. Bruno Callegher is the first in a series intended to make known the results of these excavations, and it augurs well, because the laborious publication of the volumes on the excavations of Magdala – more precisely of that area of the city, which is owned by the Custody of the Holy Land – has launched.

With painstaking detail, Prof. Callegher reconstructs the history of the excavations of the site and therefore it is preferable to leave this story and the history of Magdala/Taricheae to him. Following the careful study of the coins discovered, I limit myself to giving proper attention to the importance the city, with its vicissitudes, had between the 1st and 5th centuries within the commercial and political context of a specific geographical area. It turns out to be strategic for the exchanges between the Mediterranean and the lands beyond the lake. Furthermore, from the accurate reconstruction of Prof. Callegher, a fact of considerable importance is revealed, namely the correspondence between the scant sources on Magdala and the lively economic activity that guaranteed its discrete prosperity.

Tradition has it that this site corresponds to Mary of Magdala's city of origin. And even if the imagination has sometimes taken the upper hand in the sources that speak of it, those remains still interest us nonetheless because they are connected to this unique figure mentioned in the gospels, she who became part of the group of women who followed Jesus (Lk 8:2). This is the real reason that prompted the Custody of the Holy Land to persevere in the attempts to acquire that piece of land along the shores of Lake Tiberias. 1903 saw the first attempts but it was only in 1922 that the acquisition was finalized. Anyone who knows the history of the Custody even briefly, will also know that the Franciscan friars have always had at heart the protection of places linked to the Gospel accounts, following a centuries-old tradition that dates back to the first epoch of Christianity. Being in the vicinity of Capernaum that was preserved, Magdala too had to be preserved, and so it was.

In view of the mission entrusted to it by the Church, the Custody intended to re-evaluate the site with the aim above all, of offering pilgrims a place to visit; a place that recalls a woman whose life was transfigured by her encounter with Jesus of Nazareth and by his word.

From this point of view, archaeological investigations are certainly of great importance but they are not decisive. We have not gone in search of the home of the Magdalene, but we are also only interested in the fact that Jesus had passed through one of those streets – the layout of which has been brought to light – and that either there or elsewhere he met a woman named Mary who became his disciple, followed him to Jerusalem in the days of his Passion, and was commanded by the Risen One to go and announce to the disciples his return to the Father (Jn 20:17). Archeology directs its own course as it always has.

In 1935 Frs. Sylvester Saller and Bellarmino Bagatti visited the site for an initial reconnaissance conducted on behalf of the then Custos, Fr. Nazzareno Iacopozzi; but it was only in 1971 that the first excavation campaign was conducted by Frs. Virgilio Corbo and Stanislao Loffreda. The sole purpose of mentioning these beginnings is to remind that the later achievements were possible thanks to the pioneering work of scholars of that caliber.

The *Ancient Magdala Excavations Series* (*AMES*), which I have the honor of inaugurating with this foreword, will comprise of seven volumes. It is my personal hope that these can be published in due time.

The first volume is published by Brill | Vandenhoeck & Ruprecht. In the name of the Custody and the SBF, I express my sincere thanks to all who have worked and collaborated in various capacities to bring this challenging project to completion.

Jerusalem, 12th January 2023
Rosario Pierri, Dean SBF

Abbreviations

AASOR	The Annual of the American Schools of Oriental Research
AIIN	Annali dell'Istituto Italiano di Numismatica
AJN	American Journal of Numismatics
AqN	Aquileia nostra. International Journal of Ancient Studies on Northern Adriatic Region
ATar	Antiquité Tardive
BAAL	Bulletin d'Archéologie et d'Architecture Libanaises
BAH	Bibliothèque Archéologique et Historique. Paris
BASOR	Bulletin of American School of Oriental Research
BMC. *Phoenicia*	Hill G. F., *A Catalogue of the Greek Coins in the British Museum. Catalogue of the Greek Coins of Phoenicia*, London 1910
BMC. *The Ptolemies. King of Egypt*	BMC. *A Catalogue of the Greek Coins in the British Museum. The Ptolemies*, Kings of Egypt, London 1883
BMGS	Byzantine and Modern Greek Studies
CH	*Coin Hoards*, London 1975–
CHL	Meshorer Y., Bijovsky G., Fischer-Bossert W., *Coins of the Holy Land. The Abraham and Marian Sofaer Collection and the American Numismatic Society and the Israel Museum*, I–II, New York 2013
DOC I	*Catalogue of the Byzantine Coins in the Dumbaton Oaks Collection and the Whittemore Collection, I, Anastasius to Maurice 491–602*, Washington 1966
DOC II.1	*Catalogue of the Byzantine coins in the Dumbarton Oaks Collection and in the Whittemore Collection, Phocas to Theodosius III. 602–717, Part 1, Phocas and Heraclius (602–641)*, Washington 1968
Hadashot Arkheologiyot	Ḥadashot Arkheologiyot. Excavations and Surveys in Israel
IEJ	Israel Exploration Journal
IMJ	Israel Museum Journal
INJ	Israel Numismatic Journal
INR	Israel Numismatic Research
JAA	Journal of American Archaeology
JRA	Journal of Roman Archaeology
LA	Liber Annuus
LRBC	Carson R. A. G., Hill P. V., Kent J. P. C., *Late Roman Bronze Coinage.* I–II, London 1965
MEFREM	Mélanges de l'École française de Rome – Moyen Âge
MIB	Hahn W., *Moneta Imperii Byzantini*, I–III, Wien 1973–1981
MIBE	Hahn W., Metlich M., *Money of the Incipient Byzantine Empire*, Wien 2000
MIBEC	Hahn W., Metlich M., *Money of the Incipient Byzantine Empire Continued*, Wien 2009
NAC	Quaderni Ticinesi. Numismatica e Antichità Classiche
NC	The Numismatic Chronicle
PRQ	Palestine Exploration Quarterly
RB	Revue Biblique
RBN	Revue Belge de Numismatique
RIC	*Roma Imperial Coinage*, voll. 1–10, London 1923–1994 (and revised editions)
RIN	Rivista Italiana di Numismatica
RN	Revue Numismatique
RPC I	Burnett A., Amandry M., Pau Ripollès P., *Roman Imperial Coinage. I. From the death of Caesar to the death of Vitellius (44BC-AD69)*, London-Paris 1992
RPC II	Burnett A., Amandry M., Carradice I., *Roman Provincial Coinage*. II. *From Vespasian to Domitian (AD 69–96)*, London-Paris 1999
SC	*Seleucid Coins. A Comprehensive Catalogue*. Part 2.1. *Seleucus IV through Antiochus XIII*, Lancaster/London 2008

SICA	Album S., Goodwin T., *Sylloge of Islamic Coins in the Ashmolean, 1, The Pre-Reform Coinage of the Early Islamic Period*, Oxford 2002
SNAT 1993	Ilisch L., *Sylloge Numorum Arabicorum Tübingen: Palästina IV a Bilād aš-Šām* I, Tübingen 1993
SNG. Danish. *Egypt. The Ptolemies*	SNG. *Sylloge Nummorum Graecorum. The Royal Collection of Coins and Medals. Danish National Museum. Egypt: the Ptolemies*, Copenhagen 1977
SNG. Danish. *Syria. Seleucid Kings*	SNG. *Sylloge Nummorum Graecorum. The Royal Collection of Coins and Medals. Danish National Museum. Syria: Seleucid Kings*, Copenhagen 1959
SNG. *Israel* I	SNG. *Sylloge Nummorum Graecorum. Israel. The Arnold Spaer Collection of Seleucid Coins*, Jerusalem/London 1998
VAMZ	Vjesnik Arheološkog muzeja u Zagrebu – Journal of the Archaeological Museum in Zagreb
ZDPV	Zeitschrift des Deutschen Palästina-Vereins
ZPE	Zeitschrift für Papyrologie und Epigraphik
Τοποι	Τοποι Orient-Occident

Something more than a beginning

It was thanks to the study of the numismatic documentation of Capernaum, conducted prior to the start of the excavation campaigns of the Studium Biblicum Franciscanum (hereafter SBF)-Custody of the Holy Land, that similar research was extended to the monetary findings from the nearby site of Magdala.[1] Here, in fact, the archaeologists of the SBF[2] from the 1970s until 2013[3] carried out various excavation campaigns aimed at discovering the real extent of the archaeological remains, but also (and perhaps above all) the relationship between archaeological evidence and the written sources that had preserved records of Magdala/Migdal.[4] The task of studying this numismatic dossier was given to me by Giovanni Claudio Bottini, Dean of the SBF. At that time, the numismatic documentation only referred to the area investigated on the property of the Custody of the Holy Land. The first excavations, dated at least to 1970/71, took place in the stretch between a monastery of Byzantine layout, some Roman-era roadways, several buildings with different functions or chronology, and finally the lake port.

Later, from 1991–1992, over twenty years after those pioneering explorations, the Israel Antiquities Authority [hereafter IAA] initiated a number of archaeological excavations to the west and south of the area considered here. The aim was to verify the extent of a settlement relevant to the history of Palestine in the Hasmonean and Roman periods, widely mentioned by the historian Flavius Josephus. Additional investigations by the IAA followed in 2002. Shortly afterwards, an economic-religious development project called "Magdala Center" led to the discovery of a probable synagogue from the first century CE and one of the oldest a menorah image,[5] prompting – from 2005 – the exploration of the site that took on the dimension of a large-scale systematic urban excavation. The considerable historical-documentary significance of these discoveries caused the archaeological excavations to be extended as far as possible in order to define

1 Rahmani 1980 and subsequent clarification in Rahmani 1981 published a hoard from the Crusader period (Moneta regis), while in Wilson 1989a and Wilson 1989b both individual coin findings with a broad chronology and hoards from the Umayyad period collected in the area of the Greek Orthodox patriarchate in Jerusalem were made known. Callegher 1997, finally, edited a hoard of Byzantine gold coinage from the mid-seventh century. In general, on the numismatics of Capernaum: Tzaferis 1989; Arslan 1996a; Arslan 1996b; Arslan 1997; Arslan 2003a; Arslan 2003b; Arslan 2003c; Callegher 2007a; Callegher 2007b; Callegher 2010; Arslan 2011; Callegher 2016. A summary of all published numismatic data can be found in Mattila 2015, p. 223. Arslan 2021 recently examined some coins or roundels used as amulets.

2 This, the information provided in the foreword and the entire archaeological history of the site, will be accounted for below, especially in the notes and bibliography.

3 The first excavations were conducted by Virgilio Corbo; after about thirty years, they were resumed by Stanislao Loffreda & Michele Piccirillo, scientific heads of the Magdala Project [hereinafter MP] between 2008–2013 coordinated by the designer Stefano De Luca for whose popular reports cf. De Luca 2008; De Luca 2009; De Luca 2011; archaeological-scientific reports in Lena 2013.

4 Manns 1976a. Little added by De Luca, Leibner 2019. Essential for the contribution of economic analysis are Mattila 2013 and Mattila 2015, as they combine archaeological data and sources.

5 Preliminary reports on this part of the archaeological area in Abu-'Uqsa 2001; Abu-'Uqsa 2005; Avshalom-Gorni 2009a; Avshalom-Gorni 2009b; Avshalom-Gorni, Najar 2013.

the extent of the settlement and its function in relation to other historical sites on the shore of Lake Kinneret, and most importantly to plan a unified recovery and increase its value. Other emergency excavations, undertaken between 2009 and 2013 in collaboration with the Universidad Anáhuac México Sur and the Universidad Nacional Autónoma de México [hereinafter MAP], were motivated by the construction of tourist hotel facilities. All this took place around the area that had been acquired by the Custody of the Holy Land in 1935. As a result, the SBF was in tune with the renewed interest, not only archaeologically for the entire site of Magdala for which the urbanistic aspects and the material culture over the centuries of its frequentation remained to be defined, but also more generally its role in the framework of Hellenistic-Roman Galilee. Precisely these archaeological-historical aspects had already motivated the Corbo-Loffreda excavations in the 1970s and the recent Magdala Project [hereinafter MP].

The undoubtedly unique documentary potential of the archaeology of Magdala is confirmed by the interest shown by the numerous institutes and authorities involved. The singularity of the site is an essential motivation for any research not tainted by ideologies or uncritically constructed expectations sought to be later confirmed in the excavation. At the same time, the many stakeholders involved in each aspect of the study make it very difficult to proceed to a unitary analysis of any class of finds, in this case coins.[6] If, for the plots owned by the Custody of the Holy Land, Stanislao Loffreda's generous and profound archaeological expertise made it possible to unify the numismatic data from the 1970s excavations with those collected during the MP's long activity. The same was not possible with the same numismatic data from excavations in the surrounding areas and, generally, from the site included in the MAP. The limitation of having access only to the coins concerning a part of the site motivated the search for the sharing of numismatic data. A different approach would have prevented the reconstruction of an exhaustive monetary-economic context and reaching fully convincing conclusions regarding the frequentation of the site, the monetary stock in circulation at a certain period, and the contribution of mints from Galilee, Gaulanitis or the Decapolis. Such a collaboration was explored and attempted several times.[7] One example is the documentable fact that the unpublished catalogue created by the writer has been made available, including the photographic documentation, without any constraints to some colleagues at the IAA, while still a work in progress. That the data of this study have been made available to the archaeological community since their drafting and in the course of the work in progress is evident, *sine ullo dubio*, from the extensive and in many respects unsystematic use found in the essay by Stefano De Luca, "*La città ellenistico-romana di Magdala/Taricheae. Gli scavi del Magdala Project 2007–2009: relazione preliminare e prospettive di indagine,*" *Liber Annuus* 59 (2009), pp. 343–562.[8] In it, once the rhetoric of the formal obligation of ritually mentioning the appointee of the numismatic study had been followed, the monetary data was extensively, too extensively, used as mere chronological indicator. Such schematism, moreover justified by the user with a reference to a so-called autonomous archaeological method[9] – *utinam!* it would have been profitable for everyone if its epistemological foundations or a non-self-referential bibliography of reference had been disclosed – denotes the absence of basic competence in dealing with money in archaeological contexts. In fact, there is no archaeologist in at least the past half century who had disregarded John Casey's standard book, *Coins and the Archaeologist*, Oxford 1974 (British Archaeological Reports) or Richard Reece's numerous articles, now collected in *Roman Coins and Archaeology. Collected papers*, Wetteren 2003 (Collection Moneta 32).[10] The preliminary report of 2009 will be disregarded in

6 Several times there have been attempts to initiate a joint publication of the coin findings of the entire site, as evidenced by various emails kept in my personal archives, in particular those of 1 August 2018, when following my visit to the excavation as an anonymous visitor, I received a polite invitation from Danny Sion to tackle this proposal together because, as he recalled: "*Some years ago you suggested that we work jointly on the coins of the site*". Various coordination difficulties on the side of the excavation supervisor of the Holy Land Custody property, Stefano De Luca, procrastinated the time and research making a 'realistic joint publication' impossible.

7 E-mails stored in my personal archive.

8 In the autumn of 2008, the writer sent De Luca the catalogue of coins, a "work in progress" in need of verification, feedback and corrections at a library better equipped for numismatics than what could be consulted at the SBF. At the same time, it was suggested that he "*make use of it as he saw fit*", relying on the policy of the scientific community.

9 This singular assertion can be supported, *inter alia*, by the testimony of two professional archaeologists, not amateurs, who participated in the excavation and were present at a singular syncretum, which took place in 2009 at the SBF, during which I tried to ask for an account of the use of unpublished data: Anna Lena and Carmelo Pappalardo.

10 On the interpretative methodology of coins found both as hoards and as single finds in archaeological contexts, see now Katsari 2011, in part pp. 9–33.

this analysis because of the critical issues arising from establishing links between the dating of a coin (*terminus post quem*) and its stratigraphic contexts, the human presence on site and even with some ceramic classes. Reference to the report will be made only for elements of urban topography and sometimes for the history of archaeological excavations in Magdala.

After the MP's interruption in 2013, when the last brief numismatic survey took place, the dossier remained suspended pending the formation of an Archaeological Board of recognized value that aimed to ensure an editorial project of the entire excavation overseen by accredited specialists. As a matter of fact, this goal even today, in the spring of 2023, has remained on paper and nothing more has been heard of such a unified project.

In the meantime, numismatic finds from the nearby site of Khirbet Wadi Hamam by Gabriela Bijovsky[11] have been published, as well as the fundamental general synthesis by Danny Syon on Upper Galilee, with extensive discussion of the coinage circulating there and the monetary system in use in the region between Gamla and Tyre.[12] These contributions of undisputed standard, including analyses and syntheses on numismatic materials entirely similar to those from the Magdala Scavi Corbo-Loffreda and MP, prompted doubts and questions regarding the validity of an independent publication. The time-consuming work of classifying, compiling the catalogue, and studying such a large monetary dossier ran the risk of being repetitive, of confirming what was already known in the bibliography and demanding excessive time and energy.[13] Nevertheless, certainly well aware of all the limitations arising from a lack of a unified vision, it was decided to publish what had emerged in the archaeological section of the Custody of the Holy Land, comparing the data from the reports by fellow Israeli numismatists Gabriela Bijovsky and Danny Syon, whom I thank for making their data, some of which is still unpublished, available.

******

It is well known that coins, as archaeological finds, are potentially rich in information because they combine chronological, epigraphic, iconographic and most importantly economic data. If these sets of data are then placed in relation to each other and compared to analogous evidence from the same site and similar sites in the same area, it can be easily deduced how coins are to be placed among the most significant sources in the field of archaeology.[14] It seemed to us that this general premise was particularly relevant for the Magdala site [MP]. Moreover, the quantity of coins recovered, thanks to the combination of what was discovered in the course of various excavations, albeit directed by different archaeologists, was compelling. The potential for study, beyond the cataloguing data, would also have concerned economic aspects, in particular the function and use of the circulating stock, examined by periods or persistence of account and monetary systems, in this case quite reliable due to the extensive database available.

Acknowledgements

The long history of this work places Stanislao Loffreda at its beginning: I am grateful to him for his solicitation to study, after Capernaum, also the coins of Magdala, and for the trust he placed in me during our conversations in his archaeological laboratory at the SBF, which were always rich in information and open to scientific discussion. The entire SBF community welcomed me with warmth and cooperation during the study weeks that followed, although irregularly, between 2008 and 2015 as well as in this summer of 2022. Among them, I remember Michele Piccirillo (*sit ei terra levis*), Eugenio Alliata, Deans Giovanni Claudio Bottini, Massimo Pazzini, and Rosario Pierri. To these must be added those involved in the MP, in particular Stefano De Luca and Anna Lena to whom we owe the cleaning, the restoration of some of the coins and the references to the stratigraphic contexts, Ettore Soranzo and Angelo Tosi for the photographic campaign of the coins until 2009. Vanja Macovaz (Trieste) generously took on the propedeutic photographic optimisation to the tables, assembled by Drs. Ella Zulini, Costanza Vecchiet and Paola Maggi, collaborators at the DiSU of the University of Trieste-NummusLab. I also gratefully acknowledge my collaborators Drs. Andrea Gariboldi and Giulio Carraro who read the last version of this work before it went

11 Bijovsky 2018.

12 Syon 2015.

13 Danny Syon asked me to have the catalogue ready for publication at least by the end of 2018 and received it in the latter part of 2020 for use in his Final Report of the MAP numismatic dossier. On the other hand, he himself sent me his Report so that I could have the data from that area. I thank him.

14 Particularly significant are the considerations on the interpretation of the coin findings presented in Syon 2015, pp. 31–39 especially as they pertain to Galilee. In general, especially for the provinces of the Roman Empire see Katsari 2011, pp. 19–33.

to press. My sincere thanks also go to the translators Hannah Wilson and Michol Stocco for their meticulous work, to Jürgen K. Zangenberg for careful editing and the team at Vandenhoeck&Ruprecht for the fruitful and effective collaboration.

Special thanks go to Donald Ariel and Robert Kool, Chief Curators of the Coin Cabinet of the Israel Antiquities Authority, for their hospitality during the research of the topographical library in his office, where working on the coins found at the sites is extremely well facilitated by the excellent organisation of data and articles or monographs in alphabetical and topographical order.

I am indebted to Haim Gitler (Israel Museum) and Yaniv Schauer (Israel Museum) for the identification of the specimen *256 and to Gabriela Bijovsky (IAA) for the coins *960, *1006 and especially to Danny Syon for making his report and database of the coins found in the MAP area, which he classified, available to me and for authorizing quantitative comparisons (Syon forthcoming).

The greatest, and unpayable, debt, however, is to Rita and Dotty, who have always expressed nothing but approval for my long absences from home. They have always been with me, not only in memory, but at the heart of my thoughts.

1. Introduction

The site of Magdala is suitable for various historical and cultural investigations: firstly with an excursus on the ancient and medieval sources that mention it[1] as the possible birthplace of Mary of Magdala,[2] a central figure in the evangelical narrative;[3] then for its etymological complexity in the various sources;[4] and even for the real coincidence between ancient Magdala and the present site.[5] From other perspectives, and of no less importance, is the examination of the Greek and Latin sources, especially Flavius Josephus[6] and the Rabbinic sources, the latter being indispensable not only for topographical data but above all because they recall the existence of a synagogue and a beth-midrash in Magdala itself between the second and third centuries.[7] However, for the purposes of our study, we chose to focus on the long and arduous archaeological rediscovery of this site, as a premise for contextualizing the study of the monetary finds.

The village known as al-Majdal (but also Mejdel) during the nineteenth century, i. e. in Ottoman times, was no more than a modest agglomeration of almost uninhabited hovels, leaning against some ancient ruins.

1 Manns 1976a remains indispensable, although rarely cited in bibliographies perhaps because it is written in French, a language certainly not marginal in antiquities studies; De Luca, Leibner 2019.

2 Schaberg 2004, especially chapter two: *Meditation at Migdal*; Taylor 2014.

3 In the excursus of historical sources in Zapata-Meza *et al.* 2018, p. 83, the reference to the Polish pope John Paul II is aimed at establishing a connection between this archaeological site and Mary Magdalene as “the apostle to the apostles”. The procedure is not scientific but unmethodical because the head of the Christian Catholic religious confession has nothing to do with archaeological research and science when he speaks of religious topics.

4 It was decided to follow Manns 1976a. The Hebrew form is Migdal; the Aramaic form is known as Magdala Nunaya (Nunnaya or Nunayah meaning ‘Tower of Fish’) or Magdala Tza’baya (or Seb’iya) meaning ‘Magdala of the dyers’). Thus, it is also mentioned in the Jerusalem (Ta’anit 4.8) and Babylonian Talmud (Pesahim 46b). In Greek and Latin sources, the city is also known as Magdala/Taricheae, i. e. ‘Magdala of the fish salters’, cf. also Bauckham 2018. Kokkinos 2012 insists on an alternative location.

5 Much has been debated about Magdala’s exact location in relation to Tiberias. In this regard, the topographical conclusions shared almost unanimously in the most recent literature are accepted, to which De Luca 2009 and De Luca, Leibner 2019, pp. 407–411 add nothing new.

6 Flavius Josephus, *Jewish War, ad indicem.*

7 For the sake of correctness, not knowing Hebrew, I have referred to Manns 1976a where Tosefta Erubin 6/13, Talmud of Jerusalem (Erubin 5,22d), Talmud of Babylon (Erubin 61a) are cited, as well as passages in Bereshit Rabbah 79,6 the Pesiqta de Rab Cahana (Pisqa 10) but also Eicha Rabbati 3,8,3 and Ma’aser Scheni 5,2 are referred to for the synagogue, the beth-midrash and the scribe Nikai.

Photo 1: El-Majdal in the late nineteenth century. From the Library of Congress at Washington DC (https://en.wikipedia.org/wiki/Magdala#/media/File:Magdala_um_1900.jpg)[8].

[8]This is how eighteenth-century travelers saw it. Indeed, Ulrich Jasper Seetzen (1767–1811)[9] in 1807 stayed, without further specification, in 'the little Mahommedan village of Majdil, situated on the bank of the lake',[10] but he does not describe any monumental or archaeological finds or artefacts there. Likewise, no signs of antiquity were identified by Edward Robinson (1794–1863)[11]during his exploratory trip in 1838[12]. Reports by other travelers, such as William Francis Lynch (1801–1865),[13] Solomon Caesar Malan (1812–1894),[14] Bayard Taylor (1825–1878)[15] and Isabel Arundell (1831–1896) wife of Richard Francis Burton (1821–1890)[16] agree that the village was of miserable stone houses, mostly in ruins. In 1910 it was seen unchanged, poor and almost depopulated, by the Russian Zionists who settled not far away and founded modern Migdal. The transformations following the fall of the Ottoman Empire did not change Majdal's economy or construction, but favored, particularly during the first phase of the British Mandate, a significant population increase.[17] About a century ago, at the beginning of the 1920s, one of the first guides to be widely circulated among Christian pilgrims described it as follows: *"4 km from Tiberias, at the roots of the*

8 Petersen 2001, p. 210.
9 Kark, Goren 2011.
10 Seetzen 1810, p. 20.
11 Soler 2014.
12 Robinson, Smith 1841, p. 278.
13 Lynch 1849, p. 164; cf. also https://archive.org/stream/narrativeunited03lyncgoog#page/n202/mode/1up.
14 Malan 2012.
15 https://en.wikipedia.org/wiki/Bayard_Taylor.
16 Arundell 1875; Zilli 2019.
17 Government of Palestine, Department of Statistics. Village Statistics, April, 1945. Quoted in Hadawi, 1970, p. 122, 172. http://www.palestineremembered.com/download/VillageStatistics/Table%20II/Tiberias/Page-122.jpg; http://www.palestineremembered.com/download/VillageStatistics/Table%20III/Tiberias/Page-172.jpg.

Photo 2: Magdala before archaeological intervention by Virgilio Corbo (©SBF Photographic Archive. Virgilio Corbo, 17 February 1977).

mountain that forms the southern flank of the 'Uâdi el Hamâm, or valley of the Pigeons, one encounters a poor village called el Megidel. Near the hovels stands a small Muslim Ueli. The village bears traces of a wall and two towers, the northernmost of which was used by some dyers. El Megidel is, as we have already seen, ancient Magdala. A city of great importance was Magdala, according to the Talmud. It was divided into several quarters, among which are mentioned that of the Fish, or Migdal Numya, and that of the Dyers, or Migdal Ceboya"[18]. It was not much, but the pilgrim could see the Biblical narrative in real life and at the same time be aware of the etymological and functional complexity of the ancient site.

The aforementioned Guide also indicates an upswing in pilgrimage to the places of Christianity. So much so that new individuals had recently settled in Galilee, in particular the Franciscans, precisely to cope with and follow the influx of pilgrims. They had been dedicated for centuries to the custody of the places identifiable with those frequented by the Jew Yehoshua, the Jesus of the Gospels.[19] Between the end of the nineteenth century and 1912, they had purchased from German military engineer R[udolf?] Lendle, an archaeology enthusiast,[20] a plot of land facing the lake because there were ruins worthy of investigation which could perhaps provide some useful clues to locate another "holy" place, not far from Capernaum, in this case for Mary of Magdala.[21] It was this identical goal that motivated Bellarmino Bagatti (1905–1990)[22] and Sylvester Saller (1895–1976)[23] in 1935 to begin negotiations to extend the Franciscans' property. They met a certain Mutlaq, the head of the village with his entire family, according to Ottoman-Turkish tradition a Muhktar, who were then owners and residents of the adjoining land, but the attempts to purchase of the adjoining land was not successful.[24] The site and the Muhktar property itself

18 Meistermann 1925, p. 567.
19 Meir 1991.

20 Schaberg 2004, p. 50. I do not know any bio-bibliographical references about him and especially any accounts of his excavations. He might have been the German military engineer and cartographer Rudolf Lendl, who accompanied Alois Musil (1868–1944), an archaeologist who was particularly interested in the late antique and early Islamic archaeology of the Syrian-Palestinian region: cf. Vaselá 2012, p. 61–62, 85, 206.
21 Loffreda 1976b, p. 133.
22 Piccirillo 2001.
23 Saller 1957.
24 Bagatti 1971, p. 81.

were then affected by the events following the founding of the state of Israel and the first Arab-Israeli war in 1948 to the extent that some hovels were destroyed and the property abandoned.[25]

The 1970s marked the definitive take-off of the area, especially thanks to the Custody of the Holy Land which acquired some of the land bordering that of the first purchase and had a small building constructed there, mainly for the surveillance and conservation of the site That the area was of considerable archaeological interest was known by those interested in the historical exegesis of the New Testament, and especially by the generation of archaeologists who received consensus and expectations from the new Israeli state.[26] Thus from November 1971, and with substantial continuity in the following years until 1977, Virgilio Corbo (1918–1991)[27] and Stanislao Loffreda investigated a large part of the Franciscan property, often having to contend with inexhaustible springs and a vegetation of wild palm trees.[28] They brought to light a building that was then interpreted as a small synagogue, a water collector/cistern, mosaic fragments of buildings of various sizes and the section of a roadway. They hypothesized that ancient Magdala must have had an urban layout of considerable size, with living quarters and buildings of value, all elements consistent with a settlement with an extension and urban planning referable to a town rather than a *vicus*-village.

Photo 3a

Photo 3b

25 Bagatti 1971, p. 83; Morris 2004, p. 86: https://books.google.it/ books?id=uM_kFX6edX8C&pg=PA86&redir_esc=y#v=onepage&q&f=false. This event is briefly discussed in Testaferri 2015, p. 407.

26 However, it seems singular that in the notes and bibliography of the https://en.wikipedia.org/wiki/Al-Majdal,_Tiberias site, there is no explicit reference to the Franciscans' pioneering presence and publications in the archaeology of Magdala. Of course, as always, the motivation must be sought in the Italian language, which is also marginal in this case, but the drafters who did give evidence of knowledge of other chronicle details, rather make the impression of a deliberate removal.

27 Corbo 1974; Corbo 1976; Corbo 1978; Corbo 1989.

28 The unpublished excavation diaries are preserved in the SBF Archive: Vigilio Corbo, Diario di scavo. I. 1973–1974; Stanislao Loffreda. Excavation Diary. II. 1973–1977. I thank the director of the SBF Museum, Eugenio Alliata for this information. Bagatti 1971, pp. 68–71 and figs. 33–34.

Photos 3a–c: : Magdala during archaeological excavations by Virgilio Corbo and Stanislao Loffreda (©SBF Photographic Archive. Stanislao Loffreda, 1978?)[29].

A decade later, between 1991 and 1992, the IAA planned archaeological excavations in two areas (area A, area B)[30] outside of Corbo and Loffreda's excavation areas with the aim of partly verifying the extent of the urban area of ancient Magdala and confirming the topographical hypotheses already advanced.[31] Other interventions date back to 2002, this time in the south of area B, to which two new plots named C and D were added, in which medieval and Ottoman archaeological artefacts were found, proving a long period of frequentation.[32] Shortly afterwards, however, major urban development projects (the first called Magdala Center, the second aimed at enhancing the coastline with tourist hotel buildings) were planned by various archaeological missions for at least a decade until 2013. This was done by Israeli archaeologists both independently and in collaboration with the Universidad Anáhuac México Sur and the Universidad Nacional Autónoma de México [MAP]. Once again, those responsible were from the SBF's Department of Archaeology[33]. This is not the place for even a brief exposition of what was found, but as of 2010 it can be stated that archaeology in Magdala had radically altered what had been known about town planning until then, in particular the connection between the lake port, the road network, the settlements, and the public and private buildings.[34] Enormous and as yet unpublished is the amount of data: ceramics, transport containers, mosaics,[35] cores for pollen and palaeobotanical analyses,[36] everyday objects, the well-known 'minor objects' highly revealing regarding local taste and way of life. Since 2010, however, the locality recorded by Cassius and Cicero, Strabo and Pliny the Elder, Suetonius, Flavius Josephus, Rabbinic texts, the Synoptics and numerous late antique and medieval sources,[37] ceased to be known in a succinct manner, and the scientific community had enough elements such as to outdate all previous reconstructions. Not a village, but a typical settlement comparable with other towns on the banks of the Kinneret to be contextualized in Galilee, related to the settlements of Decapolis and the southern part of Phoenicia. Magdala emerged from historical marginality, from indeterminacy, to be confronted with the archaeology and historical investigations of numerous settlements in Galilee in order to define their constants and their diversity, not only locally, and illuminate their possible role in the economy of Galilee and the regions in various ways united by belonging to the sphere of the Kinneret.[38]

29 Corbo 1976, *passim*; Loffreda 1976a; Loffreda 1976b.
30 For the locations outside the area covered by the MP excavations and the previous excavations see the indications published in Zapata-Meza *et al.* 2018, p. 84, fig. 2.
31 Abu-'Uqsa 2001; Abu-'Uqsa 2005; Avshalom-Gorni 2009a; Avshalom-Gorni 2009b; Avshalom-Gorni, Najar 2013.
32 Testaferri 2015, p. 418.
33 Its creators were Giovanni Claudio Bottini, rector of the SBF, Stanislao Loffreda, *olim* in charge, together with Virgilio Corbo, of the 1971–1975 excavation campaigns, (+) Michele Piccirillo and the designer Stefano De Luca since 2009, *post mortem* of Piccirillo, coordinator of the MP on behalf of the SBF and the Custody of the Holy Land under whose responsibility the actual and scientific management of the site's archaeology remains to this very day.
34 The conclusions of De Luca 2009 apply.
35 De Luca, Lena 2014b.
36 Lena, Rossi, Palmieri, Marchesini 2017.
37 An exhaustive list of passages and quotations in Manns 1976a; for the Middle Ages useful De Luca, Leibner 2019.
38 Fiensy, Strange 2014; Fiensy, Strange 2015.

Photo 4a

Photos 4a–b: Magdala after the MAP archaeological excavations (©Archivio fotografico SBF. Stefano De Luca 2012).

2. Numismatics and archaeology in Magdala/Taricheae

Status quaestionis and methodological notes

As has often been the case with various localities in the Holy Land where some form of religious cult has stratified over time, it is difficult if not impossible to establish a certain point in time from which numismatic research can begin. Over the centuries, clandestine excavations, the recovery of building material, agricultural work and tampering of various degrees and nature took place in these settlements. During the first decades of the twentieth century, an increasingly rigorous application of systematic archaeological methods favored not only the protection of architectural and monumental elements, but also renewed the attention to so-called minor testimonies which also included coins. What happened in the area of Magdala over the course of many centuries is not dissimilar, and in the accounts of the pilgrims there is no mention of any archaeological excavations or coin findings, not even accidental. The earliest reports of excavated coins known to this writer, albeit in general terms, date back to the excavations of 1971–1973 because Corbo recalls that "*coins found in the same slime* [of a drainage channel] *are being studied*"[1], though many were thrown back into the lake by those same archaeologists because they were tiny, corroded and illegible.[2] It was not a great method, but that was sometimes the practice in those decades when two functions were essentially attributed to the coin: chronological and aesthetic. In reality, the information is not untrue, as a significant percentage of the numismatic specimens collected during the MP excavations conform to that narrative: many specimens are so corroded as to be unreadable, unless one wants to let the imagination run wild on the basis of the size of the coin and/or weight. As the MP archaeological excavations progressed, urbanistic interpretations of the area of the Custody of the Holy Land began to be proposed, particularly on the topography,[3] the port[4] and the mosaics.[5] No less relevant are the contributions on the remaining area of the site, excavated by the IAA in collaboration with the MAP,[6] the last of which proposes a thorough preliminary edition of the monetary finds from the 2010–2012 excavations.[7] De Luca's lengthy 2009 essay, however, as mentioned, abounded in monetary citations: the word 'coin' appears 47 times, 'coins' 27 times and 'coinage' 21 (a term used as a synonym for currency, thus without distinction between the instrument of production and the outcome of minting), the word 'nominals' is used twice, not counting citations of authorities and mints. In order for the reader to have immediate evidence of De Luca's method, I randomly quote a few passages which are all indistinctly connected by the same conviction: that the coin is merely a chronological indicator to be listed, in sequences of stratigraphic units (US), often confused with stratigraphic wall units (USM), alongside other finds. A first example:

1 Corbo 1975, p. 28.

2 Personal communication by Stanislao Loffreda. On the other side of the Mediterranean Sea, the same thing sometimes happened: in Aquileia, for example, in Brusin 1934, p. 146 we read that 1,000 small bronzes were recovered in the port area that were considered illegible and therefore, in fact, neglected and today are unrecoverable.

3 De Luca 2009.

4 De Luca, Lena 2014a.

5 De Luca, Lena 2014a; De Luca, Leibner 2019.

6 Zapata-Meza et al. 2018.

7 Syon 2018.

"Finds from the collapse disintegration layer include Late Roman ceramic fragments, with a predominance of the common tableware forms, the intact upper element of a rectangular millstone of the hopper and lever type (St 50) (Durante 2001, 78) found leaning against USM 29 near the corner of the room, and the following coins from: Alexander Iannæus (103–76 BC), Aretas IV issued in Petra (9 BC–AD 40), Trajan of the Roman mint (AD 98–117), Hadrianus of the Roman mint (AD 119–122), Trajan Decius-Volusianus of Caesarea Maritima (AD 249–253), provincial Roman mint (II–1/2 III cent. AD), provincial Roman mint with oval countermark with male head (possibly second cent. AD), provincial Roman mint with oval countermark (second–1/2 third cent. AD)".[8]

Or another passage that confuses hoard with deposit, takes the information of those who had the coins under study as their own and above all does not know the function of the punches, here confused with countermarks:

"Hidden under a stone of USM 8, at 5.50 m from the southern edge, a hoard containing 18 coins was discovered which, in ancient times, must have been accessible from the eastern compartment. At a later stage, three more coinage pieces from the same coin hoard were found in a spot not far away. The catalogue of 21 pieces includes very worn bronzes from prolonged use, originally struck by the nearby autonomous cities between the first and mid-third century AD, but which were put back into circulation after having been re-tariffed with a countermark that has yet to be studied: a fine example of a coinage from Tiberias under Claudius (AD 53), one from Tyre (55 BC–AD 87), seven of Elagabalus of which one with a figure of the emperor standing (AD 218–222), three from the mint of Nysa Scythopolis (AD 218–219; 220–221; 220–221), one from the mint of Antiochia at Hippos (AD 218–222) and another from the mint of Petra (AD 218–222), five Roman provincial issues from the second -mid third century AD, two Roman provincial issues from the mid-third century AD, one of which from a mint in the Decapolis. It is hoped that a detailed study of the punches will make it possible to trace the ***emissary*** *authority*[9] [Bold by present author]".[10]

To conclude with a last quotation as proof of the repetitive progression between coin dating and archaeological context.

The regularity and accuracy in the construction of the road conduits are in contrast to the dozens of the canal in E5 and one wonders if the latter arrangement is not a late restoration. The coin catalogue seems to confirm this. In fact, it includes: a coinage of Herod Archelaus (4 BC–AD 6 and one of Elagabalus (AD 218–222) from the dismantling of the pavement near the canal; a Tyrian mint from AD 107–108 and a provincial Roman mint from the second–third century AD on the pavement and a coin of Claudius (AD50–51) found near the mouth between E5 and E20; then there is also another mint of Herod Archelaos (4 BC–AD 6, mint of Jerusalem), one of Trajan (AD 99–100 AD, mint of Tiberias) and a provincial Roman one from the second to the first half of the third century AD from a survey in the south-east corner".[11]

The coin, like many other archaeological finds, is very talkative, as we could say in somewhat fashionable terminology. In it, individual data specific to that coin, and serial data common to other similar specimens, can indeed be identified. Among the individual features specific only to that nominal are the weight, diameter, position in the archaeological stratigraphy, state of preservation, and wear indicative of its period of circulation and use. These characteristics identify a particular specimen and that specimen alone. Alone, however, they say little on a historical-economic level. Serial data, on the other hand, increase the documentary potential of coins. They are: the type of the obverse and reverse, which together with the epigraphy help us to establish the issuing authority, the mint and the chronology. The combination of this information makes the coin a document requiring a multidisciplinary study that includes numismatic data associated with archaeological finds, historical sources and above all the comparison on a distributional basis of similar coin findings in territories belonging to the same administrative entity or monetary area. Thinking in terms of an administrative entity in ancient times, one runs the risk of applying modern criteria of exercising political power over a region and even to make explicit the central authority of a state. The relations and dependencies between the center and the periphery of a town were not structured like in a modern state and did not have an economic status even comparable to that of contemporary states or economies as they have been structured over the last five to six centuries. Actually, many regions in antiquity enjoyed relative autonomy and often had contacts with a political and administrative center only in relation to tax collection, the obligation to support the logistics of legions on

8 De Luca 2009, pp. 363–364.

9 The polysemy of the word *emissario* (emissary) in the Italian language includes meanings such as: envoy (of a person) or river that flows into a lake, for example, but never has the meaning of "monetary authority".

10 De Luca 2009, p. 367.

11 De Luca 2009, p. 414.

the move or encamped, and the maintenance of public buildings or road networks. Monetary finds can, therefore, contribute to our knowledge of ancient societies, especially through the reconstruction of the volume of coinage and its circulation away from or close to the place of actual coin production, but only if placed correctly in their general historical context.[12] However, the minted stock, which can also be described by observing the different monetary types and the choice of metals used for minting, is closely linked to its circulation: money was minted, hence money was provided if there was demand for it. Demand and supply were interdependent, and especially this relationship must be well placed in a historical epoch. With reference to the region in which Magdala was located, it is barely necessary to mention the radical difference between the epochs of the Seleucids, the Ptolemies, the Hasmoneans, the progressive Romanization up to full Roman imperial control, and finally the crisis of the Roman empire, the Byzantine and then Umayyad authorities.[13] Denominations changed; at times silver struck with large and small divisionals was favored, at other times bronze prevailed. The units of account and the physical pieces (coins) that represented them in whole or in part therefore varied.

The use of different metals poses a crucial question: whether ancient coinage always circulated with a value established by its weight and alloy, or whether it was accepted on a fiduciary basis, or better still was overvalued, because its face value was established by a civic or state authority *lato sensu* without any set standards being adhered to. This is a very complex issue because we possess few written sources, and scholarly hypotheses can only be reversed by large-scale quantitative studies. There is, however, substantial agreement that for gold and silver there was a close link between metal/weight and face value.[14] This is different for bronze. The coinage in base metal could also be exchanged with a partly fiduciary value, but not exclusively fiduciary, because in any case buying the metal, coining it and putting it into circulation required an expense so that a minting fee necessarily had to be applied especially because the quantity of bronze coins was often enormous. A productive organization with specialized artisans mastering various and not so common skills, with buildings, spaces and controls was therefore required.

Once in circulation, the coin passed from hand to hand, and on leaving its area – i. e. where pre-established values and exchange ratios were in force – it had to be confronted with a divisional responding to different values both in terms of weight and fineness, and therefore face value. This entailed either exchanges made by agents specialized in this activity or an acceptance on the money market with a different quotation, usually disadvantageous, but sometimes also advantageous especially for gold or silver coinage of excellent alloy that was collected where these metals were scarce and therefore in great demand.

In archaeological excavations, moreover, the presence of coins depends on at least three other factors: the methodology applied in the archaeological intervention (emergency excavation, systematic excavation, survey); the nature of the soils where a coin was lost; and the function, i. e. the type of frequentation of that site.[15] It is hardly worth mentioning that the recovery of numismatic documentation is strictly dependent on how one excavates because often, especially during earthworks or emergency excavations, it is the coins that suffer the most serious loss. In this case, however, during MP's campaigns, correct methodologies were followed in the excavation technique, but – as mentioned – stratigraphic units (US) were always confused with stratigraphic wall units (USM) when recording the finds, while the numbering does not always seem to be consistent or in continuity with that established in the Corbo-Loffreda intervention. Furthermore, although the excavation documentation is believed to exist, it has not been made accessible or available for inspection to the author of this publication. Thus, the entire interpretative framework and the very accuracy of the numismatic evidence suffers. As far as the stratigraphic conditions of the numismatic finds are concerned, considerable differences emerge from what has been published so far, both within the same excavation campaign and, above all, in the succession of excavations. One part of the site, in fact, was subject to heavy water infiltration, which lasted for centuries and due to the presence of limestone corroded especially the copper coins. In some sections of the site with a higher elevation, the state of preservation was better, a circumstance that also applies to the specimens that ended up in the water pipes/channels or stepped water cisterns. The extent

12 Crawford 1985; Von Reden 1995.

13 Syon 2015, pp. 31–39.

14 For methodological lucidity on this specific topic, even if focused on Constantinian and post-Constantinian times and even if written in Italian (which in the context of antiquities studies cannot be considered a marginal language at all!) cf. Carlà 2009.

15 Katsari 2011, pp. 19–34.

to which the chemical composition of soils interferes with the survival of a copper alloy roundel subject to centuries of corrosion in comparison with medieval sites,[16] is not much studied for the earliest periods, particularly in archaeological sites in the Near East. It is generally believed, though erroneously, that the absence of moisture creates the conditions that prevent corrosive interactions between soil chemistry and what falls into it and is no longer recovered. If this observation is of any value in general, it must be kept in mind that there are areas in which water was not lacking at all, or which were even marshy in the past: and it is precisely in such areas that settlements, even of considerable size, developed over the centuries. In the case of Magdala, this *communis opinio* is disproved by the recovered data, because a particularly large number of Hasmonean *prutot* or similar coinage in terms of shape or production technique is so badly preserved as to render them *de facto* unclassifiable or, at most, only generically attributable to an era, but always with many doubts.[17] Moreover, when a coin was dropped accidentally or in the course of an exchange, its recovery depended not only on its value but also on the nature of the pavement of a house, a street or a square. Perhaps archaeologists should pay attention to these facts because, obviously, if coins fell on a mosaic surface, they were readily recovered, whereas if lost on a dirt floor or in the sand, searching for them and recovering them not only became challenging, but it could also happen that the search was abandoned, especially if the lost coin was of modest value.

Finally, the presence of coins depends on their use at a particular site.[18] There are many factors to consider on this subject. First of all, circulating money was influenced by the amount of money produced in a given period and the relationship between supply and demand for divisional or small coins triggered in that site for reasons that can often only be hypothesized. In fact, when we think about exchanges in the ancient world, we are very much conditioned by our language and our experience of using money for all the transactions of our daily lives. What do we really mean when we use the terms economy, currency, exchange, market, monetary transaction to refer to the ancient world? What is the relationship between the agrarian subsistence economy and that practiced in *latifundia*? The Romans, for instance, did not monopolize land ownership in the provinces and allowed the inhabitants of the provinces to continue to have free reign to extend their holdings and cultivate according to local traditions as well as in the choice of what to cultivate and even more so in the adoption of land management techniques: a dirigiste and centralized vision was lacking. Some Roman citizens became landowners in territories they had never visited in their lives, and this allowed the formation of intermediary classes that regulated profits by directing them to the owners. In the interdependence between town and countryside, what was the mutual conditioning? I believe that in this context, rather than real trade, one should reason on the satisfaction of the essential needs of those who practiced crafts and of those who worked the land as freeholders or in servile conditions. Trade, or rather, the allocation of artefacts and agrarian product not so much according to the law of supply and demand, but of the availability of a good at that time according to the climatic seasons and the specificities of a given region could take on an irregular, periodic character and in any case be dictated by the needs of a single community. Perhaps more structured were the economic aspects of taxation or the procurement of resources for the administrative bureaucracy and especially for army logistics. It is not intended here to return to themes that gave substance to the debate on ancient economy, choosing between economists who theorized about the market's ability to regulate itself through the competition of the actors involved, and primitivists.[19] Overcoming such oppositions, often strongly ideological, happened by taking into account 'economic' components that have only been studied in recent decades such as demography, the management of the *oikos*, the application of technological innovations, and the occurrence or non-occurrence of military events that brought about profound changes in agrarian methods of production, which can, however, be prudently defined as 'crises'. In this context, the most recent studies place the use of money in the ability of an environment and its resources to allow the social organization and life of a community.[20] Numerous and increasingly accurate publications of coin findings from small sites and larger settlements that can only with some caution be defined as 'towns', have made available quantitative data capable of supporting distributional analyses that can be defined as 'mone-

16 Blackburn 1989.

17 On the technique of production by means of die casting, cf. Ariel 2012.

18 Reece 2003, pp. 335–338.

19 Finley 1973; Polanyi 1944 (ed. 2000).

20 Extremely interesting is the analysis of the history of the debate, accompanied by acute interpretative observations, in Carlà, Marcone 2011.

tary circulation'. Even if the chronological scansion, intensity and duration of the currency's presence on the market cannot be immediately associated with the quantity of specimens found, examined and published. However, such quantitative analyses should be extended to other classes of artefacts, especially those that can certainly be associated in various ways with agricultural or artisanal work or with the transfer of goods over short distances. In other words, progressive monetarization affected the territory of Galilee at least from the second century BCE, even outside the sites of greatest population concentration, as can be deduced from the large number of small coins recovered in archaeological excavations even in sites of modest size. However, one cannot define this presence per se as unitary, well-structured, continuous, and equal in all the sites in the same region. It depended on the position of a site in relation to neighboring territories, on its belonging to a well-defined monetary area and on the integration of that site into the economic system of reference, more or less open to the influences of other economic dynamics. It also depended on the greater or lesser quantity of currency struck by the mint of reference and on the reasons for the increase or decrease, which is often linked to the military or fiscal function of the currency produced. It should also not be forgotten that coinage considerations in an excavation cannot be based on the sample recovered because this can never be considered as an absolute quantitative value. In fact, the numismatic documentation of an excavation is only a part of what is potentially present because other specimens may have been found in the past and then dispersed, while others might still be waiting to be recovered in parts of the excavation not yet investigated. What can still be found is not what has been lost. Many coins lost in antiquity have disappeared through corrosion, through chemical processes of mineralization, because they returned to use in the centuries following their loss, or because they were recast as metal. These are all objective data that suggest caution in constructing interpretations on a statistical basis, caution that should also be extended to the choice of data for comparisons in contexts of the same monetary area. They are, moreover, all indicators to move from analytical data to the formulation of at least some hypotheses on the use of an instrument with a prevalent commercial function, and which must never disregard the three classic functions of the institution 'money', namely its functions as a measure of value (unit of account), as a store of value (hoarding), and as a means of settling debts and credits at all levels of exchange (monetary use/circulation).

3. Magdala in the Galilee and the specific region of Lake Kinneret

For a long time, the locality of Magdala was thought of as the village of the evangelical Mary of Magdala, a mythological approach reinforced by the image that Galilee had been a separate rural region full of farming villages. In this regard, for an analysis of the cultural tradition concerning the 'concept' of Galilee over the centuries up to most recent times, a luminous article by Zangenberg is worthy of note. Breaking with commonplaces, he attempts to pose all questions concerning Galilee from the chronology of settlements, including the interpretation of archaeological finds, to the dynamic relations with neighboring territories, the presence of different cultural and religious elements, the influence of Tyre and the Hellenistic cities of the Decapolis to the settlements along Lake Kinneret, within the peculiar geographic framework of this territory: the largest freshwater reservoir is a hinge area with easy communications in all directions, towards the Mediterranean and inland between Syria and the Red Sea along the Jordan Valley.[1] In fact, the scholar notes that for too long the interpretative *topos* had crystallized in the belief that *"Galilee has been interpreted as an integral part of Western cultural memory, as 'the land where Jesus walked', 'the cradle of early Christianity' or 'the home of the rabbis'"*. Whether a remote 'oriental utopia' where sages instructed a meek and honest audience of uncorrupted people on moral values and simple living, or a distant 'region of authentic origins', Galilee has more often been conceptualized as a myth, an ideal or a symbol than as a reality 'on the ground' that must be interpreted like any other Mediterranean area. This approach is understandable as a result of popular interest and imagination, but problematic when it comes to developing historically valid concepts about Galilean history and culture.[2] In terms of interpreting the documentation of the material cultures attested there, especially the archaeological finds, a sort of dogma has imposed itself that there was an unambiguous and indisputable relationship between documents, ethnicity, and religious cultures: *"As a consequence of this approach, scholars focused on Galilean distinctiveness by emphasising its ethnic boundaries, and thus tended to separate it from its broader geographical and cultural matrix. As a result, a geographically and culturally self-referential concept of 'Galilee' emerged, which traced pre-rabbinic and rabbinic identity constructions and emphasised the differences between the 'inside' (such as the Jewish villages and towns of the heartland) and the 'outside' (such as the non-Jewish and Greek cities of the Decapolis and the Aramaic-speaking regions of Syria to the east or the Phoenician areas along the Mediterranean coast and to the north)"*.[3] Magdala, therefore, cannot be divorced from its regional context. For this reason, numismatic evidence is of great

1 Zangenberg 2019 with an exhaustive and up-to-date bibliography on the subject.

2 Zangenberg 2019, p. 268.

3 Zangenberg 2019, p. 269. Moreover, that the tendency to mythologize the site is still an attractive option can be deduced from the statements published by Mexican excavators who, influenced by the Legionaries of Christ association (*sufficit* a few online searches), convey any link between the site of Magdala and the mythological story of Mary believed to have originated here. But Magdala is Magdala with the depth of its entire history. The rest pertains to propaganda for more or less tourist purposes.

value as it helps to establish the period when the site was first frequented, the interconnections with the cities on the coast, Tyre *in primis,* but also with the places of trade over the short distance, locally, along the shores of the lake, the true epicenter and in fact the fastest route of communication/transport. Numismatic evidence can also help clarify contacts over the long distance, with Judea and Samaria, but also with Phoenicia and Coele Syria, Hauran and the Jordan regions towards the Red Sea. Did this site, where recent archaeological excavations have contributed to a better understanding of its not insignificant size and the existence of a large lake port, a merchant area and buildings with a public function and at least one synagogue, only gained importance in the Hasmonean and later Roman period as recounted by Flavius Josephus[4], or was it precisely Magdala's strategic position on the lake and along the routes of travel in various directions that determined its vitality for several centuries?

Apart from modern definitions, the territory within which to locate Magdala and its monetary documentation was defined following the indications of Flavius Josephus, who distinguished between Upper Galilee (mountainous) and Lower Galilee (hilly and partly sloping towards the western shore of the lake), but ranging along the Bet She'an valley in the south, towards Gamla in the Gaulanitis and the northern part, that is the territory of the Jordan tributary of the lake.[5]

For the purpose of the research and to allow consistency of comparison,[6] relevant archaeological sites in the territory thus delimited are listed in the following tables.

	Location (cf. MAPS of sites 1,2)	Source/Bibliography
1	Akko Ptolemais	Syon 2016
2	Bet Yerah	Bijovsky 2017
3	Beit She'an (Nysa-Scythopolis)	Fitzgerald 1931; Sharabani 2004; Berman 2007; Berman 2015
4	Et-Tell (Bethsaida)	Meier 1995; Kindler 1999a; Ariel 2019
5	Berytos	Butcher 2003; Sawaya 2009; Sawaya 2011a; Sawaya 2016; Sawaya 2017.
6	Caesarea Maritima	Hamburger 1955; Belloni 1966; Hohlfelder 1994; Ariel 1986; De Rose Evans 2006.
7	Carmel Coast	Meshorer 2010
8	Galilee (general)	Syon 2015
9	Gamla	Syon 2014
10	Gerasa	Marot 1998; Lichtenberger, Raja 2020
11	Ginnosar	Gitler 1990
12	Gush-Halav	Bijovsky 1998
13	Hammat Gader	Barkay 1997

4 *Bellum Iudaicum* II 596–599, 634–635; III 462–465.

5 An effective delimitation, also on historical grounds, of this same territory can be found in Syon 2015, pp. 51–52.

6 For each site, the bibliography contains the coin report or some numismatic information (preliminary or final numismatic report). The numismatic documentation represents the selected background for comparison of the numismatic evidence from Magdala.

	Location (cf. MAPS of sites 1,2)	Source/Bibliography
14	Hippos	Excavation Seasons from 2001 to 2013: *courtesy of IAA (Coin Cabinet) thanks to Donald Ariel*; Solarewicz 2015
15	Omrit	Syon 2011
16	Kanaf, Horvat	Ariel 1980
17	Jerusalem	Ariel 1982; Gitler 1996; Ariel 1990; Gitler 2003; Ariel 2013; Glücksmann, Kool 1995; Ariel, Berman 2020; Ariel 2020a; Ariel 2020b; Ariel 2020c
18	Capernaum	Spijkerman 1958–1958; Arslan 1996a; Arslan 1996b; Arslan 1997; Callegher 1997; Arslan 2003b; Arslan 2003c; Callegher 2007a; Callegher 2007b; Callegher 2010; Arslan 2011; Callegher 2016; Mattila 2011; Mattila 2015
19	Kursi	Sharabani 1983
20	Magdala	Meshorer 2010; Abu-'Uqsa 2001; Arslan 2003a; Garza, Díaz Barriga 2013; Syon 2018; Garza, Diaz Barriga 2019
21	Marus, Khirbet	Bijovsky, *Report of Coins from Excavations at the Ancient Synagogue of Kh. Marus* (personal communication)
22	Meiron	Meiron 1981; Meyer, Strange, Meyers 1981; Raynor, Meshorer 1988
23	Nabratein	Bijovsky 2009
24	Nevé-Ur (Beit She'an Valley)	Berman, Bijovsky 2002
25	Nitai, Mount	Farhi, Leibner 2011–2014; Farhi 2018
26	Palestine (general)	Gitler, Weisburd 2005
27	Sarepta	Abou Diwan 2016
28	Sepphoris	Bunnel 1937; Meyers, Netzer, Meyers 1986; Ariel, Bijovsky 2018
29	Sumaqa	Kindler 1999b
30	Tabgha	Loffreda 1970
31	Tel Anafa	Meshorer 1994
32	Tel Nahariya	Ariel 1993
33	Tiberias	Hamburger 1959; Hamburger 1983; Rahmani, Sharabani 1983; Amitai-Preiss 2000; Berman 2004; Bijovsky 2004a; Bijovsky 2018
34	Tyre	Sawaya 2011b; Sawaya 2012
35	Wadi Hamam	Bijovsky, Leibner 2013; Bjiovsky 2018

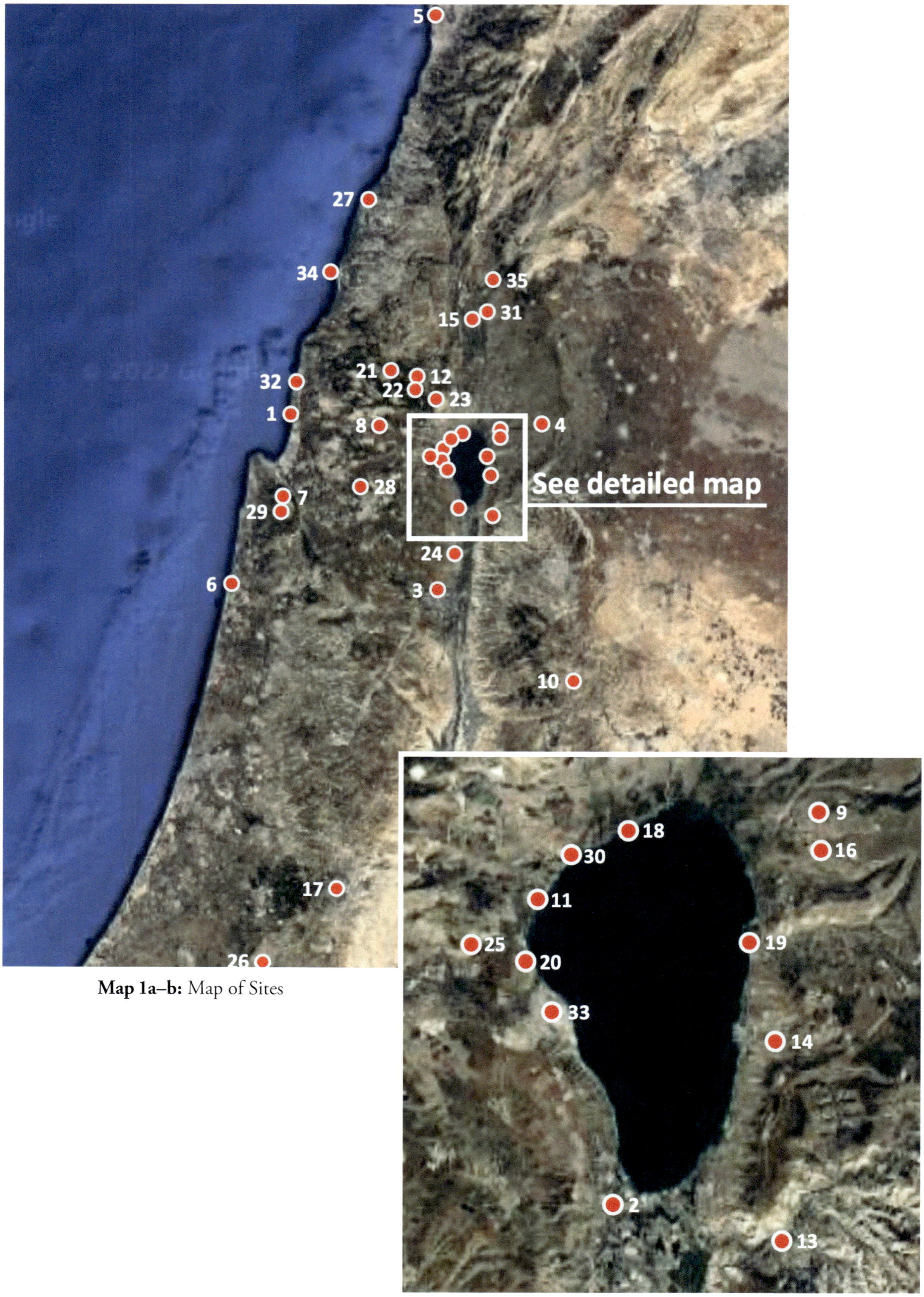

Map 1a–b: Map of Sites

Many other data are available in the numismatic bibliography of the area, but of all the publications Syon 2015 is a standard work that certainly constitutes an indispensable reference. We have chosen, as a comparison, to refer to the numismatic evidence of the following:

In our analysis, we have followed certain criteria: monetary relevance (quantitative and typological consistency, i. e. coins with a definite provenance from excavations, excluding those recovered by chance or from collections), legal relevance (i. e. relevance to the same monetary area), and finally administrative relevance, i. e. sites falling within regional units governed by the same authority, including the variation of the same authority over the centuries. However, if the choice of a coin pattern falls within the previous coordinates, comparisons with sites in a 'supra-regional' research perspective will not be disregarded.[7] The purpose hereby is to at least connect Magdala to the mints of production of the currency found there, to the current monetary system of account, and to follow broader patterns of monetary circulation so as to identify phases of lesser or greater influx and bring out their interdependencies.

In fact, alongside neighboring sites such as Wadi Hamam, Tabgha, Capernaum, et-Tell (Bethsaida?), Tiberias and Ginnosar, all of which can be directly linked to the same dynamics due to being sites on the lake and thus easily connected by navigation, we also selected sites particularly relevant for their territorial role as well as for the high consistency and reliability of their numismatic data, such as Gamla, Meiron, Beit She'an, Jerash, and sites of lesser extent but certainly indicative for establishing the actual presence and circulation of numismatic items comparable in whole or in part with those of Magdala: Gush Halav, Hammat Gader, Horvat Omrit, Horvat Kanaf, Khirbet Marus, Nabratein, Nevé-Ur, Mount Nitai and Tel-Anafa. These sites are able to illustrate the actual distribution of coinage both chronologically and quantitatively and thereby contribute to the definition of a distribution of issues on a scale beyond the case study under consideration, which only focuses on the Magdala finds.

Finally, the choice of some other sites of great historical-archaeological importance was guided by the fact that they were mints particularly active in the production of coinage, especially in copper, and sometimes played a hegemonic role in regulating the influx of coinage into the settlements of Galilee and neighboring regions. This is true of Tyre, Berytos, Caesarea Maritima, Gadara, Akko Ptolemais, Hippos, Jerusalem of course, Scythopolis, Sepphoris and close-by Tiberias.

A further element concerns the chronological periodization. Temporal extremes do not have absolute value in our case study because, as already pointed out, the date of mintage and the date of accidental loss rarely coincide.[8] As widely accepted by scholars, the chronological periodization is marked by the degrees of events that affected Galilee, Gaulanitis, and the Mediterranean coast, including Phoenicia. A chronological division is not always easy and, above all, cannot always be associated with numismatic data for the already mentioned reason of persistence in the use of the coins, and because wear and state of preservation often do not facilitate the identification of an excavated specimen. On the basis of the numismatic evidence analyzed and proposed in the catalogue and of what was possible to compare thanks to the shared numismatic data emerging from the MAP excavations at Magdala, it was decided to follow a shared periodization with the Wadi Hamam site as well. The overall data are illustrated in the following two graphs, the first (fig. 1) starting with the presence of Ptolemaic coins until the first phase of Romanization considered to have ended with Domitian; the second (fig. 2) extends from the end of the first century CE and to the subsequent coinage up to modern times, but the part of real interest can be limited to the fourth –fifth century coinage with an appendix to the Arab-Byzantine and Umayyad phases.

7 Stella 2019, p. 12.

8 On the duration in circulation of the coinage cf. Gorini 1992; Katsari 2011, chapter I which also applies to the Roman imperial provinces.

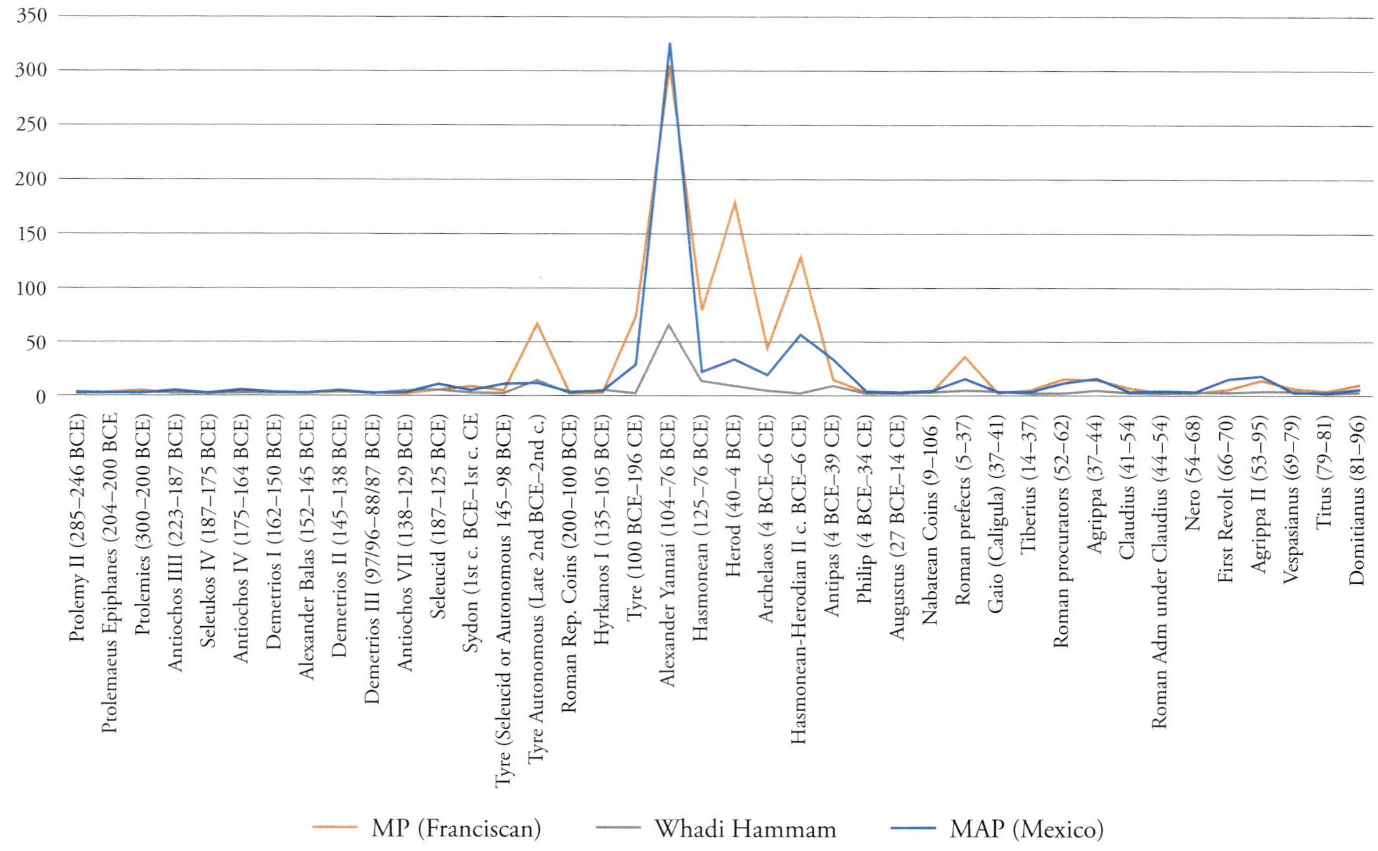

Fig. 1a: Comparison of coin quantities between Magdala (MAP), MP and Wadi Hamam from Ptolemaios II to Domitianus

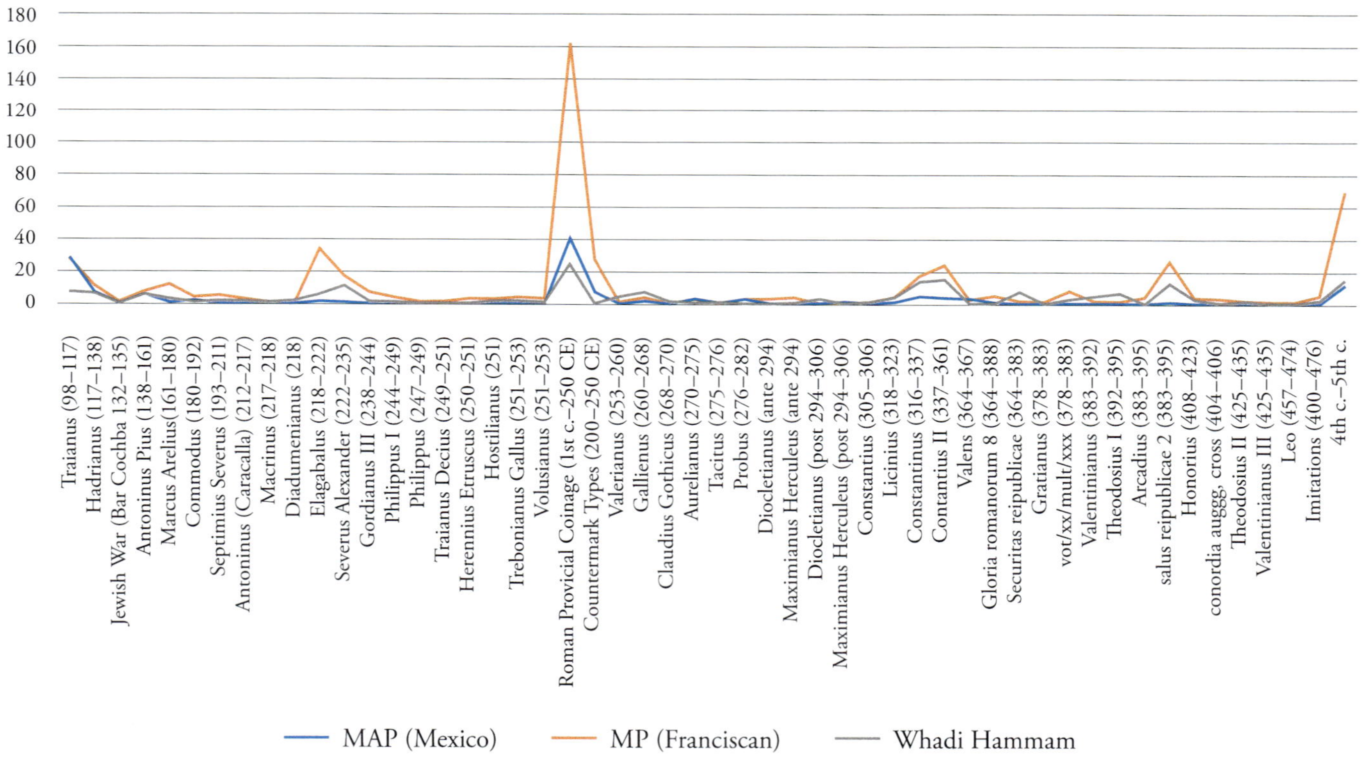

Fig. 1b: Comparison of coin quantities between Magdala (MAP), MP and Wadi Hamam from Traianus to fourth-fifth century

4. Some aspects of monetary and numismatic periodization

4.1 Third century BCE: Ptolemaic period

From the third century BCE onwards, the compositional structure of the monetary circulation of Palestine (Galilee in particular) saw a clear prevalence of coins from Tyre (rarer are those minted at Akko Ptolemais and other mints) also because the administrative-legal control of the Phoenician city extended from the coastal settlements inland, encompassing them in its own monetary area based on the Attic foot tetradrachm (17.24 g, hence on a drachma cut on the foot of 4.31 g of silver), thus asserting the supremacy of its own coinage, with the occasional inclusion of issues from Sidon and Akko.[1]

4.2 Second century BCE: Seleucid period

The Seleucid conquest of the region, which took place at the expense of the Ptolemies at the beginning of the second century BCE, led to the replacement of Ptolemaic metrology (Attic foot) by that defined as Phoenician standard, i.e. on a *tetradrachm* of 14.3 g and a *drachma* of 3.55 g of silver. Beyond the hegemonic role of Tyre and not a secondary one of Akko, the most important fact is the initiation of a copious coinage in copper, which quickly became dominant over silver and its fractions, from Phoenicia to Palestine, including inland areas. The demand for numerals of small face value, obviously intended for minute exchange as opposed to silver tetradrachms, which performed the function of a store of value, was met by the official Seleucid mints. However, especially from the reign of Antiochus IV, other mints also began to mint coinage with distinct types, giving rise to the production of copper coins known as 'municipal issues' and 'autonomous coinage', series clearly identifiable by the adoption of their own iconographic types especially on the reverse.

4.3 Hasmonean period (125 BCE–63 BCE)

In the Syro-Palestinian region, the second century had seen the establishment of Seleucid hegemony with Antiochus IV (215–164 BCE), who, however, had no successors to his military-strategic height. In fact, after his death, dynastic succession conflicts began that led to the disintegration of his state-building aimed at restoring Seleucid authority not only in the regions of Syria and Palestine, but also in Egypt. The final figure in this process of disintegration was Demetrius II (160–125 BCE), assassinated in Tyre in 125 BCE, the date from which after which the autonomous coinage of the Phoenician city began with silver (*sheqels*) and copper issues. Alongside these, albeit in later years, but as evidence of the progressive quest for civic autonomy and economic vitality in various post-Seleucid territories, Akko-Ptolemais and Askalon would start minting coins.[2] As a consequence of that crisis and

1 Elayi, A. G. Elayi 1993; bibliographical-historical synthesis in Syon 2015, pp. 51–52.

2 An effective chronological and typological excursus of issues in CHL, pp. 237–240; Syon 2015, pp. 57–61.

possible autonomy, Hasmonean coinage also began, which recent studies date to coincide with the events of 125 BCE and thus is parallel with the autonomous coinage of Tyre. After the first issues of Hyrcanus I, those of Alexander Jannaeus became dominant. His issues were copious, they spread so ubiquitously in the region that they also took on a function as identity markers, as well as an economic one, because their typology of the obverse and reverse broke with that of the Seleucid sovereigns: images, in fact, were replaced by specific, tangible objects (anchor), or natural elements (star) consistent with the rejection of images so characteristic of Hasmonean Jewish religious culture. Particular care has recently been given to the quantitative analysis of the various types of Jannaeus' coinage, in particular on the presence of the various types of his coinage in sites variously connected to the historical and military history of this central character among the Hasmoneans.[3] Assuming that excluding the type TJC L1-L6,[4] for all the others types minted in the name of Alexander Jannaeus, it is not possible to determine an absolute chronology. An attempt has been made to investigate whether the presence or absence of the various types, in particular TJC K (Type 4 in Shachar 2004) and TJC L7-L17 (Type 7 in Shachar 2004), could provide essential data for the study of Upper Galilean settlements. Given that TJC L7-L17 is by far the most widespread type in the Hasmonean territories, and in consistently surprising quantities, it does not seem entirely convincing that it was only copiously minted in the last three years of Alexander Jannaeus' reign, especially if one takes into account the previous thirty-four years of monetary projection. It might instead indicate that this type of coin was in fact minted even after the death of this Hasmonean ruler and that its presence or absence in archaeological contexts, compared to the presence/absence of Seleucid coinage, helps to establish whether a site/location was permanently inhabited or suffered discontinuity in habitation even in the phase preceding the arrival of the Romans under Pompey in 63 BCE.[5]

3 Shachar 2004, pp. 10–12.
4 Meshorer 2001.
5 On this interesting analysis of numismatic data see Shachar 2004; Ariel 2022.

4.4 Early Roman period (63 BCE–First Jewish Revolt 70 CE)

The years included in this phase are characterized by Pompey's military action, the end of the Hasmonean reign, the establishment of Herod's reign and the division of his dominion between his sons Archelaus, Philippus and Antipas. The latter was given Peraea and Galilee, i. e., the Transjordanian territory towards the Mediterranean coast, including Magdala. While the minting activity of the Jerusalem mint was central in the actual Hasmonean phase, Herod the Great opened also other minting workshops, all in the northern part of Palestine. In fact, Samaria joined Jerusalem in the start-up phase of Herodian coinage (particularly in year 3 = 40 BCE). Herod Archelaus minted in Jerusalem while Herod Antipas obtained his coinage in Tiberias between 4 BCE and 39 CE. Herod Philippus minted his series between 4 BC and 34 CE at Caesarea Philippi (Paneas), but in the name of the emperors Augustus and Tiberius, who in fact appeared on the obverse of those coins. From the same mint also came the bronze issues of Agrippa I and Agrippa II, the latter, however, was also actively minting at Sepphoris. Although with different production intensities, all rulers played a major role in the minting of copper coinage because enormous quantities of *prutot* and perhaps ½ *prutot* came out of their workshops.[6] In addition, the gradual assimilation of the Palestinian region into a Province within Roman imperial administration was accompanied by monetary coinage clearly identifiable as pertaining to the imperial procurators representing Augustus (Coponius and Ambibulus), Tiberius (Valerius Gratus, Pontius Pilatus), Claudius (Antonius Felix) and Nero (Festus). Their copper issues flanked the Hasmonean and Herodian ones in circulation, contributing to the immense stock availa-

6 The most up-to-date reference is CHL, esp. pp. 237–240 and the catalogue in this section. The existence, or rather a market price, of ½ *prutah* is not agreed upon. It is believed that the inhabitants were losing and no longer recovering *prutot* because they were worthless, especially if they were obtained with matrices and their weight dropped. Such a 'pessimistic' view on the value of bronze coinage in the ancient world goes hand in hand with the extension of maximum 'fiduciary' for coinage in base metal: the coins were worth very little and their value did not depend on the metal but on the issuing authority alone, which guaranteed their face value. They were, however, still metal, they had a value, they served to honor exchanges of goods with modest prices. And this was enough for *prutot* to first and foremost remain money in all its aspects, from minting to alloy and weight. If other denominations with equal face value but extremely different weights and alloys, however, could run on the market remains an open question.

ble at least until the First Jewish War against Rome, fought between 66 and 70/3 CE. It should also be mentioned that, as far as silver was concerned, the practical use of the *sheqel* of Tyre continued, both as a coin of account and as a high-value denomination suitable for tax collections and for larger Temple payments. In reality, even though the Romanization of the area had begun, the Roman republican and then Augustan post-reform systems began to spread slowly in Palestine, at first flanking the long-established and widely used and influential Tyre unit of account and then supplanting it in? the Flavian era, especially with Domitian (81–96). In fact, as mentioned in the previous chronological partitions, in the regions of Syria and Palestine, from the third century BCE until the end of the second century CE, silver and copper coinage was made and circulated by different authorities and in different mints, so much so that it can be said that monetary bimetallism (silver/copper) was in force in these regions. The mint of Tyre, which was joined during the first century CE by that of Antioch, played a predominant role in producing both silver (tetradrachms, tridrachms, didrachms and drachmas)[7] and bronze coins, both – as will be seen in the catalogue commentary – widely disseminated and accepted in the territory of Judea, Samaria[8] and even more in Galilee.[9] As a consequence of Augustus' reform and the full legal-administrative incorporation of these territories into the empire, various mints in the region chose to adapt the types of their bronze coinage to those of Roman bronze, as in the well-known cases of the Jewish coins from Herod Philip (4 BCE–34 CE) to Agrippa II (55/56–94/95).[10] From contemporary sources, including the *euangelion* of Levi (Matthew), it can also be deduced that units of account (talents and mines) and Greek coins (*tetradrachmas*, *didrachmas* and *drachmas*) remained in use alongside Roman units of account and circulating money (*denarii*, *asses* and *quadrans*).[11] Rabbinic texts from the same period and referring to the Herodian period or immediately thereafter hand down references about the use of coins with a lower quotation than the Roman divisionals, therefore equivalences or exchanges could require complex calculations; at the same time Roman silver had such a high value (1 *denarius* = 6 silver *ma'ot; 1 ma'ah* = 1 *obolus*)[12] to play a liberating function only for transactions with high prices.[13] However, it is the numismatic-archaeological data from the Palestinian area that enrich the information on the role of the most valuable coinage minted in Rome. For silver, the data inferred from circulation, particularly from coin findings in archaeological contexts, would indicate an unchallenged dominance of the coins minted in the local mints of the area (*tetradrachmas*, *didrachmas*, *drachmas* and *shekels*) and a marginal function of the republican and imperial *denarius* at least until the late first century CE.[14] Indeed, during the first century, despite some misgivings raised in studies from the 1960s,[15] local silver coinage spread very gradually, perhaps because, apart from the complexity arising from the exchange between the actual coinage of the Augustan system and the Hasmonean-Herodian system, various mints in the region made up for the demand for high-value coins by minting *denarii* in the style of the Roman ones and sometimes even some gold coins, the latter probably in Alexandria.[16] Moreover, the spread of imperial money, especially of Neronian standard[17] particularly from the second half of the first century CE, is related not so much to long-distance trade as to the deployment of military contingents to suppress the first anti-Roman revolt (66–70/3). For the first century, in fact, generally the composition of the hoards confirm the modest presence of Republican and Imperial Roman *denarii*: some specimens were recovered

7 Butcher 2004, pp. 49–98: "Silver and Gold Coinage".
8 Cf. Bijovsky 2021.
9 RPC, I, pp. 581–590.
10 CHL, pp. 261–266; Barkay 2012, p. 26: *"Most instances of the Roman influence on Jewish coins belong to the first group [scil. the use of Roman motifs for political reasons, BCE]. mainly because the Herodian dynasty were client kings of Rome, and thus wished to please the emperors and the Roman administration in the province".*
11 Sutherland 1967; Picozzi 1972; for a monographic study on the subject see Bijovsky 2004b, note n. 14.
12 Kindler 1967, in part. p. 181.
13 Howgego 1984–1985.
14 Levy 1995; Ariel, Fontanille 2012, pp. 34–36, in par. p. 34, Table 2.
15 Roth 1962 accepts the circulation of Roman *denarii* in Judea, but without citing examples. The absence of *denarii* of the Julio-Claudian dynasty in the repositories of the Eastern Mediterranean regions is instead affirmed in van Lassen 1971, pp. 240–241, where with some perplexity regarding the territorial spread the author writes: *"I have the following* denarii *obtained during 1939/40 in Palestine: M. Antonius (Leg. VI, very worn) from Gaza; Augustus (CL Caesares) from Jerusalem, Tiberius (Livia seated) and Vitellius* (libertas restituta) *both from Ohan in Jerusalem. The two latter may well not be of Palestinian provenance".*
16 Butcher 2004.
17 The republican *denarii* of Mark Antony's legions remained in use for a long time even in the first half of the first century almost certainly because their silver content conforms to the Neronian standard rather than the Augustan one. See Meshorer 1992; Bjovsky 2004b, p. 247.

in the Khirbet Qumran hoards in 1955,[18] at Isfiya on Mount Carmel,[19] in the Hebron district,[20] again in Hebron "spring 1990" but without any precise indications,[21] in Beit Guvrin/Eleutheropolis,[22] in Wadi Murabba'at,[23] and in hoard C from Khirbet Badd 'Issa/Qiryat Sefer[24] and in an unpublished hoard, probably found in the Gaza Strip, which appeared on the Jerusalem antiques market in late summer 2019.[25]

As for the presence of Roman gold *aurei* in this same chronological period, on the basis of the data available today, it appears to be entirely episodic compared to the enormous stock of silver and gold circulating in Palestine.[26] Therefore, it can be deduced that precious metal coinage seems to have played little role compared to silver coinage during much of the first century, so much so that it is considered a negligible presence in the composition of the money in circulation and more generally of the monetary stock in use. This holds despite Vespasian's *aurei* were probably minted in Alexandria, Vespasian's and Titus' *aurei* in a 'southern mint',[27] and despite the discovery of western *aurei* of Tiberius respectively in a Nabataean tomb at Dhat-Râs[28] and in Jerusalem (mint of Lugdunum)[29], those of Nero, Vitellius and Vespasian (mint of Lugdunum) also in Jerusalem[30], as well as those of Vespasian in Khirbet Badd 'Issa-Qiryat Sefer[31]. A hoard found in the Upper Galilee has recently been proposed, but with *aurei* dated immediately after the events of 66–70, thus attributable to a phase of more decisive influence of the Augustan-Neronian system of account.[32]

4.5 Period of Romanization (ca. 70–ca. 294)

During this period, which lasted for over two centuries, the process of full Romanization necessarily involved the coinage as well. After the events of the first anti-Roman revolt, the Augustan/Neronian system of account with coins minted in Rome became established and spread. From an administrative point of view, the region of Galilee followed the events of the relationship between Rome and Agrippa II, including the territorial partition of Judea and Syria. It was partly involved in the revolt of Bar Kokhba (132–135) whose relevance in the monetary sphere, particularly in Galilee, is analyzed by Leibner and Bijovsky who surveyed and studied the structure of monetary circulation and hoarding, revealing cases of both silver coins, mainly minted in Antioch, and mixed silver-bronze hoards, the latter coins being minted in the area, especially Akko-Ptolemais and Tiberias.[33] The evidence that can be deduced from the study of coinage is that from the first half of the second century, imperial Roman coins and coins from local mints (provincial Roman coins or city coins) circulated together, sometimes also motivated by the settlement of Roman legions, as in the case of Legio VI Ferrata. It can also be stated that from the Antonine period onwards, but especially with Septimius Severus, the whole terri-

18 Six Roman republican *denarii* are in the hoard found in Locus 120 in Khirbet Qumran during the Roland De Vaux excavations in 1955: see the manuscripts by Henri Seyrig from 1955 and Augusto Spijkerman from 1960 (Archives École Archéologique et Biblique Française and Archives Studium Biblicum Franciscanum in Jerusalem: unpublished). The arguments of Lönnqvist 2007, pp. 3–5 about the presence in this same repository of imperial *denarii* with different chronology are not well founded. See in this regard Ariel, Fontanille 2012, p. 34, Table 2.

19 After the first reports of Kadman 1960a; Kadman 1960b; Kadman 1962 and especially of Kadman 1965, this hoard has been cited as evidence of Roman coinage in trade with the East by Raschke 1978, esp. p. 998, no. 1431, or in the discussion of the concrete reference of the term *denarius* in the Gospels for which cf. Hart 1984 [there the author also refers to a letter from A. Spijkerman to Y. Meshorer in which news is given of the discovery of Roman *denarii* from the Julio-Claudian(?) era in the Jericho area why in these brackets?]. The hoard of Isfiya has been treated in a much larger recent edition than previous reports in Meir 2008; Meir 2009; Meir 2010.

20 CH III, p. 38, no. 90; Butcher 2004, p. 273, n. 28.

21 Butcher 2004, p. 274, no. 33a.

22 Butcher 2004, p. 273, no. 30.

23 Milik, Seyrig 1958. The reliability of this relic, from the Jerusalem antiquities market, remains uncertain.

24 Bijovsky 2004b, p. 247.

25 I was able to examine for myself this find of 96 Roman Republican/Imperial *denarii* and 2 *antoniniani*. For the period under examination here, there was 1 Roman Republican coin of C PISO.L.F.FRVGI Naked horseman galloping right, holding whip-above I = RRC 408/1 (and following types) but in poor condition; 4 *denarii* of Antoninus Pius; 6 *denarii* of Marcus Aurelius; 1 *denarius* of Commodus, and 5 *denarii* of the Antonine period.

26 Bijovsky 2004b, p. 247: "*In general, gold Roman coins are most unusual finds, and only four such coins are recorded from controlled archaeological excavation*".

27 Butcher 2004, pp. 96–97.

28 Zayadine 1970, p. 127, fig. 10; Butcher 1996, in part. p. 103.

29 Ariel 1982, p. 314, no. 61. Zissu *et alii* 2009–2010.

30 Zissu *et alii* 2009–2010.

31 Bijovsky 2004b, p. 247.

32 Callegher 2015.

33 Bijovsky, Leibner 2013, p. 122, note 19–21, with references to the Tiberias 1952 hoards, a tomb in the 'Akko cemetery and Kibbutz Sha'ar ha'Amaqim.

tory surrounding the Sea of Galilee, the Golan but also the confined regions of the Decapolis, Phoenicia and Syria experienced an extensive monetarization, supported by the opening or reopening of numerous mints, some continuously, others less intensively, but always in response to the increased demand for copper divisionals, proving the diffusion of the monetary instrument in the economy and in trade even of minor value. The continuity of the contribution of silver from Antioch, i. e. the tetradrachms, a reference denomination for larger values, which in fact was never supplanted by the imperial *denarius* and not even by the introduction of the *antoninianus* with Caracalla in c. 214/215, should also be mentioned. In fact, the local mints continued to strike coinage even during the great crisis of the third century, at least until the reign of Gallienus (260–268). Tyre and Akko-Ptolemais stand out among them all, as evidence of their substantially hegemonic role together with Tiberias. The reason for the success of the bronze coinage is to be found in the high quality of their alloy and in their weight trend, often close to that of the imperial *sestertius*, especially until the mid-third century, when, in the face of the devaluation of the *antoninianus*, which came to contain silver in the almost negligible percentage of between 5–3 %. The large coins of good copper were appreciated and revalued overtime, until they became the good currency of the system and were often hoarded, as shown by the data from the western part of the empire.[34] In the same period, the impact of the loss of value of silver coinage can be observed also in this region, as there are quite a number of mixed or even predominantly bronze hoards with coinage from various local mints. The phenomenon seems not to be confined to a specific episode in the Galilee area,[35] but protracted in time to intensify and stop around the time of the reign of Claudius II Gothicus (260–268) and thus shortly before Aurelian's monetary reform (274). Indeed, in addition to the cases reported in Syon's study on small change in Galilee,[36] the mixed hoard from Wadi Hamam-Unit A11 (last coins: *tetradrachms* of Claudius II Gothicus),[37] the two of Capernaum[38] and the one found there in US 8 should be added. However, it should not be forgotten that, perhaps at the same time as the loss of value of silver coinage and the revaluation of bronze coinage, in this very region, and almost certainly because of military presence, there was an extensive re-pricing of the bronze divisional through reworking of the mint and the application of different types of countermarks: with letters, images and often with small imperial portraits difficult to identify.

Aurelian's monetary reform imposed the closure of the mints of almost the entire empire, including those of Syria, Palestine and Arabia, with a notable change in the structure of the circulating currency. The presence of copper declined and that of the *antoninianus* imposed itself, albeit gradually, but devalued to such an extent that, just twenty years later, a new radical intervention occurred under Diocletianus in 294. The quantitative analysis of the presence of *antoniniani* minted between 274 and 294 will make it possible to clarify the impact of the reform on the structure of the stock in use and the consequent monetary conditions that led into the following period: the time of the formation of two monetary circuits, that of Constantinian gold, i. e. the *solidus* (ca. 310),[39] and that of the bronze coinage with increasingly vile alloy and decreasing weights, between the fourth and fifth centuries.

4.6 Between the fourth and fifth century: the decline of small coins

The long period from Diocletianus to the end of the 5fourth century will see a radical change in both the system of account and coinage. The cornerstone of the modalities of counting values and their representation in coinage will be the Constantinian *solidus*, effective as unit of account from 310. Its purity and weight stability made it a very successful currency throughout the empire. Its value was to be used to price the rare silver coins, mostly ceremonial or donative in nature, but also copper coins, exchanged according to ratios corresponding to many thousands of *denarii* of account, but also by weight at the rate of 1 *solidus* against 20 pounds of copper as the *Codex Theodosianus*

34 It is sufficient to check for this same chronological range in https://chre.ashmus.ox.ac.uk/; Walker 1978, *passim*. An account of this phenomenon, which led, for example, to the widespread distribution of bronze from Viminacium, a Balkan mint, even in the regions of *Noricum* and *Venetia et Histria*, can be found in Callegher 2018a.

35 For an updated analysis of even mixed hoarding (silver/bronze) "after 243–244 CE" in central Israel, cf Ariel, Sokolov 2018.

36 Syon 2015, p. 76.

37 Bijovsky 2018, p. 527–530.

38 Callegher 2007, pp. 71–74, known as the 'treasure of the millstone', pp. 139–141, Area A. L130.2 (with only one *tetradrachm* of Traianus Decius and all *antoniniani* up to Gallienus).

39 Confirmation of 310 as the date for the introduction of the Constantinian solid in Malingue 2018.

reminds us.[40] The high purchasing power of the *solidus* and its fractions (quite rare in the east and more frequent in the west – see below) confined it to being used in transactions of considerable amounts, in taxation and in the records of debts and credits of the great economic actors of the period: the imperial bureaucracy, tax records or army payments. One of the consequences was also a progressive differentiation between east and west. In the west, silver continued to play a significant role, later confirmed by the coinage of the Ostrogoths. The process of regionalization saw the establishment of alloy coinage (at first *folles* and fractions, then from 348 AE2, AE3, AE4) minted in eastern mints with Constantinopolis preeminent, followed by Antioch and Alexandria. Generally speaking, although the volume of issues from the various mints was enormous, especially in the second half of the fourth century for the types *fel temp reparatio* (LRBC 2625 & 2295) and *spes reipublicae* (LRBC 2504), followed by the Valentinian-Theodosian AE3 *securitas reipublicae* (LRBC 527) and *gloria romanorum* 8 (LRBC 338), all of which are evidence of an extensive inflationary phenomenon. Their diffusion in the area surrounding Lake Tiberias appears rather diversified. At some sites, considerable quantities were found, obviously in proportion to the area investigated and the function of the site itself. We mention here, by way of indication, the conspicuous presence at Capernaum,[41] Omrit[42] and Khirbet Marus,[43] but also at Meiron,[44] Nabratein,[45] Sepphoris[46] and Hippos,[47] in addition to a few smaller sites such as Horvat Kanaf.[48] By contrast, at other sites, investigated *in extenso*, the presence of numerals undergoes a rapid decrease from second – third century until they become meagre or stop altogether, like in Gamla.[49] The phenomenon is part of the process of functional diversification of certain settlements in the Galilee and the Golan, with a consequent impact on the use of circulating currency, a phenomenon that has been investigated in still valid statistical terms by Gitler and Weisburd.[50] As for the fifth century, the coins minted and in circulation in the previous fourth century continued to be widely used, in particular the type *salus republicae* 2 (LRBC 1105) joined by the types *gloria romanorum* with two/three soldiers (LRBC 1876, 2214), with *vota* of the emperor Marcian with monogram and of Leo (LRBC 2260). Along with the official coins that flowed into this area mainly from eastern mints, very ancient issues from the Ptolemaic, Hasmonean, and provincial Roman periods also began to return into circulation from the mid-fifth century, just to mention the most frequent in the excavation documentation. Above all, numerous imitations of the most common types struck between the fourth and fifth centuries appeared. In them the legends were disjointed, the images sketchy and there were even inventions that were difficult to explain.[51] Beyond the iconographic data, however, their weight is of particular importance. It tends to be about ½ of that of similar official coins, as has been verified by testing the weight data of a conspicuous number of imitative types.[52] Assuming that until the mid-fifth century, AE4 substantially respected its weight ratio with the *scruple* (1.13 g)[53] effectively representing the physical mintage of the unit of account: that is the *nummus* of account really minted. It can be hypothesized, therefore, that its face value equaled its intrinsic value in copper metal. It follows that all these imitations were mostly or predominantly fiduciary in nature and course, or at least had a price that was overvalued compared to their face value. Similar observations regarding the weight deviation concern the imitations that can be dated to the second half of the fifth century, which are also widely found in the circulation of this region. These small copper coins all have an average weight significantly lower than the reference standard. In fact, for example, the weight of the imitation *vota* is around 0.49 g; that of the small *nummus* with the cross drops to an average weight of 0.38 g.

40 Hendy 1985, pp. 291, 470 for the weight ratio of the various copper/bronze denominations.
41 Callegher 2007a; Callegher 2007b; Callegher 2010.
42 Syon 2011, particularly the graph n. 1, p. 106.
43 Thanks to Gabriela Bijovsky: personal communication.
44 Meyer, Strange, Meyers 1981, Appendix C, *passim*; Raynor, Meshorer 1988, pp. 79–83.
45 Bijovsky 2009, pp. 388–389.
46 Bunnell 1937a, pp. 62–74; Ariel, Bijovsky 2018.
47 Segal, Mlynarczyk, Burdajewicz 2000; Segal, Mlynarczyk, Burdajewicz 2001; Segal, Mlynarczyk, Burdajewicz 2002; Segal, Mlynarczyk, Burdajewicz *et alii* 2004; Segal, Mlynarczyk, Burdajewicz *et alii* 2006; Segal, Mlynarczyk, Burdajewicz *et alii* 2008; Solarewicz 2015. General Conspectus of Coins Chronology and Mints Found at Hippos: thanks to Donald Ariel, personal communication.
48 Ariel 1980.
49 Syon 2014, p. 223.
50 Gitler, Weisburd 2005, in particular the map on p. 541 and the list of sites considered, many of which pertain to the region under analysis here. Not reliable Safrai 1998 as brilliantly pointed out in Bijovsky 2000–2002.
51 Arslan 2021.
52 Carlà 2007, pp. 184–186; Carlà 2009, pp. 437–440; Asolati 2012b, pp. 283–284, in particular for the identification on both documentary and numismatic grounds between AE4 and *nummus*. For archaeometric aspects see Asolati 2012a, pp. 187–227.
53 Arslan 2011; *contra* Asolati 2012b, p. 284.

The data for the imitations of the Victory left from the period of Valentinian III are no different. In all these cases, therefore, these small coins would have been minted with a weight of at least half the acknowledged standard for the contemporary legal *nummus*. The proto-Vandal coins or the imitations of the same type Greek cross within wreath or double wreath, Greek cross and four dots, six or eight-pointed star, and type Victory left, also widely found in Palestine and Syria and almost always of Carthaginian or North African origin, would also fall within the scope of fiduciary. They are placed in the late fifth century, if not in some cases traced back to Thrasamund (496–523). However, although it seems immethodical to propose an average weight for the various proto-Vandal groupings here, it should be noted that for various types the weights are distributed with ranges between 0.21–0.45 g, 0.25–0.35 g or 0.26–0.39 g.[54] These are very low values, about half of the official *nummus*, which at that time tended to average close to, if not more than, ½ g because "*the imperial nummus* […] *had to conform to an official standard that* […] *guaranteed the monetary and account system*"[55]. The Carthaginian or North African issues, minted outside imperial control, would thus not only have seen their status as overvalued coins confirmed, but would even have been reinforced if one considers that their weight reference was not the official *nummus* but that of the Byzantine coins marked with account numbers of 40 (M), 20 (K), I (10) and E (5). In fact, the actual weight of this divisional was always lower than that which would have been obtained by adding a quantity of coins equal to the number of *nummi* indicated, even if they had had a standard weight of ca. 0.50 g. In practice, these imitations would have had their reference in an already overvalued coin as that of the first reform of Anastasius.[56] The spread of this minute divisional from Carthage along the routes of the central-eastern Mediterranean and the Syrian Palestinian regions is well known in its strictly numismatic aspects,[57] as well as for the commercial motivations reconstructed through the study of transport containers (amphorae),[58] of North African slip ware,[59] and for military reasons stemming from the strategic-military choices that involved the displacement and subsequent allocation of *numeri* and *limitanei* (Vandal *Iustiniani*) mainly in an anti-Persian function.[60] In the Syrian-Palestinian region, and also in the area under examination here, this type of numismatic documentation is very substantial, both among individual excavated finds and as a relevant component of another phenomenon typical of this area, that of the founding deposits of synagogues between the late fifth and early sixth centuries in which many thousands of these small coins are recovered.[61] It is clear from the above that all imitations at the time of their manufacture were overvalued coinage and therefore fiduciary in nature, probably in response to a demand for divisionals that the imperial mints were not taking on or were no longer able to satisfy. Despite the prohibitions (CTh. IX, 21. 10), their quantity, diversity, and diffusion attest that from the end of the fourth century and during a large part of the fifth century they were produced locally or came from other areas (Carthage or Italy). This was not by some imponderable chance, but for a necessity issues, so much so that they constituted an appreciable percentage of the stock available on the market, in this case from Galilee and Gaulanitis, without their circulation posing any particular problems of acceptance or valuation in relation to other coins.

4.7 Byzantine period (498–ca. 640)

In order to face the progressive debasement of copper coinage and its fall in weight, the reforming intervention of 498 provided for the creation of new coins quoted at de facto fiduciary values with the indica-

54 Callegher 2016.

55 Asolati 2012b, *loc. cit.*

56 Asolati 2012b, *loc. cit.*

57 For an overview of circulation and consequent issues: Morrisson 1999; Bijovsky 2000–2002; Morrisson 2003a; Asolati 2005; Asolati 2006; Prigent 2006; Asolati 2008; Morrisson 2008; Morrisson 2012; Asolati 2012a; Asolati 2012b. For the Israeli area, cf. Bijovsky 2012b, pp. 147–148.

58 Panella 1993; DeRose Evans 2006, p. 46.

59 Magness 1994, p. 134; for attestations in nearby Capernaum, see Loffreda 2008, *ad indicem*.

60 Ravegnani 2005, pp. 190–191 remember, *inter alia*, the appropriation of *numeri* at the end of the fifth century-early sixth century in the regions of Syria, Lebanese Phoenicia and Palestine; it also points to an *arithmos* of Theodosiacs in Nessana at least from 504. From 534 the appropriation of the well-known Vandal *Iustiniani*, remarks the extensive employment of Vandal soldiers in the eastern part of the empire. For monetary circulation related to the military element on the Persian-Byzantine border in the sixth century: Casey 1996. Of extraordinary relevance for the reconstruction of taxation amounts in towns and villages as well as payments of military elements in the period and territory considered here is the essay by Di Segni 2004.

61 In this regard, the data on the circulation of imitative coinage in Bijovsky 2012, pp. 102–170; Ahipaz 2013 are exhaustive. Most recently also Callegher 2019, now also see https://www.ancientsynagoguecoins.com.

tion of the value in *nummus* of account (I, K, M), but not for the disappearance of the physical *nummus*. This small divisional, in fact, continued to be minted at least in the first transitional phase and its quotation as the good coin of the system (real coinage of the *nummus* of account) even induced hoarding phenomena.[62] To this small coin was probably assigned both the task of maintaining gold-copper convertibility, especially for tax purposes, and the evident overvaluation/trustworthiness of the larger divisionals (of 40, 20, 10 and 5 *nummi*) because the weight of a number of *nummi* corresponding to the facial numerator would always give a much higher value than that of the respective multiples, the largest of which, in Anastasius' first reform, was cut at ca. 9 g.[63] In other words, the first Anastasian reform would have created the conditions for the retention or return to circulation of coins minted between the end of the fourth and throughout the fifth century. There would thus have been a substantial coincidence between the actual *nummus* and the unit of account, a condition that would have allowed the use of all the small coins then on the market, imitations, blank flans and casts included. Thanks to their weight they had namely in fact become 'good money' in relation to the fiduciary divisional.[64] From this perspective, the presence of coinage in many localities in the region and the synagogues' founding deposits may have been motivated by fiscal reasons, both towards the imperial treasury and towards the community itself in which the annual capitation was planned[65] which would be produced by taking what was available locally,[66] or returned to use purely of economic advantage. In cases of concealment, as already mentioned, one cannot think of hoards in the traditional sense because their destination under heavy paving stones *ipso facto* ruled out their recovery and monetary re-use. A question remains, however, concerning precisely the value of this coinage. That is, since it was available overvalued on the market, as the individual finds attest, why was the latter, less expensive to demonetize, not used? This question is difficult to answer. Perhaps in the divisional collection to be understood as 'community treasury/goods', only copper coinage convertible to gold was accepted and therefore of full value or less overvalued than others. It is also plausible that it was precisely between 508 and 512 that the first tensions between copper and gold were felt, generated by the gap produced by the choice made in 498.[67] Anastasius' decision to double the weight of the follis, raising it from 9 g to 18 g, had as its first consequence to make the weight difference between the *nummus* and its multiples less disadvantageous. At the same time, it would have been less profitable to keep the small coins or old denominations of lesser value still in circulation, but also less costly to use them for ritual or celebratory functions, and therefore more acceptable to demonetize them, as can be deduced from the compositional structure of various foundation deposits in Galilee-Gaulanitis and the numerous contemporary repositories in which the 40-*nummon folles* of Anastasius' first reform are completely missing.[68]

62 Asolati 2012b, pp. 285, 314–316 particularly effective for the analysis of the closed repositories between 490 and 510: 47 cases referable almost exclusively to Asia Minor, Syria-Palestine and North Africa, consisting only of AE4 and *nummi* and in which no *folles* of the first reform of Anastasius weighing ca. 9 g are reported.

63 For the relationship between the numismatics data and the sources on the Anastasian reform, in particular on the *placibilis plebi commutatio*, cf Asolati 2012b, p. 300.

64 Asolati 2012b, p. 308.

65 In this regard, one is reminded that rabbinic texts dating back to the fifth–sixth centuries recommend the collection of the annual *hekdesh* and offerings in money or goods to be allocated to the intended purposes and not be spared: *Tosefta, Baba Mesia* 143, 11.23; *Tosefta, Sheqalim* 177–178, 3.2–6.

66 In this regard, I continue to consider the correspondences between the imitations and uncoined roundels reported in Callegher 2007a, and those with the homologous specimens from the deposit, published here, as probative. The commentators seem to have overlooked e. g. the extraordinary symmetry between the individual finds from Locus L71.1 in the urban area of Capernaum (Callegher 2007a, pp. 159–161), with the statistical sequence of the coins from the deposit and their chronology. Similar correspondences can be found when comparing coins from synagogal deposits in Galilee with those from individual finds at the same sites: bibliographic indications in Ariel 1980; Bijovsky 1998; Bijovsky 2012b; Ahipaz 2013; now also see https://www.ancientsynagoguecoins.com. *Contra* Arslan 2011.

67 Asolati 2012b, p. 301 with reference to numismatic sources and data.

68 On this subject see Arslan 2011 who bases his deductions on the data of the Sardis's hoard (a site in Lydia, admittedly a little far from Galilee) and does not resort to those of, for example, Qazrin, Umm el-Qanatir, Korazin, Meiron, Bar'am, Deir 'Aziz and Horvat Marus. Arslan's assertion 2011, 159 "*Callegher's refusal to consider the assemblage as a deposit accumulated over time – with a very similar profile to the isolated finds from the city – led him to posit a currency where coins were never withdrawn from the market*", is contradicted by the timely analysis of the Galilee deposits and/or repositories, buried or concealed between 490–520 in which it would have been impossible to find late fifth–early sixth century *nummi* or AE4 if they had been withdrawn from the market 'over time', whereas their presence is conspicuous, certain proof that these coins circulated for a long time at least until the Justinian reform of 538 (for hoarding, circulation and the economic analysis cf. Asolati 2012b and Bijovsky 2012b). This obviously does not exclude some cas-

Subsequently, the various weight changes, particularly implemented during Justinian's reign, led to the cessation of minting *nummi* and an increase in the divisionals of 5 and 10 *nummi,* but the contribution of the Alexandrian *dodecanummus*, often imitated and even produced by casting in the Palestinian territories, should also be noted.[69]

In a nutshell, during the sixth century, the contribution to the circulating bronze coinage of the various emperors, albeit with some quantitative contraction particularly during the reign of Tiberius II, remained stable. Among the mints, Constantinopolis and Antioch stand out in particular.

The following century, particularly during the reign of Phocas and Heraclius, was characterized by military events with a strong impact on Galilee and the surrounding regions: the Persian occupation (610–628) was immediately followed by the start of the Arab conquest (636). The movement and succession of military contingents could not fail to be reflected in the composition of the circulating currency. For copper, the Constantinopolitan *folles* became dominant, while for gold (*solidus* and *semi-solidus*, albeit in smaller quantities) there was frequent hoarding, of various size, from a few dozen to several hundred precious coins, generally motivated by wars and the succession of different administrations or authorities rather than by economic reasons.[70]

es of their selective saving, but it certainly excludes that they were withdrawn from circulation. On this, we recommend the study by Asolati 2012b. As for the accumulation of a deposit in a manner defined as 'over time', this is considered a difficult hypothesis, a *lectio difficilior*. In such a case, it is assumed that money is accumulated/saved with the conscious purpose of depositing to retrieve it at a later time. The result would be a planned and intentional hoarding, a kind of "community or private saving deposit", for the definition of which cf. Ahipaz 2013, p. 63. Such a choice is certainly conceivable, but the intentional program of a community deposit over time would have to be demonstrated above all by disregarding the data deducible from the single finds of the various sites in a region. In addition, the methodological necessity of linking numismatic data to the economic-monetary events of the time, in this case to the value of the *nummus*, to the fiduciary nature of coins with facial value indications, and to contemporary monetary reforms, remains unavoidable.

69 Bijovsky 2012b, pp. 283–285; 299–307.

70 Bijovsky 2012b, pp. 356–360 and Appendix A, pp. 464–470. See also the subsequent hoards in Callegher 2018b, Callegher 2021.

4.8 Arab-Byzantine and early Umayyad period

As Byzantine influence in the region declined, replaced by the new Arab-Islamic authorities,[71] Byzantine gold and bronze coinage initially continued to influence the region's economy. Indeed, taxation, as had been the case during the Persian occupation between 613 and 630, continued to be calculated and almost certainly collected in *solidus*/*nomismata*. This precious metal coinage retained its status in larger transactions, e. g. in financing state or new authorities' expenditures. After the Battle of Yarmouk in 636 and for much of the seventh century, at least until the time of Emperor Constantine IV (668–685), the Constantinopolitan *solidus* remained a reference for taxation and for establishing debts and credits in a stable and shared unit. This is proven by the numerous hidden and no longer recovered hoards within the territory of Palestine, when it had already come under Arab-Islamic control.[72] It should also be mentioned that one of the most common *solidus* types, and thus most widespread at the time, was that of Heraclius with the three emperors. It is possible that it formed the bulk of the stock in use at the time of the arrival of the new conquerors and as such remained in use for a long time, so much so that it became a prototype in the Arab-Byzantine bronze coinage (e. g. three standing figures issues of Tiberias on the Jund al-Urdunn) as well as in the first dinars, perhaps minted in Damascus, around the time of the reform of Caliph 'Abd el-Malik (685–705). Equally essential was the availability of copper coinage, an integral part of the Byzantine fiscal system and often purchased from moneychangers to pay taxes with fractional value amounts compared to the gold/*solidus* unit of account. This necessity, coupled with the demand for currency for lower value exchanges, may be considered a good reason why Constantinopolitan copper continued to flow into the territories of the former dominion now subject to new authority even if in quantities not as abundant as in the past, but also why new coins were minted though inspired by imitating those then in use (e. g. the types of Constans II). In fact, from the decade 637–647, alongside the issues of Heraclius and Constans II, imitative coins appeared, but in substantial weight alignment with Byzantine metrology. Their summary style incorporated some

71 Kaegi 1992, pp. 66–111; El Cheikh 2004, pp. 21–81; Foss 2008, especially the introductory parts of the chapters.

72 Bijovsky 2012b, pp. 375–381 and Appendix A-List of Hoard. New data in Callegher 2021.

iconographic elements (emperor and value sign M) while the legends moved away from the canonical epigraphic form. The most significant change occurred in the second part of the first caliphate, between 650–660, when the images and legends moved away from Byzantine imperial prototypes that were now replaced by legends in kufic characters (e.g. the name of the Prophet). At the same time, the distinctive features of the emperor's figure faded into an almost linear form. The later copper coinage of Caliph Muʿawiya became clearly bilingual (Greek and kufic) and was produced in numerous newly opened workshops: Damascus, Jerusalem, Tiberias, Diospolis (Ludd), Baalbek (Heliopolis), Scythopolis (Bet She'an-Baisan), Jerash (Jerash), reflecting the economic centrality of Galilee and Gaulanitis, the territories of the Syrian-Jordanian-South Palestine divide. The demand for low-value currency remained substantially unchanged, in which the confirmation of the value sign M (= 40 *nummi*) referred to the units of account which continued to be those established for centuries, the Roman-Byzantine ones. The definitive change in the region's monetary structure came about with the caliphate of ʿAbd el-Malik. From this period we know of some anonymous dinars of difficult chronology, the *fals* with the three emperors, imitating Byzantine coins, and those grouped in the much-discussed series called "Standing Caliph Coinage", struck in several mints including those of the Jund al-Urdunn. The use of two metals, gold and copper, allows us to hypothesize that a bimetallic system with different purposes was preserved: fiscal for gold, with a liberating function and fiduciary value for copper.[73] The publication of coins from excavations, hoards and recent studies confirm a vast circulation of *fals* that can only be explained as a response to a substantial demand for divisionals no longer supplied by the Byzantine mints, which were in fact outside the legal administrative perimeter of the Islamic authorities.[74] The consolidation of the new monetary structure came about with the reform of ʿAbd el-Malik (H 74 = 693/694), which provided for the production of copper coinage organized at the level of the Jund, but with centralized supervision,[75] and which definitively separated the Islamic empire from the Byzantine system of account and circulating money with its issues in three metals (*dinar, dirhem, fulus*), contributing to the formation of the clear separation, also in the monetary sphere, between the two new empires. Monetary finds from Galilee are proof of this and the region became definitively part of the Umayyad domain.

4.9 Islamic coinage

Included in this definition, though admittedly imperfect because close to linguistic/religious criteria, are the issues of the various dynasties that followed one another over the centuries exercising their monetary jurisdiction in Galilee and the surrounding regions. In the second half of the seventh century, proto-Umayyad authorities emerged which established themselves definitively, from a monetary point of view, with the reform of ʿAbd al-Malik and the clear dominance of the Damascus coinage.[76] This was followed by the Abbasids, the Mamluks and finally the Ottomans. Studies and research on the issues of the various caliphs/sovereigns and the contribution of the various mints, which can be deduced from coin findings following the methodology applied for ancient coinage, are in the making. Only an accurate assessment will make it possible to delineate the exchange ratios, for example, between *fulus* and *dirhams* at a given site or their liberating function. Similarly, it would be better known, for example, the different contributions of mints, the transfer of the divisional and the reasons for it, the use of the less valuable coin in relation to the activities of a site.[77]

4.10 The *denarii* of the Latin Empire

The publications of medieval coins from archaeological excavations, alongside the coins of the various Islamic authorities/mints of the thirteenth–fourteenth centuries, make available numerous individual finds of *denarii* minted in Jerusalem by the various crusader kings. Often, their presence, especially in sites with royal or traditional memories of Christianity, are linked to pilgrimages or undefined travelers. But this hypothesis does not seem conclusive. Their number and above all the excavated contexts allow us, perhaps

73 On the debate and chronological proposals in this series, SEE Album, Goodwin 2002; Goodwin 2005; Foss 2008; Goodwin 2018 and the proceedings of *Syrian Numismatic Round Table* that are held between Cambridge and Oxford, including, in particular Goodwin T. (ed.), *Arab-byzantine Coins and History*, London 2012.

74 I am referring in particular to the current research curated by Gabriela Bijovsky, whom I thank.

75 Heidemann 1998, pp. 97–99.

76 Heidemann 1998.

77 Kool 2007; Kool 2013.

more correctly, to postulate the settlement of military contingents to give territorial depth to the control of the Latin Empire as well as the need to control peripheral areas to coastal or fortified settlements. The diffusion of crusader money, in silver and on western standards, obviously invites comparison with issues of Islamic mints with which, necessarily, that divisional coins came into contact.[78]

4.11 Evidence from the twentieth century

At the end of the First World War, Palestine passed from the Ottoman Empire to the British Mandate (1920–1948). These were years of immigration from various parts of the world, of population growth, of the movement of people in search of sites where they could finally settle in free communities. Under the aegis of the British, coins were minted from 1927 to 1946 for circulation within the Mandate. Indeed, in 1926, after a few years of transition, the British Secretary of State for the Colonies appointed a Palestine Currency Board to introduce a local currency. It was based in London and chaired by P. G. Ezechiel, with a Currency Officer resident in Palestine. The board decided that the new currency would be called the *Palestine pound*, fixed in value to the British pound and divided into 1000 *mils*, with change of 1, 2, 5, 10, 20, 50 and 100 *mils*. The 1 and 2 *mils* were struck in bronze, whereas the 5, 10 and 20 *mils* were holed, cupro-nickel coins except for during World War II when they were also minted in bronze. The 50 and 100 *mils* coins were struck in silver alloy (0.720% fine). Alongside the metal coinage they also printed 500 *mils* and 1, 5, 10 and 50 pound notes. Often, in the surface layers of archaeological excavations, specimens from this period or from other colony states are recovered, lost perhaps during visits, travels or some transaction.[79]

78 Metcalf 1995.

79 Berlin 2001.

5. Critical Analysis of single finds

On the basis of the previous methodologies and periodizations, including the critical role of gaps in the recording of excavation results, the coins found at Magdala in the area investigated by the SBF (excavations 1970/1971–2013) are 2613 to which are added 12 fragments of almost certainly coins and 2 exagia, bringing the total to 2627 items.[1] Of the 2613, only 1566 have been identified or attributed to a chronological period on the basis of a complete reading or the identification of a relevant iconographic element. A very high proportion, 1047 coins, are in such a bad state of preservation (limestone, corrosion, mineralization of the flan) that it is impossible to classify them without working on the basis of imagination and without subjecting oneself to the uncertainty of the time of a possible restoration (40 % of the specimens), which is also very costly. In fact, for only 60 %, so just over half, was a complete or partial classification possible, and in any case reliable. The numismatic material also included two hoards: one from the Roman imperial period found in H, Field 3-US 8 (21 Roman provincial coins) and one from the Arab-Byzantine period in E 11 (9 coins), which will both be described separately.

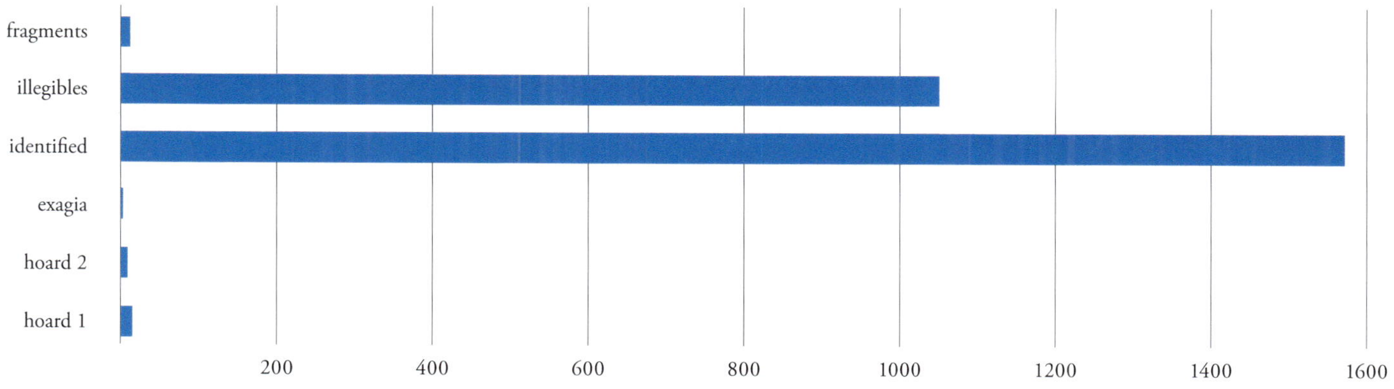

Fig. 2: General comparison of coin findings.

1 We cannot exclude some numerical discrepancies due, above all, to chronological partitioning, because some issues, especially from the transitional phase towards full control of Roman imperial authority also over Galilee, are difficult to place in one of the periods. In any case, some deviations of a few units do not change the statistical data at all.

Tab. 1: Breakdown of monetary finds by period.

Period/Ruler	Single finds	Hoard	Exagia	Fragments
Ptolemies	4			
Seleucids	7			
Hasmoneans	320			
Herodians	251			
Hasmonean/Herodian	56 + 125			
Roman Procurator (9–ca.70)	54			
First Jewish Revolt	4			
Tyre City coins (first c. BCE–second c. CE)	68			
Nabatean	1			
Roman and Roman Provincial Coins (ca. 70–294)	386	1 (15 coins)		
Late Roman Period (post 294–498)	184			
Byzantine	13			
Arab-Byzantine	15	1 (9 coins)		
Islamic Coins	68			
Crusader Period	2			
Ottomans-XX c.	2+6			
			2	
				12
Total	1566		2	12

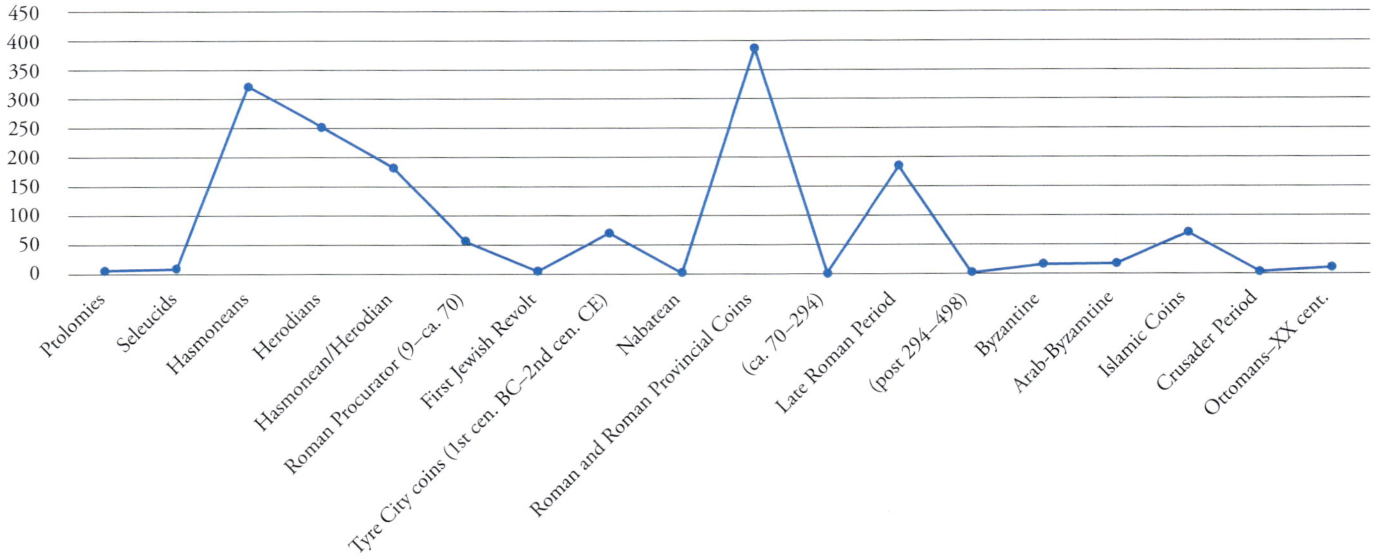

Fig. 3: Composition and Chronology of the Identified Coins.

The critical analysis of the coins will closely follow the catalogue, organized by minting areas, authorities and mints. Table n.1 shows the composition of the identifiable numismatic material.

From this summary table and graph, a substantial continuity of coin presence emerges from Alexander Jannaeus until the end of the fourth century, after which the circulating (Byzantine, Arab and Crusader) coinage declines significantly. Variations in the presence of an authority (e. g. Alexander Jannaeus) or an emperor (e. g. Trajan or Elagabalus), as well as in the mints of origin (e. g. Tyre, Jerusalem, Tiberias, etc.) will be discussed within the various sections following also the AACL statistical method,[2] in this case by comparing the MAP excavation data[3] with Wadi Hamam,[4] to extend them to a comparison with a few sites consistent in function and quantity of collected monetary documentation. However, it is necessary to recall the scope of this type of statistical calculation. This formula, in fact, expresses the diachronic distribution of coin findings considering the date of issue, but disregards the duration in circulation inferable only from the stratigraphy of the various loci of an excavation. It follows that the available data must be interpreted appropriately in light of multiple monetary factors, therefore with caution, and without any final or apodictic conclusions.

5.1 The Ptolemaic period – third century BCE (see 4.1)

Four coins are dated to this period, one of Ptolemy Epiphanes of uncertain mint, the other three of undetermined authority, all from the third century BCE, if not from its final phase. Similar finds were discovered at Wadi Hamam,[5] but especially of course in the Magdala-MAP part.[6] Coins from the Ptolemaic period are also well documented at Akko Ptolemais[7] and other sites on Lake Kinneret: for example in et-Tell (Bethsaida?),[8] in Tiberias,[9] the Gaulanitis[10] and in Gamla.[11] Tyre issues dominate these numismatic documentation[12] with some presence of coins minted in Alexandria. Already in the third century BCE, it should be remembered, the Tyrian mint exerted a hegemonic role in responding to the demand for bronze coinage. From that city, in fact, its coinage spread along the coastal settlements from Sarepta[13] to Beirut[14] and from there to the interior regions. Being bronze specimens of Tyre standard, it is not so evident that Tyrian coins arrived in the area in the early third century for trade along the Jordan Valley or inland routes; they are more likely to be connected to the movements of men and soldiers during the conflict with the Seleucids in the late third–early second century BCE. The Ptolemaic monetary presence, all in all modest, does not seem be linked in any way to the settlement's chronology; of course, any connection should possibly be sought only in connection with other classes of archaeological finds.

5.2 The Seleucid period – second century BCE (see 4.2)

A small increase is recorded with the 7 coins of the Seleucids, all in copper and among the lower-value divisionals: 1 AE of Antiochus IV from the mint of Akko-Ptolemais, 1 AE of Demetrius II from Tyre, 2 AE of Demetrius III from Seleucia-Pieria while for another 3 AE the authority and mint are uncertain. Here, again, quantitative and qualitative comparisons (authority and mint) are to be found primarily between the Magdala-MAP documentation[15] and that of Wadi Hamam.[16] The process of circulation of Seleucid bronze began, of course, where it was produced and probably spread along routes similar to those created for the small Ptolemaic divisionals, from the coastal cities towards the inland: from Tyre, from Beirut,[17]

2 Ravetz 1964, pp. 205–208; Casey 1986, pp. 89–90; Derose Evans 2006, pp. 63–70; Stella 2019, with data and method particularly reliable for the quantity of specimens considered and relevant to a single city: Aquileia. Numismatists interested in statistical studies are using the number of coins found, and how that number may compare to the number of years the ruler reigned. This equation is expressed according to this formula: (Coins of Reign/Years of Reign) × (1000/Total coins of the Site) = AACL.

3 I would like to thank Danny Syon for making the data available to me and for authorizing their use for quantitative comparisons.

4 Bijovsky 2018.

5 Bijovsky 2018, nr. 1.

6 Syon 2018, nr. 1; 4 more specimen in Syon, forthcoming. Obviously, as these are reports in progress, possible deviations are to be expected; this limitation applies to all subsequent quotations of quantitative data from these reports in progress.

7 Syon 2016: 20 specimen.

8 Meier 1995; Kindler 1999a.

9 Rahmani, Sharabani 1983, p. 71.

10 Syon 2015: map p. 135 and table pp. 137–138.

11 Syon 2014, nr. 1–14.

12 Sawaya 2011b.

13 Abou Diwan 2016, pp. 25–30.

14 Butcher 2003, pp. 44–47; Sawaya 2011a; Sawaya 2016, pp. 22–24. For an overview of production and circulation see Sawaya 2012; Sawaya 2017.

15 Syon, forthcoming.

16 Bijovsky 2018: 7 exemplars as follows: Antiochus III, Alexander Balas, Demetrius II, Antiochus VII from the mint of Tyre.

17 Butcher 2003, pp. 129–137; Sawaya 2016, pp. 106–110.

from Sarepta,[18] from Caesarea Maritima[19] up to Capernaum,[20] et-Tell/Bethsaida?,[21] Tiberias,[22] Hippos,[23] and Gamla[24] but also many other small settlements as can be seen from the detailed distributional reconstruction of Seleucid issues between 200–162 BCE, when the mint of Akko Ptolemais established itself on a large scale over all the other mints, on Tyre in particular.[25] The circulation of Akko Ptolemais coins also extended beyond Galilee, at least as far as Jerusalem.[26] Later, between 162–125 BCE, the bronze coinage of Tyre became once again considerably prevalent.[27] The different contribution to the demand for coinage between the two periods should perhaps be explained by the role of the maritime city of Akko Ptolemais as the principal city during the reigns of Antiochus III and Antiochus IV, later modified by the reorganization that begun with Demetrius I, when Tyre once again became the capital and obviously the mint of reference. However, apart from the political-military motivations, which certainly played an essential role in creating the conditions for the success of even the small divisionals, perhaps the real reason for the widespread use of Tyrian coins is to be found in the fact that Galilee still was and remained in the economic orbit of the Phoenician coast, of Tyre in particular, because it was easily connected to the Mediterranean, but above all because the Tyrian monetary and account system had already become firmly established.

This purely economic perspective also frames and explains the conspicuous number of Civic-Autonomous issues of Tyre, although subject to Seleucid authority. On the basis of the numerals present/absent on the reverse, it is not always easy to establish their chronology following the Tyre calendar. The types with Bust of Tyche or Head of Melqart and palm-tree with two branches of fruits date from the end of the second century BCE to the first century BCE, but it is a type that also reappears in the first –second centuries CE. Similar observations can be made for the coins with Head of Tyche and Galley with prow terminating in volutes in which the epigraphic part has disappeared. Their reading and attribution to a chronological period depends, therefore, on their preservation.

Alongside these, small bronzes minted in Sidon or Arados also circulated but in much smaller quantities. In the case of these civic issues – dated and undated coins – found in Magdala, in a conspicuous number (68 specimens), they are certainly not unique to the part of the area excavated by MP-SBF because numerous specimens with the same chronological scan were also recovered in various loci of the MAP excavations.[28] In addition, these small bronzes, the vast majority of which were minted in Tyre, are attested in significant quantities in Wadi Hamam,[29] Capernaum,[30] Hippos,[31] Gamla[32] and many other sites, even small ones such as Kursi,[33] in a truly large spread[34]. Their success lasted almost two centuries and resulted from the strong economic influence of the Phoenician city, but above all the advantageous relationship with other copper coinage available on the market. Thus, as the coins were issued by the authorities in Palestine (*prutot* of the Hasmoneans and of the Herodian period, coinage of the Roman procurators and even imperial Roman dials of the first phase of the second century, especially of Hadrianus), the Tyrian bronze coins maintained a quotation that guaranteed their free use, probably with a ratio of equal face value and perhaps as fractions in the case of the heavier issues. In this way, by running together with the divisional of other mints, over the course of about two centuries the Tyre mintage contributed very substantially to the stock of coinage available at the highest levels and in a very large territory, far beyond Galilee, beginning with Bet She'an (Nysa-Scythopolis),[35] at Caesarea Maritima[36] and as far as Jerusalem.[37]

18 Abou Diwan 2016, pp. 30–35.
19 Derose Evans 2006, pp. 104–105, 106–107.
20 Callegher 2007, pp. 81–82,
21 Butcher 2003.
22 Syon 2015, p. 123, with reference bibliography.
23 Segal, Mlynarczyk, Burdajewicz 2000; Segal, Mlynarczyk, Burdajewicz 2001; Segal, Mlynarczyk, Burdajewicz 2002; Segal, Mlynarczyk, Burdajewicz *et alii* 2004; Segal, Mlynarczyk, Burdajewicz *et alii* 2006; Segal, Mlynarczyk, Burdajewicz *et alii* 2008; Solarewicz 2015 and the *General conspectus of coins chronology and mints found at Hippos* thanks to Donald Ariel (May 2021).
24 Syon 2014, pp. 148–166.
25 Syon 2015, pp. 139–143 in particular the distribution maps.
26 For the presence, for example in Jerusalem, cf. Ariel 1982, p. 279; Gitler 1996.
27 Syon 2015, pp. 141–142 for the comparison of the two maps with the distribution by quantity and sites.
28 Syon forthcoming. 60 monete: Seleucid from mint of Tyre; 65 bronze coin from Tyre or/and Tyre or Sidon (first c. BCE–CE).
29 Bijovsky 2018, p. 536–537.
30 Callegher 2007, pp. 82–83.
31 General Conspectus of Coins Chronology and Mints Found at Hippos: tanks to Donald Ariel, personal communication.
32 Syon 2014, pp. 195–199.
33 Sharabani 1983, no. 1.
34 See the distribution maps in Syon 2015, pp. 172–173.
35 Sharabani 2004, p. 83.
36 Derose Evans 2006, pp. 107–108.
37 Ariel 1982, pp. 283–284, also for the relations between silver from Tyre and the taxation collected at the Temple in Jerusalem. On this site of primary importance for understanding mon-

5.3 The Hasmonean period (125 BCE–63 BCE) (see 4.3)

In the area excavated by the MP, the quantity of Hasmonean coins, almost exclusively of Alexander Jannaeus, is truly remarkable and accounts for the overall percentage of ca. 20.5% of all identified coins. However, it is highly probable that in the large number of specimens deemed unclassifiable due to their poor state of preservation, a considerable number could be placed in this chronological period. In this substantial group of 320 *prutot*, only one is attributable to John Hyrcanus I (129–104 BCE), while all the others are by Alexander Jannaeus. The issues of the first type, with anchor surrounded by Diadem and ΑΛΕΞΑΝΔΡΟΥ ΒΑΣΙΛΕΩΣ (CHL 214 ff.) are missing. The copper issues of this authority here documented belong to two other types:[38]

a) TJC K (Type 4 in Shachar 2004): in the obverse anchor) surrounded by ΑΛΕΞΑΝΔΡΟΥ ΒΑΣΙΛΕΩΣ and, in the reverse Eight-pointed star in diadem, between rays Hebrew inscription "Yehonatan the King";
b) TJC L7-L17 (Type 5 and Type 7 in Shachar 2004): in the obverse anchor in circle, in the reverse Six-pointed star, sometime the style is so crude that the anchor is represented by five dots and the star in the reverse is represented only by one spoke. This type was struck in a very small flan and no inscription is visible to the extent that it appears to be an imitation of the official types, especially when one preserves the melting tangs of the roundel which suggest the coins may have been obtained by casting moulds, therefore with a manufacturing method that do not involve the use of cones. Casting with pre-ordained moulds was more effective in responding to the demand for coinage in a market stimulated by the intensification of trade and from the logistics associated with military presence.

Since the only dated coin of Jannaeus (year 25 of his reign, i.e. 80/79 BCE), which is not identified in this group of coins, derives from the earlier type TJC L1-L6, it can be assumed that it was produced only later on a large-scale and thus be restricted to just four years. From a quantitative perspective, the stock of the two types recovered in the MP part of the excavation is composed as follows:

Tab. 2: Quantity of typology of Alexander Jannaeus's coins.

Type	Quantity	Percentage
TJC K (Type 4 in Shachar 2004)	33	11%
TJC L7-L17 (Type 7 in Shachar 2004)	269	89%

The previous data find confirmation in the MPA area of Magdala, whose numismatic report, albeit in progress, reports 9 TJC K specimens and as many as 662 of type TJC L7-L17,[39] with percentages not too dissimilar to those in the section we are dealing with, if considering that the other types of coins present in not so large quantities must be included within Jannaeus issues. Such a high percentage, close to 90 % in both areas of the site, differs from that recorded in other Galilean sites, such as Wadi Hamam where out of 67 Jannaeus coins, 16 are of the TJC K type (23 %) and 31 of the TJC L7-L17 type (42 %),[40] or Gamla, where among the 3258 coins of Alexander Jannaeus, 26 % belong to the last type of the series.[41] Percentages not very dissimilar to the latter occur in Jerusalem,[42] Meiron,[43] Horvat Mazad and Yodefat.[44] Therefore, the large number of specimens of the last type in Magdala poses a major chronological problem, the answer to which also has consequences for in the archaeology of the site and the chronology of the finds.

etary relations between the various reasons of Palestine, after Ariel 1982, one can rely on the synthesis of Gitler 1996 and numerous other numismatic contributions published in excavation reports: Gitler 2003; Ariel 2013; Ariel 2020a, 2020c; Ariel, Berman 2020. These are, of course, not the only bibliographical references. The large amount of numismatic data that has emerged from the numerous excavation campaigns in Jerusalem would require a summary similar to those published years ago by Ariel 1982 and Gitler 1996.

38 Starting with the Meshorer 2001 classification, Zlotnik 2011 and Syon 2015, pp. 162–164 and CHL propose a chronological sequence in the often difficult-to-read types of the extensive Alexander Jannaeus issue series, using year-marked specimen as a reference point L KE (= year 25: cf CHL, p. 250, no. 238 e ss.).

39 Syon forthcoming.
40 Bijovsky 2018.
41 Syon 2014.
42 Ariel 1982. Although dated, the survey retains its reliability.
43 Raynor, Meshorer 1988.
44 For these sites cf Shachar 2044, p. 10.

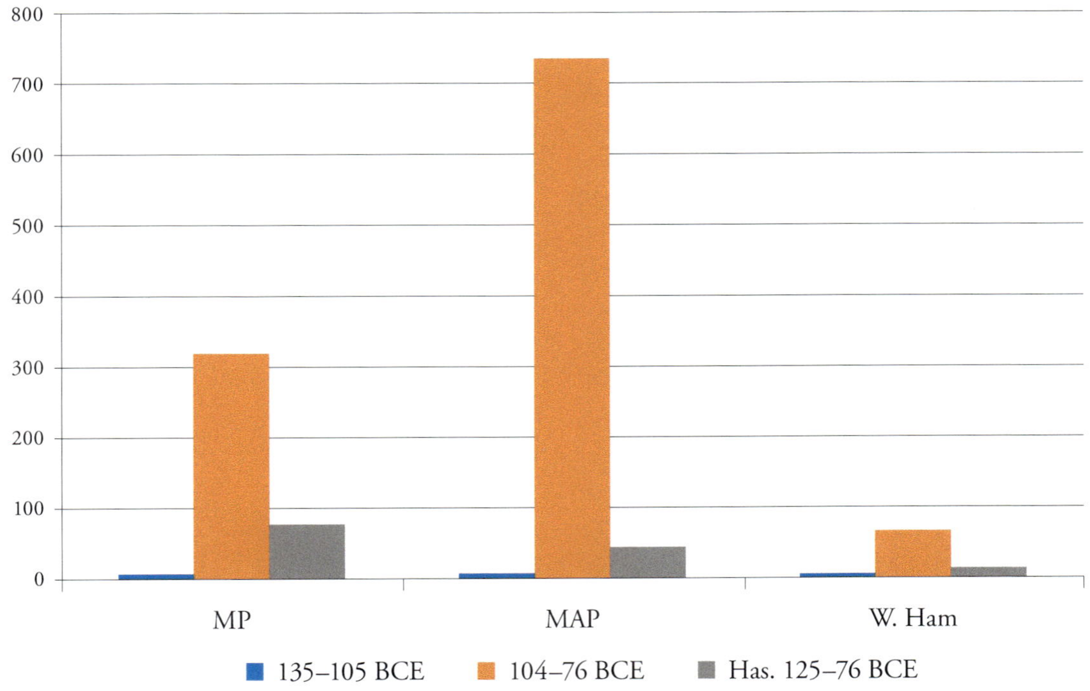

Fig. 4: Quantitative comparison between the three digs.

One wonders, in fact, whether such an enormous production could be concentrated in just a few years and also where it was coined, opening the way to the hypothesis that this degenerative series in the quality of the coinage and the alloy (often with high percentages of lead) continued at least in the first years after the death of the Hasmonean ruler. This chronological doubt leads to another question, related to site frequentation. Namely, whether such a large amount of coinage has any significance to better understand the settlement phase of the area. Following recent contributions on the documentary value of the coins of Alexander Jannaeus in archaeological excavations,[45] taking into account the persistent use in Magdala of the Seleucid divisional, the small bronze coins of Tyre autonomous city, the first coins of the Hasmoneans, Hyrcanus I, and the significant variety of the *prutot* of Jannaeus types,[46] it must be assumed that the area of Magdala must have been organized as a large settlement from at least the mid-second century BCE onwards. This intensive development, at least economically, and therefore also urban (with the semantic limits that this definition has when applied to a settlement in the ancient world), could be dated to around 90–80 BCE and continued in the following decades in the Herodian period.

Still paying attention to the quantitative data in the general context of the excavations in Madgala, the Hasmonean presence can also be examined according to the AACL method, as shown in the table that elaborates and proposes the data of both the MP and MPA and of Wadi Hamam.

Tab. 3: AACL indices for comparison between the three digs.

	MP	AACL	MAP	AACL	W.Ham	AACL
135–105 BCE	1	0,100	4	0,204	4	1,538
104–76 BCE	320	28,787	737	33,573	67	23,0082
Has. 125–76 BCE	76	3,753	43	1,075	12	2,262

45 Shachar 2004, in part. p. 11.

46 Data taken from the file made available by Danny Syon, whom I thank.

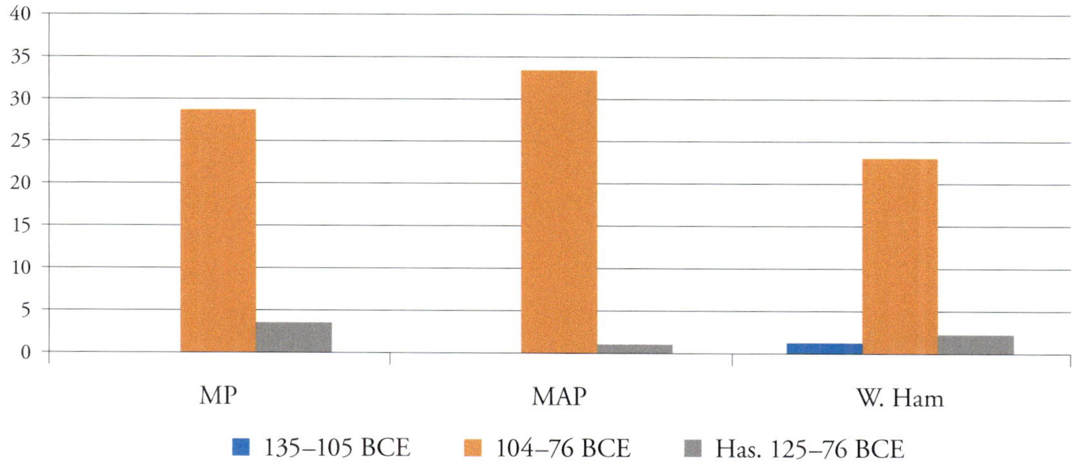

Fig. 5: Graphic rendering of the index AACL for comparison between the three digs.

In spite of the percentage deviations that are largely due to the quantity of coins recovered and catalogued which is a figure influenced by the type of use or activity practiced during the life of the archaeological site, in the graphic the peak of annual losses of *prutot* minted during the long and turbulent reign of Jannaeus is quite evident. The significance of the average annual loss index in the three contexts examined, in the MP section with an annual coefficient of 29, represents an unusual value. No less so is the value 33.5 for the MAP area and the value 23 in Wadi Hamam, both being very high. Such annual peaks are explained by the enormous stock of currency produced in the last years of this ruler's reign and circulating in this part of Lake Kinneret. This observation is logically connected to what has been hypothesized above regarding the role Magdala must have assumed following the historically documented events of the Jannaean phase of the Hasmoneans. We know, in fact, that John Hyrcanus conquered part of Samaria and Galilee between 112 and 107 BCE, especially the Greek foundation Nysa-Scythopolis. The Hasmonean expansion into Galilee was completed by Judah Aristobulus around 104–103 BCE, after whose sudden death Alexander Jannaeus succeeded as king. Militarily, Jannaeus was engaged on various fronts: against the Nabataeans, against the city of Akko-Ptolemais and against Gaza for control of the Spice Route, against Gadara east of the Jordan, in a kind of civil war between 94–84 BCE against the Pharisees and again opposed to the Nabataeans for control of the Decapolis region. In Galilee he had one of the territories of reference to organize his troops, especially mercenaries and to foster settlements for a population short of land to cultivate. Consequently, the minting and subsequently consistent circulation of *prutot* are to be connected, *in primis*, to the economic needs generated by the military campaigns and settlement strategies conducted by a sovereign who had been able to give his reign a supra-regional prominence with the monetary instrument. Magdala, perhaps even already then a port on the lake, must have been involved in the logistical needs arising from the presence and frequent movement of military contingents to, most probably, the settlement of people looking for land.[47] Moreover, as pointed out, the spread of *prutot* of the most important of the Hasmoneans is ubiquitous in much of Palestine, moreover in quantities that are always very conspicuous, often in the order of magnitude of many hundreds of specimens and, in statistical terms, often with a far greater percentage than other slightly earlier or later coinages. Leaving aside the obvious case of Jerusalem, a few random examples are worth mentioning: Samaria,[48] Jericho,[49] Masada[50] and also 'Aïn ez-Zâra/Callirrhoë place on the east coast of the Dead Sea.[51] Above all, Gabriela Bijovsky's statement, although related to the site of Wadi Hamam, is also valid for Magdala and Galilee in the first century BC: *"Jannaeus's coin belongs perhaps to his last issue, which depicts an anchor within a circle on the obverse and a star on the reverse. According to numismatic evidence from numerous other archaeological excavations, this prolific type – minted from 80/79 BCE – appears to have continued to circulate as a small denomination coin during the first century BCE, probably up to the time of the First Jewish Revolt"*.[52] A

47 Syon 2014; Syon 2021. On the relationship between monetary stocks and military and settlement strategies see Syon 2015, in part. pp. 161–170.

48 Reisner, Fisher, Lyon 1924, p. 266.

49 Meshorer 2004, pp. 292–298: 547 only coins by Alexander Jannaeus.

50 Meshorer 1989, pp. 86–87.

51 Clamer 1997, p. 91.

52 Bijovsky 2018, p. 518.

confirmation of the role as low-value coin, characteristic of a liberating function typical of an economy in which even the smallest prices are honored in cash, can also be found in the numismatic-metrological field. Indeed, the success of the TJC L1-L6 & L7-L17 types, often weighing between 1 and 2 grams, and thus lighter than the early series weighing ca. 3 grams but, in all likelihood, having the same face value, was determined precisely by their being competitive for adaptable to money market a lower weight standard.[53]

5.4 The Herodian dynasty, the Roman administration and the First Jewish Revolt (63 BCE–70 CE) (see 4.4)

The monetary documentation for this complex period is summarized in the following table, which shows the monetary evidence from the Madgala site and the nearby Wadi Hamman.

With the creation of the Province of Syria by Pompey in 64 BCE and the subjugation of Galilee and Judea to the authority of Rome, the coinage of the region and the consequent circulation underwent a considerable change. It should be noted, however, that the contribution of the numerous mints already active in Phoenicia, especially Tyre whose influence on Galilee continued to be considerable, did not diminish. In fact, the flow of bronze issues coined by Tyre as an autonomous city, as already mentioned, continued uninterrupted from the first century BCE until the second century CE. Especially noteworthy among these are the types with the Bust of Tyche looking right on the obverse and on the reverse the Galley with Greek or Phoenician inscriptions or showing the palm-tree with two branches of fruit and across field the letters as chronological indication following the Tyrian method. Sidon's monetary contribution was significant while Akko-Ptolemais remained of secondary importance[54]. Furthermore, in the sphere of what we might call "Jewish coins", the role that had

Tab. 4: Quantity and Authorities for comparison between the three digs

Authority	MP	MPA	W. Ham
Herod the Great (40–4 BCE)	175	101	9
Herod Archelaus (4 BCE–6 CE)	40	36	3
Herod the Great or Herod Archelaus (40 BCE–6 CE)		99	
Herod Antipas (4 BCE–39 CE)	23	67	8
Herod Philippus (4 BCE–34 CE)	1	2	
Ambibulus under Augustus (8–11)	8		
Coponius or Ambibulus under Augustus (5–11)	18	9	
Valerius Gratus under Tiberius (15–24)	1		
Pilatus under Tiberius (26–36)	8	23	
Agrippa I (37–44)	11	32	3
Antoninus Felix under Claudius (52–58)	5	12	
The Roman Administration under Claudius and Nero (44–68)		5	
Agrippa II (55/6–94/95)	12	36	2
Festus under Nero (58–62)	7	18	1
The First Jewish Revolt (66–70/3)	4	29	1
Uncertain Hasmonean or Herodian (first century BCE)	125	167	
"Hasmonean, Herodian, Roman Procurators, first Revolt" (125 BCE– 70 CE)		56	

53 This hypothesis, however, could be overcome if the mintage of the ½ *prutah* were to be proven, which is certainly possible, but requires a targeted metrological analysis.

54 See the distribution map of these three mints in Syon 2015, p. 173.

once been of the Hasmoneans was filled by Herod and his dynasty. Indeed, the Herodians continued the earlier tradition by minting small size copper coinage (*prutot*) and respected the prohibition of images. Instead, the issuing authority chose no anthropomorphous images: tripod with *lebes*; crested helmet; winged *caduceus*; single or double cornucopia; galley. The Jerusalem mint continued to be the reference and most active mint during the reign of Herod the Great. From 4 BCE to 6 CE it operated for Herod Archelaus. Herod Antipas minted in the fourth year of his reign (1BCE–1CE) a small issue at Sepphoris-Zippori (Diocaesara in the Roman period) while, probably from 20 CE onwards his best-known issues were made at Tiberias. Herod Philippus was active in Caesarea Paneas, introducing the portrait of Augustus on the obverse and his own on the reverse.[55] Moreover, these sovereigns exercised their jurisdiction over the territories they had divided between them, taking into account that from 5 CE onwards the imperial procuratorate was in place in Judaea, de facto respecting the others' minting rights.

What do the monetary data of these rulers, recovered in the MP area and compared with those of the MPA and Wadi Hamam, say? They fit in with and in fact confirm what has been elaborated in the most recent studies on the spread of small coinage in Galilee.[56] The *prutot* minted in Jerusalem by Herod the Great, especially the type with double cornucopia and anchor, and by Herod Archelaus, especially the type with Bunch of grapes/Crested helmet, arrived and circulated in Galilee, flanking and perhaps progressively replacing the earlier Hasmonean coinage of Alexander Jannaeus. As for the other two sovereigns responsible, respectively, for what was coined in the mints of Tiberias and Caesarea Paneas, the Magdala data confirm a sort of regional circulation, linked to the territory of the two Herodians. *Prutot* from Herod Philip/Caesarea Paneas appear to be rather scarce within the territory ruled by Antipas. Similarly, what was done under his rule in Tiberias seems to have been accepted or used almost exclusively within his territory. Since, on a metrological basis, no competition can be assumed between the

Tab. 5: AACL indices for comparison between the three digs

Authority	MP	MPA	W.Ham
Herod the Great (40–4 BCE)	11,09	4,05	9,25
Herod Archelaus (4 BCE–6 CE)	9,13	5,20	11,11
Herod the Great or Herod Archelaus (40 BCE–6 CE)	0	3,11	0
Herod Antipas	1,2	2,25	6,89
Herod Philippus (4 BCE–34 CE)	0,06	0,07	0
Ambibulus under Augustus (8–11)	6,08	0	0
Coponius or Ambibulus under Augustus (5–11)	6,84	2,16	0
Valerius Gratus under Tiberius (15–24)	0,25	0	0
Pilatus under Tiberius (26–36)	1,82	3,32	0
Agrippa I (37–44)	3,58	6,60	15,87
Antoninus Felix under Claudius (52–58)	1,90	2,89	0
The Roman Administration under Claudius and Nero (44–68)	0	0,30	0
Agrippa II (55/6–94/95)	0,68	1,30	1,85
Festus under Nero (58–62)	3,99	6,50	9,25
The First Jewish Revolt (66–70)	2,28	10,47	9,25
Uncertain Hasmonean or Herodian (first century BCE)	2,85	2,41	0
"Hasmonean, Herodian, Roman Procurators, first Revolt" (125 BCE–70 CE)	0	0,41	0

55 CHL, plate 211, no. 117.

56 Syon 2015, pp. 174–179, in particular distribution maps figs. 44, 45.

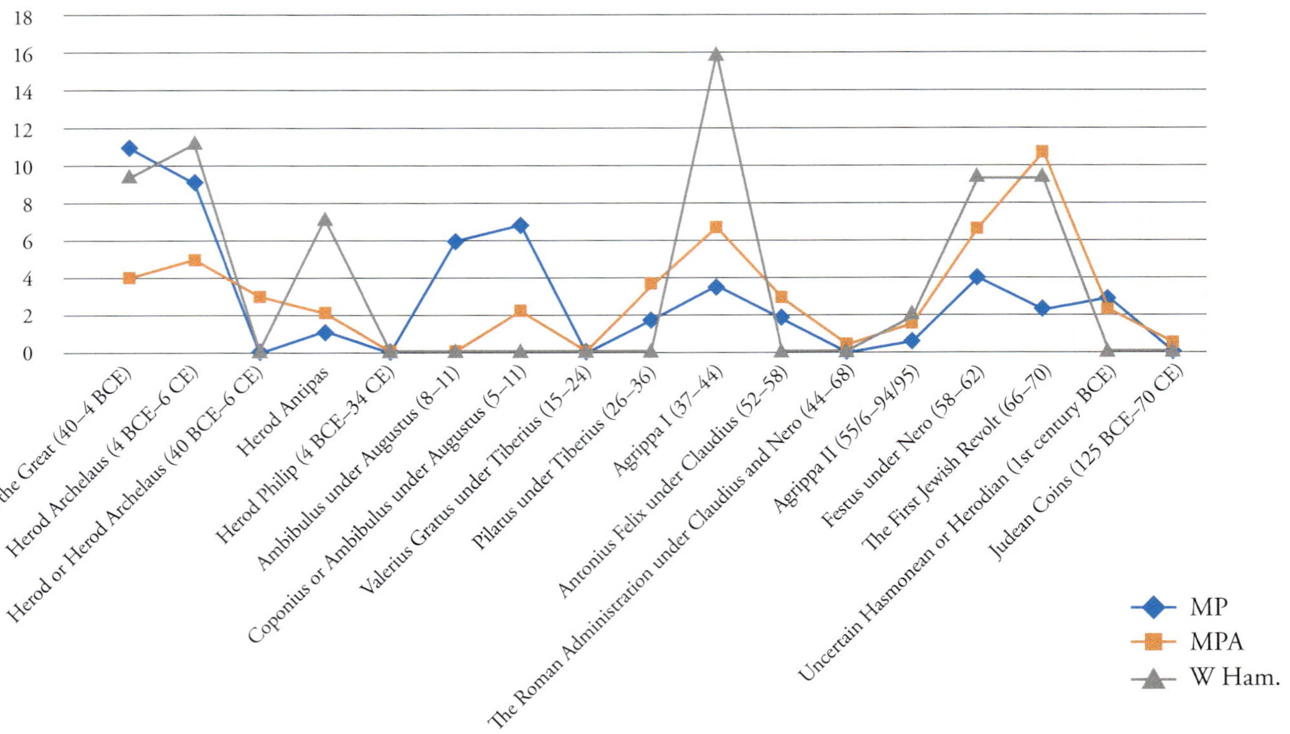

Fig. 6: Graphic rendering of the index AACL for comparison between the three digs.

various *prutot* because they in fact belong to a single account system, nor even a fiduciary and competitive rate in their respective legal-territorial spheres. A possible explanation for this distribution is to be sought in the most-lively trade network around Lake Kinneret and towards the Mediterranean rather than towards the hills of the Transjordan region. An explanation of an economic nature which, on the basis of the quantitative data and the intensity of trade as indicated by AACL proposed below, would make Magdala one of the most active centers documented to date in Galilee.

It can be observed, in fact, that the annual loss index, from which the intensity of coin passages with relative losses can be deduced, is particularly high in certain chronological periods and roughly coincides in the three sites considered. The data must be examined as a whole, period by period, because internal differences are due to the different functions of what was found in the specific part and extent of the archaeological site excavated. Regarding the quantity of coins found, the stock of coins minted by the various mints must also have had some significance, because on a chronological basis, the mints of Tiberias and Caesarea Paneas produced coins in limited continuity, so as to assume that they had to compete on the market with those of the Procurators of Rome minted in almost the same years. On the basis of the Magdala data, we can also assume that these two mints did not play a very relevant role in this period in meeting the demand for divisional coinage with a liberating function in the dynamics of trade, particularly within the Magdala settlement.

In sum: Despite of different provenances, a lot of small value coinage arrived and circulated in Magdala also between the mid-first century BCE and the mid-first century CE.

In detail, in the MP area Herod the Great is attested with a few specimens of the type with Greek inscription-X within diadem/table flanked by two palm branches, but conspicuously almost entirely by the type with anchor/double cornucopia with caduceus. Despite his short reign, between 4 BCE and 6 CE, the coinage of Herod Archelaus is also very well documented, especially by the type Wine branch with bunch of grapes/Crested helmet. Of Herod Antipas there are both full value coins and fractions of ¼. According to the cadence of the years of activity of the Tiberias mint, i. e. the years 19/20, 28/29, 28/30 and 30, both Archelaus is attested by the palm branch or palm tree type: coins of evident Tyre influence in the choice of iconography, with Greek legends referring both to the tetrarch and to the city seat of the mint. The only specimen found of Herod Philippus, struck at Caresarea Paneas and with a weight close to that of the Roman imperial axis rather than of the *prutah* (6.5 g), documents an epochal change by the use of a human portrait, in this case the portrait of Augustus, on the obverse of a coin produced in a Judaean

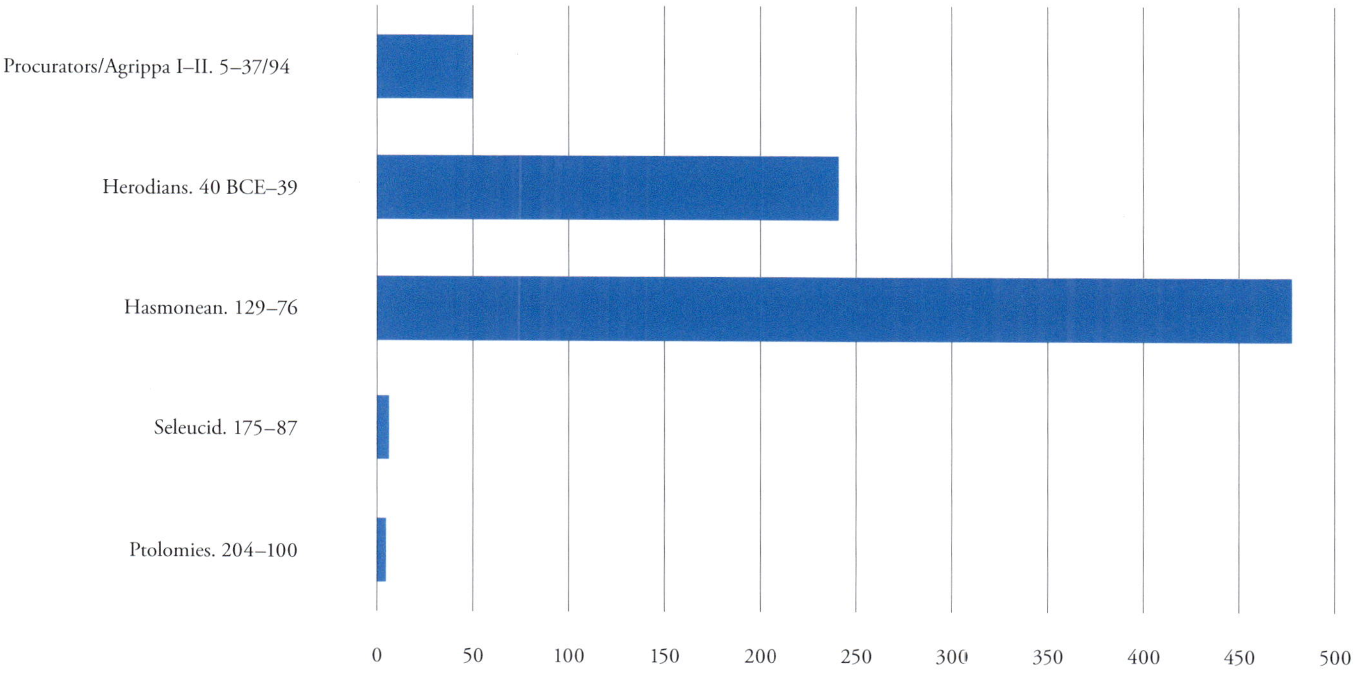

Fig. 7: Quantitative distribution by periods (second century BCE-ca. 55 CE).

environment, while the reverse shows the facade of tetrastyle temple.[57]

A significant contribution was also made by the *prutot* of the Roman Procurators, in this part of the Magdala area present in the series from Augustus (Coponius and Ambibulus), Tiberius (Valerius Gratus and Pontius Pilatus), to Claudius (Antonius Felix) and Nero (Porcius Festus).[58] The total, including some specimens of unclear attribution, amounts to 43 coins while the issues of Antipas and Philippus number 24, about half in that chronological range.

Starting in the year 41/42, Agrippa I issued a copper coin through the mint of Jerusalem with a weight standard close to that of the *prutah* (2.5–1.5 g) of the canopy/three ears of grain type. Later, Agrippa II, by the mint of Caesarea Paneas, chose to strike the portrait of the emperor – his protector – Nero accompanied by legends in Greek. He repeated the hommage with subsequent emperors Titus and Domitian whose faces appeared on bronze coins from the same mint. All these types have been recovered in the MP area in statistically appreciable quantities. It can therefore be seen that in this period the volume of circulation in the MP section, all in all not too extensive when compared to the entire area excavated on the MAP, nevertheless appears to be substantial in percentage terms and regarding its distribution over a time span of about a century and a half.

The quantitative peaks indicate real fluctuations in the temporal succession within the period considered. However, the currency's contextualization in the market isn't leading topic because the long permanence in use of the coin, especially the bronze coins, cannot be ignored. In fact, the flow from Jerusalem especially of small copper coins, being the most suitable for exchanges with goods and commodities of modest value, remained constant as can be seen in the following graph. In this graph, the quantities are grouped by macro-periods and, we repeat, do not take into account either the continuity of use or the contemporaneity of coinage in the post-Herodian-Roman Procurators phase. In fact, on the basis of the persistence in use, if one adds the data from 40 BCE to those of the Procurators/Agrippa I and II, the quantitative basis of the circulating stock does not vary so as to assume interruptions with fewer or more divisional arrivals in the same place.

An epochal shift in Palestine's first phase of Romanization, also in the monetary sphere, was brought about by the events of the First Jewish Revolt against the Roman authority. As is widely known, in the years 66–70/3 the rebels initiated an autonomous coinage series in silver and bronze, adopting the Palaeo-Jewish script combined with identity symbolism: the vine leaf, a cup, the palm and the pomegranate.[59] Recent articles have confirmed that the most abundant *pru-*

57 Barkay 2012.
58 Kokkinos 2012.
59 Noy 2013 with bibliography.

tot coinage dates from the second year (67 CE) of the revolt,[60] and they are also attested, albeit not in great quantities, in Galilee between the provinces Syria and Judaea. In the sites around Lake Kinneret they are present in Hippos,[61] Tiberias,[62] Capernaum,[63] Wadi Hamam[64] and Gamla in the form of local coinage,[65] and of course, in the most conspicuous quantity to date, in the MAP part of Magdala.[66] In our area, there are 4 *prutot* from the second year, complementing what has already been pointed out and contributing to a significant change in the consistency of the insurgents' circulation, which, confirming the direction of the coin's arrival from Jerusalem towards Galilee, would indicate that this region was involved in the war *"because Galilee was still more or less free during the first half of the second year of the revolt (until the fall of Gamla on October 10, 67 CE)"*.[67] It should be added that the finds suggest that Magdala took on a central role in the context of the arrival and use of these issues with respect to the whole of Galilee. In fact, the census and its distribution map proposed in Syon 2015 counted 94 *prutot* from the years of the First Revolt distributed over 31 sites. An additional 34 of them (26.5 %) out of 128 attestations were found in the MAP part of Madgala including as many as 23 from 67 CE.[68]

The coins defined as Provincial and Autonomous also deserve some consideration, such as the mints that minted copper coinage in the same period and whose issues reached and were used in this region. We refer, above all, to Akko-Ptolemais and Sepphoris-Diocaesarea without neglecting other mints. In the MP part, for the period ending with the events of 70 CE the picture is as follows: In addition to the already mentioned coins from Tyre, whose chronology extends to almost the entire second century, there is 1 bronze coin of Tiberius from the mint of Antioch of Commagene, 1 City coin of Antioch of Syria, 1 Autonomous coin of Aradus, and 1 Civic coin of Akko Ptolemais, 1 of Caesarea Maritima, 3 of Tiberias (Claudius) and 2 of Gadara, on the whole a presence that can be defined as marginal compared to the circulating stock.[69] The issues of the Nabataeans had similar marginalization (only one coin of Aretas IV was attested in the MP area),[70] and had to enter the circulation from Transjordan, where they are quite numerous between Gamla[71] and the area of Caesarea Paneas,[72] perhaps because they are quoted at the value of 1 *prutah*.

5.5 The Romanization of currency: Roman coins and Roman provincial coinage (ca. 70–ca. 294) (see 4.5)

The disastrous outcome of the first Jewish revolt profoundly altered the structure of coin circulation in Galilee, even though the competitive confrontation with the Jerusalem mint had begun at least a few decades earlier, starting with the strategic development of Tiberias and the production of its first bronze coin (probably an *as*) in the name of the emperor Claudius. This same emperor as well as Nero coined in Caesarea Paneas and Caesarea Maritima, confirming the ideological innovation of the portrait of the sovereign on the coin and the production of bronze divisionals with weight standards close to Roman metrology rather than *prutot*. The coins of Agrippa II from the mint of Sepphoris- Diocaesarea are also part of the progressive adaptation to the monetary system of the victors, the imperial Roman armies. The decisive turning point for coinage in Galilee was the defeat of the insurgents and the consequent closure of the Jerusalem mint at least for a few years, even if some continuous use and survival of previous coinage needs to be taken into account. Another consequence was a somewhat more substantial arrival of coins minted in Rome, perhaps due to the transfer/allocation of legions to cope with the challenge against Roman authority, especially of the right to levy taxes, by an entire population.

60 Syon 2015, pp. 186–188, in particular the distribution map fig. 49.
61 From *General Conspectus of Coins Chronology and Mints found at Hippos* (IAA) (for references: Segal, Mlynarczyk, Burdajewicz 2000; Segal, Mlynarczyk, Burdajewicz 2001; Segal, Mlynarczyk, Burdajewicz 2002; Segal, Mlynarczyk, Burdajewicz *et alii* 2004; Segal, Mlynarczyk, Burdajewicz *et alii* 2006; Segal, Mlynarczyk, Burdajewicz et alii 2008) and former excavated finds kept at the IAA.
62 Syon 2015, pp. 186–189.
63 Callegher 2007a.
64 Bijovsky 2018, p. 541, no. 127.
65 Syon 2014, pp. 189–190, nos. 4481–4487.
66 Syon forthcoming.
67 Syon 2015, p. 189.
68 Syon 2012.
69 MAP reports many coins from Tyre, but also from Akko-Ptolemais, Sepphoris-Diocaesarea, Gadara, Gerasa and Caesarea (Syon forthcoming). The coins confirm the marginal influx of coinage from other mints than Jerusalem and attest to first Hasmonean and then Herodian supremacy and that of the Roman Procurators thereafter.
70 Syon forthcoming. 1 Nabatean copper coin of unsure chronology is also attested in Wadi Hamam: Bijovsky 2018, p. 541, no. 130.
71 Syon 2014, pp. 221–2223, nos. 5873–5887.
72 Syon 2015, p. 194.

5.6 Phoenicia and Syria

The supply of bronze coinage was provided, with quantitative differences, by cities in the provinces of Phoenicia and Syria, Galilee and Samaria, Decapolis and Arabia.[73] In the data summarized in the following tables a continuous and consistent flow of small Tyre bronzes can be observed according to the previous territorial division, characterized by the Tyche and the palm with the years of issue according to the calendar of that city. The contribution of this city, moreover, is not limited to civic coinage, but continues at least until Elagabalus. The other mint that seems to have played a non-secondary role is Akko Ptolemais, with a good chronological duration from Hadrianus to Philippus I. From the others (Antioch, Damascus, Aradus, Tripolis) divisional coinage arrived sporadically, particularly during the first half of the third century. This confirms, therefore, whose presence in an area between Gaulanitis and Caesarea Paneas mostly with single coins, but in fact also their absence in coastal sites of the Lake Kinneret area,[74] as it has already been hypothesized regarding the Sidon issues.

5.7 Roman imperial coinage, Galilee and Samaria

Evidence from the excavations suggest that the contribution of Urbs minting (Rome) did not increase significantly after the conclusion of the Revolt (70 CE), but remains an episodic presence. The most present coin is the *denarius*, a silver coin intended primarily for the payment of the legions, but there is no lack of small bronze coins either, i. e. the *quadrantes*. Their diffusion is probably to be ascribed to the presence and settlement of the legions that faced the Bar Kokhba Revolt. Indeed, the *quadrantes* of Traianus and the *denarii* of Hadrianus are well documented in MP Magdala, as they are also in the MAP area and at Wadi Hamam.[75] Rather than a direct involvement of this region in the events of 132–135, it is possible that the coins were lost during the settlement or passage of the legions, and in this sense scholars are inclined to believe that Galilee was not involved in these events.[76] Some hoards, however, closed around 135 could, due to their composition, be described as emergency hoards.[77] Some relation to the military sphere is suggested by a bronze with the countermark of *Legio VI Ferrata*, but also by

Tab. 6: Distribution by mints and authorities.

Authority	Antioch	Damascus	Aradus	Akko Ptolemais	Tyre	Sydon	Tripolis
City/Civic Coinage			1	2	54	1	
Domitianus	1						
Traianus					2		
Hadrianus				2			
Caracalla				1	2		
Macrinus				1			
Elagabalus				1	4		1
Philippus I		1		1			
Herennius Etruscus	1						
Gallienus					1		

73 The Tyre *tetradrachms* and *didrachms* are not considered here because they are absent in this part of the MP excavation, whereas they are present in the vast archaeological area of MAP.

74 Syon 2015, p. 203.

75 See following tables 7–9.

76 Syon 2012, pp. 60–62.

77 Bijovsky 2018, p. 523.

the large number of coins of Traianus. The fact is that in the MP area a small coin of the 132–135 insurgents was found, showing on the obverse the palm tree and on the reverse the bunch of grapes (Cat. no. 934). It is certainly a clue, but too little to be used as proof of Magdala's direct involvement in the last violent anti-Roman opposition. Rather, the coin should be interpreted as a usual, circulating and accepted coin, despite the strong ethnic connotation – or maybe just because of it, as it can be compared to similar coins from other mints and authorities weighing between 2 and 3 grams. Among the mints active in the same period are Tiberias, Sepphoris and Caesarea Maritima with a significant concentration precisely corresponding to the two emperors Traianus and Hadrianus.

Neapolis contributes to the circulation structure of the late second to mid-third century with as many as 6 bronzes of Elagabalus while Caesarea Maritima contributes 8 coins of Alexander Severus. The other mints (Dora, Aelia Capitolina, Ascalon and Gaza) are documented here especially for the first century, but mostly with single specimens.

Tab. 7: Distribution by mints and authorities.
D = denarius, wQ = quadrans, S = sestertius

Authority	Rome	Caesarea Maritima	Dora	Neapolis	Sepphoris	Tiberias	Aelia Capitolina	Ascalon	Gaza
Agrippa II Period					4				
City/Civic Coinage								1	1
Claudius		1				3			
Vespasian								3	
Titus	2D	1							
Traianus	5Q	2	1		4	4			
Hadrianus	2D	2				3	1		
Antoninus Pius	1D				2		1		
Marcus Aurelius									1
Commodus						3			
Elagabalus				6	1	2			
Volusianus	1S								
Alexander Severus		8							
Philippus I				1					
Philippus II				1					
Herennius Etruscus							1		
Traianus Decius		1							
Hostilianus		1					2		
Trebonianus		1		1					
Volusianus		2							

5.7 The Decapolis and Provincia Arabia

Mints in the Decapolis and Arabian area are equally present; some of them even offer a long chronological perspective as in the case of Gadara: from civic issues to Gordian III, although with single coins and a small increase with the latter emperor. Hippos is also well documented. In fact, the two cities were not far from the Kinneret area, although they belonged to territories on the eastern shore. Still, the arrival of coins from Hippos or Gadara on the western shore cannot be ruled out as result of *mercatores* or travelers or some commercial activity between Magdala and its territory with Transjordan. The 9 bronzes of Septimius Severus from Bostra clearly stand out and might only be explained from the perspective indicated above or perhaps because of some military movement following the reorganization of the regional army with the strengthening of the *limes Arabicus*. In a general Roman coinage perspective, this peak could be a reflection of the massive production of bronze coinage in the mints of Septimian period Syria. This money then entered the economic circuit for the management of military logistics, or the redistribution of what was produced in *latifundia* or by local craftsmen. But this is only a research hypothesis which should be deepened with a survey of the presence of this emperor in sites located in Transjordan and towards the provinces of Syria/Palestine.

Other mints like Capitolias, Esbous, Nysa-Scythopolis, the distant Petra and Pella to the south-east and Philippopolis in the Jebel Hauran to the north-east are attested in Magdala with a few specimens that can be traced back to bronze circulation on a fiduciary basis.

Tab. 8: Distribution by mints and authority.

Authority	**Bostra**	**Capitolias**	**Esbous**	**Gadara**	**Hippos**	**Nysa-Scythopolis**	**Pella**	**Petra**	**Philippopolis**
City/Civic Coinage				1					1
Tiberius				1					
Antoninus Pius					1 + 3				
Marcus Aurelius	1			1	2		1		
Lucius Verus				1	1				
Septimus Severus	9			1				1	
Macrinus		1							
Elagabalus			1		1+1			1	
Gordianus III				4		1			
Philippus I									1

5.8 Uncertain Mints or Authority (MP)

Finally, the large number of highly corroded medium and small bronzes is worth mentioning. Often an imperial bust on the reverse, a male or female figure, a temple or other types of imagery are barely distinguishable so that a definite attribution cannot be reached. In the MP area as many as 151 cases (not insignificant 42 %) cannot be related to any mint or authority due to corrosion, limescale encrustation and a generally poor state of preservation. Overall, there are 362 Roman provincial coins or coins from mints that worked independently, but were in fact part of the empire. Of these, 212 (58 %) have been identified, while the other 151 are illegible, with a distribution percentage of 58 % and 42 % respectively.

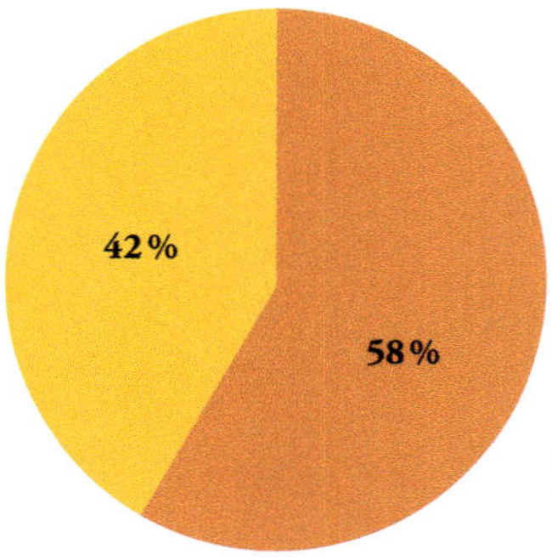

Fig. 7: Identified percentages of Roman Provincial Coins.

On the whole, three quantitative peaks emerge in this MP area, including the uncertain specimens reported in the *Uncertain Mints and Authority* scheme (Tab. 9): the small bronze coins of Tyre, the coins of Traianus and Hadrianus and the increase of the Severan period (Septimius Severus, Elagabalus and Alexander Severus).

It could be asked whether the finds from this part of the site are peculiar due to the proximity to the lake port, active at least since the first century BCE the presence of structures/warehouses connected to it and the function of exchange rather than habitation of some of the area. Alternatively, the monetary data might lack peculiarity because they are entirely similar to those of the other areas excavated by MAP and even comparable to those of Wadi Hamam. This doubt arises especially when comparing the unidentified specimens: 151 in MP and only 34 in MAP. Of course, the classifier's inexperience, mine of course, prevented a more certain attribution of a large number of these 151 uncertain coins, but in fact even a greater number of resolved doubtful cases would not have changed the number of Roman Provincial coins recovered in MP. The answer can be searched in the comparison between data sets in the following tables and graphs which follow the territorial partitions suggested. The quantities are compared by issuing authority and mints distribution in the three regional areas. The ellipse highlights the peaks in presence.

Tab. 9: Distribution by mints and authorities: Uncertain mints or authority.

	Tyre/Sidon	Caesarea Maritima	Dora	Sepphoris	Gadara	Uncertain Mint
City/Civic Coinage	4				1	
Domitianus						1
Domitianus/Traianus				2		6
Traianus						1
Hadrianus						1
Traianus/Hadrianus			1			
Antoninus Pius						1
Septimius Severus						1
Elagabalus						6
Elagabaus/Gordianus III						1
first century/middle third century						149
second century/ middle third century		1		1		
Countermarked coins	3	1		1		25

Tab. 10: Distribution by mints and authority for comparison between the three digs. Phoenicia and Syria (MP [white], MAP [yellow] and Wadi Hamam [blue])

	Antiochia			Damascus			Aradus			Akko Ptol.			Tyre			Sidon			Tripolis			Beirut		
City/ Civic Coins							1			2	1		54	60	13	1	4	1						
Claudius																								1
Domitianus	1																							
Traianus											1		2											
Hadrianus										2		1												
Macrinus										1					1									
Caracalla										1		1	2											
Elagabalus										1		1	4		2		1		1	1				
Diadumenianus															2									
Philippus I			1	1						1														
Herennius Etruscus	1																							
Gallienus													1		2									

Tab. 11: Distribution by mints and authority for comparison between the three digs.
Roman Imperial Coinage, and Galilee and Samaria (MP [white], MAP [yellow] and Wadi Hamam [blue])

	Rome			Caesarea Maritima			Dora			Neapolis			Sepphoris			Tiberias			Aelia Capitolina			Ascalon			Gaza		
Agrippa II													4														
City/Civic Coinage													4									1			1		
Claudius				1												3											
Vespasianus			2D																			3					
Titus	2D			1																							
Domitianus		2 As																									
Traianus	5Q	1 S +10Q	1D + 3Q	2			1		1				4	4		4	13	3									
Hadrianus	2D			2	2	3			2							3	13	1	1							1	
Antoninus Pius	1D	2 D	1D						1				2		1		2		1				3				
Marcus Aurelius																									1		
Commodus																3											
Elagabalus										6			1			1		1									
Caracalla									1																		
Volusianus	1S																										
Alexander Severus				8		4																					
Philippus I										1																	
Philippus II										1																	
Herennius Etruscus																			1								
Traianus Decius				1		1																					
Hostilianus				1		2													2								
Trebonianus				1		1			1	1																	
Volusianus				2		1																					

Tab. 12: Distribution by mints and authority for comparison between the three digs Decapolis and Arabian Province (MP [white], MAP [yellow] and Wadi Hamam [blue])

Authority	Bostra			Capitolias			Esbous			Gadara			Hippos			Nysa Sc.			Pella			Petra			Philippopolis			Gaba		
	MP	MAP	WH	MP	MAP	WH	MP	MAP	WH	MP	MAP	WH	MP	MAP	WH	MP	MAP	WH	MP	MAP	WH	MP	MAP	WH	MP	MAP	WH	MP	MAP	WH
City/Civic Coinage										1															1					
Tiberius										1	1																			
Nero											1			2																
Titus											1																			
Domitianus														2	1					1										
Hadrianus																													1	
Antoninus Pius													4		1															1
Marcus Aurelius	1									2	1	1	3		1			1	1											
Commodus														2	1														1	
Septimius Severus	9									1		1										1		1						
Macrinus				1																										
Elagabalus		1					1						2		2							1								
Alexander Severus			5																											
Gordianus III										4		1				1														
Philippus I																									1					

A substantial constant can be observed in the various graphs, regardless of the mint of origin: The greatest intensity of coinage loss as a result of demand and exchange occurs in two cases: during the Antonine emperors between Traianus to Commodus and with the Severans from Septimius Severus to Alexander Severus. Regarding the motivations, we cannot refrain from postulating a significant contribution of the legions on the move or stationed in the western area of the Kinneret, as we will discuss in a moment by examining, once again comparatively, the countermarked coins.

For now, we are looking for a visual confirmation of the varying stock found in Magdala between the first century CE, particularly after 70, and up to Gallienus. The particular densities are well shown in the following graph, relating to the MP area only.

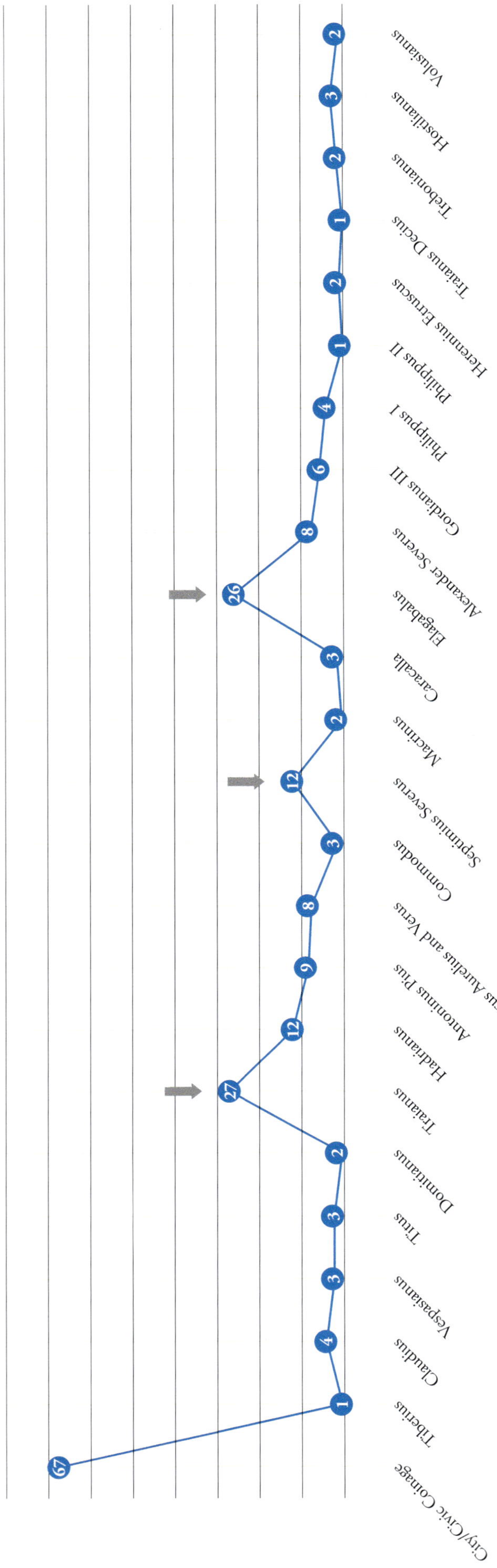

Fig. 8: Chronological histogram of emperors and number of coins.

Once again, of interest for a general and reliable reconstruction of the monetary stock in use in Magdala is the comparison with MAP data and neighboring Wadi Hamam.

The data confirm a substantial quantitative coincidence between the two areas of Magdala and the neighboring site of Wadi Hamam with the large influx of provincial Roman coinage from the nearest mints at Tiberias, Gadara, Hippos, Sepphoris and Caesarea Maritima, thereby relegating the others to a role that can be defined as complementary.[78]

In addition, the data tell us that the stock of recovered coins after the events of the 70s and up to Gallienus amounted to approximately 590 coins (including the undetermined and with a few incursions into the earlier phase of the first century because provincial Roman coinage could have remained in use for a long time). They are distributed as follows: 363 in MP, 142 in MAP and 86 in Wadi Hamam. The analysis of the AACL (tabs. 14 and 15; fig. 10), then, confirms particular intensity of monetary transactions in the following periods: Traianus – Antoninus Pius (Antoninian Emperors), Macrinus – Elagabalus (Severian Emperors), with truly remarkable coefficients for the years 249–251 (Philippus I, Herennius Etruscus, Trebonianus, Hostilianus and Volusianus). Similar AACL coefficients are typical of the large urban areas, in which the liberating function was based on the value of circulating bronze denominations, quoted with a certain degree of overvaluation with respect to its weight and alloy, accepted because the coins corresponded to a system of account in use.

Finally, in the absence of stratigraphic data at least for the MP part, higher or lower concentrations do not allow the determination of the function of individual sectors within the area, at least not on a numismatic basis.

Tab. 13: Distribution by authority for comparison between the three digs.

Authority	MP	MAP	WHam
City/Civic Coinage	67	65	14
Tiberius	1	1	
Claudius	4		1
Vespasianus	3		2
Titus	3	1	
Domitianus	2	3	1
Traianus	27	29	8
Hadrianus	12	17	7
Antoninus Pius	9	7	5
Marcus Aurelius and Verus	8	1	3
Commodus	3	3	1
Septimius Severus	12		2
Macrinus	2		1
Caracalla	3		1
Elagabalus	26	2	6
Diadumenianus			2
Alexander Severus	8		5
Gordianus III	6		1
Philippus I	4		1
Philippus II	1	2	
Herennius Etruscus	2		
Traianus Decius	1		1
Trebonianus	2		2
Hostilianus	3		1
Volusianus	2		1
Gallienus	1		2

78 Similar remark in Bijovsky 2004b for the site of Badd 'Issa-Qiryat Sefer.

Emperors/Number of coins of the MP, MAP, W. Hamam

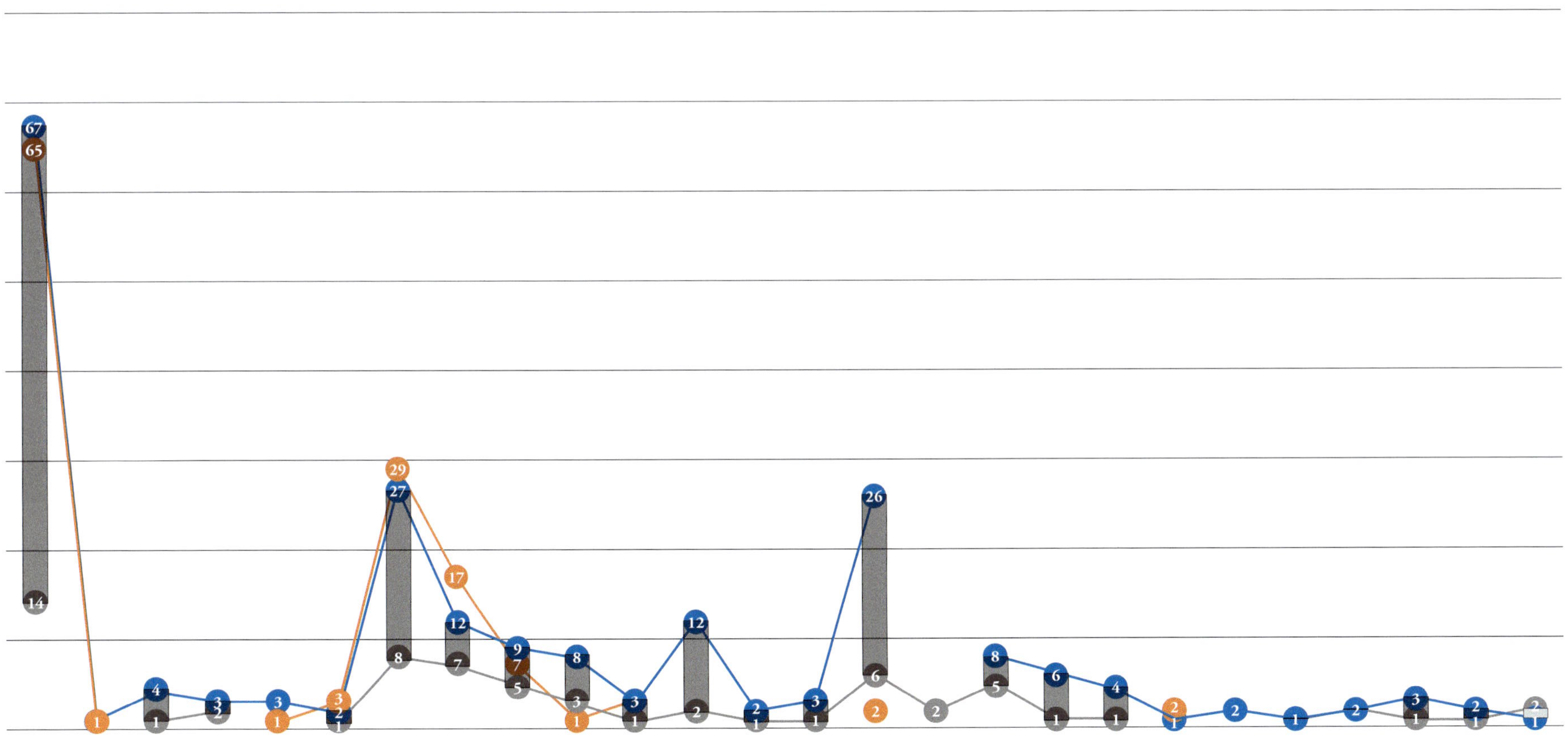

	City/Civic Coinage	Tiberius	Claudius	Vespa-sianus	Titus	Domi-tianus	Traianus	Hadrianus	Antoninus Pius	Marcus Aurelius and Verus	Commo-dus	Septimius Severus	Macrinus	Caracalla	Elagabalus	Diadu-menianus	Alexander Severus	Gordianus III	Philip-pus I	Philip-pus II	Herennius Etruscus	Traianus Decius	Trebonia-nus	Hosti-lianus	Volusianus	Gallienus
Serie 1 = MP	67	1	4	3	3	2	27	12	9	8	3	12	2	3	26		8	6	4	1	2	1	2	3	2	1
Serie 2 = MAP	65	1			1	3	29	17	7	1	3				2					2						
3 = W. Hamam	14		1	2		1	8	7	5	3	1	2	1	1	6	2	5	1	1			1	2	1	1	2

Fig. 9: Distribution by authority for comparison between the three digs.

Tab. 14: Distribution by authority for comparison between the three digs and AACL.

	MP		MAP		WHam	
Authority	**N. coins**	**AACL**	**N. coins**	**AACL**	**N. coins**	**AACL**
City/Civic Coinage	67	0,9	65	2,3	14	0,8
Tiberius (14–34)	1	0,1	1	0,4	0	0,0
Claudius (41–54)	4	0,8	0	0,0	1	0,9
Vespasianus (68–79)	3	0,8	0	0,0	2	2,1
Titus (79–81)	3	2,8	1	2,3	0	0,0
Domitianus (81–96)	2	0,4	3	1,4	1	0,8
Traianus (98–117)	27	3,9	29	10,7	8	4,9
Hadrianus (117–138)	12	1,6	17	5,7	7	3,9
Antoninus Pius (138–161)	9	1,1	7	2,1	5	2,5
Marcus Aurelius and Verus (169–180)	8	2,0	1	0,6	3	3,2
Commodus (180–193)	3	0,6	3	1,6	1	0,9
Septimius Severus (193–211)	12	1,8	0	0,0	2	1,3
Macrinus (217–218)	2	5,5	0	0,0	1	11,6
Caracalla (211–217)	3	1,4	0	0,0	1	1,9
Elagabalus (218–222)	26	17,9	2	3,5	6	17,4
Diadumenianus (218)	0	0,0	0	0,0	2	23,3
Alexander Severus (222–235)	8	1,7	0	0,0	5	4,5
Gordianus III (238–249)	6	1,5	0	0,0	1	1,1
Philippus I (244–249)	4	2,2	0	0,0	1	2,3
Philippus II (247–249)	1	1,4	2	7,0	0	0,0
Herennius Etruscus (251)	2	5,5	0	0,0	0	0,0
Traianus Decius (249–251)	1	2,8	0	0,0	1	11,6
Trebonianus (251–253)	2	2,8	0	0,0	2	11,6
Hostilianus (251)	3	8,3	0	0,0	1	11,6
Volusianus (251–253)	2	2,8	0	0,0	1	5,8
Gallienus (260–268)	1	0,3	0	0,0	2	2,9
Unidentified coins (70–268)	151	2,1	34	1,2	25	1,5

Tab. 15: (ca. 70–268) AACL indices for the three digs.

Authority	MP	MAP	WHam
City/Civic Coinage	0,9	2,3	0,8
Tiberius (14–34)	0,1	0,4	0,0
Claudius (41–54)	0,8	0,0	0,9
Vespasianus (68–79)	0,8	0,0	2,1
Titus (79–81)	2,8	2,3	0,0
Domitianus (81–96)	0,4	1,4	0,8
Traianus (98–117)	3,9	10,7	4,9
Hadrianus (117–138)	1,6	5,7	3,9
Antoninus Pius (138–161)	1,1	2,1	2,5
Marcus Aurelius and Verus (169–180)	2,0	0,6	3,2
Commodus (180–193)	0,6	1,6	0,9
Septimius Severus (193–211)	1,8	0,0	1,3
Macrinus (217–218)	5,5	0,0	11,6
Caracalla (211–217)	1,4	0,0	1,9
Elagabalus (218–222)	17,9	3,5	17,4
Diadumenianus (218)	0,0	0,0	23,3
Alexander Severus (222–235)	1,7	0,0	4,5
Gordianus III (238–249)	1,5	0,0	1,1
Philippus I (244–249)	2,2	0,0	2,3
Philippus II (247–249)	1,4	7,0	0,0
Herennius Etruscus (251)	5,5	0,0	0,0
Traianus Decius (249–251)	2,8	0,0	11,6
Trebonianus (251–253)	2,8	0,0	11,6
Hostilianus (251)	8,3	0,0	11,6
Volusianus (251–253)	2,8	0,0	5,8
Gallienus (260–268)	0,3	0,0	2,9
Unidentified coins (70–268)	2,1	1,2	1,5

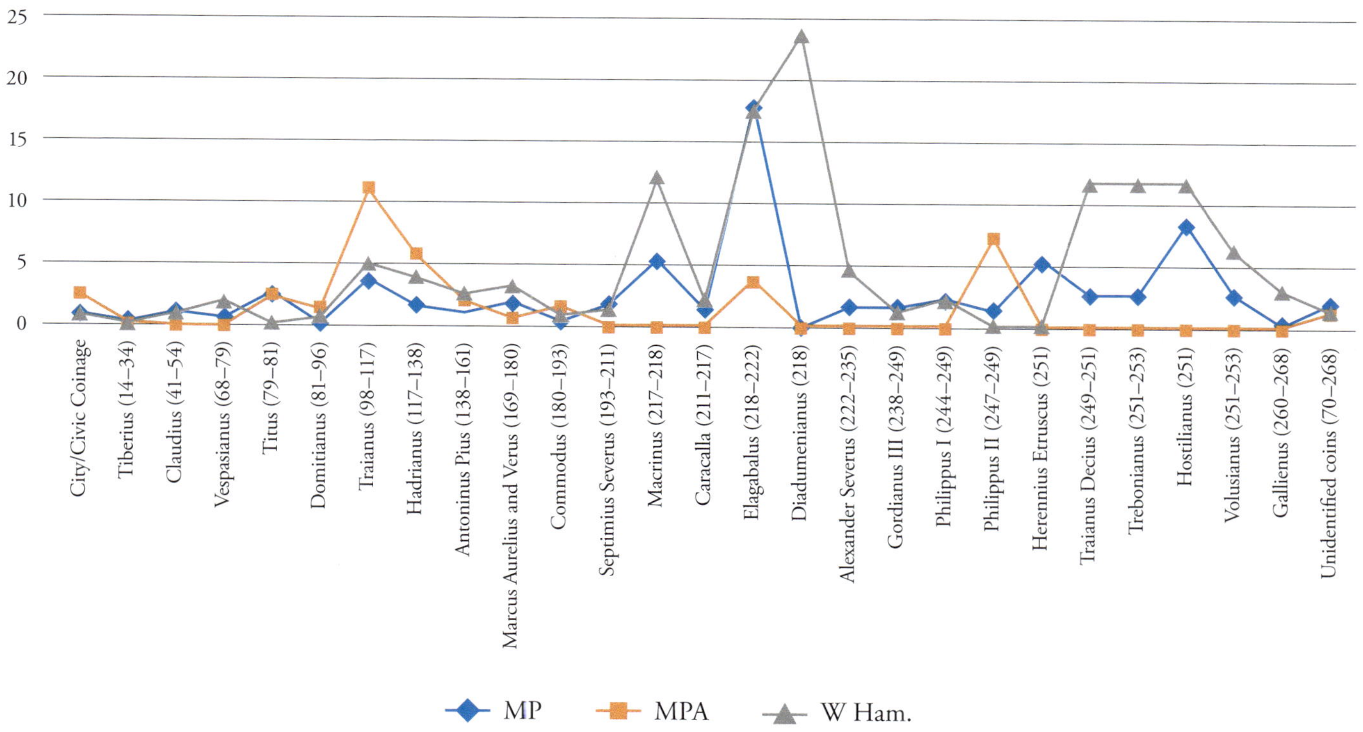

Fig. 10: (ca. 70–268) Graphic rendering of the index AACL for comparison between the three digs.

5.9 Countermarked coins

As mentioned above, there are various questions to which it is difficult to give convincing and well-founded answers, especially about the reasons for such a large quantity of Roman provincial coinage. A possible answer can perhaps be sought by analyzing countermarked coins found at this site in numbers that are perhaps unmatched by any other, at least in Galilee and Gaulanitis.

It is well known that countermarks were applied to the roundels of almost always worn or fairly worn coins in order to give a higher or lower price than the circulating coin with a different weight and sometimes with a different fineness. In each case the countermark turned the old coin into a new issue,[79] although countermarks with explicit reference to a value/quote are quite rare. The phenomenon has been known since the Hellenistic period, but became very common among provincial Roman coins from the late second century onwards and intensified in the Severan period. It is still not clear, however, whether the application of a punch with the image of a deity, emperor or other symbol revalued or adjusted downwards that specific coin because the starting price is unknown. Depending on the circumstances of a city or territory (money supply and demand), it is not excluded that an old coin was put back into circulation rather than being considered out of circulation. Countermarking meant establishing a new relationship with the newly minted coin, officially issued by the local authority. But even in this case it is very problematic to opt for a supportable explanation of devaluation/revaluation. We can be guided into some further investigation by the fact that the application of countermarks on the mint was not widespread throughout the Roman Empire, but happened on a regional basis, in this case part of the Province Syria and Palestine. In these territories copper coinage was conspicuous and produced in many mints. Moreover, we do not know for sure whether there were different metrologies for the *assarion* that was minted in several mints often very close to each other. Howgego writes: *"The bronze currencies in the cities of Asia Minor in the third century must have been very confusing. The coins current in a city came from many mints and included a great variety of sizes and weights. It seems certain that the countermarks represent attempts to restore some order to the situation, but it is not known whether these attempts were made independently by the city or were inspired by Roman administration".*[80]

79 On countermarks and their historical-economic interpretation, it is still fundamental Howgego 2005.

80 Howgego 2005, p. 10.

It can be deduced that the use of countermarking was intended to bring some order into a circulating currency that could escape the control of a city's authority. This, of course, raises other important questions like who decided and controlled the application of countermarks and for what monetary purpose, because it is not even conceivable, in a field so relevant to the determination of monetary values, that the application of punches/countermarks was beyond the control of at least some authority.

Action was taken on local or foreign coins especially if their weight deviated positively or negatively from the circulating analogue, either because they met foreign metrological standards, or because of changes in the value standards in use in a city. All these explanations, however, assume that the monetary authorities of a city have control over emissions and money in circulation.

There is, however, another possibility: that the countersigns were applied on small coins destined for the payment of legions on the move in a territory, or at least to allow the transformation of silver wages into coinage appropriate to the rate of the place where the military contingent (*legio*, *vexillatio*, *auxilia*) had settled, was stationed or was passing through. The hypothesis is certainly interesting, but on the basis of the finds in such a case one would have to follow the movement of the soldiers and at the same time assume that the right of minting was taken away from the various workshops while it was applied in legal autonomy according to circumstances at the various military detachments.[81] Despite these critical issues, it cannot be ruled out that it was the instances that led the authority of the city to intervene on the bronze coinage which could create a 'very confusing' situation.

Before moving on to the analysis of the extensive documentation of countermarked coins in the MP area of Magdala, a final technical remark. It is believed that the application of the countermark was mostly on worn coins. In some cases, however, it cannot be ruled out that the obverse and reverse images were heated to the point where they disappeared, so that the countermarked coin was to all intents and purposes a new mintage, with a new and different value, with no connection to what the previous images, which mainly identified the city of origin, might have suggested. In the MP site, not many of the coins that support this hypothesis have a rounded shape typical of a recast minting, and in them the disappearance of the previous minting can only have been achieved by a process of almost-recasting rather than by wear through circulation.

In the MP area, as many as 30 coins with a countermark were recovered. In some cases, it has been possible to identify the coinage pre-countermark: 2 specimens of Elagabalus and 1 uncertain between Caracalla/Elagabalus struck in Tyre with Melqart (Heracles) punch on the right; 1 of Caesarea Maritima; and 1 with doubt between Neapolis or Sepphoris.

In all the other 25 cases it was not possible to trace the authority or the mint before the countermark because the coins were worn or partly almost remelted to make the pre-existing types disappear. They were grouped on the typological basis of the punch:

a) Male head with uncertain inscription or naming Emperors
b) Male head facing right on oval/circular punches
c) Unclear oval or circular punches

The roundels of these three groupings, due to the style of the imperial heads or other barely perceptible iconographic elements, may be considered to be earlier coinages from mints of Phoenicia or provincial cities of Palestine or/and South Arabia.

But beyond general considerations of the countermark phenomenon, in and around Magdala as well as in the sites chosen for comparison,[82] the most striking fact is the number of attestations, making this sample the most conspicuous known so far from the whole of Galilee. In addition to the 30 countermarks mentioned by MP, there are 15 from MAP in which the punches are predominantly elliptical in shape and applied to coins struck in Tiberias by Traianus and Hadrianus, and in Hippos by Nero, but in many cases the determination of mint and authority remains uncertain. The common element, in the vast majority of cases, seems to be the application of an elliptical countermark with a male head (of an emperor or a deity, often indistinguishable). It seems as if in this area it had been necessary to put the quotations of various *assaria* in order that were brought to Magdala by *mercatores* or, more probably, *milites* following movements along the *limes arabicus* who might have chosen the region because of its favorable position on the lake and a certain ease of supply.[83]

81 For possible legionary rebellions and related consequences to the coinage, cf. Eadie 1996.

82 I'm referring to the sites listed on Maps 1 and 2.

83 In the area of Neapolis Samariae (Nablus), not very far from Magdala, the presence of the *Legio II Cyreniaica* was proposed on the base of the countermarks: Kindler 1980. Regarding the movement of the *Legio X Fretensis* through countermarks, cf. Barag 1967.

That the presence and connection with the military is more than a hypothesis could be inferred from a bronze found in the Burnt House Hoard (area B) of Wadi Hamam.[84] The two impressed countermarks, in this case rectangular, clearly read *L VI F*, an abbreviation of *Legio VI Fulminata.*[85] It is believed that this punch 'was applied in Palestine' during its transfer from Syria to Arabia or in connection with the events of the second anti-Roman revolt, between Traianus and Hadrianus as confirmed by the closure of the hoard around 123–135 CE. Admittedly, the chronology of the legionary countermark compared to that of the other elliptical countermarks with male figures is a century earlier. But one cannot rule out at least some continuity in the economic importance of these coins in the Magdala territory, both because of the already mentioned singular quantity (45 attestations) and because of their hoarding, of which at least two cases are known[86]:

a) the hoard discovered on the land of a farmer at Migdal, where *"of the coins in this hoard, 24 are so worn that identification is impossible. This group is characterized by countermarks depicting emperor's heads"* and it is reported that "most of the coins from this group originated in the Tyre mint" dated to the end of the second century but still in use at the time of the concealment set by the coins of Elagabalus around 222[87];
b) the hoard from H-Field 3/Locus 8- MP area,[88] whose composition is shown in the table below.

Tab. 16: Distibution for Authority and Mints

	Tyre	Tiberias	Abila	Gadara	Hippos	Nysa-Scytho-polis	Petra	Uncertain Mint
City/Civic Coinage	1							
Claudius		1						
Traianus		2						
Marcus Aurelius and Verus			1	1				
Commodus						1		
Septimius Severus						1		
Elagabalus		1			1	2	1	2
first century/ middle third century								4
Countermarked coins								2

84 Bijovsky, Leibner 2013; Bijovsky 2018, p. 563, no. 435.
85 Howgego 2005, no. 134 but above all pp. 250–251.
86 Bijovsky publishes another hoard also from Wadi Hamam with 37 coins, but with a later chronology (Gallienus) and without countermarked specimens.
87 Meshorer 1976.
88 It is the same hoard published in https://chre.ashmus.ox.ac.uk/hoard/8012.

We note the consistency of the mints with the previous case: Tyre, Abila, Tiberias, Gadara, Hippos, Nysa-Scythopolis with the only difference being a coin of Elagabalus from Petra. There are also 2 coins with countermarks, again with Male head facing on oval punch, confirming a common characteristic of the area.

Of course, a detailed examination of the various punches would be essential for the attribution of a coin to an emperor or male deity. However, such a formal constant and the large number of attestations lead to point to a monetary specificity in the Migdal area in the first decades of the third century, for reasons that can be conjectured. A possible starting point is the value of the coin before being countermarked and the subsequent higher or lower quotation within exchange ratios between the *assaria* of the numerous mints active in the area, particularly in the Severan period. As for the causes of the concealment, the small number of coins, most of them in bronze, suggests an accumulation of savings by someone who later failed to retrieve them rather than the circumstances peculiar to emergency hoards.

5.10 A noteworthy *assarion* of Gallienus

In the large number of provincial Roman coins, one appears singularly worthy of some independent consideration. The *assarion* is described as follows[89]:

D/[IM]P C P LIC GALL [IENVS AVG]. Bust of Gallienus right, radiate, wearing paludamentum and cuirass. R/[CO]L TYRO METR; two prize crowns, inscribed on sunk panel the initial letters of the games, but not clearly legible. Possible one of the two following ways: – AKT(IA) and/or KOM(ODEIA) and/or HPA(KLIA) and/or OLY(MPIA). Between the two crowns, Hercules' club between two palm branches. Below, murex shell.

89 I am indebted to Alessandro Cavagna, University Statale di Milano, for his validation of the attribution to Gallienus.

The identification of the emperor is also certain on an epigraphic basis because in front of the C of the legend Caesar we see a vertical bar very similar to that of another coin of this emperor. It is the type D/Laureate and cuirassed bust right; R/Olive tree between two baetyls (the Ambrosial Rocks); in exergue, hound of Hercules before murex shell.[90]

(© Classical Numismatic Group > Auction 102, 18 May 2016, lot 756. https://www.coinarchives.com/a/openlink.php?l=891130|1683|756|3e64ec5b079c76f3b7e06e18febc67ac).

The type on the reverse is known from the *assaria* of the Colony of Tyre minted by Philippus I for Severa Otacilia[91] and Trebonianus Gallus for Volusianus.[92] I have found no comparisons for the association of the obverse of Gallienus with the reverse mentioned present on other Tyrian issues either in the British Museum's catalogues or in the online site of today's reference: https://rpc.ashmus.ox.ac.uk/search/browse?q=agonistic+tyre.

However, our coin is mentioned in the Rouvier catalogue as belonging to his collection, but does not appear in the plates.[93] We propose here, probably for the first time, not an entirely unpublished specimen, but certainly one that has so far not been accompanied by an image.

5.11 From Gallienus to Diocletianus

During the reigns of Valerianus and Gallienus (253–268)[94] and then of Claudius Gothicus (268–270) another remarkable change in the circulating paradigm occurred. The opening of many mints in the Near East, or rather, the fact that in many of them the minting of the *antoninianus* in a good silver mixture was started, supplied the money market with this

90 Rouvier 1900–1904, no. 2560; not in BMC *Phoenicia*.
91 https://rpc.ashmus.ox.ac.uk/type/6508.
92 https://rpc.ashmus.ox.ac.uk/coins/9/2012; https://rpc.ashmus.ox.ac.uk/coins/9/2013.
93 Salonina: Rouvier 1904, 108 Nr. 2571.
94 Butcher 1996.

denomination in conspicuous quantities and caused at the same time a decrease in the minting of *assaria*, with a strong competition between these two coin denominations. But the general devaluation pressure of that phase of the Roman Empire even affected both the *antoniniani* and the Tyrian *tetradrachms*, which very quickly underwent such a process of debasement that it can be assumed that their value was no longer accepted on a legal basis but was fixed in the exchange market, according to the quotations of the divisionals at the exchange rate on that particular day. They did not, therefore, have a legal quotation defined by law, but their value depended on the circumstances of the place and the relationship created on the market with other coins, especially with the *aureus*.[95] If we analyze what happened in Palestine in the twenty years preceding Aurelian's reform, we are not unaware of a certain tendency to hoard both *antoniniani* and *assaria*, sometimes even in mixed repositories, as if some distrust in the legal value of the silver circulating was spreading since it was becoming more and more debased. Mention should be made, for example, of the cache of Syrian tetradrachms and Tyrian bronze coins at Gush Halav 1948 (closed by coins of Severus Alexander and Philippus I),[96] in Jenin of only *antoniniani* with a last date of ca. 270 (Valerianus-Claudius Gothicus),[97] in Hippos of Quietus *antoniniani* (260–261)[98] and in Horbat Qastra in 1994 with a small hoard still of only *antoniniani* struck between 255 and 271.[99] In Yafiah the significant repository closed after Aurelian's reform in 286 with 55 Syrian *tetradrachms* (Caracalla to Trebonianus Gallus) and 104 *antoniniani* (Trebonianus Gallus to Maximianus), found in a pot in an underground room beneath a church in Iafa (Bet Shean 1871)[100]. Another small group of 22 *antoniniani* is dated between the reigns of Valerian, Gallienus and Claudius Gothicus (268–270),[101] being similar to the case of the Mount of Olives-Jerusalem assemblage comprising 14 *antoniniani* dated between 260/1 and 270 CE.[102] In the face of the debasement of the silver divisional, some hoards may be indicative of renewed appreciation of copper coinage compared to the *antoninianus* and perhaps even the *tetradrachms* of Tyre. In fact, silver coinage had undergone progressive decreases in its precious metal content, which first dropped from 50 % to 42 % and in the years of Valerianus and Gallienus decreased both in its weight (ca. 2.5 g compared to the previous 5–4.5 g) and in its fineness (ca. 3 %). In the west, the rapid loss of value of silver coinage resulted in the revaluation of bronze coinage, especially the *sestertii*. Similarly, if one accepts a devaluation of the *antoninianus* minted in the east, though not as dramatic as in the west, a revaluation of the bronze divisional becomes plausible, which would explain its concealment in repositories of bronze coinage alone and together with silver alloy coins. The phenomenon could even date back to the beginning of the reign of Valerianus and Gallienus, as would be evident in the cases of Paneas,[103] Gelilot,[104] Bet She'an 2002[105] and El-Qabu[106]. In this context of profound changes, similar monetary dynamics fully affected also the area of Galilee close to Magdala, as shown by the hoard of The Burnt Room (Unit A11) in Wadi Hamam[107] and the big hoard of Capernaum[108] both closed between 268–270 and containing good *antoniniani* of Caracalla, *tetradrachms* of Tyre and various bronze coins of good weight. Also from Capernaum is the smallest hoard found in Locus 130.2 in Area 5, of only *antoninians*, the last of which were those of Gallienus.[109]

In this hoard there are, for example, the *antoniniani* minted in Antioch or Asia (a topographical definition adopted in the absence of more precise reference to a specific place of issue). And this in some ways anticipates the role Antioch, or the generically defined mints from Asia, would play once the peripheral organization of the mints was revolutionized with the reforming intervention of Aurelian. Its central significance is confirmed by individual finds from the Magdala-MP area, in the thirty-year period from Valerianus to Diocletianus. Gallienus is attested with 2 *antoniniani* issued in Asia (plus two uncertain ones), Aurelianus with 2 *antoniniani* from Antioch and 1 from Rome, Probus with 1 *antoninianus* from Antioch, Maximianus Herculius with 2 *antoniniani*

95 On these themes see Elliott 2014.
96 Waner, Safrai 2001, no. 25; https://chre.ashmus.ox.ac.uk/hoard/5502.
97 https://chre.ashmus.ox.ac.uk/hoard/6942.
98 https://chre.ashmus.ox.ac.uk/hoard/7707.
99 https://chre.ashmus.ox.ac.uk/hoard/7711.
100 Waner, Safrai 2001, no. 32; https://chre.ashmus.ox.ac.uk/hoard/8081.
101 Waner, Safrai 2001, no. 27; https://chre.ashmus.ox.ac.uk/hoard/8174.
102 Waner, Safrai 2001, no. 31; https://chre.ashmus.ox.ac.uk/hoard/8183.
103 https://chre.ashmus.ox.ac.uk/hoard/7650.
104 https://chre.ashmus.ox.ac.uk/hoard/7652.
105 https://chre.ashmus.ox.ac.uk/hoard/7709.
106 https://chre.ashmus.ox.ac.uk/hoard/7721.
107 Bijovsky 2018, pp. 529–530.
108 Spijkerman 1975, pp. 71–99, last *antoninianus* of Claudius Gothicus of Antioch.
109 Callegher 2007a, pp. 139–141.

from Antioch and 1 from Alexandria while Diocletianus with 2 from Antioch. Almost mirroring, but of lesser consistency, is the data from the MAP area, while for this same period the numismatic evidence from Wadi Hamam is more consistent in quantitative terms, with an *antoninianus* of Probus from Tripolis, but above all for the provenance from Antioch of all the other *antoniniani.* Substantially in line with what was observed in Magdala for this period are the data from Capernaum,[110] of Meiron[111] and of Khirbet Marus[112] given the extent of the areas investigated and the function of the various sites.

The next phase involved the whole empire, following the reform of Diocletianus in 294, with the attempt to restore a trimetallic system with denominations in a fixed and constant relationship. In particular, after the catastrophic devaluation of the *antoninianus*, a new coinage was started with the standard of the Neronian *denarius*, the *argenteus* characterized by a very high denomination, around 94/95 % cut off at 1/96 of a pound. Three minor denominations followed, the large laureate (*follis*), the radiate fraction (fraction of *follis*) and the small laureate. This momentous intervention, however, seems to have left little numismatic trace in Galilee. There are few laureates of the tetrarchs, mostly after the reform of 306 (*follis* weighing c. 5–6 g), mainly from Antioch which in fact became the first mint to supply for the small-currency demand. It almost seems as if Antioch had replaced Tyre to which can be added a few sporadic contributions from Alexandria, Cyzicus, Ostia. For this epoch, the presence of Constantinian *folles* in MP is in general very modest like in MAP[113] and also in Wadi Hamam, in Capernaum and Meiron.[114] This decrease of circulating money is often interpreted as a generalized economic crisis involving an entire area to the point of causing the abandonment of all or part of a site. Such a deduction, however, seems a little too mechanical, as if in the economy of the ancient world there was a direct, almost cause/effect relationship between monetary circulation and the vitality/crisis of the so-called economic dynamics of a region. Applying our categories, and even our language or *forma mentis* to the ancient world is misleading. The decrease of the circulating currency, as inferred from the occasional losses that distributed in an AACL scheme depended on several factors: the competition between currencies during reforms, the non-involvement in actions/transfers of legions, perhaps a loss of centrality of an area with respect to events that involved other territories more directly with a relative presence of currency. In the Magdala area, the shortage of *folles* and fractions of the Tetrarchs is not sufficient to support either a generalized economic contraction, abandonment or a radical discontinuity. Rather, perhaps parts of the area of this vast settlement underwent functional transformations with settlement changes and perhaps the city itself temporarily lost its economic role, which it had kept at least until the second half of the third century, due to shifting trade axes or strategic-military choices at least until the reunification of the empire in 324 with the defeat of Licinius and the return to a single emperor, Constantinus. What is certain is that in the period from Valerianus to Diocletianus the monetary flow, though less substantial, did not stop. At the same time, Galilee had entered the late imperial Antiochian orbit to remain there until the Byzantine era.

5.12 The decline of small currency during the Late Roman period: fourth-fifth century (cf. 4.6)

As observed for the Tetrarchic period, small value coinage continued to flow into Magdala in the following decades, but in smaller quantities. Notable is the absence of *folles* with large modulus and traces of silvering still clearly discernible, and the absolute prevalence of small laureate fractions or *folles* of reduced weight, often not well attributable to a specific mint. Below is a summary and comparison with a similar period from Wadi Hamam and Capernaum, chosen here because of the prominence of that site during the Late Roman period.[115]

110 Callegher 2007a, pp. 92–93.

111 Meyer, Strange, Meyers 1981; Raynor, Meshorer 1988, pp. 47–49.

112 Personal communication of Gabriela Bijovsky: manuscript *Coins from Excavations at the Ancient Synagogue of Kh. Marus. Catalogue of isolated Coins*, p. 16.

113 Syon forthcoming.

114 A bibliographic check ok Bjiovsky 2018, Callegher 2007a and Raynor, Meshorer 1988 can confirm that.

115 Callegher 2007a, pp. 39–41. The data available in Syon, forthcoming, are even more limited than in the MP, covering only about 25 coins from between the fourth and fifth century.

Tab. 17: Distribution by authority and mints.

Authority	MP	W. Hamam	Capernaum
Constantius I	1 Alexandria	1 Cyzicus	
Licinius I	1 Siscia 1 Heraclea **1 Antioch**	1 Rome **3 Antioch**	2 Cyzicus **1 Antioch** 1 Arelate
Constantinus I	1 Trier 1 Rome **1 Antioch** 1 Indeterminate	1 Ostia 1 Areate 1 Constantinopolis 1 Indeterminate	1 Londinium 1 Arelate 3 Lugdunum? 2 Ticinum 4 Rome 2 Thessalonica 2 Heraclea 1 Constantinopolis 1 Nicomedia 1 Cyzicus **3 Antioch** 1 Alexandria
Constantinus II	1 Cyzicus	1 Nicomedia **1 Antioch**	1 Ticinum 2 Rome 1 Constantinopolis 1 Cyzicus **3 Antioch** 1 Alexandria
Family of Constantinus I	1 Arelate 3 Identerminate **1 Antioch**	1 Nicomedia	2 Nicomedia **1 Antioch** 1 Cyzicus
Urbs Roma	1 Indeterminate		1 Thessalonica 1 Indeterminate
Constantinopolis		1 Cyzicus	1 Nicomedia 1 Indeterminate
gloria excercitus 2 standards (LRBC 60)	1 Indeterminate	1 Cyzicus **3 Antioch**	**3 Antioch** 2 Indeterminate
gloria excercitus 1 standard (LRBC 1028)	3 Indeterminate		1 Cyzicus **7 Antioch** 7 Indeterminate

These issues are produced largely following the reforming intervention of Constantinus I, 310–311. That emperor, in fact, sought to remedy the devaluation, which was undermining the value of the Tetrarchic currency in circulation, causing prices to soar and impoverishing the public treasury, at the time engaged in enormous expenditures to reinforce the defensive lines at the empire's borders, including the eastern ones, and to pay the stipendium to the soldiers. Constantinus radically changed the previous Diocletianus system by anchoring it to a new gold coin, the *solidus*.[116] He also acted, however, on the *follis* whose weight and alloy were reduced compared to the previous standard.[117] After 313, the dissemination of this coin resumed, not documented at our site, but present in the *soli invicto comiti* type dated 313–318 at Wadi Hamam, Capernaum and various

116 Hendy 1985, pp. 462–467.

117 The devaluation of *follis* during the fourth century is analyzed in Depeyrot 1992 and, most recently, with an extension to a similar phenomenon during the fifth century, especially in Asolati 2005, pp. 56–63.

other excavations in the Upper Galilee and the neighboring regions: Sepphoris[118] and Megiddo,[119] Dor,[120] Meiron,[121] in the Roman military camp of Ḥorvat 'Eleq,[122] in the synagogues of 'En Nashut,[123] Khirbet Shema'[124] and Korazim,[125] and on Lake Kinneret[126] as well as in the harbour of Caesarea Maritima.[127] The type is also attested in Transjordan in the *Macellum* and in the settlement of Gerasa[128] and the city of Pella.[129] Again, for Magdala, at least in the MP part, there are several absences compared to other sites in the same region. In fact, the number of Constantinian *folles*, minted 313–335, remains modest. It should be noted, however, that this regressive phase seems to be characteristic only of this part of the site because a similar rarefaction of the monetary flow does not seem to extend to the whole of Palestine and in particular to Galilee. These regions, during the fourth century had been confirmed *territorium legionis*, the hinterland of the most advanced military camps and fortifications towards the East.[130] This economic and strategic function, in fact, influenced the level and composition of the circulating currency. Perhaps this function can also be traced in Magdala, not so much in the quantitative aspect, but in the great variety of mints, particularly for the issues of Constantinus. This emperor's *folles* came from Trier or Rome, but also from other western mints: Arelate, Ticinum and Ostia. The clear predominance, however, and this applies to the entire Constantinian period in the area, lay with the eastern mints, especially Antioch.

5.13 From the monetary reform of Constantius II (348) to the end of the fourth century

In the post-Constantinian phase, the issuing authorities changed the weight and alloy of the *follis* several times in attempts to stabilise its quotation and cope with its progressive devaluation. The old issues remained in use at a fixed legal value until new specimens with a different iconography attempted to replace them.

For this period, we see the contribution of the western mints gradually decrease in our site (cf. tabs. 18, 19). This process corresponds to a strengthening of the role of Antioch for all monetary types like at Capernaum[131] and Wadi Hamam,[132] but also in other significant archaeological-urban sites, such as in Caesarea Maritima,[133] Pella,[134] Gerasa[135] and, to remain in possible contact with the Syrian region, in Beirut[136] and Apamea.[137]

As early as between 348–349, two types of *maiorina* were struck, whose modulus, weight and type led them to be called AE2. They then became the reference of the new system, albeit cut on different feet according to the various mints and in any case generally around

118 Bunnell 1937a, pp. 57–58, 61–63.
119 Newell 1938, p. 203.
120 Meshorer 1995, nos. 114–115.
121 Raynor, Meshorer 1988, nos. 325–348.
122 Barkay 2000, p. 386.
123 Ariel 1987, p. 156.
124 Hanson, Bates 1976, pp. 155–156.
125 Ariel 2000, p. 34.
126 Berman 2004, p. 228.
127 Belloni 1966, p. 231; Ariel 1986, p. 140; Derose Evans 2006, pp. 134–139.
128 Marot 1998, nos. 53–60; Olavarri Goicoechea 1986, nos. 12–14.
129 Pella 2001, nos. 019–034.
130 Beginning with Diocletianus, continuing with Galerius Maximianus and throughout the entire fourth century, the eastern *limes* of Syria, Palestine and Arabia were profoundly reorganized with an extensive system of fortifications and the consequent redeployment of some legions, in particular *legio VI Ferrata* and *legio X Fretensis*. These military interventions have recently been investigated in Cotton 2000 (presence of *legio VI Ferrata* in Upper Galilee), Dabrowa 2000 (displacements of *legio X Fretensis*), Findlater 2002 (military on the *limes Arabicus*), Gichon 2002 (relations between the legions and nomadic tribes), Lewin 2004 (military organization in the fourth century with the creation of soldiers distinguished into *limitanei* and *comitatenses*). More generally cf. Leadbetter 2002, Lewin 2002, Parker 2002. For the economic-numismatic aspects Gichon 2002, pp. 195–196 has investigated the relations between the displacement of the *legio X Fretensis* and the territorial enlargement of the Province of Palestine, which Diocletianus probably enacted in order to better provide for the fiscal needs for the payment of the troops; Chameroy 2004 has studied the coinage in military contexts-sites, as an indicator of *donativa* or *stipendium*, but also of a possible contribution of individual mints close to the investigated area, without excluding that coins were transported by *milites* during the transfers of their legion. The fiscal and economic impact resulting from the presence of the legions in the fourth century in Syria and Palestine is discussed in Liebeschuetz 1990, XII–XIII and in Roth 2002, pp. 382–386, although these essays lack precise data on the monetary circulation along the *limes Palaestinae*.
131 Callegher 2007a, pp. 40–49.
132 Bijovsky 2018, pp. 553–558.
133 Derose Evans 2006, pp. 153–167.
134 *Pella* 2001, pp. 86–87.
135 Marot 1998, p. 78.
136 Butcher 2003, pp. 84–85.
137 Callu 1979, pp. 15–24.

Tab. 18: Distribution by Authority and Mints.

Authority	MP	W. Hamam	Capernaum
Costantius II	2 Constantinopolis **3 Antioch** 1 Heraclea	**7 Antioch** 1 Thessalonica 1 Cyzicus 1 Alexandria 1 Indeterminate	2 Thessalonica 25 Constantinopolis 2 Nicomedia **8 Antioch** 2 Alexandria 21 Indeterminate
fel temp reparatio (LRBC 2625,2295)	10 Indeterminate	3 Indeterminate	6 Thessalonica 6 Constantinopolis 3 Heraclea 3 Nicomedia 2 Cyzicus **22 Antioch** 9 Alexandria 77 Indeterminate
spes reipublice (LRBC 2504)	8 Indeterminate	3 Indeterminate	8 Indeterminate
Valens	1 Constantinopolis		2 Rome 1 Constantinopolis 2 Indeterminate
Valentinianus I	1 Indeterminate		1 Rome 1 Constantinopolis 2 Indeterminate
Gratianus	1 Indeterminate		1 Antiochia 1 Oriental mint
Valentinianus II	**2 Antioch**	1 Thessalonica 5 Indeterminate	1 Heraclea 6 Constantinopolis 2 Nicomedia **6 Antioch** 2 Alexandria 10 Indeterminate
Theodosius I	**1 Antioch**	**1 Antioch** 1 Cyzicus 1 Alexandria 4 Indeterminate	2 Rome 3 Constantinopolis 2 Cyzicus **4 Antioch** 2 Alexandria 5 Indeterminate
securitas reipublicae (LRBC 527)	2 Indeterminate	8 Indeterminate	1Aquileia 5 Constantinopolis **1 Antioch** 4 Alexandria 27 Indeterminate
gloria romanorum 8 (LRBC 338)	5 Indeterminate		3 Roma 1 Heraclea 1 Constantinopolis **2 Antioch** 23 Indeterminate

Authority	MP	W. Hamam	Capernaum
vot xx/mult xxx	**1 Antioch** 9 Oriental mint	3 Indeterminate	1 Constantinopolis 1 Nicomedia 2 Cyzicus **1 Antioch** 1 Alexandria 13 Oriental mint 1 Indeterminate
Arcadius	**3 Antioch** 1 Indeterminate	1 Costantinopolis **1 Antioch** 2 Indeterminate	1 Rome 1 Thessalonica 1 Heraclea 3 Constantinopolis 2 Nicomedia **6 Antiochia** 6 Indeterminate
Honorius	1 Rome/Aquileia	1 Rome **1 Antioch** 3 Indeterminate	1 Rome 1 Constantinopolis 1 Cyzicus **1 Antioch** 2 Alexandria 4 Indeterminate
salus reipublicae (LRBC 1105)	1 Alexandria **1 Antioch** 24 Indeterminate	**1 Antioch** 15 Indeterminate	1Thessalonica 9 Constantinopolis 4 Nicomedia 6 Cyzicus **31 Antioch** 3 Alexandria 75 Indeterminate
Theodosius II	6 Oriental mint	1 Oriental mint	29 Oriental mint
Valentinianus III	1 Rome		11 Rome 13 Oriental mint 6 Indeterminate
Leo	1 Oriental mint		1 Constantinopolis 6 Oriental mint
Imitations	5 AE		
Indeterminate authority and mint (fourth-fifth century)	68 AE 4	16 AE 4	523 AE 4

a weight value of 1/60 of a pound.[138] This new coin struggled to enter circulation, as it can be seen also in the sites chosen for comparison, to the extent that it was replaced by an AE3 struck at approximately 1/120 of a pound. Dating to this early phase of the monetary dynamics of the reign of Constantius II are the AE3s of the type *fel temp reparatio*/soldier piercing fallen enemy (LRBC 2625, 2295), in Magdala mostly of Antiochian mintage. Also, during the empire of Constantius around 355, another intervention was made on the copper coinage by issuing another AE3 of the *spes reipublice* type (LRBC 2504) with a decreasing weight compared to the previous ones. These were the most widespread devalued coins (type LRBC 2625, LRBC 2295, LRBC 2504) in many Magdala *loci*.

Later, Valentinianus I and Valens also proceeded with new copper issues and interventions on their alloy composition. As Callu's studies have shown, the

138 About the weight trends of the various mints, the denominations and types adopted for the coins, cf *RIC*, VIII, pp. 35–40, 61–67.

blanks for the manufacture of these coins contained only a certain percentage of copper and were completely devoid of silver, a metal that was present, however, though in minute quantities, in earlier coins.[139] The first series of AE3 types *securitas reipublicae*/Victory on the left with laurel wreath (LRBC 527) and *gloria romanorum*/Emperor with labarum and prisoner (LRBC 338) retained the weight standard of the last issues of Constantius II, i. e. a ratio to the pound of about 1/130 or 1/132, corresponding to a theoretical weight oscillating between 2.47 and 2.49 g. These choices helped to give stability to the system, diminished inflationary expectations and ensured that earlier types of equal weight continued to be legal tender. In this era, Antioch and Constantinopolis were the mints that contributed most to the supply of numerals in the Syro-Palestinian sites.

The most recent researches have analyzed the different circulation of the types *gloria romanorum* and *securitas reipublicae* in the area of Phoenicia, Syria and Transjordan near Lake Kinneret, leading to the hypothesis of a sort of territorial division in the distribution of these two types of currency.[140] To the north, in Syria and the Phoenician coast, AE3 LRBC 338 predominated, in particular due to the minting of Antioch. To the south, in the provinces of Palestine and Arabia, AE3 LRBC 527 from the Alexandria mint prevailed. However, the few data from Magdala as well as from the sites chosen for comparison, especially Capernaum, do not point to an indisputable prevalence of one of the two types, but instead confirm the coexistence of various mints and a consistently prominent role for Antioch or Alexandria. The documentary bases for such quantitative-distributive analyses are, not only in this site, rather uncertain for two reasons. First of all, statistical comparisons are distorted by the number of specimens in which, due to corrosion or poor preservation, it is impossible to identify any sign or letter that would help to trace a mint or authority (Valentinianus I, Valens, Gratianus, Valentinianus II, Theodosius I).[141] The other element concerns the sample chosen and its location, i. e. whether it relates to a town, a military settlement or a village in the countryside, because the number of surviving specimens depends, as illustrated in the introduction, largely on the function of a site and the economic activities and exchanges that took place there.[142]

In the period 378–388, various types of AE4 of lower modulus and weight than the AE3 also circulated. A few *vot × mult xx* and *vot xx mult xxx*, produced only in eastern mints between 378–383 are reported in Magdala.

Between the end of the fourth century and the fifth decade of the fifth century a small coin weighing slightly more than a gram appeared: the AE4 type *salus reipublicae* 2 (LRBC 1105), whose chronology in the East seems to end around 395.[143]

Very often it has not been possible to go beyond the determination of the type alone. This type of small currency was undoubtedly among the most common recovered in excavations and also in hoards from the fifth century, but they are also often the most insidious to read due to their poor state of preservation and the ease of making errors in correctly

139 Callu 1980.

140 The distributional analysis of Butcher 2003, pp. 87–88, with reference to the cities of Sardis, Antioch, Beirut and Jerash is valid. The author points out, in fact, that *"When the data from Antioch and Beirut are added, there appears to be a divide between the north, where GLORIA ROMANORVM predominates, and the south, where SECVRITAS REIPVBLICAE predominates"*.

141 Marot 1998, pp. 86–87, explains the poor legibility of the letters or marks of the *gloria romanorum* type with *"la finalidad de transformar los AE3 en AE4. Esta prática, documentada en abundantes tesoros y hallazgos acqueológicos, impide la conservación de la marca de la ceca situada en el exergo, y dificulta enormemente la documentación de la procedencia del numerario"*. The fact is that the very poor state of preservation makes a complete identification of both the AE3 *securitas reipublicae* and the AE3 *gloria romanorum* in Magdala uncertain if not impossible, as they are present in only modest quantities. In the case, then, of a quotation of the latter AE3 equal to that of an AE4, one would have to conclude that a very disadvantageous issue for the state treasury would have taken place, with the consequence of provoking the immediate and widespread phenomenon of hoarding only of the *gloria romanorum* type. To the best of my knowledge, however, this does not seem to have occurred except in association with other coins, especially with the AE3 *securitas reipublicae* (cf. example of the treasury of Haifa in Butcher 2003, p. 88). On the possible weight reduction from 1/130–1/132 lb to 1/192 lb for both types of AE3 in the final phase of their minting cf. Depeyrot 1984, p. 210 and Depeyrot 1992, p. 82. Finally, I would like to point out that in the west the weight trend of the two series is, in some cases, opposite to that observed in the Syro-Palestinian area: cf. Callegher 1998, pp. 47–49.

142 The numerous contributions collected in Reece 2003, which analyse the relationship between coin findings, the methodology of archaeological excavation, the function of a site, and the chronological reliability of numismatic data, constitute a methodological reference even if they deal with contexts and data mainly from Britain and the western part of the empire. For the application of statistical methods in the processing of numismatic data, cf. the critical remarks in De Callataÿ 1987.

143 The usual dating 383–395 has been extended to 402–403 in RIC X, pp. 375–376. For the small coinage of this period, cf. Bijovsky 2012b.

identifying them.[144] In many cases, in fact, the legend *salus reipublicae* and the various mintmarks in the exergue or field are missing because they are worn, badly minted or obliterated by corrosion. However, relying on some traces of the iconography on the reverse (Victory on the left with a staff on her shoulder, prisoner on the right; in the field on the left christogram or cross, the latter used especially in Nicomedia and Antioch[145]), a large number of specimens are attributed to this series. A case in point is the discovery of a small hoard of 84 AE3/4, generally of poor conservation, during the 1973 archaeological campaign. In the publication, it was noted that the coins *"were not in obvious association with each other, but neither were they associated with any other monetary species. Considered as a coherent core, they proposed a composition in many respects anomalous"*[146]. In fact, the majority type is 'camp gate' of Magnus Maximus, Flavius Victor, Valentinianus II and Valentinianus III, coined in western mints (Arelate, Aquileia and Rome) and also in Thessalonica.[147] If it was a hoard (doubts remained even to its editor), it was hidden or abandoned around the mid-fifth century and was the result not so much of a collection of small bronzes circulating in the area as of a purse belonging to a *viator* or a poor *peregrinus* perhaps from the west. Apart from this singular finding, the attestations in Magdala diminish so drastically in the course of the fifth century that only an AE4 of Emperor Leo I (457–474) and a few locally minted imitations can be reported. This evidence also testifies to a collapse of bronze coinage, which was beginning to be exchanged by weight and not by number.[148]

It has been argued, on the basis of the quantitative data and from the second half of the third century onwards, that there was a progressive reduction in the contribution of circulating bronze and thus a weakening of the significant economic role of at least the area investigated with the MP. Raw data like the numbers of coins recovered between the fourth and fifth centuries including unidentified types, however, could confirm a possibly even more modest flow. Confirming a negative, or if one prefers non-enthusiastic reading of the monetary data, one should consider the value in *nummi* of account of these coins over a period of almost two centuries, but even more so their copper solidus in comparison with gold unit of account: the cut at 1/72 of a pound (4.45 g). Throughout the first half of the fourth century *follis* (if this was the common name for the increasingly vile bronze coins) meant 12500 *denarii* of account.[149] And it may be of relevance to recall that the sources agree in indicating in assigning a value equivalent to 1/24 of the *solidus* to the *siliqua* and the *carat*, that is in copper weighing 1/6 of a gram, so a quantity of copper weighing 0.18 g or 1/1728 of a pound. If we compare these units of weight with Codex Theodosianus XI, 21, 2 *pro viginti quinque libris aeris solidus a possessore reddatur*, which states that the amount of gold of 1 solidus (4.45 g) by law should be exchanged for 25 pounds of copper (= 8.1 kg) corresponding to ca. 7200 *nummi* of account, it is understandable *ipso facto* that the few coins recovered at the Magdala site, spread over a chronological span of c. 200 years, represent a less than modest and irrelevant value; thus the only possible economic deduction concerns a very limited recourse to small divisional, and above all in a context of exchanges or production that were also very limited, typical of a marginal settlement. By contrast, in Capernaum, and in some other sites in Galilee (e.g. Korazim,[150] Horvat Kanaf,[151] Tiberias,[152] Gush Halav[153]) the exchange in actual numerals was certainly more frequent and conspicuous.[154]

144 The spread of this AE4 can be seen in the large documentary evidence (*Hoards of bronze coins*) in *RIC*, X, pp. cxxviii–clxx.
145 *RIC*, IX, p. 262 (Nicomedia), pp. 292–293 (Antiochia).
146 Arslan 2003a, p. 33.
147 An AE of Magnus Maximus, mint of Rome, type *spes romanorum*/Camp gate (387–388) = LRBC 795 was found in Wadi Hamam: Bijovsky 2018, no. 332.
148 Callegher 2016, precisely with references to imitations in the Galilee between the fourth and fifth centuries.
149 Carlà 2009, p. 164.
150 Ariel 2000.
151 Ariel 1980.
152 Rahmani, Sharabani 1983; Bijovsky 2004a; Bijovsky 2008; Ariel 2019.
153 Bijovsky 1998.
154 Callegher 2007a, in part. pp. 52–56 for the comparison between currency and the founding deposit of the synagogue of Capernaum and other synagogues in Galilee; Arslan 2003c; Arslan 2011; Callegher 2016, in particular pp. 165–167. The substantial marginality of the settlement is reflected in Zangenberg 2010.

5.14 Notes on a Phoenician lead weight[155]

In the course of cataloguing MP coins, a lead weight was identified, which is described below following the method proposed in an updated study on this particular class of materials.[156] It has a quadrangular shape; its state of preservation is quite good, and on its surface there are numerous cuts at the base and along the margins. It weighs 53.75 g. On the obverse, there is a geometric figure attributable to Tanit.

Type and Date: This type of lead weights, be they truncated cone, animal, talus, rectangular or square in shape, is known mostly through collecting or fleeting appearances at public auctions, and it is believed to have been produced either in the Phoenician area or in towns on the Syro-Palestinian coast.[157] In general, precisely because of the absence of archaeological contexts, their dating remains approximate because it is based on their inclusion in some weight scale, on the presence of legends referring to cities, authorities or magistrates, or on Palaeographic features. On the basis of iconography, for example, the plummet weights with the emblem of Tanit are placed in the Hellenistic period by comparison with similar finds in locations in the Syro-Lebanese area.[158] They have a rather broad time span, difficult to distinguish whether of production or use, between the fourth century BCE and the first century CE. In some cases, however, epigraphic elements have been decisive in establishing a reliable chronology. One weight, for instance, records Antiochus IV (175–164 BCE); others give the date of the era of a city as in the case of Antioch (63–62 BCE and 58–57 BCE) or Gaza (154–155 and 226/227 BCE)[159]; still others are dated by the presence of the name of an authority and the years of its government placed on the obverse, while on the reverse are the names of the *agoranomoi*, officials in charge of overseeing the accuracy of weights and measures.[160] I recall, among these, two specimens with the name of Agrippa II whose provenance is believed to be from Magdala, distinguished by striking similarities in shape, size, ductus and epigraphic setting. The first, indicating year 22 of Agrippa II corresponding to 70/71 or 81/82, bears on the reverse side the names of two Roman citizen *agoranomoi*, *Rufus* and *Iulius*.[161] On the second, dated to year 23 of Agrippa II i. e. 71/72 or 82/83, we read of two local *agoranomoi*, *Iaesaias son of Mathias* and *Animos son of Monimos*.[162] In the absence of elements similar to those in the two cases just cited, it remains somewhat difficult to date both the period of production and the period of use of most of this group of Phoenician lead weights. In this context, the safe provenance from a systematic excavation makes this Magdala weight of considerable interest. It was in fact discovered

155 The specimen was already published in Callegher 2008.

156 All this documentation was recently reviewed by Elayi, A. G. Elayi 1999. A number of suggestions for the future: cf. Finkielsztejn 2007, but above all Finkielsztejn 2014.

157 See, for example, the specific sections edited by S. Qedar, *Münz-Zentrum Auktion 32: Gewichte aus drei Jahrtausenden*, Köln 1978, in part. no. 76; S. Qedar, *Münz-Zentrum Auktion 37: Gewichte aus drei Jahrtausenden*, II, Köln 1979, in part. nos. 4091, 4093; S. Qedar, *Münz Zentrum. Auction 49: Gewichte aus drei Jahrtausenden*, IV, Köln 1981, in part. pp. 31–43 and nos. 95–96; S. Qedar, *Münz-Zentrum. Auktion 49: Gewichte aus drei Jahrtausenden*, IV, Köln 1983. Other data in: J. L. Malter, *Auction VII*, April 22, 1979, no. 8 and nos. 9 (a-c), further. Elayi, A. G. Elayi 1997, cf. also I. Vecchi, *Nummorum Auctiones 13*, London 4th September 1998, p. 56, no. 1338; I. Vecchi, *Nummoroum Auctiones 17*, London 15th December 1999, p. 34, no. 1224; *Archaeological Center. Auction no. 40 part II. The Arnold Spaer Collection of Hellenistic and Roman Lead Weights and Byzantine and Crusader Lead Bullae*, Tel Aviv 4th April 2007, in part. nos. 384–420.

158 Elayi, A. G. Elayi 1997, pp. 265–279 (Antiochia, Seleucia Pieria, Tyre), but above all Finkielsztejn 2007.

159 All these data are published in Qedar 1986–1987; Barag, Qedar 2003–2006. Also known is a weight of a certain Marcus from Laodicea of Syria, datable to the early first century: Le Rider, Seyrig 1968 in part. p. 33.

160 On the tasks and status of these controllers cf. PWE, s. v. ἀγορανόμοι, cc. 883–885; Migeotte 2005.

161 Kushnir-Stein 2002; SEG, no. 1693.

162 Qedar 1986–1987, pp. 30–32, reconsidered in Kushnir-Stein 2002 and in SEG, no. 1694.

in situ, in area H field 3-US 83, where bronze coins of the Jerusalem mint, issued during the reign of Herod the Great (40/37–4 BCE) (2 *prutot*[163]), as well as coins from the Roman procurator Pontius Pilate (26–36 CE) (1 *prutah*[164]), Emperor Claudius made by the mint of Tiberias (53 CE) (1 AE)[165] and Tyre as an autonomous city (93–196 CE) (2 AE[166]) were collected. These specimens are distributed between the middle of the first century BCE to the end of the second century CE. It is not certain, however, that a similar chronology for the lead weight can be deduced symmetrically from this association. In fact, its loss in the ground could have occurred at any time during the decades covered by the coins. In any case, however, the monetary date represents a safe *terminus post quem*, capable of making a convincing contribution to subsequent chronological comparisons of similar lead weights.

Iconography: The image of Tanit is composed by a Δ surmounted by a small circle and a horizontal line to simulate the head and arms, while at the base there is an apex with two divergent signs on either side. In its essential elements, such a design is well documented, particularly in the square lead weights produced or used in the city of Arados (Phoenicia) during the Hellenistic phase, thus in a period entirely corresponding to the one inferred here thanks to the associated numismatic material.[167] However, even in its simplicity, the iconography of this specimen does not seem to overlap precisely with any of the numerous types which appear in the most up-to-date illustrative tables of signs/figures attributable to Tanit.[168]

Metrology. The identification of its standard weight is particularly difficult because it lacks signs or other epigraphic elements that can be interpreted as numerals or as indicators of some kind of measurement. As far as the metrology of square lead weights is concerned, for this region recent studies propose the existence of various weight systems in force during the Hellenistic period. The first, of ancient origin, would have had as its basic unit a shekel of 9.40 g defined as the Syrian or Micro-Asian foot.[169] The second weight system refers to the region of Tyre where lead weights would have been produced on a foot/cycle between 8.90 g and 9.30 g, the sub-multiple of a *mina* ranging between 445 g and 465 g.[170] Finally, the third, system is that of the city of Arados, depending on the Tyre *mina* with lead weights aligned to a foot/shekel of between 9.25–9.59 g equivalent to c. 1/50 of a *mina* with values between 462.5 g and 479.5 g. Again, also this shekel would be equivalent to ca. 1/50 of a slightly modified *mina*.[171] During the first century the imperial authorities gradually imposed the weight standard of the Roman pound of c. 327.45 g or 324.[172] This means that while the ancient weights continued to be used according to their own scale of values, they could fit into the new Roman system, especially to even outweigh fractions on the scales.

The Magdala specimen, with a weight of 53.75 g, does not immediately fit into the average values of any of the first three systems mentioned. However, if it were given a hypothetical value of 1/10th of a *mina*, it would relate to the heavier weight standard of Arados, for which a *mina* of 479.5 g was assumed. In this case, the calculation would give the following equivalence: 479.5 g (Arados *mina*): 10 = 47.95 g. Compared to this theoretical value, the weight deviation of the specimen under examination here is + 5.8 g, i. e. a deviation of just over 10 %, a threshold not too far off from the average weight of the 1/10th weights of the Arados *mina*.

If, on the other hand, we compare it to the Roman pound system of 327.45–324 g, then its weight of 53.75 g is very close to that of two ounces (27.29 g × 2 = 54.58 g), a difference of less than a gram.

It should be noted, however, that in general small weight denominations were overvalued compared to their theoretical value, perhaps because they were intended to favor product weighing and their fractional interchange.[173]

Provenance. The iconography and metrology of the Tanit weight do not allow for an unambiguous interpretation. The image of Tanit in the cartouche and

163 Cf. Area H-Field 3 US 7; cat. no. 518, 512.

164 Cf. Area H-Field 3, US 11, cat. no. 904.

165 Cf Area H-Field 3, US 8, cat. no. 1238.

166 Cf Area H-Field 3, US 8, cat. nos. 123 and Area H-Field 3, US 11, cat. no. 68.

167 The attribution to this city is based on the reading of the monogram *rwd* which appears on the square weights with the sign of Tanit. On this subject cf. most recently Finkielsztejn 2007, p. 49.

168 Elayi e A. G. Elayi 1997, p. 386, fig. 18 for comparison with nos. 394–402. Concerning the dissemination of representative models of this deity also on other media, such as on stone material as far afield as the regions of North Africa and the western Mediterranean, cf. Avaliani 1999; Elayi 1998, in part. tab. III, nos. 7.8. See also Wolff, Erlich 2018.

169 Parise 1984; Parise 1991. The Syrian standard would also have had a use in the monetary sphere because the first issues of Byblos would have conformed to it, cf. Sole 2000.

170 Finkielsztejn 2007, pp. 42–45.

171 Cf. Elayi, A. G. Elayi 1997, pp. 320–321.

172 This hypothesis is suggested in Qedar 1986–1987, p. 34.

173 Finkielsztejn 2007, p. 50.

the shape of the artefact would point to Arados as the city of origin, not without some prior reflection as to whether in the ancient world a city's weights were used outside of its sphere of influence. In general, the application of a weight system entailed forms of control of standards with considerable legal implications, aimed at avoiding falsification or damage to property, so much so that it was precisely to ensure such guarantees that there was a tendency to diversify the respective metrological systems. It is therefore logical to assume that weights remained within the city/region. Itinerant trade, on the other hand, had to provide for the transport of certain weights, usually the smaller values of the metrological scale, both for verification and for the necessary feedback when changing from one system to another.[174] Based on the data available to date, it seems that a possible mobility of lead square weights was prevalent in the cities or coastal ports of Syria, Phoenicia and Palestine:[175] Laodicea, Arados, Marathos, Tripolis, Byblos, Tyre, Umm el-'Amed, Ashdod,[176] Ascalon[177] and Gaza.[178] There is, however, no lack of evidence in the hinterland like Judea, Samaria and Galilee, areas in which the Phoenician influence on lead square weights lasted for a long time, from the third century BCE until the entire second century CE, both in metrology and in the choice of images.[179] Finds of *plumbum* weights from the Herodian and post-Herodian periods are known from excavations in Jerusalem,[180] but the Magdala area has also provided evidence as has already been reported. In addition to the one published here, while this book was being written, SBF archaeologists recovered another specimen precisely in this locality, now being under restoration.[181] If we add to these two the lead of Agrippa II with the name of the local *agoranomoi Iaesaias* son of *Mathias* and *Animos* son of *Monimos*, indicated as coming from Magdala though decontextualized,[182] and that of *Rufus/Iulius*, for which production in Tiberias is assumed,[183] the use of such metrological instruments is confirmed in Herodian and/or post-Herodian times perhaps along the routes through Samaria that connected Judea with Upper Galilee,[184] but especially due to the existence of a market near the harbor on Lake Kinneret in the town of Magdala itself.

On the basis of these observations, the possibility that the weight discovered in Magdala is a local production should be ruled out. Instead, it seems more likely that it arrived and/or was used there by some merchant in contact with the towns on the Phoenician coast, or that it was used in the market place as part of the weight and monetary system specific to Phoenician Tyre. Moreover, it is precisely the study of coin findings that has made it possible to clarify that towards the end of the second century BCE to the first half of the first century CE a vast territorial area was formed, including Upper Galilee, in which copper coins minted according to Tyre's own metrology ran.[185] That being said, the square lead weight published here can certainly be linked to the Phoenician types from Arados in terms of its iconography, and such an affinity suggests a consequent metrological connection. It is conceivable, therefore, that even in Magdala standards proper to the Phoenician cities or even in use in the area between Tiberias and Magdala were followed for weighing operations in the context of market exchanges under the control of *agoranomoi*. Only from the first century CE onwards did these standards

174 On this topic see Hachens, Moucharte 1993; Elayi, A. G. Elayi 997, pp. 266–267; Duyrat 2005.

175 Finkielsztejn 2007, p. 56, fig. 4.

176 Even if with some doubt, a lead square weight with an image of Tanit may have been discovered in the excavations at Ashdod-Yam: cf. Dotan 1974, no. 14; Elayi, A. G. Elayi 1997, p. 268.

177 For connections between images stamped on lead weights and coins in Ascalon cf. Kushnir-Stein 2006.

178 This is confirmed, for example, by the Phoenician weights preserved in the Museum of the *Studium Biblicum Franciscanum* in Jerusalem. They come in part from the collection of Godfrey Kloetzli (1916–1992): cf. *Acta Custodiae Terrae Sanctae* 37 (1992), pp. 386–387. His collecting activities, in particular at the Terra Sancta College Museum, are mentioned in *Acta Custodiae Terrae Sanctae* 26 (1991), p. 241. Manns 1976a, p. 6 states that Kloetzli collected these finds in Gaza, thus at a coastal site. The aforementioned study was published in monographic form as Manns 1984 already edited in Manns 1976b. More data from Gaza and Palestine in general in Kushnir-Stein, Gitler 1999.

179 Based on iconographic attributes and epigraphy Finkielsztejn 2007, p. 39 assigns two Seleucid-era weights to the city of Gerasa and Caesarea Maritima (with doubt) respectively. The scholar also confirms as erroneous the attribution of a weight to Dor and accepts the conclusions by Kushnir-Stein 1997, p. 90.

180 Qedar 1986–1987, p. 35. Gatier 2014 holds a different opinion, considering these weights not to date from the Hellenistic period.

181 Information by Stefano de Luca on May 21, 2008.

182 Qedar 1986–1987, p. 31 tells us that *"the weight was found at Migdal (ancient Magdala/Taricheae), 5 km. north-west of Tiberias"*, without additional information.

183 Kushnir-Stein 2002, p. 297; the datum is accepted in *SEG*, no. 1693 while the place of discovery is noted as unknown.

184 Qedar 1986–1987, pp. 29–30; Elayi, A. G. Elayi 1997, pp. 265–285, p. 391, fig. 23. More generally on the road system in the region from the Persian era to the Roman and Byzantine empires, cf. Roll 2005 with bibliography on the topic.

185 Hanson 1980; Barag 1982–1983; Callegher 2007a.

begin to be gradually supplanted by the metrology of the Roman empire. At the time of Agrippa II, however, the transition to the Roman pound had not yet fully taken place, as can be seen from the two weights of the *agoranomoi Rufus/Iulius* and *Iaesaias/Animos*, both of which bear no relation to the standard of the pound (327.45 g) and the ounce (27.29 g).

5.15 Byzantine period and at the beginning of Arab-Byzantine coins (see 4.7–4.8)

Among the isolated finds from Magdala MP, the Byzantine coins are all bronze and their number, although not particularly high compared to other Palestine sites, documents what was in use at least until the second half of the seventh century. This presence is part of the profound changes that, following the reform of Anastasius in 498, helped stabilize the price of the bronze divisional after the chaotic phase at the end of the fifth century.[186]

Tab. 19: Distribution by Authority and Mints.

Justinianus	1 K	Salona
Justinus II	1 M	Constantinopolis
	2 M	Nicomedia
	1 M	Antioch
Mauritius Tiberius	1 M	Cyzicus
	1 K	Indeterminate
Heraclius	1 M	Constantinopolis
	1 K	Constantinopolis
	12N	Alexandria
Constans II	1 M	Constantinopolis
	1 M	Imitative *follis*

Such a small number of coins matched by an equally small value in *nummi* of account (only 392 *nummi* of account distributed over more than a century!) can perhaps be explained, at least in the early part of the sixth century, by the continued use of coinage[187] not only in large cities, but also in small villages as Migdal had perhaps become by then and where a monastery had been built as early as the fifth century.[188] This statement, however, would need to be verified by having the exact association in stratigraphic units between the Byzantine *folles* and fractions with other coins, especially those of the fourth –fifth century. Regarding the modest value, it should be noted that *Codex Justininanus* X.73.2 established a gold *solidus*/copper exchange rate of 1 to 20 pounds, i. e. 4.45 g of gold against 6.48 kg of copper, so that the 12 gold coins found in the MP excavations area equal 392 *nummi* of account and therefore correspond to essentially insignificant values.

The Byzantine numismatic documentation of the MP part of Magdala begins with a singular presence of a ½ Justinian *follis* probably minted in Salona whose circulation is almost exclusively limited to the Adriatic Sea region.[189] With Justinus II and up to Constans II, the higher-value coins of 40 and 20 *nummi* prevail. As far as the contribution of mints is concerned, Constantinopolis prevails, while other mints, even territorially closer such as Antioch or Alexandria, seem to have played a marginal role here. If the data on emperors and mints are compared with similar data from other localities, it is possible to observe a considerable inhomogeneity that cannot be easily explained.[190] For the supply of coinage, some settlements or cities appear to be tributary to Antioch, others to Nicomedia, in others still none of the then active mints prevails. These differences may be due to diverging trade contacts between cities, to the particular function of a site, or to the extent of the excavated area. I believe, however, that such a question is of limited importance because Byzantine copper coinage, like Roman imperial coinage, circulated with values dependent not so much on having been struck in one of the various mints, but

186 For the reform, mentioned in various contemporary written sources, cf. most recently Zuckerman 2004, pp. 65–66.

187 This observation is confirmed by the graphs proposed for Jerash (Marot 1998, pp. 147–166), in the numismatic commentary on the Pella excavations (*Pella* 2001, p. 44) and Beirut (Butcher 2003, p. 102), but also in numerous other smaller sites, some of which are mentioned here as examples: Ramat Hanadiv-Ḥorvat ʿEleq (Barkay 2000); Hammat Gader (Barkay 1997); Korazim (Ariel 2000, pp. 38–42); Caesarea Maritima (Ariel 1986, p. 144; De Rose Evans 2006), Capernaum (Callegher 2007a, pp. 58–61), Wadi Hamam (Bijovsky 2018, 2 *folles* of Justinus II, Constantinopolis and Antioch), MAP (3 Byzantine coins) but above all in Bijovsky 2012b, the standard work on these issues for the entire Palestinian region; see also recently Bijovsky 2021, *ad indicem*.

188 De Luca, Leibner 2019. On the changing economy and the impact on the use of money cf. Liebeschuetz 2000 and Liebeschuetz 2001.

189 On the debate between the Ravenna or Salona issue, cf. Callegher 2013 and Prigent 2021.

190 See cf. Butcher 2003, p. 103, fig. 75; Bijovsky 2012b, in particular in sixth century, see the sections dedicated to *"Distribution in Neighbouring Regions"*.

on a 'fiduciary base' within quotations or values guaranteed by the imperial authority accepted in a single monetary area in which the greater or lesser use of the various coinage types depended on the different metrology of the prices. The different provenance of a *follis* and the varying issuing authorities were therefore of secondary importance, while the value marks/minting in numerals of account and compliance with the weight standard were essential. Only the correct ratio of face value to weight ensured that the coin was exchangeable throughout the empire.[191] For comparisons with similar occurrences at sites in the Magdala range, the data of Capernaum,[192] Khisas,[193] Gush Halav,[194] 'En Nashut,[195] Korazim,[196] Tiberias,[197] and Hamat Tiberias,[198] Beth She'an (Nysa-Scythopolis),[199] Sepphoris,[200] Tabgha[201] and although distant but of extreme interest for the quantities and the role played by the town in the phase immediately preceding the end of Byzantine jurisdiction, Caesarea Maritima.[202]

5.16 Arab-Byzantine coinage

After the Byzantine defeat at the Yarmuk River (c. 636), the Lake Kinneret region first came under control of the Orthodox Caliphs and later the Umayyads. The political-administrative change caused the end of circulation of Byzantine coinage, which however occurred gradually as it continued to be accepted and exchanged for a rather prolonged period that numismatists tend to fix in the eighth decade of the seventh century[203] on the evidence of both hoarding and circulating currency.[204] For much of the second half of the seventh century, despite the loss of imperial control in Syria and Palestine, the values and coins representing them remained deeply influenced by the system of account and the actual currency of Constantinopolis. Indeed, at least until 680/681, the eastern Empire continued to supply the lost territories with gold and copper currency. The supply of gold took place through the payment of tributes established in *solidi* of account and honored mostly in *solidi* and less in *tremisses*. The enduring supply of Byzantine gold coinage is also evident from the composition of numerous other hoards recovered in the region, in particular in comparison with those of Nikertai,[205] Horvat Kab[206] and Beth She'an,[207] maybe from Gaza,[208] to which must be added the unpublished one from Jordan sealed with a *dinar* from the first Umayyad issues.[209] In all these hoards there is a substantial correspondence in the percentage distribution of coins, mint and issuing authorities.

The monetary relations of the caliphate with Byzantium also continued in the area of copper coins. For several decades, the newly conquered towns and villages continued to use Byzantine coinage because they were in fact included in that money market.[210] Only from ca. 650 onwards, following the opening of local mints, were the Byzantine *folles* progressively joined

191 Bijovsky 2012b for the summary on circulation, the contribution of metals and coins as well as mints.
192 Callegher 2007a, p. 59.
193 Syon 2000, p. 6.
194 Bijovsky 1998.
195 Ariel 1987, p. 151.
196 Ariel 2000.
197 Berman 2004, pp. 229–230; Bijovsky 2004a, pp. 169–171; Bijovsky 2008.
198 Amitai-Preiss 2000, nos. 1–7.
199 Fitzgerald 1931, p. 60; Sharabani 2004, p. 86; Berman 2015, pp. 260–266.
200 Bunnel 1937, pp. 75–76.
201 Loffreda 1970, pp. 172–173.
202 Derose Evans 2006, pp. 180–203. Above all the chapter *"Numismatic Profiles of the Sites"* in Bijovsky 2012b p. 448.
203 Oddy 2004, in part. p. 130. On the basis of an extensive and up-to-date bibliography, the article clarifies the various problematic aspects of this particular coinage series: definition of 'Arab-Byzantine' coinage, issues between the Byzantine wars with the Persians (611–628) and the start of Umayyad coinage (post-697), proposals for new attributions and new mints with their chronology, reforms by 'Abd al-Malik (685 for the issuance of the *fals* with a standing caliph; 696–697 for the intervention on the *dinar*, *dirhem* and *fals*); cf. also Heidemann 1998; Foss 2008; Walmsley 2010; Bijovsky 2015; Schulze & Schulze 2020.
204 Philipps 2004, in part. pp. 23–24, with insightful observations on the political control and fiscal function of money in the transitional phase between Byzantine authority and caliphate. See also Bijovsky 2012b, pp. 375–380.
205 Morrisson 1972.
206 Syon 2000–2002.
207 Bijovsky 2002 combines the edition of the hoard with an exhaustive survey of contemporary finds of gold coins in the Syrian-Palestinian area. On the merits of the chronological deductions concerning the contribution of Byzantine gold coinage, among other things found in the chronological analysis of numerous hoards, see Philipps 2004, pp. 22, 25. He proposes to set the interruption of the Byzantine gold contribution at the year 680 (death of Mu'āwiya) since, after that event, Constantinopolis would have stopped paying tribute.
208 Callegher 2021.
209 The hoard was first made known at an Arab-Byzantine Symposium at Dumbarton Oaks in Washington. The study assignment was recently given to me by Eugenio Alliata of the *Studium Biblicum Franciscanum* in Jerusalem.
210 Foss 2003; Philipps 2004 and Morrisson 2004, p. 410, where it is claimed *"La persistance de l'arrivée d'AE byzantins jusque vers 659"*. The relationships between Byzantine, Proto-Arab and Umayyad numerals are also discussed in Heidemann 1998 and in Walmsley 1999.

and then replaced by the first Arab coins, with iconography and value indications borrowed from the equivalent copper coins or even from Constantinopolitan solids. In fact, to produce the Arab-Byzantine coins, mints were engraved to closely resemble the Byzantine typology. On the obverse, between one and three standing 'emperors' appeared, while on the reverse, the 40-nummi value sign (M) was accompanied by identifying elements such as the cross, the christogram, and legends in Latin or Greek script alongside the Arabic ones indicating the year and mints.[211]

The characteristics and chronology of the 'Arab-Byzantine' coinage series remain controversial due to the difficult distinction between pseudo-Byzantine types, one with an Umayyad imperial image and the other with a standing caliph, in a complex interdependence of transitional, imitative, autonomous and proto-Umayyad issues.[212]

Among the specimens documented in the Magdala MP area, there is first of all a small group of *fals* minted in Tiberias/Tabariya of the type Three standing figures/emperors and M/mixed Greek and kufic legend *tabaryya* and then another 15 *fals*, variously distributed in the pre-reform of 'Abd al-Malik period.

The small hoard, type Foss 2008 no. 81 and SICA 587–591, was spotted during the first excavation campaigns, in the corner of a flight of stairs. The archaeological context indicates either an intentional concealment or perhaps the misplacement of a purse.[213] The *fals* date from the period 660–680 (caliphate of Mu'āwiya) and constitute one of the rare cases of bronze hoards from this transitional phase,[214] perhaps motivated more by sudden events such as the well-known earthquake of 659/660 rather than by economic dynamics.[215] In this case, the historical-earthquake data would confirm the chronology of this series and the specimens found would consequently place themselves in the first phase of minting the series 'Thee emperors/M mixed Greek and Kufic legend *tabaryya*'.

As for the individual finds, they are distributed in chronological sequence beginning with the earliest Arab-Byzantine coins, a Cyprus copper imitation/three standing emperors perhaps the first type of *fals* produced in the new post-Constans II regime. The flan is cut and the coinage is a 'crude' imitation of the prototype.[216] Specimens were found both in hoards (Hama and Syria), but also among the single finds in circulation (Apamea, Resafa, Bethlehem).[217] This is followed by four imitative *fals* with the imperial standing figure [EN TOY TO NIKA] with decorative elements as described in Foss 2008 p. 125. Their chronology lies between c. 647–670, and it is still *sub iudice* whether they are products of official mints or of some local mints because of their poor quality and the great variation in the mints. The range of their circulation is also rather wide: from Antioch to Pella, passing through numerous sites in Galilee.[218] The later phase is attested in Magdala by 3 forgeries from the First Bilingual Series with standing imperial figure, by 1 *fulus* from the Main Bilingual Series-standing imperial figure with ΔAM in exergue and by 4 forgeries with three standing figures holding the globus cruciger and TIBEPIAΔOI in exergue. About their diffusion around Lake Kinneret[219] and neighboring territories, they are known in Capernaum,[220] Tiberias,[221] Jerash,[222] Bet She'an (Nysa Scythopolis),[223] Hammat Gader,[224] Nabratein[225] and Bet She'an.[226] Closing the Arab-Byzantine series is the interesting and much discussed Caliph standing type probably coined at Halab in the *Jund of Qinnasrin*. Also this *fulus*, coined almost at the time of the reform of 'Abd al-Malik, represents the definitive departure from Byzantine iconographic modes for the totally different figure compared to the attributes of the standing emperor, and for the replacement of the cross on the reverse with

211 On the iconographic evolution of coins prior to the 696–697 reform cf. the introductory summary in Marot 1992, but above all in *SICA*, pp. 1–9 and the observations of Foss 2003, pp. 748–760; an overview is offered by Foss 2008. On the type of the standing Caliph cf. Morrissson, Prigent 2013.

212 On this subject, see the bibliographical summary by Morrisson 2003b, p. 349 and the update on the status of these studies in Oddy 2004, in part. pp. 132–133.

213 Albeit from a few decades later, but with a similar explanation (purse) is the small Umayyad-era hoard from the not-so-distant Baysân (Bet She'an): Schindel 2006b.

214 To the best of my knowledge, I do not know of a similar case. Similar hoarding, but not so homogeneous in the typology of *fals*, in Bijovsky 2012a, p. 150.

215 Russell 1985, pp. 46–47.

216 Foss 2008, p. 23.

217 Bibliographic references in Foss 2008, p. 22 and pp. 163–175: "Coins from Hoards and Excavations".

218 Foss 2008, pp. 28–35.

219 Gitler 1990, pp. 105–106.

220 Callegher 2007a, p. 63 with distribution table for pre-reform Arab-byzantine coins sites (c. 640–696/697).

221 Berman 2004, pp. 230–244; Bijovsky 2004a, pp. 171–175.

222 Olavarri Goicoechea 1986, p. 44 with summary tables; Foss 2008, pp. 42–43, 47.

223 Foss 2008, p. 45; Berman 2015, p. 266.

224 Barkay 1997.

225 Bijovsky 2009.

226 Amitai-Preiss 1999, p. 612; Mazor 2007; Newell, Witschonke 2008, nos. 95–97; Berman 2011, p. 114.

a Φ on three steps and the definitive adoption of the *shahadah*. For this epoch, the numismatic data from Magdala MP confirm how the opening of numerous decentralized coinage workshops contributed to maintaining an acceptable availability of copper coinage throughout the area destined, however, for local exchange and not for wider circulation.[227] As far as continuity of use is concerned, the coexistence of Byzantine and Arab-Byzantine copper coinage in some parts of this area of the site is conceivable. It was certainly in decline compared to the vitality of the previous centuries, at least until the mid-third century, but not yet completely imploded, perhaps also due to the emergence, with its own economic function, of two sites in the same period that were quite lively in the monetary sphere: Capernaum and Tiberias. All these autonomous or imitative coinages of Byzantine prototypes show that the demand for copper denominations remained rather sustained for local trade in the *Bilād al-Shām* and *Jund Filasṭīn* until the end of the seventh century (696/697), when caliph ʿAbd el-Malik implemented his monetary reform, an event that marks the end of the influx and circulation of Byzantine coinage in Palestine.

5.17 Arab-Byzantine and Arabic coins (see 4.8–4.9)

Arianna D'Ottone

The work entitled *al-Masālik wa-l-mamālik* by the Cordovan al-Bakrī (432–487 AH/1040–1094 CE)[228] is one of the few Arabic medieval sources that mentions the town (Ar. *qarya*) of Magdala (Ar. *al-Majdal*).[229] According to al-Bakrī, there was a church in Magdala dedicated to Mary (Ar. *kanīsaᵗ Maryam*), and he also says that Magdala was the scene of the miracle – recorded in all four Gospels – where Jesus blessed five loaves and two fish and fed five thousand of his followers.[230] The mosque of al-Khaḍir, al-Bakrī says, was just a few kilometres (one *farsanj*) from Magdala.

The forty-two Arabic coins found in archaeological excavations[231] at this site are all copper (Ar. *fals/fulūs*) and minted in other cities, as no mint is recorded as ever having existed in Magdala itself. Most of the seventeen readable specimens in this group date back to the Umayyad period and are post-reform issues (Cat. nos. 2–32). The very fact that we have a group of bronze coins – most likely caused by accidental loss[232] – dating back to the Umayyads and from the province of Damascus, merits our attention.[233]

The nucleus of this post-reform Umayyad group is chronologically preceded by a piece that has tentatively been attributed to the transitional Umayyad period (Cat. no. 1) and is followed by a few ʿAbbasid (Cat. nos. 33–37), Mamluk (Cat. nos. 38–40) and Ottoman issues (Cat. nos. 41–42). Twenty-five exemplars are no longer readable since they are too worn/corroded.[234] The specimens for which identification was possible or a tentative suggestion made – that is, those specimens in which the mint was recorded and was readable or where it was possible to identify the specific type of the piece – provide us with interesting information regarding the circulation of Islamic copper coins, particularly in the first three centuries of the Hijra (early seventh – early tenth century CE).

For the Umayyad period, the area of production of the *fulūs* found in Magdala corresponds to that of three military districts (*jund*) of the province of

227 Philipps 2004, p. 27 supports the possible use of bronze money in the payment of taxes, at least in the area or with local destination.

228 Cf. Brockelmann 1898, p. 476: no. 2.

229 Cf. al-Bakrī 2003, vol. 2, p. 45.

230 However, in the Gospel of Luke the miracle is said to take place in Bethsaida (Ar. *Bayt Ṣaydā*), cf Luke 9:12–17. The confusion and conflation of Magdala with another village (Bethany), also extends to the identification of Mary Magdalene with Mary of Bethany. Magdala is also mentioned in Nikos Kazantzakis' historical novel, *The Last Temptation of Christ*, added to the *Index Librorum Prohibitorum* in 1955.

231 For a brief overview of the various archaeological missions that have worked in different areas of Magdala, cf. Garza-Díazbarriga 2019. On the Magdala Archaeological Project, cf. Zapata-Meza *et al.* 2018. For a detailed account of the *Studium Biblicum Franciscanum* (SBF) archaeological mission, cf. Callegher *supra*.

232 On Umayyad copper coin findings cf. Ilisch 2010, p. 126. The fact the loss of the copper coins found in Magdala was accidental seems confirmed by the extent of the area excavated and the fact that the coins were not found in groups; cf. Callegher *supra*. This is very different from the silver hoards found in Damascus as regards the nature of the collection, the circumstances of the find and the metal of the coins. The Damascus finds contained Sasanian drachms and Arabic dirhams of the early Islamic period; cf. Al-ʿUsh 1972; Gyselen, Kalus 1983.

233 On the usefulness and importance of archaeological data from excavations in the *Bilād al-Shām* area cf. Schindel 2006a, p. 141. On the interest of copper coin findings from this area, cf. Walmsley 2010, pp. 412–413.

234 These worn/corroded exemplars correspond to photograph nos. 21; 532; 533; 628; 755; 804; 830; 1550; 1766; 327L; 338; 422; 444L; 448L; 451L; 453L; 455L; 456L; 519L; 102L; 122L; 134L; 159L; 175L; 215L9. On unreadable coins found in Magdala in the excavations of 1971–1973 that were deemed useless and thrown into the lake, cf. Callegher *supra*.

al-Shām: *Filasṭīn* (corresponding to Byzantine *Palaestina Prima*),[235] *al-Urdunn* (corresponding to Byzantine *Palaestina Secunda*)[236] to which *al-Majdal* belonged, and *Dimashq*.[237] It is therefore not totally unexpected to find copper coins – meant for small exchange – struck locally (in Ṭabariyya, al-Urdunn), in the capital of the adjacent *jund Filasṭīn* (ar-Ramla)[238] or in the caliphal mint of Damascus.

The post-reform types attested by the specimens identified can be compared with the Umayyad *fulūs* found at other sites such as Jerusalem at the Greek-Orthodox Church of St. John the Baptist (*Prodromos*), St. Hilarion, Jericho, Tall Jawa, Bet She'an, Hippos and Baʿalbek[239].

Unfortunately, the state of conservation of the ʿAbbasid *fulūs* group makes precise identification impossible. However, their relatively small number seems consistent with a period of economic crisis in the area after the ʿAbbasid Revolution and the subsequent transfer of the capital from Damascus to Baghdad.

This major political and regional shift, together with the natural disasters that affected *Bilād al-Shām* in the first half of the second century AH (mid-eighth century CE) help to explain, together with the relative small size of the town, the large chronological gap – of almost three centuries – that divides the Umayyad and the ʿAbbasid group of *fulūs* from the late seventh-eighth AH (thirteenth–fourteenth century CE) Mamluk issues found in Magdala.[240] The Mamluk bronze coins from Magdala were all struck in Damascus, the second most important mint in the Mamluk realm, which produced coins in the three metals.[241]

From a geographical point of view, the site of *(Qalʿat)* Bālis in northern Syria is further away, which is where Roman, Byzantine and Islamic coins were found. However, the comparison with the Arabic pieces from Magdala is interesting, since in both cases the finds are made up of only copper coins dateable up to the time of the Ottoman empire.[242]

5.18 Crusader period (see 4.10)

Some continuity of currency use in the Magdala MP area occurs at the end of the eleventh century with modest quantities of silver. The formation of the crusader kingdoms made the adoption of currency systems peculiar to their countries of origin, particularly the French area, thus in continuity with the Carolingian system.[243] Undoubtedly, to entail the use of currency and its diffusion, there was a need to create a system of defensive-preventive fortifications along the borders, the provisioning of the military component, as well as, of course, the accidental losses by *mercatores* or pilgrims in transit to Jerusalem or from there to the locations of the fortifications or settlements within the territory of the kingdom.[244] Evidence of this is the discovery of Latin reign *denarii* at Magdala MP. These are two *denarii* minted in Jerusalem during the reign of Amalricus (1163–1174). As mentioned, similar or contemporaneous finds are not uncommon. At sites close to the one under consideration here, crusader-era *denarii* are known from nearby Capernaum (1 hoard),[245] in Khirbet Marus[246] and Wadi Hamam[247] and in Caesarea Paneas,[248] but in the not too distant Caesarea Maritima which at that time certainly played an important role from various points of view: especially harbor and economic[249]. Other finds of crusader-era *denarii* are reported in Jaffa[250] and Ibelin/Yibna 20 km south

235 Cf. Sourdel 1991.
236 Cf. Cobb 2000.
237 Cf. Elisséef 1991, esp. pp. 280–281.
238 On the Palestinian mints of Ṭabariyya, al-Urdunn and al-Ramla cf. Shamma 1400/1980, pp. 69–70.
239 Cf. respectively: Callegher and D'Ottone Rambach 2016, esp. p. 424; D'Ottone Rambach 2022; Vorderstrasse 2015; Berman 2015, pp. 266–267; Solarewicz 2015, p. 46 and Al-Akra 2016, pp. 93–98. Of course, the comparison only regards the type rather than the number of coins found, since neither the size nor the importance of these other sites is comparable with that of the small town of Magdala.
240 Cf. Schindel 2006a.
241 Cf. Balog 1964, p. 51. Similar pieces were found at the Lebanese sites of Baʿalbek and Sarepta/Sarafand, though in greater quantities; cf. Abou Diwan 2016, p. 18; Al-Akra 2016, pp. 155–176.
242 However, the numismatic finds from Bālis attest to a wider range of dynasties – Seljukids of Rūm, Artuqids, Zanjids and Ayyubids – than those indicated by the Magdala specimens. On the other hand, the Ottoman coins from Bālis are comparable with those from Magdala, cf. Hennequin, Al-ʿUsh 1978, pp. VIII–IX and pp. 100–101. Ottoman numismatic evidence has also been found in Jerusalem in the area of the Greek-Orthodox Church of St. John the Baptist; cf. Callegher, D'Ottone Rambach 2016.
243 Metcalf 1995; for metrological and weight analyses of Amalricus emissions cf. Metcalf 2002.
244 For the distribution-circulation of the issues of the Crusader kingdoms, cf. Kool 2002, Kool 2007, but especially Kool 2013.
245 Callegher 2007a, p. 141.
246 Bijovsky, personal communication: 1 denarius of Balian, mint of Jerusalem.
247 Bijovsky 2018, nos. 374–375: 2 denarii di Amalricus, mint of Jerusalem.
248 Berman, Bijovsky 2008, p. 14 and catalogue.
249 Hohlfelder 1980, pp. 127–131; Lampinen 1994; Metcalf, Holland 1994–1999; Kool 2007; Kool 2013.
250 Metcalf 2003–2006.

of Yafo, the latter in a mixed repository of Crusader *denarii* and Ayyubid *dirhams* from the Sultanate of Egypt.[251]

5.19 Modern period (see 4.11)

During the twentieth century, the Upper Galilee was affected by the first phase of Zionist settlement and the events that led to the creation of the British Mandate from 1927 to 1946. Indeed, in 1926, the British Secretary of State for the Colonies appointed a Palestine Currency Board to introduce a local currency. It was based in London and chaired by P. G. Ezechiel, with a Currency Officer resident in Palestine. The board decided that the new currency would be called the Palestine pound, fixed in value to the British pound and divided into 1000 *mils*. Evidence of the inclusion of the British Palestine within this monetary system are some modern coins, respectively two fractions of 1 *mil* from 1927 and 1940, 1 coin of 100 *mils*, all fractions of the major denomination of 1000 *mils* (thousandths) also known as the Palestine pound (*juniah filistini*/from the English word *guinea* or maybe *foont palestina'i*).[252] Added to these is the 1923 US 5 cents nickel coin, this one perhaps brought to the area by some researcher on the site's archaeological ruins or by some wayfarer.

5.20 Conclusions: From money to economy

The long *excursus* commenting on the coin findings in the MP area of Magdala has revealed periods of greater and lesser presence/circulation of coinage, always of modest value. The data can be observed in the two initial graphs relating to two phases: the first illustrating the quantities from the earliest numismatic attestations up to ca. 70 CE, the second from the end of the first century CE up to the fourth–fifth century. The numismatic evidence, of course, has its own value in this specific field, but we cannot fail to transfer this data to some economic considerations because, as already mentioned in the opening section, the coin is first and foremost a document that speaks to us, informing us about the economy of a site during the various periods of its frequentation, especially as numismatic data interact with other sources (historical, literary, archaeological or modern analyses, e. g., pollen or soil layers). Sources and coinage suggest that at the site investigated, at least in the MP part closer to the lake harbor, there was an intense phase of frequentation (and thus accidental loss of the proverbial *prutah*) starting in the last decades of the second century BCE. The number of issues of Alexander Jannaeus is undoubtedly the largest percentage. But beyond the quantities, which are certainly related to frequent exchanges/losses (cf. AACL: figs. 4–5; tab. 3), the modest value of these *prutot*, which are often not very heavy and were made of vile metal and thus devalued compared to a reference unit (the first type of *prutah*, made of excellent copper and good minting, with a generally stable weight) is of great economic importance. This same mass of coin discoveries confirms that finding a convincing and non-ideological explanation for the fall in weight and fineness of the TJC K and TJC L *prutot* of Jannaeus, which were, moreover, disseminated in many thousands throughout Palestine, is an extremely interesting subject, especially in economic terms proving an extremely lively and shared circulation. During the reign of this Hasmonean ruler, Magdala was undoubtedly an important town, inhabited by a large community that was involved in military events leading to the Hasmoneans' confrontation with the Romans. Thus, the town fulfilled a military function, but also supported one of the two sides – in the end the side that lost. The logistics of the military contingents had to be supported and it is probable that the agricultural products of the fertile Ginnosar plain with its freshwater springs and the abundance of fish in the lake whose preservation with salt made it a center of reference.[253] The very name of the site is Tarichéa, i. e., the place where fish is salted. We know that during the 1st century armies and people resisting the new Roman rule faced each other in the area by the lake, at Magdala, from a letter that Cassius sent to Cicero from the 'camp' of Tarichea (Cicero, *Ad Familiares* 12,11), where the Jewish forces were barricaded, under siege. Flavius Josephus confirms such an involvement when he recalls the capture and enslavement of 30,000 people[254] from this site, which cannot have been very small if it was also equipped with a hippodrome where his opponents gathered.[255] In fact, after the fall of Joppa (Jaffa) emperor Vespasian faced the Tarichean rebellion and established his military camp between Tiberias and Tarichea/Magdala. Sources claim that 6,500 people died

251 Kool, Uzi'ad 2016.
252 Shneydor 2009.

253 Strabon, *Geogr.* XVI, 2.45.
254 Flavius Josephus, *Jewish Antiquities* 14:120.
255 Flavius Josephus, *Jewish War* 2:598.

in the clash.[256] Another, economically even more interesting piece of information concerns the fishing activity. We know, in fact, that as many as 250 fishing boats operated from the shores of the lake. Their landing alone demanded adequate space, and even more so the treatment of the fish, which was not consumed immediately but processed and preserved with salt: it was an activity so intense and widely practiced that it became eponymous for the site itself.[257] And what about salt, which had to be transported there, perhaps from the Mediterranean coast or along the Jordan valley from the Dead Sea (in Hebrew *Yam ha-Melah*, literally 'Sea of Salt'), thus activating a network of exchanges in both directions? The large number of Hasmonean and Herodian coins must therefore be placed within these economic and military dynamics. Moreover, since they were divisional coins of the lowest value, it must be assumed that the price level must not have been very high and that the exchange of agricultural products (figs, spelt and perhaps also wine) and the preservation (salted fish) could be honored at a price accessible to all, since the huge quantity of *prutot*, overvalued in relation to the alloy and their weight, were available to the entire population.[258] This economic status did not change in the Herodian period (Tab. 5 and Figs. 6–7), perhaps not even until the time of the Antonine and Severan emperors in the mid-third century when copper coins were once again very common (cf. Tabs. 10–12, Figs. 10) and the number of countermarked specimens soared, suggesting a sustained demand for currency which was met by re-pricing previous coins to market value by means of a hallmark. As for the cultural component, we are limited to mentioning the existence of a *beth midrash* next to the synagogue where the scribe Nikai was active, perhaps in the second half of the third century, and in which other famous rabbis were trained also dating from the third and fourth centuries: Isaac and Judan.[259] The Midrashim, then, mention Magdala Sebayah for its opulence and immorality of customs, but also for being one of only three cities to send taxation to the temple in Jerusalem by chariot, only possible in a city or territory that is very active and lively in terms of functions, human presence and thus also economic activity.[260]

What historical-economic information, in this albeit synthetic framework of sources, do the monetary finds offer us? Let us indicate them briefly:

1. The amount of coinage is so abundant in at least three phases (Hasmonean, Herodian and Severan) that accidental losses must be ruled out, identifying them instead as a consequence of an intense exchange of goods for currency.[261]
2. The value of the recovered currency is almost always modest, often very modest.
3. It is possible to place the surplus of the small-denomination divisional in certain market occasions or periodic fairs, while for accounting (recording debits and credits) a good, stable silver coin was used: the Tyrian tetradrachm.
4. The coins come from various mints such as Tyre between the first century BCE and the second century CE; from Jerusalem in the Hasmonean period; from nearby Caesarea Paneas, Tiberias and Sepphoris in the Herodian period; from the mints of the Decapolis and Galilee between the mid-second –mid-third century. From this we deduce that circulation was ensured by the nearest monetary workshops, probably because the quotation of *assaria* was common in those mints and also accepted in Magdala.
5. The contribution of more distant mints, including Rome, remains very limited and from the fourth century onwards it was the coins of Antioch and then Constatinopolis that reached Magdala.
6. Some archaeological finds, in part definable as paramonetary (Tyre ambit weights; fourth-fifth century exagrams, tiles with *agoranomoi* names) allow us to deduce, rather than postulate, the operation of a market in some square/space of the site where coinage in a certain continuity was used with a liberating function.
7. It is more than conceivable that the mercantile function, evidenced by the large quantity of coinage, is to be linked to the presence of military contingents with stable or temporary settlement in the area of Magdala, as can be deduced from the Latin and Rabbinic sources concerning this site.

256 Flavius Josephus, *Jewish War* 3:532–542.

257 Flavius Josephus, *Jewish War* 3:462–470.

258 With regard to plants and their fruits, analyses by Lena, Rossi, Palmieri, and Marchesini 2017, have shown the large quantity of seeds of *ficus carica* (fig tree), *vitis vinifera* (wine grape vine) and *triticum dicoccum* (spelt). The ecosystem for flora had been analyzed and described, for example, at Hesban (Esbous) east of the Dead Sea where among the cultivated and fruit plants are *triticum aestivum, triticum dicoccum, vitis vinifera* and *ficus carica*: Crawford 1986; Gilliland 1986.

259 Baba Metzia 25a; Manns 1976a, p. 325.

260 Eicha Rabbah 2,2,4; J. Ta'anit 4,69, cf. also Manns 1983, p. 326.

261 Of considerable interest are the arguments concerning a definition of the economic structure of Palestine in the first century CE, in particular the chapter *Growth of Market Activity in First-Century Palestine* in Noell 2007.

On a monetary basis, therefore, Magdala must be considered one of the most important and active settlements between the first century BCE and much of the third century CE on Lake Kinneret, a place of production and trade, supplier to military contingents, certainly in contact with other trading places probably located on the Mediterranean coast. Nevertheless, in a 'market' perspective Magdala was quite different from our current experience and even from the semantic content of this word, often misused with a broadening that does not correspond to the experience of the ancients. Its monetary decline began as early as the early fourth century, when the economic and monetary strategies of the Constantinian era shifted the flow of money to other routes, especially between the great port cities of the Mediterranean.[262]

262 For the trade and markets/fairs in Galilee cf. Syon 2015, pp. 183–186.

Catalogue

In the catalogue, the distribution of coins follows the chronological sequence and series proposed in the main repertories (e.g. SNG, BMC, RIC, CHL, LRBC, MIB, MIBE). The material in this volume is arranged as fellow:

- Greek coins and Roman provincial coins of Syria and Phoenicia;
- Hasmonean and Herodian dynasty coins;
- Roman procurators and Jewish wars against Rome;
- Greek coins and Roman provincial coins of Palestine and South Arabia;
- Roman imperial coins;
- Byzantine coins;
- Arab-Byzantine and Islamic coins;
- The Latin kingdom of Jerusalem;
- Modern coins

Whenever possible, within the coin series, for each coin are indicated:

in vertical sequence: the administrative or issuing region; the mint following the main repertories; the issuing authority; a broad or specific year of issue; the metal (AR = silver; AE = bronze); obverse and reverse description (not repeated in the case of specimens of the same type);

in horizontal sequence: the progressive number in the general catalogue; the metrological data (the weight expressed in grams, with no more than two numbers after the comma, diameter in mm and sometimes the dies orientation). This is followed by the bibliography, the reference to the Locus or the Stratigraphic Unit, and the excavation inventory number. In this case the number is alphanumeric for the coins recovered in the Corbo-Loffreda excavation campaigns (= number followed by L) and only numeric for the numismatic material collected in the excavations conducted by the Migdal Project. An asterisk accompanies some of these numbers to indicate that the coin has been reproduced in the plates. A similar asterisk marks the corresponding numbers in the general catalogue.

Greek coins and Roman provincial coins of Syria and Phoenicia

Coins of the Ptolemies

Uncertain Mints
Ptolemaeus Epiphanes (204–181 BCE)
AE
O/Head of Zeus Ammon r.
R/Eagle l. on thunderbolt; to l. lotus; ΠΤΟΛΕΜΑΙΟΥ ΒΑΣΙΛΕΩΣ

1	H, Field 2 Locus 4	1,06	23	↑	BMC. *The Ptolemies, King of Egypt*, 28–35	*68

Uncertain Authority (III–II BCE)
AE
O/Head r. with diadem
R/Eagle l. on thunderbolt; wings open

2	E, Field 11 Locus 303	9,85	24	↑	BMC. *The Ptolemies, King of Egypt*; SNG. *Danish. Egypt: the Ptolemies*?	*280

AE
O/Bust r.
R/Eagle l. on thunderbolt; l. club

3	H, Field 1 Locus 39	14,2	26	↑	BMC. *The Ptolemies, King of Egypt*; SNG. *Danish. Egypt: the Ptolemies*?	*172

AE
O/Bust r.
R/Eagle l.

4	C, Field 3 Locus 738	2,4	14	↑	BMC. *The Ptolemies, King of Egypt*; SNG. *Danish. Egypt: the Ptolemies*?	*403

1

2

3

4

Seleucid kings

Mint of Ptolemais-Acre
***Antiochus* IV** (175–164 BCE)
AE
O/Radiate head of Antiochus IV; behind monogram no. 2?
R/Veiled goddess holding in r. hand long sceptre; ΒΑΣΙΛΕΩΣ on r.; ΑΝΤΙΟΧΟΥ on l.

5	E, Field 4	2,7	14	↑	SNG. *Danish. Syria: Seleucid Kings*, 198; SC II.1, p. 92, 1479	*288 L

Tyre
***Demetrius* III**, first reign (146–145 BCE)
AE
O/Diademed head of Demetrius r.; dotted border
R/Palm tree, across lower field, date: ΙΞ/Ρ; dotted border; ΒΑΣΙΛΕΩΣ ΔΗΜΗΤΡΙΟΥ

6	H, Field 1, Locus 0	1,85	13	↑	SNG. *Israel* I, 1681–1683; 1691–1695 *SC* II.1, p. 304, 1970.1	*85

Mint of Seleucia Pieria
***Demetrius* III** (97/96–88/87 BCE)
AE
O/Diademed head of Demetrius III r.; [---]
R/Winged thunderbolt placed on table; above ΒΑΣΙΛΕ[ΩΣ] ΔΗΜΗΤΡ[ΙΟΥ] ΦΙΛΟΜΗΤoΡ[ΟΣ];
below, ΕΥΕΡΓΕΤΟΥ ΚΑΛΛΙΝΙΚΟΥ

7	H, Field 1, Locus 94	6,06	21	↑	SNG. *Danish. Syria: Seleucid Kings*, 419; *SC* II.1, p. 588, 2447	*215
8	H, Field 3, Locus 67	6	21	↑	same	*500

Seleucid kings?

Uncertain authority and mint (2nd century BCE)
AE
O/Radiate head
R/Poorly preserved and garbled; serrated flan

9	F, Field 19, Locus 353	1,65	12	SNG. *Danish. Syria: Seleucid Kings*?	*393

AE
O/Laureate? Head; [---]
R/Poorly preserved and garbled; [---]

10	M	3,55	17	SNG. *Danish. Syria: Seleucid Kings*?	*501
11	A, Field 6 Locus 1196	2,5	13	SNG. *Israel* 1, Antiochus VII?	1

5

6

7

8

9

10

Syria

Mint of Antiochia Commagene
Tiberius
AE (14–37)
O/Laureate head r.; [---]
R/ Double cornucopia with caduceus; [---]

12	V, Field 3 Locus 676	12,5	29	↑	Butcher 2004, pl. 4, 68; *RPC* I, 3869	*1006

Mint of Antiochia
City coinage (11–14)
AE
O/Laureate head of Zeus r.
R/Ram running r., head reverted: above: star; [ΑΝΤΙΟΧΕΩΝ ΜΗΤΡΟΠΟΛΕΩΣ]

13	F, Field 3 North	7,92	21	↑	SNG. *Danish. Syria: Cities*, 95–99	*606L

Domitianus (81–96)
AE (quadrans?) (83?)
O/Laureate head of Domitianus l.; IMP DOMITI [---]
R/CAES AVG GERMANICVS; winged caduceus

14	D, Field 1	2,05	13	↑	RPC I, 2025; McAlee 413	*196L

Herennius Etruscus (250–251)
Billon Tetradrachm
O/Bust r.; ЕРЕΝΝ ЕТРОΥ МЕ КΥ ΔΕΚΙΟC ΚΕCΑΡ
R/Eagle l., standing on palm branch, holding wreath on beak; ΔΗΜΑΡΧ ΕΞΟΥCΙΑC; in ex. SC

15	A, Field 6	13	26	↑	SNG, *Danish, Syria. Cities*, 286; McAlee 2007, 1153a–g	*101L

Mint of Damascus
Philippus* I** (244–249) for ***Otacilia Severa (244–249)
AE
O/Draped bust right, wearing stephane and set on crescent; M OTACILIA SEVERA AVG [---]
R/Magna Mater (Cybele) seated r. on rock, raising hand to lips; at feet, lion standing right; COL [---]RA METRO

16	E, Field 11 Locus 302	15,4	30	↓	Rosenberger 1978, p. 28, 37; see also Israel Museum (Coin Cabinet: IM 82.4280)	*256

12

13

14

15

16

Phoenicia

Mint of Arados
Autonomous (first century BCE)
AE (48–46 BCE)
O/Laureate male head r.
R/AΣ Prow of galley l.

17	H, Field 2 Locus 34	2,6	14		BMC. *Phoenicia*, pl. III, 13	*121

Mint of Ptolemais-Acre
Civic Coinage (40–39 BCE)
AE
O/Jugate busts of Tyche and Zeus r.; border of dots
R/Tyche, holding cornucopia and aplustre; [ΠΤΟ/ΛΕΜΑ/ΕΩΝ] date: LI/KAI AΣY

18	H, Field 1 Locus 86	9,9	24	↑	CHL, pl. 6–7, 111–114	*143

Colonial coinage (1st century)
AE
O/Laureate head of Zeus r.
R/Club downwards; COL PTO

19	E, Field 11 Locus 303	2,3	16	↓	BMC. *Phoenicia*, p. 131, 15; CHL, pl. 7, 129–130	*285

Hadrianus (117–138)
AE
O/Laureate head of Hadrianus r.; IMP CAES TRAI. H [---]
R/Tyche of the city, seated r. on rock; half- figure of river-god swimming r.; COL PTOL

20	E, Field 11 Locus 303	8,85	25	↓	BMC. *Phoenicia*, p. 132, 24, pl. 16, 12 CHL, pl. 8, 139–140	*250
21	D, Filed 10 Locus 784	9,10	24	↑	CHL, pl. 8, 139–140	*1064

Caracalla (198–217)
AE
O/Bust of Caracalla, laureate, r.; [IMP CAE] M AVR ANT [---]
R/Emperor in military dress on horseback to left, holding sceptre; COLO [---]

22	F, Field 27 Locus 999	13,7	27	↑	BMC, *Phoenicia*, p. 134, 34; pl XVII.2	*1697

17

18

19

20

21

22

Macrinus (217–218)
AE
O/Laureate and draped bust of Macrinus; IMP CM MACRIN
R/Perseus? nude, standing l. holding r. head of Gorgon? COL PTOLEM

23	A, Field 7	11	24	↑	CHL, pl. 11, 187	*103L

Elagabalus (218–222)
AE (220)
O/Laureate head of Elagabalus r. [---] NTONIN [---]
R/Hexastyle temple within Tyche l. crowned by Nike, standing in a temple; in ex.: HEC

24	B, Field 1	8,89	26	↓	CHL, pl. 12, 192	*110L

***Philippus* I** (244–249)
AE
O/Laureate bust of Philippus r. wearing paludamentum and cuirass; IMP M IVL PHILIPPVS P F AVG
R/Frontal temple of Astarte on podium of step, with six columns. COL TV RO [---]

25	E, Field 11 Locus 301/302	15,5	28	↓	CHL, pl. 15, 246–247	*343

Mint of Tyre
City coinage
DATED COINS
AE (99/98 BCE)
O/Head of Melqart r., laureate
R/Palm-tree with two branches of fruit; Phoenician inscriptions. Linear circle and concave flan.

26	F, Field 18 Locus 325	2,85	14	↑	BMC. *Phoenicia*, p. 254, 251, pl. 31, 5	*350

AE (82/81 BCE?)
O/Head of Tyche r., wearing turreted crown; behind, palm branch
R/Galley l., with prow terminating in volute; Phoenician inscriptions. L E M /A/ IEPAΣ-V

27	F, Field 7	7,12	21	↑	BMC. *Phoenicia*, p. 255, 252	*550L

AE (80/85)
O/Head of Tyche r., wearing turreted crown; behind, palm branch
R/Galley l., with prow terminating in volute; Phoenician inscriptions. [---]/ A-Y

28	E, Field 20 Locus 327	8,15	20	↑	BMC. *Phoenicia*, p. 256, 263–266	*429

23

24

25

26

27

28

AE (104/105)
O/Bust of Tyche r.; turreted crown, veil; behind palm branch; border of dots.
R/Palm-tree with two branches of fruits; across filed: date; around inscr. ΔΛ Τ ΜΗΤΡΟΠΟΛΕѠΣ ΙΕΡΑΣ
across field, date: Λ/Σ

29	H, Field 4 Locus 117	3	15	↑	BMC. *Phoenicia*, p. 265, 338	*157
30	V, Field 2 Locus 273	2,9	15	↑	same	*484

AE (107/108)
O/Bust of Tyche r.; turreted crown, veil; behind palm branch; border of dots.
R/Palm-tree with two branches of fruits; across filed: date; around inscr. ΔΛ Τ ΜΗΤΡΟΠΟΛΕΩΣ ΙΕΡΑΣ;
Across field, date: Γ/ΛΣ

31	E, Field 5 Locus 342	1,85	16	↑	BMC. *Phoenicia*, p. 265, 339	*40

AE (104/166–167)
O/Bust of Tyche r.; turreted crown, veil; behind palm branch; border of dots.
R/Palm-tree with two branches of fruits; across filed: date; around inscr. ΔΛ Τ ΜΗΤΡΟΠΟΛΕΩΣ ΙΕΡΑΣ;
Across field, date; ΓΜ/Σ (?)

32	E, Field 36 Locus 319	2,35	14	↑	BMC. *Phoenicia*, p. 265–267, 338–355	*430

AE (195/196)
O/ Head of Tyche r.; wearing turreted crown; behind, palm branch
R/Galley l. with prow terminating in volute; Greek inscription: AKT/TIEPAC/MHTPOΠO/ΛΕΩC;
Phoenician inscription

33	H, Field 2 Locus 4	4,15	18		as SNG. *Danish. Phoenicia*, p. 264, 328–329	*116
34	F, Field 25 Locus 351	3,5	17		same	*696

Undated Coins
AE (c.98/97 BCE – 84/85)
O/Head of Tyche r.; wearing turreted crown; behind, palm branch
R/Galley l. with prow terminating in volute; Phoenician inscription; [-] ΙΕΡΑΣ

35	H, Field 2 Locus 34	6,8	19	↑	BMC, *Phoenicia*, pp. 255–256, 252–267, pl. 31, 6–8	*115
36	D, Field 6 Locus 863	6,38	18	↑	same	A25.1
37	F, Field 5 - under stone pavement II	6,31	19	↑	same	638L
38	E, Field 32 Locus 355	5,9	20	↑	same	*544
39	E, Field 12 Locus 261	5,56	19	↑	same	*541

29

30

31

32

33

34

35

38

39

40	F, Field 7 NE	5,47	18	→	same	*832L
41	F, Field H Locus 290	5,45	19	↑	same	*458
42	G, Field 9 Locus 1051	5,30	21	↑	same	*1270
43	G 100 Sector N	4,66	20	↑	same	*850L
44	V Field 2	4,54	19	↑	same	143L
45	E, Field 13 Locus 357	4,45	20		same	547
46	D, Field 9 Locus 716	4,45	18		same	1009
47	H, Field 4 Locus 117	4,25	21	↑	same	*158
48	E, Field 5	4,07	18	↑	same	*302L
49	E Field 3 Locus 1092	4,75	19		BMC, *Phoenicia*, pl. XXI, 7–8, 17–19	*1506
50	Without context	3,5	18	↑	same	452
51	V, Field 2	2,31	16	↑	same	*150L
52	F, Field 20/22 Locus 298	5,75	19		BMC, Phoenicia, tav. XXII, 5–6, tav. XXXI, 7 or 17	*782

AE (c.55/54 BCE – 86/87)
O/Head of Melqart r., laureate
R/Within an oak-wreath, club downwards; on r. Phoenician inscription

53	E, Field 9 Locus 452	9,4	25	↑	BMC. Phoenicia, p. 257, 268–274, pl. 31, 10	*28

AE (c.18/17 BCE – 114/115)
O/Head of Tyche r., wearing turreted crown, veil; behind, palm branch
R/Palm-tree with two branches of fruit; across field: date; monogram of Tyre and inscription. Border of dots.

54	H, Field 2 Locus 6	2,5	17	↑	BMC. *Phoenicia*, pp. 258–259, 275–287, pl. XXXI, 11–13	*89
55	E, Field 22a Locus 308	2,5	12		same	656
56	C, Field 31 Locus 698	2,15	15		same	1022
57	H, Field 2 Locus 33	2,05	14	↑	same	*88
58	F 100:1	1,25	12		same	*480L
59	H, Field 3 Locus 21	0,45	11		same	*111

40

41

42

43

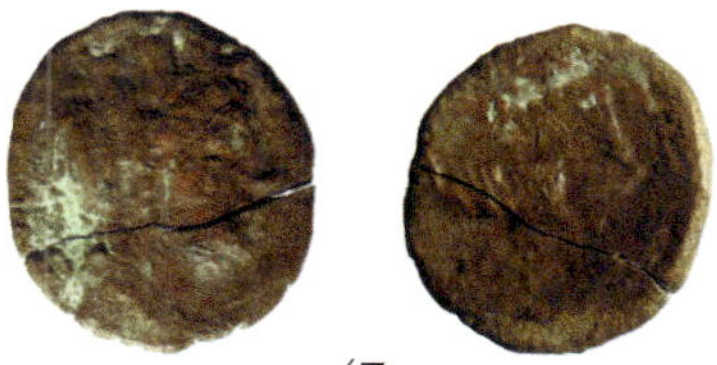
47

48

49

51

52

53

54

57

58

59

AE (93/94–153/4)
O/Head of Tyche r.; wearing turreted crown, veil; behind, palm branch; border of dots
R/Galley l.; on it, Astarte (or Tyche?), turreted, standing l.; date and monogram not preserved

60	F, Field 25 Locus 571	1,6	13	↑	BMC. *Phoenicia*, pp. 261–262, 299–312; SNG, *Danish, Phoenicia*, pl. 10, 356–358	876

AE (c. 93/94–195/196)
O/Head of Tyche r.; wearing turreted crown; behind, palm branch
R/Galley l. with prow terminating in volute; Greek inscription: [---]/ΙΕΡΑΣ/ΜΗΤΡΟΠΟ/ΛΕΩΣ;
Phoenician inscription

61	F, Field 28 Locus 551	6,35	19	↑	BMC. *Phoenicia*, pp. 262–264, 313–330, pl. 31, 17	*1092
62	E, Field 7 Locus 815	6,15	21	↑	same	*33
63	H, Field 3 Locus 82	5,1	19	↑	same	*136
64	E, Field 11 Locus 303	5	20	↓	same	254
65	C, Field 31 Locus 664	4,2	18	↑	same	983
66	V, Field 3 Locus 767	4,15	18	↑	same	*14
67	E, Field 12, Locus 1205	3,44	16	↑	BMC. *Phoenicia*, pp. 262–264, 313–330, pl. 31, 18–19	*44
68	H, Field 3 Locus 11	3,4	18	↑	same	*73
69	F, Field 3 East	2,76	13	↓	same	881L
70	D, Field 1	2,71	18	↑	same	*232L

61

62

63

66

67

68

70

AE (c. 104/105–166/167)
O/Head of Tyche r.; wearing turreted crown; behind, palm branch
R/Palm-tree with two branches of fruit; across field: date. Around insc. [---]Τ ΜΗΤΡΟΠΟΛΕΩΣ ΙΕΡΑΣ

71	E, Field 19 Locus 534	5	19	↑	BMC. *Phoenicia*, pp. 266–267, 347–355; SNG, *Danish, Phoenicia*, 347–355	814
72	E, Field 11, Locus 305	2,4	14	↑	same	300
73	C, Field 3 Locus 713	2,3	14	↑	same	1008
74	H, Field 1 Locus 87	2,25	13	↓	same	142
75	H, Field 1, Locus 110	2,1	15	↖	same	*174
76	H, Field 1, Locus 0	2	13		same	213
77	D, Field 3 Locus 346	1,7	14	↑	same	*442
78	F, Field 27 Locus 620	1,65	15	↑	same	530
79	B, Field 5	1,14	14	↑	same	*128L

AE (c. 112/113–183/184)
O/Head of Melqart r., with slight whisker, laureate.
R/Club downwards; across field inscription and date.

80	E, Field 6 Locus 1076	4,7	21	BMC, *Phoenicia*, pl. XXI, 7	829
81	C, Field 15 Locus 754	2,65	17	BMC, *Phoenicia*, pl. XXXII, 6	838

AE (Undated coins)
O/Head of Tyche r.; wearing turreted crown; behind, palm branch
R/Palm-tree with two branches of fruit; across field (date: incompletely preserved).

82	F, Field 28 Locus 970	4,45	18	BMC, *Phoenicia*, pl. XXI, 7–8, 17–19	1237
83	F, Field 13 Locus 964	2,65	14	BMC, *Phoenicia*, pl. XXXII, 2–3	*1199
84	C, Field 15 Locus 589	2,4	15	BMC, *Phoenicia*, pl. XXXII, 2–3, but flan some garbled	*1754
85	C, Field 15 Locus 589	2,3	16	BMC, *Phoenicia*, pl. XXXI, 11	*1753
86	C, Field 15 Locus 589	1,10	14	BMC, *Phoenicia*, pl. XXXII, 2–3	1748
87	F, Field 25 Locus 351	1,55	13	Palm tree, but very little flan (Tyre?)	1558
88	C, Field 6 Locus 747	1,3	14	Same	837

75

77

79

83

84

85

Roman provincial coinage

Traianus (98–117)

AR. Tetradrachm (110–114)

O/Laureate head of Traianus r.; AYTOKP KAIC NEP TPAIANOC CEB [---]

R/Laureate head of Melqart r.; ΔΗΜΑ ΠΧ ΕΞ ΙΔ ΥΠΑΤΕ

89	H, Field 2 Locus 32	13,8	25	↓	BMC. *Phoenicia*, p. 301, 15	*75

AR. Tetradrachm (111–112)

O/Laureate head of Traianus r.; AYTOKP KAIC NEP TPAIANOC CEB [---]

R/Tyche of Antiochia seated r., on upper part of river-god swimming r.; ΔΗΜΑ ΠΧ ΕΞ ΙΔ ΥΠΑΤ [---]

90	H, Field 2 Locus 13	13,95	23	↓	BMC. *Phoenicia*, p. 302, 30	*80

Caracalla (198–217)

AE

O/Laureate bust of Caracalla r.; [---]

R/Bull walking r.; in background, standard inscribed [LEG III GAL]; ex. [CO]LON[I]

91	E, Field 11 Locus 303	14,25	30	↓	BMC. *Phoenicia*, p. 271, 377–378	*266

AE

O/ Laureate bust r.; [---]

R/Temple seen in perspective (five columns in front, eight columns at the side); [---]

92	E, Field 11 Locus 303	4,9	22	↓	BMC, *Phoenicia*, pp. 271, 376, pl. 32, 12	*267

AE

O/Laureate bust Caracalla r.; [---]

R/Agonistic table with four legs; upon two prize crowns; [---]; [SEP] TVRVS METRO COLONI, agonistic table with two prize crowns; ERACL[IA] in exergue

93	B, Field 1	9,61	25	↑	BMC. *Phoenicia*, 379; Rouvier 1903–1904, 2324?	*113L

89

90

91

92

93

Elagabalus (218–222)
AE
O/Laureate bust of Elagabalus r. wearing paludamentum; [---]
R/Astarte placing r. on trophy, crowned by Nike; exergue: COLO

94	F, Field 25 Locus 351	13,9	29	↑	BMC. *Phoenicia*, p. 273, 389	*686

AE
O/Laureate bust of Elagabalus r. wearing paludamentum; [---]
R/Temple of Astarte with six columns; within, Astarte placed right; before the temple, in exergue, altar between palm-tree and murex-shell.

95	E, Field 2	7,77	24	↑	BMC, *Phoenicia*, p. 276, 404; pl. 33, 3 SNG. *Danish. Phoenicia*, 366	*269L

AE
O/Laureate bust of Elagabalus r., wearing paludamentum; [---]
R/Ovoid baetyl, encircled by serpent; on l. palm-tree on murex-shell; around, TV RI ORVM

96	V, Field 3	16,6	28	↓	BMC. *Phoenicia*, p. 278, 413, pl. 33, 8	*165L
97	E, Field 11 Locus 302	11	28	↑	same	*258

***Gordianus* III** (238–244)
AE
O/Bust of Gordianus r. laureate, wearing paludamentum and cuirass; [---] VS PIVS [---]
R/Melqart-Heracles, nude, standing to front, looking l., in r. he holds club and lion-skin, with l. he pours libation ovr altar; in field l. two baetyls: [---] T VR [---]

98	D, Field 1	6,27	23	↑	BMC. *Phoenicia*, p. 281, 427, pl. 33, 13	*197L

Gallienus (260–268)
AE
O/Laureate bust of Gallienus r., wearing paludamentum and cuirass; IMP C P LIC GA [---]
R/Two prize crowns, inscribed on sunk panels AKT; between them, above, club downwards and two palm-branches; [---] TV ROME

99	E, Field 11 Locus 302	10,85	29	↑	BMC. *Phoenicia*-; SNG, *Danish, Phoenicia*-; Rouvier 1900–1904, n. 2560	*298

94

95

96

97

98

99

Mint of Sidon
City coinage
AE (98/97–11/10 BCE)
O/Bust of Tyche r.; wearing turreted crown laureate.
R/War-galley l.; stem terminating in volute at bow; on it, Astarte standing l., wearing long chiton; below, in two lines, Greek and Phoenician inscriptions: ΣΙΔΩΝΙΩΝ

100	F, Field 23 Locus 507	5,45	21		BMC. *Phoenicia,* pp. 163–164, 130–136; SNG, *Danish, Phoenicia*, pl. 6, 218–220	*792

AE (78/77–46/45 BCE)
O/Bust of Tyche r.; wearing turreted crown laureate
R/War-galley l.; stem terminating in volute at bow; Greek and Phoenician inscriptions

101	H, Field 1 Locus 94	7,5	21		BMC. *Phoenicia,* pp. 164–165, 137–142	152

AE (77/78–117/118)
O/Head of Tyche r.
R/Galley l.; ΣΙΔΩΝΟΣ ΘΕΑΣ

102	B, Field 5	2,28	14	↑	SNG, *Danish, Phoenicia*, 242–245 BMC. *Phoenicia*, pp.172–174, 179–191	*119L

Roman provincial coinage
Mint of Tripolis
Roman provincial coinage
Elagabalus (218–222)
AE (220–221?)
O/Undraped, laureate bust of Elagabalus r. [---]
R/Temple of Astarte with central porch, the Goddess standing to front (but incompletely preserved); [---]

103	B, Field 1	7,39	23	↑	SNG. Danish, *Phoenicia*, 291 BMC. *Phoenicia*, p. 223, 118, pl. 28, 5	*114L

100

102

103

Mint of Tyre or Sidon

AE (first century BCE – first century CE)
O/Head of Tyche r., wearing turreted crown
R/War galley l.; below, perhaps, Phoenician or Greek inscriptions

104	E, Field 8 Locus 1064	3,35	16		BMC, *Phoencia,* tav. XXII, 5–7, tav. XXXI, 4, 11–16, XXXII, 2–3 (Tyre)	*1311

Mint of Tyre, Sidon or Ascalon

AE (first century BCE – first century CE)
O/Head of Tyche r.
R/Galley l.

105	F, Field 1 Locus 91/94	6,45	20		Cfr. BMC. *Phoenicia*; BMC. *Palestine*	192
106	C, Field 30 Locus 688	3,9	17		Same	1001

AE (first century BCE – first century CE)
O/Head of Tyche r.
R/Corroded

107	C, Field 31 Locus 664	3,25	19		Cfr. BMC, *Phoenicia*, BMC. *Palestine* and SNG. ANS, *Palestine-South Arabia* only for obv. head of Tyche	*984

AE
Time of Vespasian (72/73; 76/77)
O/Head of Tyche r
R/Galley sailing r

108	C, Field 32 Locus 709	2,18	14	↑	SNG.ANS, *Palestine-South Arabia*, 679–687	A26

104

107

Hasmonean and Herodian dynasty coins

Hasmonean

Mint of Jerusalem
John Hyrcanus I (129–104 BCE)

AE (prutah)
O/Inscription in five lines, in wreath
R/Double cornucopia with pomegranate

109	A, Field 4 Locus 1195	1,9	15	Meshorer 2001, p. 203, D4; CHL, p. 242, 6 ss.	647

Mint of Jerusalem
Alexander Jannaeus (103–76 BCE)

AE (prutah)
O/Anchor, surrounded by inscription: ΑΛΕΞΑΝΔΡΟΥ ΒΑΣΙΛΕΩΣ (sometimes incompletely preserved)
R/Eight-pointed star, between rays, Palaeo-Hebrew inscription (Yehonatan the King), sometimes incompletely preserved; linear border.

110	H, Field 1 Locus 1	4,35	16	SNG. ANS, *Palestine-South Arabia*, 55–76; CHL, pl. 200, 221–227	*82
111	H, Field 3 Locus 7	3,35	18	same	762
112	V, Field 1	2,95	18	same	131L
113	H, Field 1 Locus 94	2,95	15	same	227
114	H, Field 3 Locus 78	2,5	16	same	*130
115	H, Field 2 Locus 31	2,3	15	same	*103
116	H, Field 1 Locus 94	2,2	15	same	*226
117	H, Field 1 Locus 94	2,15	15	same	*228
118	H, Field 1 Locus 94	1,8	15	same	*225
119	H, Field 1 Locus 94	1,7	15	same	*150
120	D, Field 1	1,7	12	same	216L
121	H, Field 2 Locus 32	1,5	14	same	*125
122	H, Field 1 Locus 39/98	1,5	13	same	*186
123	H, Field 1 Locus 91	1,15	15	same	*199
124	F, Field C Locus 317	1,15	13	same	751

110

114

115

116

117

118

119

121

122

123

125	H, Field 1 Locus 91	0,95	14	SNG. ANS, *Palestine-South Arabia*, 55–76; CHL, pl. 200, 221–227	*198
126	H, Field 3, Locus 67	2	16	same	*499
127	D, Field 4 Locus 770	0,75	14	same	741
128	V, Field 2 Locus 1052	3,35	15	same	*1260
129	E, Field 39 Locus 812	2,37	18	same	A44.9
130	F, Field 27 Locus 999	2,3	15	same	*1698
131	F, Field 31 Locus1158	2,20	16	same	1623
132	I, Field 3 Locus 274	2,2	16	same	*506
133	H, Field 2	1,9	15	same	*79

AE (prutah)
O/Anchor, surrounded by inscription: ΑΛΕΞΑΝΔΡΟΥ ΒΑΣΙΛΕΩΣ or ΒΑΣΙΛΕΩΣ ΑΛΕΞΑΝΔΡΟΥ (sometimes incompletely preserved);
R/Eight-pointed star; sometime flan as SNG. ANS, *Palestine-South Arabia*, 95

134	E, Field 6 Locus 1076	1,9	14	SNG. ANS, *Palestine-South Arabia*, 95; CHL, pl. 201, 236	1495
135	F, Field 19 Locus 353	1,35	13	same	*394
136	H, Field 3 Locus 48	1,35	13	same	*108
137	E, Field 4	1,35	14	same	*297L
138	H, Field 1 Locus 94	1,35	14	same	*229
139	E, Field 8 Locus 1063	1,3	15	same	1100
140	H, Field 1 Locus 94	1,15	14	same	*184
141	F, Field 14 Locus 921	1,15	14	same	1141
142	H, Field 1 Locus 91/94	1,1	15	same	*217[1]
143	H, Field 1 Locus 91/94	1,1	13	same	*218
144	D, Field 2 Locus 255	1,1	14	same	1606

1 Overstruck on CHL, pl. 200, 221–227.

125

126

128

130

132

133

135

136

137

138

140

142

143

145	V, Field 3 Locus 713	1,05	16	SNG. ANS, *Palestine-South Arabia*, 95; CHL, pl. 201, 236	*20
146	E, Field 32 Locus 320	1,05	16	same	1097
147	H, Field 1 Locus 94	1	14	same	*246
148	F, Field 18 Locus 325	0,95	13	same	*409
149	V, Field 2 Locus 279	0,9	14	same	*203
150	F, Field 18 Locus 329	0,85	12	same	420
151	H, Field 1 Locus 94	0,8	13	same	*183
152	H, Field 1 Locus 96	0,8	13	same	205
153	H, Field 1 Locus 91/94	0,75	14	same	219
154	F, Field 3 E Locus 291	0,55	11	same	*472
155	H, Field 3 Locus 11	0,45	11	same	*112
156	V, Field 3 Locus 713	0,4	11	same	*15
157	H, Field 1 Locus 94	0,4	11	same	*182
158	D, Field 2 Locus 254	2,95	15	SNG. ANS, *Palestine-South Arabia*, 55–95, or 96	858
159	F, Field 21 Locus 297	2,45	16	same	768
160	H, Field 2 Locus 4	2,35	15	same	590
161	H(2013)	2,3	15	same	
162	H, Field 2 Locus 5	2,25	16	same	*124
163	F 100:1	2,03	15	same	483L
164	G 101	1,99	15	same	777L
165	E, Field 20 Locus 327	1,95	15	same	818
166	F, Field 30 Locus 1115	1,93	14	same	1773
167	C, Field 15 Locus 897	1,8	16	same	844
168	F, Field 5 Locus 288	1,8	14	same	1081

145

147

148

149

151

154

155

156

157

162

169	E, Field39/41 Locus 814	1,69	11		SNG. ANS, *Palestine-South Arabia*, 55–95, or 96	A21.2
170	D, Field 3	1,63	12		same	266L
171	Cardo	1,61	15		same	725L
172	G, Field 1 Locus 268	1,55	15		same	594
173	G (2013)	1,55	15		same	
174	F, Field 3 Locus 902	1,5	13		same	1108
175	F, Field 4	1,47	15		same	367L
176	F, Field 20 Locus 502/503	1,4	12		same	803
177	E, Field 42 Locus 873	1,39	15		same	A11
178	F, Field 5 – under stone pavement II	1,36	13		same	667L
179	E, Field 8 Locus 1064	1,35	16		same	1288
180	F, Field 27 Locus 625	1,33	13		same	A19.1
181	F, Field 1	1,26	14	↓	same	402L
182	E, Field 22	1,2	15		same	356L
183	A, Field 7	1,15	13		same	*510
184	E, Field 6 Locus 1085	1,15	13		same	*34
185	G Locus 455	1,15	14		same	1235
186	F 100:2	1,14	13		same	742L
187	F, Field 8 Locus 356	1,12	10		same	*411
188	F, E Field 34 Locus 320	1,10	12		same	*456
189	H, Field 1 US 111	1,05	13		same	*243
190	D, Field 4 Locus 770	1,05	14		same	*27
191	H, Field 1 Locus 96	1,05	14		same	*204
192	E, Field 26 Locus 919/920	1,05	13		same	1150
193	F 100:1	1,02	14		same	464L
194	A, Field 7 Locus 1197	1,01	12		same	1494

183

184

187

188

189

190

191

195	H, Field 1 Locus 94	1	13	SNG. ANS, *Palestine-South Arabia*, 55–95, or 96	*230
196	C, Field 26 Locus 684	1	13	same	1046
197	V, Field 2 Locus 279	0,95	13	same	*485
198	V, Field 2 Locus 279	0,95	13	same	*482
199	V, Field 2 Locus 458	0,95	13	same	*523
200	F, Field 7	0,95	14	same	577L
201	C, Field 31 Locus 698	0,95	12	same	1035
202	H, Field 2 Locus 5	0,95	11	same	*113
203	F, Field 25 Locus 1100	0,95	13	same	1563
204	F, Field 31 Locus 1163	0,95	14	same	1680
205	H, Field 1 Locus 91/94	0,95	12	same	221
206	E, Field 42 Locus 873	0,94	12	same	A27.3
207	F 100:1	0,93	12	same	492L
208	D, Field 1	0,92	13	same	218L
209	F, Field 7	0,91	11	same	584L
210	C, Field 4 Locus 766	0,9	14	same	748
211	F, Field 18 Locus 324	0,9	13	same	*413
212	H, Field 1 Locus 0	0,9	13	same	*214
213	H, Field 3 Locus 1132	0,9	13	same	1591
214	F, Field 3 Locus 902	0,9	13	same	1112
215	G, Field 8 Locus 939	0,90	12	same	1161
216	E, Field 8 Locus 1064	0,9	13	same	1316
217	F, Field 31 Locus 1158	0,90	13	same	1625
218	E, Field 29 Locus 832	0,89	12	same	A39.1
219	F 100:1	0,88	12	same	468L

195

197

198

199

202

211

212

220	G 101	0,88	14	SNG. ANS, *Palestine-South Arabia*, 55–95, or 96	778L
221	C, Field 30 Locus 672	0,85	17	same	982
222	E, Field 29 Locus 804	0,85	13	same	892
223	F, Field 7 Locus 282	0,85	14	same	*168
224	F, Field 18 Locus 329	0,85	12	same	1391
225	F, Field 18 Locus 325/329	0,85	13	same	1396
226	E, Field 8 Locus 1064	0,85	13	same	1292
227	E, Field 7 Locus 1073	0,85	12	same	1367
228	G, Field 7	0,85	11	same	1712
229	B, Field 5	0,82	12	same	*124L
230	E, Field 13 Locus 357	0,8	12	same	*549
231	F, Field 28 Locus 329	0,8	12	same	649
232	C, Field 27 Locus 650	0,8	13	same	962
233	E, Field 31 Locus 789	0,8	15	same	*528
234	C Locus 595	0,8	15	same	854
235	H, Field 1 Locus 86	0,8	14	same	*147
236	A, Field 5 Locus 269	0,8	14	same	526
237	E, Field 36 Locus 376	0,8	14	same	1127
238	F, Field 14 Locus 921	0,8	12	same	1142
239	G 101	0,79	12	same	779L
240	F 101:1	0,78	12	same	479L
241	F, Field 5 under stone pavement II	0,78	11	same	660L
242	G, Field 6 Locus 1194	0,75	14	same	*12
243	V, Field 2 Locus 279	0,75	14	same	*177
244	M, Field Locus 999	0,75	11	same	*31

223

229

230

233

235

242

243

244

245	E, Field 21 Locus 357	0,75	14	SNG. ANS, *Palestine-South Arabia*, 55–95, or 96	574
246	H, Field 1 Locus 94	0,75	13	same	*236
247	M	0,75	13	same	643
248	F, Field 25 Locus 554	0,75	13	same	694
249	E, Field 46 Locus 917	0,75	12	same	1144
250	E, Field 8 Locus 1063	0,75	13	same	1346
251	E, Field 7 Locus 1071	0,75	12	same	1417
252	F, Field 25 Locus 351	0,75	11	same	1620
253	E, Field 20	0,74	11	same	334L
254	F 100:1	0,74	11	same	475L
255	F 100:1	0,74	12	same	485L
256	E, Fieldn29 Locus 832	0,74	13	same	A40.1
257	F 100:1	0,72	13	same	518L
258	F, Field 2, trench 1	0,72	14	same	713L
259	F, Field 7 North	0,72	14	same	814L
260	F, Field 4	0,72	12	same	379L
261	F 100:1	0,7	12	same	508L
262	F, Field 1	0,7	16	same	383L
263	E, Field 31 Locus 789	0,7	11	same	890
264	F, Field 18 Locus 325/329	0,7	12	same	1397
265	F, Field 3, Locus 902	0,7	11	same	1116
266	G 101	0,68	13	same	702L
267	G 101	0,67	12	same	703L
268	F, Field 19 Locus 253/354	0,65	12	same	*398
269	E, Locus 804	0,65	12	same	891
270	E, Field 37 Locus 785	0,65	12	same	1087
271	E, Field 10 Locus 453	0,65	11	same	612
272	C 30, Locus 672	0,65	11	same	1089

246

268

273	H, Field 1 Locus 94	0,65	13	SNG. ANS, *Palestine-South Arabia*, 55–95, or 96	*241
274	E, Field 8 Locus 1064	0,65	13	same	1312
275	G, Field 7	0,65	12	same	1713
276	E, Field 42 Locus 873	0,65	13	same	A27.6
277	F, Field 1	0,63	12	same	378L
278	E, Field 29 Locus 832	0,63	13	same	A39.3
279	D, Field 6 Locus 863	0,62	13	same	A6.1
280	G 101	0,61	12	same	776L
281	F, Field 25 Locus 251	0,61	11	same	*509
282	M, Field 20	0,6	12	same	*26
283	F, Field 21 Locus 297	0,6	11	same	767
284	H, Field 1 Locus 94	0,6	13	same	*244
285	H, Field 1 Locus 0	0,6	13	same	587
286	C, Field 22 Locus 595	0,6	13	same	919
287	F, Field 25 Locus 351	0,6	12	same	*358
288	C, Field 19 Locus 596	0,6	12	same	949
289	E, Field 33 Locus 320	0,6	12	same	1075
290	H, Field 2 Locus 4	0,6	12	same	850
291	H, Field 2 Locus 4	0,6	12	same	848
292	F, Field 6 Locus 1079	0,60	14	same	1502
293	E, Field 46 Locus 917	0,6	11	same	1136
294	G, Field 8 Locus 1046	0,6	11	same	1245
295	E, Field 8 Locus 1063	0,60	12	same	1349
296	M (2013)	0,6	12,5	same	
297	H (2013)	0,6	13	same	
298	F 100:1	0,59	13	same	509L

273

281

282

284

287

299	E, Field 39/41 Locus 814	0,59	10	SNG. ANS, *Palestine-South Arabia*, 55–95, or 96	A4.1
300	F, Field 1	0,58	12	same	398L
301	F 100:1	0,57	12	same	472L
302	F, Field 18 Locus 325	0,55	12	same	*415
303	H, Field 1 Locus 39/98	0,55	14	same	*181
304	D, Field 4 Locus 770	0,55	12	same	680
305	F, Field 23 Locus 509	0,55	11	same	800
306	H, Field 1 Locus 0	0,55	10	same	588
307	F, Field 25 Locus 1101	0,55	11	same	1642
308	F, Field 3, Locus 902	0,55	11	same	1114
309	E, Field 5 Locus 956	0,55	12	same	1188
310	F, Field 31	0,55	11	same	1639
311	F, Field 31 Locus 332	0,55	12	same	1665
312	F, Field 16 Locus 1157	0,55	11	same	1676
313	H (2013)	0,55	10	same	
314	F, Field 7 North	0,54	12	same	825L
315	E, Field 20	0,53	12	same	333L
316	D, Field 3	0,52	12	same	265L
317	F, Field 7	0,51	12	same	591L
318	G 100, North	0,51	13	same	851L
319	E, Field 29 Locus 832	0,51	12	same	A39.6
320	E, Field 39 Locus 812	0,51	14	same	A44.7
321	F, Field 18 Locus 329	0,5	13	same	*421
322	F 100:1	0,5	11	same	504L
323	C, Field 26 Locus 684	0,5	11	same	1040
324	F, Field 20 Locus 299	0,5	11	same	776
325	F, Field 11 Locus 970	0,50	11	same	1228

302

303

321

326	G, Field 9 Locus 1211	0,5	12	SNG. ANS, *Palestine-South Arabia*, 55–95, or 96	1273
327	E, Field 8 Locus 1064	0,50	11	same	1331
328	E, Field 8 Locus 1063	0,50	12	same	1347
329	E, Field 6 Locus 1079	0,5	12	same	1469
330	H, Field 1 Locus 91/94	0,5	12	same	191
331	F 100: 1	0,49	11	same	513L
332	F, Field 5, under stone pavement II	0,48	12	same	675L
333	F, Field 7 North	0,47	13	same	828L
334	F 100:1	0,47	11	same	477L
335	F, Field 7	0,47	11	same	567L
336	F, Field 1, filling trench A	0,46	14	same	623L
337	F, Field 7 North	0,45	12	same	824L
338	F, Field 7	0,45	11	same	569L
339	G, Field 9 Locus 1047	0,45	11	same	1250
340	E, Field 7 Locus 1073	0,45	10	same	1365
341	E, Field 22a Locus 316	0,45	12	same	1702
342	D, Field 1	0,43	11	same	219L
343	F, Field 4	0,42	15	same	*368L
344	H, Field 1, US 94	1,1	14	same	*232
345	F, Field 1, filling trench A	0,4	12	same	633L
346	F, Field 4	0,4	11	same	369L
347	F, Field 5, under stone pavement II	0,4	11	same	661L
348	F, Field 5, under stone pavement II	0,4	8	same	683L
349	D, Field 4 Locus 770	0,4	11	same	740
350	F, Field 25 Locus 1109	0,40	11	same	1650

343

344

351	F, Field 3, Locus 902	0,40	10	SNG. ANS, *Palestine-South Arabia*, 55–95, or 96	1115
352	F, Field 13 Locus 963	0,40	11	same	*1216
353	E, Field 8 Locus 1064	0,40	10	same	1341
354	F 100:1	0,39	10	same	512L
355	F 100:1	0,38	11	same	510L
356	F 100:1	0,38	9	same	506L
357	F, Field 7 North	0,36	10	same	812L
358	H, Field 1 Locus 0	0,35	11	same	*210
359	F, Field 7 Locus 282	0,35	10	same	*164
360	E, Field 29 Locus 804	0,35	10	same	895
361	F, Field 25 Locus 556	0,35	10	same	883
362	F, Field 18 Locus 325/329	0,35	11	same	1399
363	F, Field 30 Locus 1093	0,35	11	same	1516
364	E, Field 1 Locus 1088	0,35	11	same	1493
365	E, Field 39 Locus 812	0,35	9	same	A44.4
366	F, Field 13 Locus 963	0,35	10	same	1215
367	E, Field 8 Locus 1064	0,35	13	same	1297
368	E, Field 8 Locus 1064	0,35	10	same	1326
369	E, Field 7 Locus 1071	0,35	9	same	1426
370	E, Field 7 Locus 1071	0,35	12	same	1430
371	E, Field 19 Locus 527	0,35	9	same	A12.2
372	E, Field 39 Locus 812	0,34	12	same	A44.1
373	F, Field 4	0,33	11	same	371L
374	F, Field 1	0,32	15	same	380L
375	F, Field 1	0,32	13	same	390L
376	F, Field 1	0,32	9	same	377L
377	F 100:1	0,31	10	same	488L

352

358

359

378	H, Field 2 Locus 34	0,3	10	SNG. ANS, *Palestine-South Arabia*, 55–95, or 96	*104
379	E, Field 20 Locus 618	0,3	10	same	936
380	E, Field 1 Locus 1087	0,3	10	same	*43
381	H, Field 2 Locus 4	0,3	10	same	852
382	F, Field 25 Locus 522	0,3	9	same	903
383	V, Field 2 Locus 276	0,3	11	same	519
384	E, Field 26 Locus 919	0,3	11	same	641
385	G, Field 9 Locus 1051	0,3	10	same	1276
386	F, Field 5, under stone pavement II	0,29	11	same	637L
387	F 100:3	0,29	12	same	528L
388	F 100:1	0,28	12	same	515L
389	F, Field 27 Locus 625	0,28	10	same	A19.2
390	E, Field 31 Locus 789	0,25	11	same	889
391	E, Field 33 Locus 320	0,25	9	same	1069
392	E, Field 7 Locus 1073	0,25	10	same	1369
393	E, Field 25 Locus 929	0,25	10	same	1156
394	F, Field 13 Locus 963	0,25	11	same	1214
395	F, Field 13 Locus 963	0,25	9	same	1220
396	F, Field 3 North	0,24	13	same	598L
397	F, Field 23 Locus 507	0,2	12	same	793
398	E, Field 13 Locus 357	0,2	11	same	561
399	E, Field 39 Locus 812	0,18	5	same	A44.2
400	F 100:1	0,17	9	same	491L
401	F, Field 25 Locus 552	0,15	11	same	898

378

380

402	E, Field 8 Locus 1090	0,15	11		SNG. ANS, *Palestine-South Arabia*, 55–95, or 96	1387
403	F, Field 13 Locus 963	0,15	8		same	1221

AE (prutah)
O/Palaeo-Hebrew inscription in wreath
R/Double cornucopia with pomegranate in between the horns.

404	H, Field 1 Locus 63	2,21	15		SNG. ANS, *Palestine-South Arabia*, 118;	631

AE (prutah)
O/Palaeo-Hebrew inscription (sometimes incompletely preserved), all within wreath
R/Double cornucopia; in center: pomegranate

405	F, Field 18 Locus 325	2	16		Meshorer 2001, P; CHL, p. 251, 274 ss.	*418
406	C, Field 10	1,71	14		same	186L
407	F, Field 30 Locus 1102	1,7	14		same	1571
408	F, Field 18 Locus 325	1,5	13		same	*432
409	F 100:1	1,46	13		same	473L
410	E, Field 1	0,38	11		same	268L

John Hyrcanus* I** (129–104 BCE) or ***Alexander Jannaeus (103–76)
AE (prutah)
O/Palaeo-Hebrew inscription
R/Double cornucopia; in center, pomegranate

411	H, Field 1 Locus 39/98	2,15	14		SNG. ANS, *Palestine-South Arabia*, 97–134, 135–138, 139–182	*195
412	F/B, Field 30 Locus 281	1,85	14		same	477
413	V, Field 2 Locus 276	1,8	13		same	515
414	H, Field 1 Locus 94	1,65	13		same	242
415	H, Field 1 Locus 96	1,65	13		same	*179
416	M Locus 999	1,65	13		same	502
417	H, Field 1 Locus 94	1,5	13		same	*216
418	E, Field 13 Locus 357	1,25	13		same	557
419	F, Field 30/32 Locus 1094	1,71	15	←	SNG. ANS, *Palestine-South Arabia*, 163	*1774

405

408

411

415

417

419

420	F, Field 3 Locus 902	1,3	12	↓	SNG.ANS, *Palestine-South Arabia*, 135–138, 139 ss.	*1111

AE (prutah)
O/ and R/ incompletely preserved, but iconography perhaps identical.

421	V, Field 2 Locus 278	2,25	15	SNG. ANS, *Palestine-South Arabia*, 97–182	488
422	G 101	1,77	15	same	775L
423	G 100:2 on the wall	1,73	15	same	843L
424	F, Field 2, trench 1	1,66	15	same	714L
425	D, Field 4 Locus 770	1,6	13	same	745
426	F, Field 19 Locus 353	1,4	14	same	395
427	F, Field 13 Locus 266	1,3	16	same	187
428	E, Field 17 Locus 381	1,2	13	same	1080
429	C, Field 27 Locus 808	1,7	14	same	*960

420

429

HASMONEAN PERIOD?

AE (prutah)
O/ and R/ incompletely iconography and inscriptions poorly preserved and garbled; typical flan i.e. SNG. ANS. *Palestine-South Arabia*, 95

430	F, Field 27 Locus 999	2,5	13	SNG. ANS, *Palestine-South Arabia* 95 for a flan	1699
431	G, Field 8 Locus 1043	2,15	16	same	1248
432	M, Field 2 Locus 999	2,1	14	same	626
433	F, Field 18/25 Locus 325	2	16	same	1553
434	F, Field 3 Locus 902	1,55	14	same	1109
435	F, Field 3 Locus 902	1,55	13	same	1110
436	H, Field 1 Locus 109	1,4	14	same	*171
437	E, Field 8 Locus 1064	1,3	14	same	1289
438	D, Field 5 Locus 781	1,2	15	same	1063
439	F, Field B Locus 281	1,15	16	same	*464
440	C, Field 33 Locus 712	1,1	14	same	1055
441	F, Field 18 Locus 553	1,1	13	same	1548
442	E, Field 8 Locus 1064	1,1	10	same	1294
443	F, Field 30/32 Locus 1094	1,03	9	same	1775
444	C, Field 8 Locus 809	1	14	same	1085
445	F, Field 30 Locus 1115	1	10	same	1780
446	E, Field 8 Locus 1064	0,95	14	same	1291
447	F, Field 3 Locus 908	0,95	12	same	1125
448	E, Field 8 Locus 1064	0,90	12	same	1330
449	E, Field 8 Locus 1064	0,85	14	same	1295

436

439

450	V, Field 2 Locus 931	0,8	12	SNG. ANS, *Palestine-South Arabia* 95 for a flan	1171
451	C, Field 29 Locus 667	0,75	16	same	987
452	E, Field 28 Locus 370	0,75	14	same	1096
453	V, Field 3 Locus 767	0,7	17	same	1002
454	H, Field 2 Locus 65	0,7	11	same	*546
455	D, Field 9 Locus 716	0,6	11	same	1058
456	F, Field 3 Locus 902	0,60	14	same	1113
457	E, Field 13 Locus 357	0,55	13	same	*444
458	C, Field 33 Locus 712	0,55	13	same	1094
459	G, Field 8/9 Locus 939	0,55	12	same	1241
460	D, Field 9 Locus 718	0,5	11	same	1053
461	E, Field 13 Locus 357	0,5	15	same	*559
462	E, Field 13 Locus 357	0,5	14	same	*551
463	V, Field 2 Locus 930	0,5	11	same	1181
464	E, Field 13 Locus 357	0,45	11	same	*563
465	E, Field 13 Locus 357	0,45	12	same	*560
466	F, Field 1 Locus 991	0,45	11	same	1232
467	E, Field 6 Locus 1079	0,45	12	same	1473
468	C, Field 26 Locus 704	0,4	11	same	1018
469	E, Field 35 Locus 320	0,4	12	same	1079
470	F, Field 13 Locus 963	0,40	9	same	1217
471	F, Field 11 Locus 970	0,4	11	same	1236
472	E, Field 13 Locus 357	0,35	10	same	*565

454

457

461

462

464

465

472

473	D, Field 9 Locus 718	0,35	12	SNG. ANS, *Palestine-South Arabia* 95 for a flan	1052
474	G, Field 8/9 Locus 939	0,35	10	same	1242
475	F, Field 3 Locus 902	0,35	10	same	1117
476	F, Field 13 Locus 963	0,3	10	same	1218
477	F, Field 1 Locus 991	0,3	10	same	1233
478	E, Field 8 Locus 1064	0,30	10	same	1324
479	F, Field 3 Locus 902	0,3	9	same	1118
480	F, Field 1 Locus 991	0,25	10	same	1234
481	E, Field 8 Locus 1064	0,25	9	same	1332
482	F, Field 7 North	0,22	12	same	818L
483	V, Field 2 Locus 276	0,2	11	same	*520
484	V, Field 3 Locus 767	0,2	9	same	1003
485	V, Field 2 Locus 937	0,2	12	same	1170
486	V, Field 2 Locus 258	0,15	9	same	1168

483

Herodian dynasty

Herod the Great (40/37–4 BCE)
Mint of Samaria (40 BCE)
AE
O/Tripod with lebes [---] ΒΑΣΙΛΕΩΣ; LΓ
R/Uncertain ceremonial object (apex) flanked by two palm branches

487	D, Field 1	5,36	23	↓	SNG. ANS, *Palestine-South Arabia*, 195–200; Meshorer 2001, n. 44; CHL, pl. 207, 1–7	*193L
488	E, Field 39/41 Locus 814	5,11	23	↓	same	A21.1

Mint of Jerusalem (40 BCE)
AE
O/Greek inscription ΗΡΩΔΟΥ ΒΑΣΙΛΕΩΣ; X within diadem
R/Table flanked by two palm branches

489	H, Field 2 Locus 62	1,5	16	↑	SNG. ANS, *Palestine-South Arabia*, 203–205; Meshorer 2001, 53a; CHL, pl. 207, 18–27	*139
490	H, Field 1 Locus 1	1,35	16	↑	same	*84
491	G, Field 8 Locus 1044	1,25	12	↓	same	1283
492	E, Field 4	1,11	18	↑	same	*298L

AE
O/ΗΡΩ/ΒΑCΙ; Anchor
R/Double cornucopia with caduceus

493	C, Field 3 Locus 270	2,65	16		SNG. ANS, *Palestine-South Arabia*, 206–218; CHL, 208, 28 ss	974
494	F, Field 3 North	2,52	16		same	601L
495	H, Field 2 Locus 4	2,3	15		same	853
496	C, Field 15 Locus 597 897	2,1	15		same	843
497	G, Field 1 Locus 268	1,95	17		same	*535
498	H, Field 1 Locus 94	1,65	15		same	*185
499	H, Field 7 3 Locus 7	1,65	15		same	1015
500	F, Field 4, under stone pavement II	1,65	14	↓	same	653L

487

489

490

492

497

498

501	F, Field 30 Locus 1096	1,65	13		SNG. ANS, *Palestine-South Arabia*, 206–218; CHL, 208, 28 ss	1757
502	C, Field 19 Locus 596	1,6	16		same	916
503	F, Field 25 Locus 552	1,6	13		same	901
504	F, Field 7 North	1,55	14		same	809L
505	H, Field 2 Locus 4	1,5	15	↙	same	*155
506	F, Field 7	1,5	14		same	565L
507	F, Field 3 North	1,49	15		same	602L
508	H, Field 1 Locus 94	1,45	15	↑	same	*209
509	E, Field 33 Locus 320	1,45	12		same	*1073
510	H, Field 1 Locus 0	1,45	16		same	*118
511	F, Field 5, under stone pavement II	1,44	14	↑	same	672L
512	H, Field 3 Locus 21	1,4	15		same	*138
513	V, Field 1 Locus 267	1,4	15		same	*540
514	F, Field 25 Locus 560	1,4	15		same	885
515	E, Field 36 Locus 785	1,4	14		same	821
516	H, Field 3 Locus 1133	1,40	15		same	1595
517	F, Field 2 West	1,37	14		same	796L
518	H, Field 3 Locus 7	1,35	15	↑	same	*110
519	F, Field 25 Locus 557	1,35	14		same	1691
520	F, Field 5, under stone pavement II	1,33	13	↑	same	646L
521	F, Field 5, under stone pavement II	1,3	15		same	691/A1
522	F, Field 5, under stone pavement II	1,3	16	↑	same	648L

505

508

509

510

512

513

518

523	H, Field 4 Locus 117	1,3	14	↓	SNG. ANS, *Palestine-South Arabia*, 206–218; CHL, 208, 28 ss	*156
524	F, Field 20 Locus 299	1,3	16		same	771
525	F, Field 31 Locus 1158	1,30	14		same	1671
526	E, Field 7 Locus 1071	1,3	13		same	*1418
527	F, Field 5, under stone pavement II	1,27	13	↑	same	662L
528	F, Field 25 Locus 558	1,25	16		same	886
529	F, Field 30 Locus 1104	1,25	14		same	1568
530	F, Field 25 Locus 1101	1,25	13		same	1641
531	F 101, on the pavement	1,24	13		same	883L
532	F, Field 5, under stone pavement II	1,23	14	↓	same	649L
533	F, Field 7	1,22	14		same	581L
534	F, Field 1	1,21	14		same	399L
535	C, Field 31 Locus 698	1,2	14		same	1036
536	C, Field 20 Locus 618	1,2	12		same	935
537	F 100:1	1,17	14		same	505L
538	F 100:1	1,17	12	↑	same	467L
539	F, Field 7	1,16	13		same	785L
540	F, Field 7	1,16	13		same	562L
541	F, Field 3 North	1,15	14		same	599L
542	C, Field 26 Locus 704	1,15	15		same	1049
543	F, Field 31	1,15	14		same	1636
544	F, Field 4, near the wall	1,14	15		same	697L
545	F, Field 5, under stone pavement II	1,14	13		same	676L
546	F, Field 5, under stone pavement II	1,14	6	↓	same	652L
547	B, Field 5	1,12	14	←	same	*125L

523

526

547

548	B, Field 5 Locus 296	1,1	15	SNG. ANS, *Palestine-South Arabia*, 206–218; CHL, 208, 28 ss	537
549	F, Field 8 Locus 329	1,1	15	same	426
550	C Locus 595	1,1	15	same	855
551	E, Field 13 Locus 357	1,05	15	same	443
552	E, Field 13 Locus 357	1,05	14	same	*562
553	F, Field 23 Locus 509	1,05	14	same	787
554	C, Field 31 Locus 700	1	13	same	1032
555	V, Field 2 Locus 278	1	14	same	489
556	F Field 10 Lo-cus 289	1	14	same	606
557	E, Field 34 Locus 320	1	14	same	608
558	F, Field 20 Locus 298	1	14	same	614
559	C, Field 20 Locus 298	1	14	same	934
560	F 100:2	0,99	14	same	735L
561	F, Field 5, under stone pavement II	0,99	15	same	678L
562	F, Field 5, under stone pavement II	0,99	14	same	681L
563	G 101	0,98	11	same	699L
564	F, Field 5, under stone pavement II	0,96	15	same	641L
565	F, Field 23 Locus 507	0,9	14	same	791
566	C, Field 26 Locus 684	0,9	14	same	1029
567	F, Field 20 Locus 299	0,9	13	same	773
568	C, Field 26 Locus 684	0,9	12	same	*1042
569	C, Field 31 Locus 700	0,89	14	same	1031
570	F, Field 2, trench 1	0,87	15	same	715L

552

568

571	F 110: 4	0,86	13		SNG. ANS, *Palestine-South Arabia*, 206–218; CHL, 208, 28 ss	763L
572	F, Field 7 Locus 282	0,85	13		same	165
573	C, Field 29 Locus 667	0,85	13		same	986
574	F, Field 5, under stone pavement II	0,85	11		same	689L
575	F, Field 7 Locus 282	0,85	16	↓	same	*170
576	C, Field 26 Locus 684	0,85	12		same	1027
577	C, Field 6 Locus 589	0,85	12		same	1724
578	G 101	0,84	14		same	700L
579	F, Field 19 Locus 353	0,8	15		same	391
580	I, Field 3 Locus 274	0,8	15		same	504
581	F, Field H Locus 290	0,8	14		same	*459
582	F, Field 22 Locus 511	0,8	14		same	811
583	H, Field 3 Locus 1144	0,80	12		same	1597
584	F, Field 31 Locus 1158	0,8	14		same	1672
585	F, Field 32 Locus 1152	0,80	10		same	1679
586	F, Field 7 Locus 282	0,75	14		same	*167
587	C, Field 26 Locus 684	0,75	14		same	1047
588	E, Field 13 Locus 357	0,75	13		same	553
589	C, Field 26 Locus 684	0,75	13		same	1028
590	C, Field 24 Locus 655	0,75	13		same	968
591	C, Field 26 Locus 684	0,75	12		same	1025
592	E, Field 33	0,75	12		same	1714
593	F, Field 19 Locus 353	0,7	14		same	396
594	E, Field 19 Locus 520	0,7	15		same	816

575

581

586

595	E, Field 11 Locus 301/302	0,65	14	SNG. ANS, *Palestine-South Arabia*, 206–218; CHL, 208, 28 ss	340
596	E, Field 13 Locus 357	0,65	14	same	550
597	C, Field 26 Locus 684	0,65	13	same	1041
598	C, Field 30 Locus 672	0,65	12	same	999
599	H, Field 1 Locus 91/94	0,62	12	same	190
600	V, Field 2	0,61	13	same	148L
601	C, Field 20 Locus 601	0,5	13	same	913
602	C, Field 26 Locus 684	0,4	12	same	1026
603	C, Field 26 Locus 684	0,4	12	same	1045

AE
O/[---] Anchor?
R/Double cornucopia with caduceus?

604	V, Field 2 Locus 930	2,05	14	SNG. ANS, *Palestine-South Arabia*, 206–218?	1182
605	E, Field 39 Locus 825	1,94	16	same	A34
606	G, Field 9 Locus 1211	1,7	13	same	1272
607	E, Field 8 Locus1067	1,5	13	same	1358
608	V. Field 1 Locus 267	1,5	15	same	*536
609	G, Field 8 Locus941	1,4	14	same	1243
610	F, Field 28 Locus970	1,35	14	same	1238
611	G, Field 9 Locus1050	1,35	13	same	1259
612	E, Field 20 Locus 327	1,3	14	same	1286
613	E, Field 6 Locus 1079	1,3	15	same	1468
614	D, Field 11 Locus 816	1,24	16	same	A43.1
615	E, Field 42 Locus 873	1,23	14	same	A27.4

608

616	V, Field 2 Locus 932/937	1,2	14	SNG. ANS, *Palestine-South Arabia*, 206–218?	1177
617	V, Field 2 Locus 937	1,15	14	same	1166
618	E, Field 42 Locus 873	1,15	14	same	A23.2
619	D, Field 6 Locus 863	1,1	13	same	A25.2
620	E, Field 29 Locus 832	1,08	15	same	A39.4
621	F, Field 13 Locus 963	1,05	12	same	1208
622	E, Field 7 Locus 1071	1,05	14	same	1421
623	E, Field 29 Locus 832	1,04	14	same	A42.4
624	F, Field 12 Locus 902	1,01	14	same	1129
625	E, Field 8 Locus 1064	1	15	same	1313
626	E, Field 7 Locus 1071	1	13	same	1412
627	E, Field 6 Locus 1076	1	12	same	1481
628	V, Field 2 Locus 933	0,95	13	same	1160
629	G, Field 8 Locus 942	0,95	13	same	1254
630	E, Field 8 Locus 1064	0,95	13	same	1318
631	E, Field 8 Locus 1064	0,90	14	same	1290
632	E Field 8 Locus 1063	0,85	12	same	1103
633	F, Field 13 Locus 964	0,85	12	same	1201
634	E, Field 6 Locus 1079	0,85	15	same	1467
635	E, Field 29 Locus 832	0,82	15	same	A42.1
636	E, Field 39 Locus 812	0,82	14	same	A44.6
637	E, Field 7 Locus 1071	0,80	13	same	1422
638	E, Field 7 Locus 1071	0,8	12	same	1442

639	E, Field 6 Locus 1076	0,8	13	SNG. ANS, *Palestine-South Arabia*, 206–218?	1482
640	C, Field 20	0,78	12	same	A31.2
641	E, Field 37	0,76	15	same	A38.5
642	E, Field 46 Locus 917	0,75	12	same	1135
643	E, Field 6 Locus 1079	0,75	11	same	1471
644	C, Field 20	0,72	13	same	A31.1
645	F 100:1	0,7	14	same	474L
646	H, Field 2 Locus 4	0,70	13	same	1587
647	F, Field 13 Locus 963	0,7	13	same	1211
648	E, Field 8 Locus 1064	0,65	14	same	1315
649	E, Field 6 Locus 1079	0,60	14	same	1466
650	E, Field 42 Locus 873	0,59	14	same	A17
651	D, Field 6 Locus 874	0,59	12	same	A22
652	D, Field 6 Locus 865	0,56	13	same	A37.1
653	E, Field 8 Locus 1064	0,55	12	same	1317
654	E, Field 13 Locus 357	0,5	12	same	*554
655	E, Field 26 Locus 919/920	0,5	10	same	1151
656	F, Field 13 Locus 963	0,5	12	same	1212
657	E, Field 8 Locus 1064	0,5	11	same	1322
658	E, Field 7 Locus 1071	0,5	14	same	1423
659	E, Field 6 Locus 1076	0,5	12	same	1484
660	E, Field 8 Locus 1063	0,45	13	same	1348
661	E, Field 8 Locus 1064	0,20	8	same	1325

654

AE
O/BACI/HPΩΔ; Single cornucopia
R/Eagle standing r.

662	D, Field 2 Locus 255	0,40	12		*SNG. ANS, Palestine-South Arabia*, 220–226; CHL, pl. 208, 56–57	*1607

Herod Archelaus (4 BCE–6 C.E.)
AE
O/Anchor; around, HPΩ/Δ/OY (sometimes incompletely preserved)
R/Double cornucopia with caduceus between horns; EΘ/PAN/YOX sometimes abbreviated) within wreath

663	F 100:1	1,37	14		SNG. ANS, *Palestine-South Arabia*, 251–254; MESHORER 2001, n. 69	502L

AE
O/H/P/Ω Prow of galley l.
R/EΘN/A within wreath

664	F 101 N	0,94	14		SNG. ANS, *Palestine-South Arabia*, 246; MESHORER 2001, n. 72	838L
665	F, Field 1	0,73	13		same	832L
666	F 100:1	0,47	12		same	503L

AE
O/Wine branch with bunch of grapes and small leaf; above HPΩΔ/OY (sometimes incompletely preserved)
R/Crested helmet with two cheek pieces; to l, downward, small caduceus and inscription EΘNAPX (sometimes abbreviated)

667	C, Field 31 Locus 698	2,35	17	↑	SNG. ANS, *Palestine-South Arabia*, 255–260; MESHORER 2001, n. 73; CHL, pl. 209, 81–85	*1021
668	B, Field 5	2,32	15	↑	same	*118L
669	F 110:4	2,19	17		same	761L
670	F, Field 5, under stone pavement II	2,11	15	↓	same	663L
671	C, Field 15 Locus 749	2	17		same	*833
672	F, Field 33 Locus 298	1,9	16		same	1137
673	E, Field 7 Locus 1071	1,9	17		same	*1408
674	E, Field 6 Locus 1079	1,9	13		same	1457
675	F, Field 1 trench A, near BB	1,87	15	↖	same	611L
676	F, Field 31 Locus 1158	1,8	16		same	1622
677	E, Field 34 Locus 320	1,75	13		same	609

662

667

668

673

678	E, Field 29 Locus 832	1,72	16		SNG. ANS, *Palestine-South Arabia*, 255–260; Meshorer 2001, n. 73; CHL, pl. 209, 81–85	A40.2
679	F, Field 22 Locus 511	1,7	15		same	808
680	F, Field 4	1,65	15	↓	same	*372L
681	C, Field 27 Locus 808	1,65	16		same	*959
682	F, Field 7 NE	1,59	18		same	833L
683	D, Field 2	1,58	17	↑	same	243L
684	E, Field 33 Locus 320	1,55	16		same	1068
685	E, Field 37	1,47	15		same	A38.6
686	F, Field 4, under stone pavement	1,43	13		same	*696L
687	E, Field 5 Locus 342	1,4	16		same	*575
688	F 100:2	1,39	16		same	737L
689	E, Field 5 Locus 342	1,35	16		same	*543
690	F 110:4	1,32	13		same	765L
691	D, Field 3 Locus 450	1,3	15		same	*48
692	E, Field 21	1,3	15		same	*1711
693	E, Field 7 Locus 1071	1,25	13		same	1410
694	Without context	1,23	15	↓	same	169L
695	F 100:1	1,19	15	↑	same	493L
696	F 102 East, in a wall break	1,18	16		same	855L
697	C, Field 26 Locus 704	1,15	14		same	1016
698	F 100: 3	1,09	13		same	524L
699	V, Field 2 Locus 258	1,03	16		same	1167
700	E, Field 1	0,94	13	↑	same	*267L
701	F, Field 23 Locus 509	0,85	13		same	790
702	F, Field 28 Locus 970	0,85	14		same	1239
703	E, Field 6 Locus 1079	0,75	12		same	1500

680

681

686

687

689

691

692

700

Mint of Tiberias
Herod Antipas (4 BCE–39 CE)
AE (19/20)
O/HPΩΔOY TETPAPXOY, but sometimes incompletely struck or preserved; palm or tree
R/TIBE/PIAC and ΓAI/ΩKA/CAP in different combinations, within wreath

704	E, Field 11 Locus 301/302	6,55	19		SNG. ANS, *Palestine-South Arabia*, 228–229; Meshorer 2001, n. 81; CHL, pl. 209, 88–89	*330
705	E, Field 7 Locus 1071	5,15	19		same	*1441
706	G, Field 9 Locus 1051	3,65	16		CHL, pl. 209, 90–91	1269
707	F, Field 13 Locus 963	3,15	14		same	1203
708	F, Field 13 Locus 963	3	14		same	*1206
709	E, Field 11 Locus 305	2,1	12		same	301
710	V, Field 2 Locus 1011	1,05	11		same	1227
711	E, Field 6 Locus 1076	1,05	15		same	1374

AE (28/29)
O/HPΩΔOY TETPAPXOY, Palm branch; in field L/ΛΓ
R/TIBE/PIAC in wreath

712	D, Field 6 Locus 863	8,75	21	↑	CHL, p. 16, n. 93, pl. 210, 93	A5
713	E, Field 6 Locus 1076	6	19	↑	CHL, pl. 210, 95	1373

AE (28/29–29/30)
O/Palm branch; around Greek inscription: HPWΔOY TETPAPXOY; date: L A Γ
R/Inscription in wreath. TIBE/PIAC

714	F, Field 25 Locus 558	12,65	24	↑	SNG. ANS, *Palestine-South Arabia*, n. 227, 229; Meshorer 2001, nn. 79, 83	*870
715	F, Field 25 Locus 558	11,7	25	↑	same	*877

AE (1/4 or 1/8 denomination?) (28/29–29/30)
O/Palm branch; around Greek inscription; date: L A Γ
R/Inscription in wreath: T/C

716	F, Field 1	1,52	12		Meshorer 2001, 78, 82, 86, 90, 94	397L
717	C, Field 13 Locus 636	1,06	12		same	747
718	V, Field 2 Locus 258	1,05	13		same	598

704

705

708

714

715

AE (1/4 or 1/8 denomination?) (19/20–38/39)
O/Palm branch; around Greek inscription; date: L A Γ
R/Inscription in wreath

719	F, Field 18 Locus 324	6,35	19	↑	SNG. ANS, *Palestine-South Arabia*, 229	*427
720	E, Field 28	3,37	19	↓	SNG. ANS, *Palestine-South Arabia*, 229, 232	*361L
721	F, Field 4	4,14	12	↓	SNG. ANS, *Palestine-South Arabia*, 228	*373L
722	F, Field 4	4,13	14	↑	same	374L
723	H, Field 2 Locus 62	1,6	12	↑	Meshorer 2001, nn. 78–82; SNG.ANS, Palestine-South Arabia, 228 L K Δ (19/20)	*123
724	H, Field 2 Locus 12	1,4	12	↓	Meshorer 2001, nn. 78, 82, 86, 90, 94; SNG.ANS, Palestine-South Arabia, 228 L K Δ (19/20)?	*145

AE (quarter denomination?) (39)
O/Palm tree with seven branches; around Greek inscription; date: ETO/M Γ
R/Inscription in wreath

725	D, Field 2 Locus 254	3,5	15	↑	CHL, pl. 210, 107–108	857
726	F, Field 3 Locus 265	2,8	15	↑	CHL, pl. 210, 116	1131

Herod Philippus (4 BCE–34 CE)
Mint of Caesarea Philippi (Paneas)
AE
O/Head of Augustus r., laureate [KAICAPI CEBACTΩ]
R/Facade of tetrastyle temple; [---] TETPA [---]

727	H, Field 2 Locus 10	6,5	20	↑	CHL, pl. 211, 119 e ss.	*105

719

720

721

723

724

727

Mint of Jerusalem
***Agrippa* I** (37–43)
AE (41/42)
O/ΒΑCΙΛΕΩC ΑΓΡΙΠΑ Canopy
R/Three ears of grain; l. L r. ς

728	C, Field 34 Locus 820	2,5	16	↑	SNG. ANS, *Palestine-South Arabia*, 262–272; Meshorer 2001, n. 120; CHL, pl. 212, 153–160	A29.1
729	E, Field 6 Locus 1079	2,15	15	↑	same	1379
730	F, Field 18 Locus 331	2,1	17	↑	same	*417
731	F, Field 25 Locus 552	1,95	16	↑	same	1575
732	C, Field 24 Locus 655	1,9	17	↑	same	*954
733	V, Field 3	1,87	15	↓	same	*151L
734	E, Field 7 Locus 1070	1,85	17		same	1404
735	E, Field 8 Locus 1063	1,65	17		same	1287
736	D, Field 2 Locus 255	1,4	17		same	*1601
737	D, Field 6 Locus 865	1,13	16		same	A37.2
738	F, Field 18 Locus 330	1,05	16		same	1556

***Mint of Jerusalem*?**
***Agrippa* I** (37–43)?
AE (42)?
O/Corroded flan
R/Three ears of grain?

739	V, Field 3 Locus 767	0,9	15		SNG. ANS, *Palestine-South Arabia*, 262–272?	621

Mint of Caesarea Paneas *(under Nero)*
***Agrippa* II** (50–95)
AE (61)
O/Bust of Nero; [ΣΕΒΑΣΤΟΣ]
R/Inscription in wreath; [ΕΠΙ ΒΑCΙΛΕ …]

740	D, Field 2 Locus 255	9,4	24		SNG. ANS, *Palestine-South Arabia*, 275 ss; poorly preserved	1098

730

732

733

736

(under Titus)

AE (86–87)
O/Bust of Titus r. laureate; AYTOKP TITOC [KAICAP CEB]
R/Nike advancing r, holding wreath and palm branch ETO [BA AΓPIΠΠA]

741	F, Field 18 Locus 329	10,5	24		SNG. ANS, *Palestine-South Arabia*, 289; CHL, pl. 216, 229–230	*1555

(under Domitianus)

AE (78/79)
O/Bust od Domitianus r., laureate; ΔOMETIANOC KAI C AP
R/Galley with oars and rudder sailing l.; above inscription in wreath; ETO/IΘ BA A/ΓPIΠΠA

742	H, Field 2 Locus 36	3,5	15	↑	CHL, pl. 215, 205–206	*101
743	G, Field 2/3 Locus 1028	2,45	15	↑	same	*3
744	F, Field 13 Locus 963	2,95	15	↓	same	*1204

AE (84/85)
O/Bust of Domitianus r., laureate; ΔOMET KAICAP ΓEPMANI
R/Nike standing l; inscription in wreath; ETO/KΔ BAA/ΓPIΠΠA

745	C, Field 22 Locus 595	5,6	20		SNG. ANS, *Palestine-South Arabia*, 296–297; CHL, pl. 215, 210–211; *RPC* I, 2263	*917

AE (84/85)
O/Bust of Domitianus r., laureate; ΔOMETIANOC KAICAP
R/Nike standing l.; inscription in wreath; ETO/KΔ [BAA/ΓPIΠΠA]

746	E, Field 33	4,27	13	↑	SNG. ANS, *Palestine-South Arabia*, 299–302; CHL, p. 215, 212–213; RPC I, 2264	*A30

Domitianus (81–96)
AE
O/Bust of Domitianus r., laureate; ΔOMET KAIC ΓEPM
R/Palm-tree, with two bunces of fruit; across field, in four lines, inscription and date;
ETKE/BA C-AΓP/IΠ

747	C, Field 31 Locus 698	3,2	15	↑	RPC II, pl. 98, 2267	*1020

741

742

743

744

745

746

747

HASMONEAN OR HEROD THE GREAT (FIRST CENTURY BCE)

Mint of Jerusalem?

AE

O/and R/incompletely preserved, but the iconography perhaps anchor; in the obverse: double cornucopia/pomegranate in the reverse. Crude style; inscription poorly preserved

748	F, Field 25 Locus 558	2,45	16	↑	As SNG. ANS, *Palestine-South Arabia*, nn. 95 or 206	872
749	F, Field 7	2,4	14	↑	same	783L
750	F, Field 31 Locus 1158	2,20	16	↑	same	1624
751	C, Field 15 Locus 897	1,8	16	↑	same	860
752	G 101	1,73	12	↑	same	782L
753	F, Field 18 Locus 317	1,7	15	↑	same	750
754	F, Field 25 Locus 351	1,55	15	↑	same	703[2]
755	V (2013)	1,5	14	↑		
756	E, Field 22a Locus 308	1,45	16	↑	same	655
757	H, Field 1 Locus 94	1,45	15	↑	same	*208
758	H, Field 2 Locus 6	1,45	12	↑	same	*72
759	F, Field 7	1,42	15	↑	same	564L
760	M, Field 9 Locus 999	1,4	12	↑	same	667
761	H, Field 1 Locus 91	1,4	13	↑	same	200
762	F, Field 7	1,34	13	↑	same	566L
763	F, Field 20 Locus 298	1,3	14	↑	same	616
764	F 100:2	1,27	14	↑	same	739L
765	F 110:4	1,23	14	↑	same	760L
766	F, Field 7	1,18	12	↑	same	561L
767	F 100:1	1,15	14	↑	same	511L
768	V, Field 2 Locus 258	1,15	14	↑	same	600
769	B, Field 5 Locus 296	1,15	14		same	605
770	C, Field 12 Locus 596	1,1	15		same	873

2 Double cornucopia?

757

758

771	F, Field 3, under stone pavement II	1,07	15	As SNG. ANS, *Palestine-South Arabia*, nn. 95 or 206	884L
772	H, Field 1 Locus 39	1,05	14	same	*178
773	F, Field 7	1,04	13	same	571L
774	F, Field 3 East	0,99	12	same	790L
775	F, Field 5, under stone pavement II	0,96	12	same	640L
776	F, Field 1, trench BB	0,95	15	same	614L
777	F, Field 7	0,92	11	same	574L
778	F, Field 110	0,9	15	same	755L
779	F, Field 18 Locus 325	0,9	13	same	*431
780	D, Field 4 Locus 770	0,9	14	same	744
781	D, Field 4 Locus 770	0,9	13	same	681[3]
782	F, Field 5, under stone pavement II	0,88	12	same	670L
783	F 110	0,88	13	same	751L
784	D, Field 1	0,85	13	same	*8
785	F 110:4	0,85	11	same	773L
786	F, Field 25 Locus 351	0,85	12	same	868
787	F, Field 2, trench 1	0,82	13	same	709L
788	F 100:3	0,8	14	same	523L
789	G 101	0,78	12	same	707L
790	E, Field 3	0,76	11	same	272L
791	F, Field 10 Locus 286	0,75	13	same	634
792	F, Field 20 Locus 298	0,75	13	same	615
793	F 100:2	0,73	13	same	740L
794	E, Field 9	0,72	12	same	306L
795	F 100:1	0,72	12	same	476L
796	F 100:1	0,71	12	same	517L
797	H, Field 1 Locus 91/94	0,7	12	same	*220

3 Anchor?

772

779

784

797

798	F, Field 9 Locus 298	0,7	13	As SNG. ANS, *Palestine-South Arabia*, nn. 95 or 206	765
799	F, Field 7 North	0,67	11	same	819L
800	F 5, under stone pavement II	0,66	13	same	679/aL
801	D, Field 4 Locus 770	0,65	11	same	743
802	F, Field 2, trench 1	0,65	13	same	717L
803	V, Field 2 Locus 279	0,65	13	same	596
804	E, Field 34 Locus 320	0,65	12	same	672
805	V (2013)	0,65	13		
806	F, Field 5, under stone pavement II	0,63	15	same	656L
807	F 110:4	0,62	10	same	768L
808	F, Field 7	0,62	11	same	588L
809	C, Field 1 Locus 755	0,6	12	same	*7
810	F, Field 25 US 544	0,6	12	same	888
811	F, Field 5, under stone pavement II	0,59	13	same	674L
812	F 100:3	0,59	11	same	539L
813	F, Field 7 North	0,56	13	same	817L
814	F, Field 7	0,55	10	same	589L
815	F, Field 20 Locus 299	0,55	11	same	774
816	E (2013)	0,55	13		
817	F, Field 7 North	0,52	13	same	813L
818	F 100:1	0,52	10	same	514L
819	F 100:3	0,51	13	same	530L
820	F, Field 7	0,5	12	same	556L
821	F, Field 7	0,5	12	same	592L
822	F, Field 7 North	0,5	12	same	810L
823	F, Field 7 Locus 282	0,5	8	same	160

809

824	D, Field 4 Locus 770	0,5	12		As SNG. ANS, *Palestine-South Arabia*, nn. 95 or 206	739
825	B, Field 3 Locus 1198	0,5	8		same	*11
826	F, Field 25 Locus 558	0,5	12		same	884
827	D, Field 6 Locus 872	0,50	13	↑	same	A18
828	F 110:4	0,49	12		same	771L
829	G 101	0,49	11		same	701L
830	Cardo	0,46	11		same	727L
831	F, Field 5, under stone pavement II	0,46	11		same	659L
832	F, Field 5, under stone pavement II	0,46	11		same	677L
833	H, Field 1 Locus 91/94	0,45	12		same	*222
834	F, Field 28 Locus 329	0,45	12		same	650
835	F, Field 2, trench 1	0,44	11		same	718L
836	F, Field 5, under stone pavement II	0,44	12		same	664L
837	G 101	0,42	11		same	708L
838	F, Field 2 West	0,41	12		same	801L
839	F, Field 3 North	0,41	12		same	605L
840	F, Field 2, trench 1	0,41	11		same	719L
841	H, Field 1 Locus 94	0,4	13		same	*235
842	C, Field 32/34 Locus 702	0,40	11			1708
843	F 100:1	0,38	12		same	495L
844	F, Field 5, under stone pavement II	0,37	11		same	671L
845	F, Field 1, trench A	0,36	11		same	632L
846	F, Field 5, under stone pavement II	0,36	12		same	669L
847	F, Field 7	0,36	10		same	784L

825

833

841

848	F, Field 5, under stone pavement II	0,34	11	As SNG. ANS, *Palestine-South Arabia*, nn. 95 or 206	666L
849	F, Field 5, under stone pavement II	0,33	9	same	655L
850	F, Field 5, under stone pavement II	0,32	9	same	668L
851	F, Field 5, under stone pavement II	0,32	9	same	685L
852	Cardo	0,32	12	same	730L
853	V, Field 2 Locus 279	0,3	12	same	637
854	V, Field 2 Locus 271	0,3	8	same	*505
855	H, Field 1 Locus 0	0,3	10	same	673
856	V, Field 2 Locus 258	0,3	11	same	597
857	F, Field 22 Locus 514	0,3	12	same	810
858	V (2013)	0,3	11		
859	E, Field 42 Locus 873	0,29	9		A27.2
860	F 100:2	0,28	12	same	747L
861	F, Field 4	0,28	11	same	695L
862	F, Field 7 NE	0,28	9	same	836L
863	F 100:1	0,27	11	same	486L
864	F, Field 7 NE	0,27	10	same	835L
865	F, Field 1	0,24	10	same	375L
866	F, Field 7 North	0,22	12	same	818L
867	F, Field 5, under stone pavement II	0,16	7	same	686L

854

Hasmonean or Herod the Great (first century BCE)?

AE (prutah)
O/ and R/ incompletely iconography and inscriptions poorly preserved and garbled; typical flan

868	M, Field 3 Locus 999	1,6	14	SNG. ANS, *Palestine-South Arabia*?	602
869	M (2013)	1,6	14	same	No nr.
870	F 100:2	1,01	14	same	747L
871	E, Field 31 Locus 791	0,95	13	same	1086
872	E, Field 34 Locus 320	0,85	13	same	607
873	E, Field 20	0,52	10	same	336L

Roman procurators and the Jewish wars against Rome

Roman procurators

Ambibulus (9–12) *(under Augustus)*
O/KAICAPOC Ear of grain
R/Palm tree
AE (9) LAΘ

874	F, Field 7	1,93	16	↑	SNG. ANS, *Palestine-South Arabia*, 326–330; CHL, pl. 219, 3–8; RPC I, 4955–4957	*563L
875	D, Field 1	0,93	16	↑	same	*217L

AE (10) LMA

876	F, Field 4, lower structure	2,24	12	↑	SNG. ANS, *Palestine-South Arabia*, 331; CHL, pl. 219, 6–7; RPC I, 4956–4957	*694L
877	F, Field 7	2,23	14	↑	SNG. ANS, *Palestine-South Arabia*, 331–332	*551L
878	Without context	1,5	15	↑	SNG. ANS. *Palestine-South Arabia*, 326–336	*29

AE (9–12)

879	F, Field 3 Locus 902	1,95	16	↑	SNG. ANS, *Palestine-South Arabia*, 326–330; RPC I, 4956–4957	1107
880	F, Field 18 Locus 330	1,5	15	↑	SNG. ANS. *Palestine-South Arabia*, 336; RPC I, 4956–4957	1690
881	F, Field 25 Locus 351	0,55	15	↑	SNG. ANS. *Palestine-South Arabia*, 326–336; RPC I, 4956–4957	701

Coponius or ***Ambibulus*** (6–12)
AE
O/Ear of grain
R/Palm tree

882	E, Field 42 Locus 873	2,84	16	↑	SNG. ANS. *Palestine-South Arabia*, 321–325; 329–336; CHL, pl. 219, 1–8	A23.1
883	E, Field 5	2,22	12	↑	SNG. ANS, *Palestine-South Arabia*, 321–325? CHL, pl. 219, 1–8	300L
884	H, Field 1 Locus 39	1,7	17	↑	SNG. ANS. *Palestine-South Arabia*, 329–336; CHL, pl. 219, 1–8	87
885	H, Field 1 Locus 94	1,75	13	↑	SNG. ANS. *Palestine-South Arabia*, 321–325; 329–336; CHL, pl. 219, 1–8	245
886	F, Field 19 Locus 353	1,45	17	↑	CHL, pl. 219, 1–8	*392
887	C, Field 15 Locus 897	1,45	15	↑	same	842
888	E, Field 8 Locus 1064	1,4	16	↓	same	1314

874

875

876

877

878

886

889	F, Field 7 Locus 353	1,35	15	↑	CHL, pl. 219, 1–8	*390
890	F, Field 4	1,31	18	↓	same	693L
891	D, Field 1	1,3	15	↑	same	*227L
892	F, Field 1	1,25	12	↑	same	405L
893	E, Field 6 Locus 1076	1,2	12		same	1496
894	E, Field 19 Locus 534	1,15	6	↓	same	815
895	F 100:1	1,08	14	↑	same	466L
896	F, Field 1, trench A, near BB	0,89	12	↑	same	613L
897	C, Field 6 Locus 589	0,55	11	↑	same	1732
898	G, Field 9 Locus 1051	0,50	11	↑	same	1262
899	C, Field 6 Locus 589	0,3	10	↑	same	1730

Valerius Gratus (15–26) *(under Tiberius)*

AE (16)
O/KAI/CAP within wreath
R/TIB, double cornucopia with L Γ

900	F, Field 5 under stone pavement II	1,89	16	↓	SNG. ANS, *Palestine-South Arabia*, 341–343; CHL, pl. 219, 15–17	*636L

Pontius Pilatus (26–36)

AE (29)
O/TIBEPIOV KAICAPOC; LIϛ; Simpulum
R/IOVΛIA KAICAPOC; Three ears of grain

901	E, Field 7 Locus 1071	1,1	15	↑	SNG. ANS, *Palestine-South Arabia*, 367–372; CHL, pl. 219, 34–35	*1409

O/TIBEPIOY KAICAPOC; LIϛ lituus
R/Date within wreath
AE (30–31)

902	E, Field 12 Locus 263	1,05	15	↑	SNG. ANS, *Palestine-South Arabia*, 373–386	*573

889

891

900

901

902

AE (26–36)

903	F, Field 14 Locus 921	1,65	15	↑	SNG. ANS, *Palestine-South Arabia*, 373–387; CHL, pl. 220, 38–46	1139
904	H, Field 3 Locus 11	1,3	15	↑	same	*74
905	E, Field 7 Locus 1071	1,05	13	↑	same	1411
906	C, Field 6 Locus 589	1,05	14	↑	same	1721
907	D, Field 2 Locus 255	0,95	15	↑	same	1602
908	V 2	0,77	13	↑	same	*137L

Antonius Felix (52–59) *(under Claudius)*
O/IOV/ΛΙΑΑΓ/ΡΙΠΠΙ/ΝΑ within wreath
R/TIKΛAVΔIOCKAICAP Two palm branches crossed
AE (54)

909	E, Field 6 Locus 1076	1,7	17	↑	SNG. ANS, *Palestine-South Arabia*, 388–396	45
910	C, Field 19 Locus 596	1,55	15		same	*950

AE (52–59)

911	E, Field 8 Locus 1063	2,85	14	↑	SNG. ANS, *Palestine-South Arabia*, 397	1101
912	C, Field 15 Locus 749	2	17	↑	SNG. ANS, *Palestine-South Arabia*, 397	*831
913	D, Field 1	1,49	14	↑	SNG. ANS, *Palestine-South Arabia*, 397–404	*233L

904

908

910

912

913

Porcius Festus (59–62) *(under Nero)*
AE
O/NEP/ΩNO/C within wreath
R/LE KAICAPOC palm branch

914	F, Field 25 Locus 554	2,75	17	↑	SNG. ANS, *Palestine-South Arabia*, 412–418	*695
915	E, Field 42 Locus 873	1,71	15	↑	same	A27.5
916	C, Field 31 Locus 698	1,55	15	↓	same	*1030
917	E, Field 11 Locus 301/302	1,5	15	↑	same	678
918	F, Field 18 Locus 331	1,15	15	↑	same	*389
919	C, Field 24 Locus 655	1,05	14	↑	same	953
920	D, Field 2 Locus 255	0,80	14		same	1605

Roman procurators (15–62)
AE; O/ and R/ incomplete iconography and inscriptions poorly preserved and garbled (legend within wreath)

921	E, Field 35 Locus 320	1,05	13	SNG. ANS, *Palestine-South Arabia*, 339–418	1077
922	E, Field 2/7 Locus 350	1,1	11	same	*569[4]
923	E, Field 11 Locus 303	0,75	13	same; R/Palm tree (?)	*255

4 Perhaps Coponius or Ambibulus under Augustus (6–9; 9–12) or Antonius Felix under Claudius (52–59), cf. SNG, ANS, Palestine-South Arabia, 321–325 or 397–404.

914

916

918

922

923

Herod the Great or Roman procurators

Mint of Jerusalem? (40 BCE–62 CE)
AE
O/ and R/ incomplete iconography and inscriptions poorly preserved and garbled

924	H, Field 1 Locus 93	2,15	14		SNG. ANS, *Palestine-South Arabia*?	*189
925	M, Locus 999	2,1	15		same	46
926	E, Field 5	1,67	19	↑	same	299L

Jewish wars against Rome: First revolt

AE (67)
O/Palaeo-Hebrew inscription. Amphora
R/Palaeo-Hebrew inscription. Vine leaf with tendril

927	V, Field 3 Locus 767	2,45	16	↓	SNG. ANS, *Palestine-South Arabia*, 427–443	*19
928	D, Field 1	2,24	18	↓	same	229L
929	F, Field 23 Locus 509	2,2	17	↓	same	788
930	B, Field 5	1,64	16	↓	same	120L

Roman administration: Domitianus Judaea coinage

931	E, Field 8 Locus 1065	7,95	20	↑	Meshorer 1982, pl. 36, n.8; SNG. ANS, *Palestine-South Arabia*, 495–498; CHL, pl. 226, 30–32; *RPC* II, 2306	1309
932	G, Field 9 Locus 1048	6,30	17	↑	same	1265
933	G, Field 2/3 Locus 1028	4,35	20	↑	same	*2

Jewish wars against Rome: Bar Kokhba War

AE (132–135)
O/Palaeo-Hebrew inscription and SM'W/N; Palm tree
R/Palaeo-Hebrew inscription; Bunch of grapes

934	E, Field 5 Locus 956	2,45	19	↑	SNG. ANS, *Palestine-South Arabia*, 590–592	*1187

924

927

933

934

Greek coins and Roman provincial coins of Palestine and South Arabia

Galilee and Samaria: Provincial city coins

Mint of Caesarea Maritima

Claudius (45–54)

AE

O/Laureate head of Claudius r. [CLAVDIVS CAESAR AVG PM TR P IMP PP]

R/Anchor within wreath

935	E, Field 11 Locus 303	13,5	27	↑	SNG. ANS, *Palestine-South Arabia*, 744; CHL, pl. 231, 88–89?	*299

Titus (79–81)

AE

O/Laureate head of Titus, r. [AVTOKP ΤΙΤΟΣ ΚΑΙΣΑΡ

R/Trophy, to l. Jewess seated l. [ΙΟΥΔΑΙΑΣ ΕΑΛΩΚVΙΑC]

936	E, Field 2 Locus 1003	12,2	24	↑	SNG. ANS, *Palestine-South Arabia*, 481–482	*1383

Traianus (98–117)

AE

O/Laureate bust of Traianus r. [---]

R/Emperor standing l. sacrificing over the altar; COL PRI FL AVG [---]

937	E, Field 11 Locus 302	10,25	25	↓	SNG. ANS, *Palestine-South Arabia*, 762–763; CHL, pl. 23, 22–23	264
938	H, Field 3 Locus 21	9,75	27	↑	SNG. ANS, *Palestine-South Arabia*, 762–763; CHL, pl. 23, 22–23; CHL, pl. 23, 22–23	*134

Hadrianus (117–138)

AE

O/Laureate bust of Hadrianus; IMP TRA HADRIANUSO CA

R/Tyche standing l., holding bust and sceptre, but resting her foot on harbour-god; CIF AVG CAESAR

939	F, Field 18 Locus 325/329	8,5	24	↑	SNG. ANS, *Palestine-South Arabia*, 768–770; CHL, pl. 24, 28–29	*1395
940	E, Field 11 Locus 302	6,45	22	↑	same	*286

935

936

938

939

940

Alexander Severus (222–235)
AE
O/Laureate head of Alexander Severus r. [---]
R/Inscription SPQR within wreath supported by eagle looking l. CIF [AFCAE METROPOLIS]

941	B, Field 5	9,54	21	↑	SNG. ANS, *Palestine-South Arabia*, 807–816; CHL, pl. 27, 84–87	*127L
942	D, Field 1	8,82	18	↑	same	211L
943	H, Field 1 US 90	7,45	23	↑	same	*194
944	V 1	5,75	20	↑	SNG. ANS, *Palestine-South Arabia*, 812–816; CHL, pl. 27, 89–91 (small denomination)	132L
945	B, Field 1	4,42	20	↓	same	*106L
946	E, Field 7 Locus 1068	3,5	19	↑	same	1363

Alexander Severus (222–235)?
AE; O/ and R/ incomplete iconography and inscriptions poorly preserved and garbled

947	E, Field 11 US 301/302	5,3	21		SNG. ANS, *Palestine-South Arabia*, 807–812	*321
948	E, Field 36 Locus 321	4,05	24		same	731

Elagabalus (218–222) or ***Alexander Severus*** (222–235)
AE
O/Laureate bust of emperor r.
R/Crown supported by eagle

949	D, Field 1	6,32	18	↑	SNG. ANS, *Palestine-South Arabia*, 803–804; 815–816	*254L

Traianus Decius (249–251)
AE
O/Draped bust of Traianus Decius
R/Bust of Tyche r.

950	H, Field 3 Locus 78	4,2	19	↓	SNG. ANS, *Palestine-South Arabia*, 821	*131

941

943

945

947

949

950

Hostilianus (251)
AE
O/Draped and radiate bust of Hostilianus r.
R/Bust of Tyche l.

951	D, Field 6 Locus 784	7,5	19	↑	SNG. ANS, *Palestine-South Arabia*, 846–848	*1088

Trebonianus Gallus (251–253)
AE
O/Draped bust of Trebonianus Gallus r.
R/Vexillum between two eagles

952	E, Field 11 Locus 302	11,5	23	↙	SNG. ANS, *Palestine-South Arabia*, 851; CHL, pl. 32, 152	*262

Volusianus (251–253)
AE
O/Laureate bust of Volusianus r. [---]
R/Dionysus reclining l. on panther advancing r.

953	E, Fiel 11 Locus 302	9,35	23	↗	BMC. *Palestine*, 214–217; SNG. ANS, *Palestine-South Arabia*, 856–857; CHL, pl. 23, 173	*263

AE
O/Draped bust of Volusianus, radiate, r.
R/Altar [---]

954	F, Field 25 Locus 552	10,65	22	↑	CHL, pl. 34, 177–178	*900

Uncertain mint* (Caesarea Maritima?) *and authority (second–mid-third century)
AE
O/Draped female (?) bust r.
R/Bust of Tyche r.

955	E, Field 11 Locus 303	20	15	↑	SNG. ANS, *Palestine-South Arabia*?; CHL, pl. 31, 141; pl. 32, 151, 153?	*278

Mint of Dora
Traianus (98–117) or ***Hadrianus*** (117–138)
AE
O/Imperial bust, laureate, r.; [---]
R/Galley sailing l; above ΔΩPA IEPA

956	C, Field 32 Locus 669	3,2	16	↓	CHL, pl. 40, 32 or 35	*998

951

952

953

954

955

956

Mint of Neapolis
Elagabalus (218–222)
AE
O/Laureate, draped bust of Elagabalus r.; [---]
R/Tetrastyle temple; within Tyche standing facing; [---]

957	V, Field 3	8,41	23	↓	SNG. ANS, *Palestine-South Arabia*, 996; CHL, pl. 52, 104–108	*162L
958	D, Field 1 Locus 1199	7,9	20	↑	same	545
959	E, Field 30 Locus 260	7,8	23	↑	same	584
960	D, Field 1	7,2	18	↑	same	*195L
961	B, Field 1 Locus 262	5,75	20	↑	same	578

AE
O/Bust of Elagabalus r. laureate; inscription incompletely preserved
R/Tyche standing facing, holding rudder and cornucopia; inscription, perhaps, ΦΛΝΕ CVP Π

962	C, Field 33 Locus 713	3	18	↑	SNG. ANS, *Palestine-South Arabia*, 1007; CHL, pl. 52, 109–111	1060

Philip I (244–249)
AE
O/Draped and radiate bust of Philip r.; inscription incompletely preserved; [IMP M IVL PHILIPPVS AVG]
R/COL [SERG NEAPOL] within wreath

963	D, Field 1	10,89	23	↑	CHL, pl. 55, 163	*203L

Philip II (247–249)
AE
O/Draped bust of Philip II r. [IMP C M IVL PHILIPPO PF AVG]
R/Eagle with spread wings standing facing, looking r.

964	E, Field 11 Locus 302	18,35	30	↑	CHL, pl. 59, 213	*257

Trebonianus Gallus (251–253)
AE
O/Bust of Trebonianus Gallus r.
R/Mount Gerizim surmounted by temple and altar, stairway leads to temple, colonnade below mountain; all supported by facing eagle; inscription incompletely preserved: ΦΛ ΝΕΑC ΠΟΛΕΩC

965	E, Field 11 Locus 302	9,7	23	↑	CHL, pl. 59, 216–218	*259

957

960

963

964

965

Mint of Sepphoris (Diocaesarea)
Period of Agrippa II
AE (67–69)
O/Double cornucopia; in center: caduceus; Greek inscription
R/ΝΕΡΩΝΟ/ΚΛΑΥΔΙΟ/ΚΑΙCΑΡΟ/C; all within wreath

966	Surface, NE of mosaics	8,61	22	↑	SNG. ANS, *Palestine-South Arabia*, 1085; CHL, pl. 213, 173	888L
967	H, Field 2 Locus 6	8,3	24	↑	same	*99
968	E, Field 11 Locus 301/302	7,05	28	↑	same	307

AE (68–69)
O/Border of dots; legend, in center: large SC, around Greek inscription
R/Circle surrounded by wreath tied at bottom; legend within in five lines [---] C

969	V, Field 2	6,82	20	↑	Kindler 1974, p. 135; Meshorer 1982, II, pl. 29, 9; *RPC* I, 4850	*144L

Traianus (98–117)
AE
O/ΤΡΑΙΑΝΟΣ ΑΥΤΟΚΡΑΤΩΡ ΕΔΩΚΕΝ incompletely preserved. Laureate head of Traianus r.
R/ΣΕΠΦō/ΡΗΝōΝ within wreath

970	C, Field 29 Locus 667	12,9	27	↑	SNG. ANS, *Palestine-South Arabia*, 1086–1087; CHL, pl. 64, 1	*985
971	C, Field 13 Locus 596	11,7	25	↑	same	*912

AE
O/Head of Traianus; [ΤΡΑΙΑΝΟΣ ΑΥΤΟΚΡΑΤΩΡ ΕΔΩΚΕΝ,]
R/ΣΕΠΦ Ω ΡΗΝΩΝ palm tree

972	D, Field 3 Locus 346	9	24	↑	SNG. ANS, *Palestine-South Arabia*, 1088–1091; CHL, pl. 64, 2	*441
973	V, Field 3	7,49	22	↑	SNG. ANS, *Palestine-South Arabia*, 1088–1091; CHL, pl. 64, 2	*152L

Antoninus Pius (138–161)
AE
O/Laureate head of Antoninus Pius r.; ΑΥΤΟ ΚΑΙ [ΑΝΤΩΝΙΝΩ ΕΥ]
R/Tetrastyle temple, within Tyche standing r. holding scepter and cornucopia; ΔΙΟ ΚΑΙ [ΙΕΡ ΑCΥ ΑΥΤΟ]

974	E, Field 2 Locus 259	7,4	22	↑	SNG. ANS, *Palestine-South Arabia*, 1095–1096; CHL, pl. 64, 6–7	585
975	B, Field 1	5,55	21	↑	same	*115L

967

969

970

971

972

973

975

Elagabalus (218–22)
AE
O/Draped bust of Elagabalus r., radiate; [AYT K M AY ANTΩN]
R/Zeus seated in a tetrastyle temple; [ΔIOK AYT ACYΛ]

976	B, Field 6 Locus 454	10,35	24	↑	CHL, pl. 65, 17–19	*827

Mint of Neapolis or ***Sepphoris (Diocaesarea)***
Domitianus (81–96) or ***Traianus*** (98–117)
AE
O/Laureate head r.
R/Palm tree

977	E, Field 5 Locus 958	7,5	23	↑	SNG.ANS, *Palestine-South Arabia*, 962–963 (Domitian); SNG.ANS, *Palestine-South Arabia*, 1088–1090 (Traianus)	

Mint of Tiberias
Claudius (41–54)
AE
O/KΛAYΔIOY KAICAPOC Palm branch
R/TIBE PIAC within wreath

978	B, Field 1	10,67	21	↓	SNG. ANS, *Palestine-South Arabia*, 1097; CHL, pl. 221, 79–80	*111L
979	F, Field 31 Locus 1158	7,5	19	↑	same	*1621
980	C, Field 34 Locus 820	1,5	12	↑	same, but SNG. ANS, *Palestine-South Arabia*, 1098 (the half denomination)	A29.2

Traianus (98–117)
AE (99/100)
O/Laureate bust of Traianus r. [AYTOKP KAIC NEP TPAIANOC CEB ΓEPM]
R/Double cornucopia crossed, in center: palm branch; [ET AΠ]

981	E, Field 11 Locus 303	4,85	21	↑	BMC. *Palestine*, p. 7, nn. 14–17; pl. 1, nn. 12–13; CHL, pl. 65, 3–4	*275
982	E, Field 5 Locus 342	4,3	18	↑	same	*542

AE (108/109)
O/Laureate bust of Traianus r. [AY KAI NE TPAIANOC CE ΓE ΔA]
R/Anchor; TIBEP KΛAY; ΛAч

983	C, Field 13 Locus 636	2,1	12	↙	SNG. ANS, *Palestine-South Arabia*, 1105–1108; CHL, pl. 66, 7–9	*746
984	C, Field 23/25 Locus 596	2	14	↓	same	*1704

976

978

979

981

982

983

984

Hadrianus (117–138)

AE (120)
O/Laureate bust of Hadrianus r.; [AYT TPA AΔPIANΩ KAI CEB]
R/Tetrastyle temple, within, Zeus seated l., holding small eagle; [TIBEP KΛAYΔ]

985	E, Field 11 Locus 303	8,9	24	↑	SNG. ANS, *Palestine-South Arabia*, 1109–1111; CHL, pl. 66, 10	*277
986	E, Field 11 Locus 303	8,85	25	↑	same	*296
987	V, Field 2 Locus 277	6,45	24	↑	same	*492

Commodus (177–192)

AE (188–189)
O/Laureate bust of Commodus r.; [AYTOKP KAI KOMMOΔOC]
R/Hygieia standing, feeding a snake from a bowl; TIB KΛ CVP ΠAΛ [ETPO]

988	E, Field 11 Locus 303	13,7	27	↑	BMC. *Palestine*, p. 10, n. 37; CHL, pl. 66, 15	*251
989	H, Field 2 Locus 1121	9,75	22	↑	BMC. *Palestine*, p. 10, n. 38; CHL, p. 66, 17	*1588
990	E, Field 33 Locus 320	8,15	22	↑	BMC. *Palestine*, p. 10, n. 38; CHL, p. 66, 17	*1072

Elagabalus (218–222)

AE (218)
O/Draped bust of Elagabalus, laureate, r.; [---]
R/Asklepios l. and Hygieia r. [TIBE?]

991	V, Field 2	10,43	26	↑	CHL, pl. 66, 19	*149L

AE
O/Radiate bust of emperor r. [---]
R/Poseidon on galley l.; [TIB KΛAYΔ]

992	V, Field 1	14,07	22	↑	Kadman 1957, 90; Kindler 1961, 17–18, pl. IV; CHL, pl. 67, 21, 25–26	*133L

985

986

987

988

989

990

991

992

City coins of Judaea, Idumea and Philistia

Mint of Aelia Capitolina

Hadrianus (117–138)

AE
O/Laureate bust of Hadrianus r.
R/Boar standing r.; COL [--_]

993	M, Locus 999	2,3	15	↑	BMC. *Palestine*, p. 83, n.3; pl. 8, n. 18; CHL, pl. 71, 6	*522

Antoninus Pius (138–161)

AE
O/Draped bust of Antoninus Pius, laureate, r.; IMP CAES H ANTONINO
R/Boar standing r.; KAC

994	C, Field 6 Locus 589	2,8	14	↑	BMC. *Palestine*, p. 87, n.29; CHL, pl. 73, 36	*1718

Herennius Etruscus (250–251)

AE
O Draped bust r., radiate; [---]
R/Serapis standing l. [---]

995	F, Field 25 Locus 351	10,4	25	↑	SNG. ANS, *Palestine-South Arabia*, 631; CHL, pl. 80, 149	867

Hostilianus (251)

AE
O/Draped bust of Hostilianus r., radiate
R/She-wolf r., suckling Romulus and Remus; eagle or legionary standard?; [---]

996	C, Field 3 Locus 738	14,5	29	↑	CHL, p. 81, 162–163	*407
997	F, Field 18 Locus 324	9,65	25	↓	SNG. ANS, *Palestine-South Arabia*, 632–633; CHL, pl. 81, 162	434

Mint of Ascalon

Autonomous (first century BCE)

AE
O/Bust of Tyche?
R Prow of galley; [A]Σ

998	F 100:1	1,12	11		SNG. ANS, *Palestine-South Arabia*, 641–647; CHL, pl. 88, 39–40 and 44,45	*490L

993

994

996

998

Time of Vespasian (72–77)
AE
O/Head of Tyche r.
R/A Σ Galley sailing r., with cruciform standard [ςOP or ΠP]

999	G, Field 7 Locus 1032	5,75	21	←	SNG. ANS, *Palestine-South Arabia*, 679–687; BMC. *Palestine*, p. 108, nn. 23–25	6
1000	E, Field 11 Locus 306	4,5	20	↑	SNG. ANS, *Palestine-South Arabia*, 679–682 (A.D.72/73)?; BMC. Palestine, p. 108, nn. 23–25	659
1001	B, Field 5	2,24	14	↑	SNG. ANS, *Palestine-South Arabia*, 679–687; BMC. *Palestine*, p. 108, nn. 23–25	*123L[5]

Mint of Gaza
Marcus Aurelius (178–179)
AE
O/Draped and laureate bust of Marcus Aurelius r.
R/Apollo, nude, standing l. pouring libation and holding branch

1002	H, Field 2 Locus 4	3,95	18	↑	SNG. ANS, *Palestine-South Arabia*, 932; CHL, pl. 111, 123–126	*78

Uncertain authority
AE
O/Bust r.
R/Male figure walking l.

1003	D, Field 6 Locus 884	1,08	11	↓	SNG. ANS, *Palestine-South Arabia*, 987?	*A15

5 The galley is not clearly distinguishable; the attribution was chosen in caparison with CHL table 215.

1001

1002

1003

The Decapolis and Provincia Arabia

Mint of Bostra

Marcus Aurelius (161–180) or **Commodus** (177–192)
AE
D/Laureate bust r.
R/Bust of Tyche r.

1004	D, Field 1	6,95	22	↓		*198L

Alexander Severus (222–235)
AE
O/Laureate and draped bust of Alexander Severus r.; [IMP CAES M AVR SEVV ALEXANDER AVG]
R/Bust of Tyche l., cornucopia over l. shoulder [COLONIA BOCTRA]

1005	H, Field 3 Locus 78	5,1	20	↑	SNG. ANS, *Palestine-South Arabia*, 1219–1221; CHL, pl. 130, 43	*132
1006	H, Field 2 Locus 10	4,8	20	↑	SNG. ANS, *Palestine-South Arabia*, 1219–1221; CHL, pl. 130, 43	*100
1007	E, Field 11 Locus 301/302	6,4	21	↓	SNG. ANS, *Palestine-South Arabia*, 1219–1221; CHL, pl. 130, 43	*305
1008	V, Field 3	2,14	19	↓	SNG. ANS, *Palestine-South Arabia*, 1219–1221; CHL, pl. 130, 43	*163L

AE
O/Laureate and draped bust of Alexander Severus r.; [IMP CAES M AVR SEVV ALEXANDER AVG]
R/Bust of Zeus-Ammon r.; COLONIA BOCTRA

1009	F 101, up to the pavement	4,86	19	↓	SNG. ANS, *Palestine-South Arabia*, 1222–1226	*856L
1010	F, Field 25 Locus 351	4,05	19	↓	SNG. ANS, *Palestine-South Arabia*, 1222–1226	684
1011	E, Field 2	3,65	19	↓	SNG. ANS, *Palestine-South Arabia*, 1222–1226	*1745

Alexander Severus (222–235) for ***Julia Mamaea***
AE
O/Draped bust of Julia Mamaea r., crescent [IVLIA MAMAEA AVGVSTA]
R/Bust of Zeus-Ammon r.; COLONIA BOSTRA

1012	E, Field 11 Locus 301/302	5	21	↓	SNG. ANS, *Palestine-South Arabia*, 1237–1241; CHL, pl. 131, 49–50	*326
1013	E, Field 11 Locus 301/302	3,85	20	↓	SNG. ANS, *Palestine-South Arabia*, 1237–1241; CHL, pl. 131, 49–50	*316

1004

1005

1006

1007

1008

1009

1011

1012

1013

Mint of Capitolias
Macrinus (217–218) or ***Elagabalus*** (218–222)
AE
O/Laureate bust r.; [---]
R/Octastyle temple; [---]

1014	E, Field 11 Locus 303	8,95	24	↑	SNG. ANS, *Palestine-South Arabia*, 1275–1276	*273

Mint of Esbous?
Elagabalus (281–222)?
AE
O/Draped and cuirassed bust of Elagabalus (?), laureate r.; [AVT C M AVP ANTONINVC]
R/Tyche standing l. in tetrastyle temple; in exergue: [---] CBOV?

1015	E, Field 3	6,32	23	↓	CHL, pl. 135, 4–5	*270L

Mint of Gadara
Pseudo-Autonomous (First century BCE)
AE
O/Veiled Tyche r.; behind shoulder, palm branch
R/ΓΑΔΑ ΡΕΩΝ; cornucopia

1016	V, Field 2 Locus 277	5,9	23	↑	CHL, pl. 135, 3–4	*493

Tiberius (14–37)
AE (28–29?)
O/Bare bust of Tiberius r.; TIBEPIΩ
R/ΓΑΔΑ; Two cornucopia crossed; date [---]

1017	E, Field 5/20 Locus 342	2,45	13	↑	Spijkerman 1978, 12; RPC I, 4813; CHL, pl. 135, 11	*36

Marcus Aurelius (161–180)
AE
O/Draped and cuirassed bust or Marcus Aurelius, laureate, r. [---]
R/Tyche standing r. [---]

1018	E, Field 27	6,66	28	↑	CHL, pl. 138, 41?	*360L

1014

1015

1016

1017

1018

Marcus Aurelius and ***Lucius Verus*** (161–169)
AE
O/Draped bust of Lucius Verus, laureate; [ΑΥΤ ΚΑΙCΑΡ Λ ΑΥΡ ΟΥΗΡΟC]
R/Laureate bust of Heracles, draped in lion skin; [ΓΑΔΑΡΕΩΝ ΕΚC]

1019	E, Field 3	5,68	22	↑	Spijkerman 1978, p. 123, 37; SNG. ANS, *Palestine-South Arabia*, 1311; CHL, pl. 139, 53–56	277L

Septimius Severus (193–211)
AE
O/Bust of Septimius Severus r, laureate; ΑΥΤ Κ Λ CΕΠΤ CΕΒ.
R/Laureate bust of Heracles r., lion's skin knotted around neck; [ΓΑΔΑΡΕѠΝ ΒΞC]

1020	D, Field 2	10,96	29	↑	CHL, pl. 140, 71	*237L

***Gordianus* III** (238–244)
AE
O/Draped bust r. [ΑΥΤ Κ Μ ΑV ΑΝΤ ΓΟΡΔΙΑΝΟC]
R/Three Graces; ΠΟΜΠ; in exergue ΓΑΔΑΡ[ΕѠΝ]

1021	E, Field 33 Locus 320	7,8	22	↑	SNG. ANS, *Palestine-South Arabia*, 1331, 1341; CHL, pl.142, 100–101	*1067

AE
O/Draped bust of Gordianus r.; radiate [ΑΥΤΟΚ ΜΑΡ ΑΝΤѠ ΓΟΡΔΙΑΝ]
R/Galley r.; row of horsemen; navigator in stern and captain in prow; [ΠΟΜΠ ΓΑΔΑΡΕѠΝ]

1022	E, Field 11 Locus 301/302	15	26	↑	SNG. ANS, *Palestine-South Arabia*,1332–1338; CHL, pl. 142, 102–103	*344
1023	E, Field 11 Locus 301/302	10,9	25	↑	SNG. ANS, *Palestine-South Arabia*,1332–1338; CHL, pl. 142, 102–103	*345
1024	C, Field 6	8,94	29	↑	SNG. ANS, *Palestine-South Arabia*,1332–1338; CHL, pl. 142, 102–103	*179L

Mint of Hippos (Antiocheia ad Hippum)
Antoninus Pius (138–161)
AE
O/Laureate bust of Antoninus Pius r.; ΑΥΤΟΚΡ ΚΥΡ ΑΝΤѠΝΕΙΝΟC
R/Tyche standing facing, holding bridled horse and cornucopia; [ΑΝΤΙΟ ΤѠ ΠΡΙ ΤΗC ΙΕΡ Κ ΑCΥΛΟΥ]

1025	E, Field 4	9,03	23	↑	SNG. ANS, *Palestine-South Arabia*, 1136–1138; CHL, pl. 145, 11	*289L

1020

1021

1022

1023

1024

1025

Marcus Aurelius (161–180)
AE
O/Draped and cuirassed bust laureate of Marcus Aurelius; [AVT KAIC M AVP ANTΩN]
R/Tyche standing facing, holding bridled horse and cornucopia; [ANTIOX ΠP IΠ IEP ACYΛOY]

1026	D, Field 1 Locus 1191	7,9	24	↑	Spijkerman 1978, p. 172, 8; CHL, pl. 145, 12	*582
1027	D, Field 4 Locus 770	7,5	25	↑	same	*23

Lucius Verus (161–169)
AE
O/Laureate bust of Lucius Verus r. cuirassed; AVT KAIC Λ AVP OVHPO.
R/Tyche standing facing, looking l., holding bridled horse and cornucopia; [ANTIOX ΠP IΠ IЄP ACYΛOY]; exergue: OKC

1028	C, Field 18 Locus 608	9,85	25	↑	SNA, *Palestine – South Arabia*, 1139–1141; CHL, pl. 146, 17	*922

Antoninus Pius (138–161) or ***Marcus Aurelius*** (161–180) or ***Lucius Verus*** (161–169)
AE
O/Laureate bust r.; [---]
R/Tyche standing facing, holding bridled horse and cornucopia; [---]

1029	E, Field 34 Locus 320	6	24	↑	SNG. ANS, *Palestine-South Arabia*,1136–1141; CHL, pp. 175–176	610
1030	E, Field 11 Locus 303	4,15	22	↑	same	*271
1031	E, Field 11 Locus 301/302	2,8	21	↑	same	335

Elagabalus (218–222)
AE
O/Draped and cuirassed bust of Elagabalus, laureate, r.; AYT K M AY ANTωNEINOC
R/Tetrastyle temple within Zeus standing l.; [ANTIOX ΠP IΠ IЄP ACYΛ]

1032	C, Field 3 Locus 738	13,55	27	↑	Spijkerman 1978, n. 27; CHL, pl. 146, 30	*406

***Mint of Antiocheia ad Hippum*?**
Elagabalus (218–222)?
AE
O/Bust r.
R/Pegasus with head reverted?

1033	V, Field 2	7,54	21	↑	SNG. ANS, *Palestine-South Arabia*, 1148–1152? CHL, pl. 147, 32–34?	*140L

1026

1027

1028

1030

1032

1033

Mint of Nysa-Scythopolis
***Gordianus* III** (238–244)
AE
O/Laureate bust of Gordianus III r.; [AVT K M ANT ΓΟΡΔΙΑΝΟC CEB]
R/Dionysus, nude, advancing r., holding thyrsus and placing hand on head of small reclining figure; [NVC CK VIEP AC]

1034	E, Field 11 Locus 302	11,75	24	↑	SNG. ANS, *Palestine-South Arabia*, 1054–1055; CHL, pls. 151–152, 59–64	*261

Mint of Pella
Marcus Aurelius for ***Lucilla*** (177/178)
AE
O/Draped bust of Lucilla r.; [ΛΟΥΚΙΛΛΑ ΑΥΓΟΥCTA]
R/Tyche seated r., extending hand over figure river god swimming at her feet; in exergue [date]; [---]

1035	E, Field 3	7,93	24	↑	CHL, pl. 154, 4–5	*276L

Mint of Petra
Septimius Severus (193–211)
AE
O/Laureate bust of Septimius Severus r.; [ΚΛ CΕΠ CEOYHPOC]
R/Tyche seated l. within distyle temple with pediment; [ΑΔΡΙ ΠΕΤΡΑ ΜΗΤ]

1036	E, Field 11 Locus 301/302	6,7	27	↑	Spijkerman 1978, pl. 50, nn. 34–34a; CHL, pl. 157, 34	*325

Elagabalus (218–222)
AE
O/Laureate bust of Elagabalus with incomplete legend not preserved; [IMP C M AV ANTΩN]
R/Founder ploughing r. with bull and cow; in exergue: COLON [I]

1037	D, Field 1	4	17	↑	SNG. ANS, *Palestine-South Arabia*, 1373–1377; CHL, pl. 158, 53–55	*199L

Mint of Philippopolis
The Roman Period with Imperial Portraits
Pseudo-autonomous (164–165)
AE
O/Veiled bust of Demeter r. [ΦΙΛ ΚΟΙ C ΥΡΙ]
R/Cista mystica; [ETOYC SKC]

1038	C, Field 15 Locus 589	1,85	14	↑	SNG.ANS, *Palestine-South Arabia*, 1379	*1737

1034

1035

1036

1037

1038

***Philip* I** (244–249)

AE

O/Laureate and draped bust of Philip r.; [AYTOK K M AOYΛI ΦΙΛΙΠΠΟC CEB]

R/Roma seated l., holding eagle supporting two small figures and spear; [ΦΙΛΙΠΠΟ ΠΟΛΙΤΩΝ ΚΟΛΩΝΙΑC; SC]

1039	E, Field 11 Locus 301/302	12,75	28	↑	SNG. ANS, *Palestine-South Arabia*, 1403–1405; CHL, pl. 162, 3–4	*304

1039

Nabatean coin

Mint of Petra
***Aretas* IV** (9 BCE–40)
AE
O/Jugate busts of Aretas and Shuqailat r.
R/Nabataean inscriptions

1040	H, Field 2 Locus 10	2,6	19	↑	SNG. ANS, *Palestine-South Arabia*, 1438–1443; CHL, pl. 187, 66–69	*96

Roman provincial coins: Uncertain mint and/or uncertain authority and mint

Mint of Adraa? or ***Gadara?***
Pseudo-Autonomous (*post* 106)
AE
O/Helmeted head r.
R/Traces of iconography not identifiable

1041	G, Field 1 Locus 1024	0,9	12		SNG. ANS, *Palestine-South Arabia*, 1129 Spijkerman 1978, pl. 30, 64, pl. 57, 34	4

Mint of ***Neapolis*** or ***Sepphoris?***
Domitianus (81–96) or ***Traianus*** (98–117)
AE
O/Laureate head of Domitianus or Traianus
R/Palm-tree; [---]

1042	D, Field 2	6,19	22	↑	SNG. ANS, *Palestine-South Arabia*, 962–963; 1088–1091	*246L

Uncertain authority (second–second half of third century CE)
AE
O/Laureate head r.; [---]
R/Head r; [---]

1043	C, Field 7	5,4	18	↑	SNG. ANS, *Palestine-South Arabia*?	*184L

Uncertain mint
Domitianus (81–96)
AE
O/Laureate head r.
R/Corroded flan

1044	F, Field 25 Locus 552	2,6	18		SNG. ANS, *Palestine-South Arabia*?	1574

1040

1042

1043

Traianus (98–177)
AE
O/Laureate head r.
R/Corroded flan

1045	G, Field 8 Locus 1044	14,5	15		SNG. ANS, *Palestine-South Arabia*?	1282

Domitianus (81–96) or ***Traianus*** (98–117)
O/Laureate head of Domitianus or Traianus
R/Corroded flan

1046	E, Field 2 Locus 984	8,34	21		BMC. *Phoenicia*? RPC I? SNG. ANS, *Palestine-South Arabia*?	1385
1047	E, Field 11 Locus 303	7,35	24		same	660

AE
O/Laureate bust r.
R/Figure seated? l. Illegible inscriptions

1048	C, Field 3 Locus 738	9,8	23		SNG. ANS. *Palestine-South Arabia*? BMC. *Phoenicia*?	*404
1049	E, Field 33 Locus 320	8,9	20		same	1071
1050	E, Field 11 Locus 303	4,55	16		same	*284
1051	C, Field 27 Locus 639	4,4	16		same	965

Hadrianus
AE
O/Imperial bust r.; [---]
R/Cista mystica in middle torches [---]

1052	E, Field 8	3,75	18	↑	SNG. ANS, *Palestine-South Arabia*, pl. 26, 842?	*304L

Antoninus Pius (138–161)
AE
O/Laureate head of Antoninus Pius; [---]
R/Corroded flan

1053	B, Field 1 Locus 262	11,45	26		SNG. ANS, *Palestine-South Arabia*? BMC. *Phoenicia*?	*577

1048

1050

1052

1053

Septimius Severus (193–211)
AE
O/Laureate bust of Septimius Severus r.
R/Corroded flan

1054	F, Field 25 Locus 552	11,5	30	SNG. ANS, *Palestine-South Arabia*? BMC. *Phoenicia*?	896

Elagabalus (218–222)
AE
O/Laureate head of emperor r.; [---]
R/Traces not distinctly identifiable

1055	F, Field 25 Locus 351	19,35	30	SNG. ANS. *Palestine-South Arabia*? BMC. *Phoenicia*?	685
1056	E, Field 36 Locus 319	6,75	20	same	736
1057	E, Field 5 Locus 342	6,6	22	same	*576
1058	H, Field 3 Locus 7	5,5	20	same	*129
1059	F, Field 18/25 Locus 330	5,15	19	same	1552[6]

Elagabalus (218–222) or ***Gordianus*** III (238–244)?
AE
O/Draped bust of emperor r.; [---]
R/Traces not distinctly identifiable

1060	E, Field 11 Locus 301/302	5,65	24	SNG. ANS. *Palestine-South Arabia*? BMC. *Phoenicia*?	*332

6 R/ perhaps male figure standing l.

1057

1058

1060

Roman provincial coins or provincial city coins of Syria and Palestine or of the Decapolis and Provincia Arabia (Second – second half of third Century CE)

AE
O/Laureate bust of rulers or princes sometimes incompletely preserved; traces of Greek or Latin inscriptions
R/Traces of iconography not always identifiable

1061	D, Field 2 Locus 255	4,05	15		RPC; SNG. ANS, *Palestine-South Arabia*? CHL?	1603
1062	E, Field 42 Locus 355	2,43	25		RPC; SNG. ANS, *Palestine-South Arabia*? CHL? O/Bust r.	A7
1063	E, Field 36 Locus 376	6,81	23		same O/Head r.; R/Inscription and type garbled	A20
1064	C, Field 35 Locus 817	2,42	14		same O/Head r.; R/Corroded	A35
1065	E, Field 29 Locus 832	6,6	25	↑	same O/Imperial bust, laureate r.; R/Tetrastyle temple	A40.3
1066	E, Field 37	1,79	16		same O/Head (laureate?) r.; R/Corroded	A38.8
1067	C, Field 6	7,31	24	↑	same O/Imperial bust r.; [---]; R/Tetrastyle temple, within the female figure?; [---].See also Spijkerman 1978, pl. 8, 19.	*176L
1068[7]	E, Field 11 Locus 302	19,1	29	↑	same R/Apollo standing l. Altar in center, female figure r.	*297
1069	C, Field 3	7,38	28	↑	same O/Bust of imperator r.; R/Eagle r.	*170L
1070[8]	F, Field 31 Locus 1158	5,15	19		same O/Laureate head r.; R/Eagle?	1669
1071	D, Field 10 Locus 883	6,97	12		same O/Laureate head r.	A13
1072	G 100; Cardo	4,57	22	↑	O/Laureate head r. R/Head? or Two male figures, standing facing each other	*848L
1073	V, Field 3	4,75	21		O/Head, female, with crescent?	*164L
1074	D, Field 1	12,02	28	↑	R/Figure, standing	205L
1075	F, Field 7	5,94	21		Corroded	*552L
1076	E, Field 30 Locus 260	12,65	26	↓	same	*583
1077	F, Field 4	3,49	18	↓	same	364L
1078	V, Field 2 Locus 277	4,9	18		R/Figure, male, standing l.	*494

7 This may be an Akko Ptolemais issue, with on the obverse Philip I (cf. CHL, pl. 15, 249–250) and on the reverse Otacilia Severa (?) standing right, clasping hands with Philip I (?) in military dress, standing left, holding scepter; between them, caduceus and lighted altar (cf. CHL, pl. 17, 272, but in this case the coin is of Otacilia Severa).

8 The eagle spreading wings on the reverse could refer to a coin of Antioch, perhaps of Philip I.

1067

1068

1069

1072

1073

1075

1076

1078

1079	E, Field 11 Locus 303	11,75	24	↑	O/Laureate head r.	*268
1080	F, Field 31	1,8	11	↑	O/Laureate head r.; R/Female figure standing	*1637
1081	C, Field 15 Locus 589	1,15	15	↑	Corroded	*1749
1082	C, Field 15 Locus 897	5,5	24		O/Laureate bust r.	862
1083	F, Field 20 Locus 299	7,65	21		O/Bust r. (radiate?)	785
1084	E, Field 11 Locus 303	8,76	24		O/Head r.	679
1085	E, Field 11	7,57	26		Corroded; with hole	*325L
1086	E, Field 22a Locus 308	3,45	21		Corroded	657
1087	C, Field 32 Locus 669	6,8	23		Corroded	997
1088	C, Field 30 Locus 688	5,75	22		Corroded	*1000
1089	V, Field 3 Locus 677	3,55	22		same	990
1090	F, Field 23 Locus 509	3,2	17		same	*798
1091	C, Field 15 Locus 749	3,55	16		same	832
1092	D, Field 2 Locus 254	2,95	16		same; R/Galley r.?	856
1093	D, Field 4 Locus 770	12,45	27	↓	Corroded	*22
1094	E, Field 11 Locus 301/302	3,6	18		O/Head r.; R/Corroded	*337
1095	E, Field 11 Locus 301/302	1,25	14		Corroded	*339
1096	F, Field 30 Locus 1104	2,7	14	↑	O/Head r.; R/Corroded	*1567
1097	V, Field 2	7,11	22		Corroded	*142L
1098	C, Field 30 Locus 270	10,9	22		O/Corroded; R/Laurel wreath?	978
1099	D, Field 2 Locus 255	6,64	19		O/Corroded; R/Laurel wreath?	1778
1100	C, Field 18 Locus 595	2,7	16		R/Double circle dots (or laurel crown?) around the flan	910
1101	F, Field 1	1,31	12		O/ and R/dot within circle	404L
1102	V, Field 2 Locus 279	7,6	23		R/Greek legend in three lines? [-]Π[-]	638

1079

1080

1081

1085

1088

1090

1093

1094

1095

1096

1097

1103	E, Field 11 Locus 303	13,4	27	↑	O/Bust or head r.; R/Corroded	*252
1104	D, Field 2	12,38	27		same	*242L
1105	E, Field 11 Locus 303	11,45	29		O/Head r.; R/Corroded	*276
1106	E, Field 11 Locus 301/302	9,8	2,5		same	*324
1107	D, Field 1	9,55	25		same	202L
1108	D, Field 1	9,16	25		same	213L
1109	F, Field 1	8,19	26		same	*401L
1110	H, Field 3 Locus 78	7,9	23		same	*133
1111	E, Field 11 Locus 303	7,7	21		same	*270
1112	E, Field 5 Locus 342	6,8	24		same	*570
1113	V, Field 3	6,73	23		O/Head r.; R/Corroded	*157L
1114	D, Field 1	6,54	21		same	204L
1115	E, Field 11 Locus 302	6,25	25		same	*293
1116	D, Field 1	6,25	22	↓	same	846L
1117	D, Field 1	6,01	24		same	*234L
1118	E, Field 4	6,01	19		same	292L
1119	V, Field 2	5,68	21		same	*138L
1120	D, Field 1	5,61	23		same	847L
1121	V, Field 2 Locus 258	5,6	22		same	601
1122	E, Field 11 Locus 301/302	5,55	20		same	*333
1123	V, Field 3	5,25	23	↑	same	*155L
1124	E, Field 11 Locus 303	4,7	20		Corroded	*274
1125	V, Field 2	4,39	18	↑	O/Head r.	*141L[9]
1126	C, Field 6	4,38	19		same	177L
1127	D, Field 1	4,32	19		same	207L
1128	D, Field 1	4,16	17		same	214L
1129	H, Field 3 Locus 21	3,9	18	↑	same	*135
1130	E, Field 11 Locus 301/302	2,65	19		same	*334
1131	V, Field 2 Locus 276	2,6	17		same	*514

9 Wreath with inscription? See SNG. ANS, *Palestine-South Arabia*, pl. 8, 296–297: Caesarea mint under Domitian?

1103

1104

1105

1106

1109

1110

1111

1112

1113

1115

1117

1119

1122

1123

1124

1125

1129

1130

1131

1132	E, Field 4	2,28	18	↓	O/Head r.	*286L
1133	E, Field 36 Locus 321	2	13		same	733
1134	F, Field 31 Locus 282	1,9	13		same	677
1135	E, Field 34 Locus 257	1,2	19		same	737
1136	V, Field 3 Locus 270	0,6	22		same	*507
1137	D, Field 2	1,65	14	↑	O/Bust or head r.; R/Δ in field r.?	*1613

AE
O/Laureate bust of rulers or princes sometimes incompletely preserved; traces of Greek or Latin inscriptions
R/Traces of temple not distinctly identifiable

1138	E, Field 11 Locus 301/302	5,25	24	↓	SNG. ANS, *Palestine-South Arabia*? BMC, *Phoenicia*? R/Temple, distyle with central arch?	*327
1139	E, Field 11 Locus 303	15,35	24	↑	SNG. ANS, *Palestine-South Arabia*? BMC, *Phoenicia*? R/Temple, distyle?	*253
1140	E, Field 20 Locus 327	9,15	23	↑	SNG. ANS, *Palestine-South Arabia*? BMC, *Phoenicia*? O/Head r-; R/Temple, distyle?	*433
1141	F, Field 18 Locus 325	8,23	24	↑	SNG. ANS, *Palestine-South Arabia*? BMC, *Phoenicia*? O/Head r.; R/Temple, tetrastyle within figure, standing?	*349
1142	D, Field 1	6,76	22	↑	SNG. ANS, *Palestine-South Arabia*? BMC, *Phoenicia*? O/Head r.; R/Temple, tetrastyle?	*212L
1143	D, Field 1	5,95	23	↓	BMC, *Phoenicia*, pl. 32, 12, 14–15? O/Head r.; R/Temple, tetrastyle?	*201L
1144	C, Field 6	3,21	15	↑	SNG. ANS, *Palestine-South Arabia*? BMC, *Phoenicia*? R/Temple?	*178L

AE O/ and R/Traces of inscriptions, imperial head and other images, but corroded by rust

1145	E, Field 19 Locus 534	15,6	25		SNG. ANS, *Palestine-South Arabia*? BMC, *Phoenicia*? Corroded	813
1146	E, Field 2 Locus 1003	14,2	25		same	1384
1147	E, Field 11 Locus 302	12,75	25		same	*292
1148	B, Field 5	12,5	24		same	121L
1149	C, Field 33 Locus 677	11,6	27		same	1062
1150	D, Field 2 Locus 255	11,5	23		same	1598
1151	F, Field 13 Locus 1012	11,2	25		same	1198
1152	E 4	10,7	25		same	290L

1132

1136

1137

1138

1139

1140

1141

1142

1143

1144

1147

1153	D, Field 6 Locus 865	10,24	23		SNG. ANS, *Palestine-South Arabia*? BMC, *Phoenicia*? Corroded	A37.4
1154	C, Field 6 Locus 589	9,7	23		same	1716
1155	C, Field 6 Locus 589	9,7	23		same	1715[10]
1156	B, Field 1	9,57	25		same	107L
1157	F, Field 32 Locus 1152	9,15	25		same	1612
1158	E, Field 11 Locus 303	8,65	25		same	*295
1159	D, Field 2 Locus 255	8,55	20		same	*1599
1160	C, Field 16 Locus 572	8,2	24		same	1083
1161	H, Field 1 Locus 86	7,7	23		same	*144
1162	C, Field 1	7,61	29		same	*168L
1163	E, Field 5 Locus 958	7,35	21		same	1193
1164	E, Field 4	7,22	27		same	291L
1165	E, Field 2 Locus 981	7,2	22		same	*38
1166	G, Field 9 Locus 1050	7,1	20		same	1278
1167	B, Field 6 Locus 1212	6,65	25		same	*436
1168	E, Field 33 Locus 320	6,55	21		same	1070
1169	E, Field 2 Locus 979	6,45	22		same	*37
1170	F, Field 11 Locus 993	6,4	22		same	1231
1171	G, Field 9 Locus 1047	5,95	21		same	1249
1172	G, Field 9 Locus 1051	5,9	22		same	1271
1173	D, Field 1	5,84	24		same	251L
1174	E, Field 11 Locus 303	5,8	17		same	*269
1175	D, Field 1	5,71	20	↑	same	200L
1176	F, Field 20 Locus 299	5,7	22		same	786

10 Perhaps Tiberias as SNG.ANS, *Palestine South Arabia* n. 1114?

1158

1159

1161

1162

1165

1167

1169

1174

1177	G, Field 9 Locus 1048	5,65	22		SNG. ANS, *Palestine-South Arabia*? BMC, *Phoenicia*? Corroded	1264
1178	V, Field 1	5,6	21		same	129L
1179	D, Field 1	5,51	20		same	208L
1180	H, Field 2 Locus 13	5,4	20		same	*93
1181	C, Field 4	5,39	16		same	172L
1182	D, Field 2	5,01	21		same	*241L
1183	C, Field 5	4,77	16		same, cut flan	174L
1184	D, Field 2	4,72	22		same	*240L
1185	D, Field 2 Locus 255	4,5	20		same	1600
1186	H, Field 2 Locus 1121	4,45	19	↑	same	*1586
1187	E, Field 3	4,39	21		same	*278L
1188	H, Field 1 Locus 1	4,3	17		same	*114
1189	D, Field 3	4,16	22		same	239/1L
1190	E, Field 4	4,12	23		same	296L
1191	D, Field 3	4,1	24		same	239L
1192	F, Field 13 Locus 962	4,1	19		same	1194
1193	D, Field 2	3,8	23		same	261L
1194	H, Field 1 Locus 39	3,8	22		same, cut flan	*197
1195	E, Field 11 Locus 301/302	3,8	18		same	*328
1196	V, Field 3	3,78	18		same	156L
1197	H, Field 2 Locus 4	3,7	18		same	*97
1198	C, Field 6 Locus 589	3,55	15		same	1717
1199	E, Field 5 Locus 342	3,25	23		same	*41
1200	F, Field 2, Trench 1	3,05	23		same, cut flan	710L
1201	E, Field 20 Locus 327	3	15		same	817
1202	B, Field 1 Locus 262	2,85	17		same	*579
1203	E, Field 12 Locus 261	2,85	15		same	*39
1204	C, Field 13 Locus 593	2,69	15		same	*914

1180

1182

1184

1186

1187

1188

1194

1195

1197

1199

1202

1203

1204

1205	Without context	2,59	18	SNG. ANS, *Palestine-South Arabia*? BMC, *Phoenicia*? Corroded	*166L
1206	C, Field 6	2,38	21	same	*181L
1207	C, Field 18 Locus 608	2,35	15	same	920
1208	D, Field 1 Locus 1206	2,15	21	same	*5
1209	C, Field 15 Locus 589	2,10	16	same	1747
1210	H, Field 1 Locus 94	1,6	19	same	*153

1205

1206

1208

1210

Roman provincial coins: Countermarks

Countermark types

Heracles (Melqart), bust r.
Tyre
Elagabalus (218–222)

1211	E, Field 11 Locus 301/302	9,05	28	↑	BMC. *Phoenicia*, pl. 33, 2; Howgego 1985, 15	*320
1212	Cardo	8,42	25	↑	same	*723L

Caracalla (198–217) – ***Elagabalus*** (218–222)

1213	G, Field 8 Locus 942	6,9	25		Overstruck on imperial head (Hadrianus?) Howgego 1985, 15	*1281

Male head with uncertain inscription or naming emperors

1214	E, Field 11 Locus 303	4,9	22		Howgego 1985, 37–38	*281

Male head facing r.: Oval, circular punches
Mints of provincial cities of Palestine and South Arabia?

1215	H, Field 2 Locus 10	7,6	23		Howgego 1985, 65–76; 104–105	*77
1216	E, Field 4	5,68	21		Howgego 1985, 100–101, 105	*293L
1217	H, Field 2 Locus 10	11,8	26		Howgego 1985, 121–128	*95
1218	E, Field 4 Locus 451	11,25	27		same	*42
1219	V, Field 3	11,14	26	↑	same	*158L
1220	B, Field 1	7,8	18		same	*109L
1221	D, Field 2	7,02	26		same	260L
1222	B, Field 5	6,75	22		same	*116L
1223	C, Field 3 Locus 738	6,5	22		same	*405
1224	D, Field 2	6,27	26		same	*259L
1225	V, Field 3	4,76	21		same	*160L
1226	V, Field 3 Locus 713	7,5	26		Howgego 1985, 145 e ss	*623
1227	H, Field 2 Locus 12	2,25	16		same	*146

1211

1212

1213

1214

1215

1216

1217

1218

1219

1220

1222

1223

1224

1225

1226

1227

Unclear oval and circular punches

Mints of provincial cities of Palestine and South Arabia?

1228	C, Field 22 Locus 607	6,7	22	Howgego 1985, p. 145 e ss.; Oval with a head?	*923
1229	E, Field 35 Locus 320	11,3	24	same; oval with a little head	*1076
1230	C, Field 31 Locus 698	7,85	22	same; oval with lituus? Howgego 1985, p. 185, 5?	* 1019
1231	F, Field 11	7,3	22	same; oval with imperial head	*1122
1232	C, Field 24 Locus 655	7,1	23	same; oval with head	*956
1233	E, Field 37	6,69	19	same; countermark in center of flan: oval with head	A38.7
1234	H, Field 2 Locus 1121	6,65	21	same; oval with imperial head	*1594
1235	G/I	5,90	24	same; oval with imperial head?	*1758
1236	C, Field 15 Locus 589	5,85	22	same; oval with imperial head?	*1746

1228

1229

1230

1231

1232

1234

1235

1236

Roman provincial hoard (US 8)

Mint of Tyre
City coinage
DATED COINS
AE (c. 55/54 BCE – 86/87)
O/Head of Melqart r., laureate
R/Within an oak-wreath, club downwards; on r. Phoenician inscription

1237	H, Field 3 Locus 8	5,85	20		BMC. *Phoenicia*, p. 257, 268–274, pl. 31, 10	*58

Mint of Tiberias
Claudius (41–54)
AE
O/ΚΛΑΥΔΙΟΥ ΚΑΙCΑΡΟC palm branch
R/ΤΙΒΕ ΡΙΑC within wreath

1238	H, Field 3 Locus 8	6,9	19	↑	SNG. ANS, *Palestine-South Arabia*, 1097; CHL, pl. 221, 79–80, pl. 221, 81–82 for weight	*91

Traianus (98–117)
AE (99/100)
O/Laureate head of Traianus r. [ΑΥΤ ΚΑΙ ΝΕΡ ΤΡΑΙΑΝΟC CΕΒ ΓΕΡ]
R/Hygieia seated r. in rock below which water in flowing

1239	H, Field 3 Locus 8	8,15	23	↑	CHL, pl. 65,2	*63

AE (108/109)
O/Laureate bust of Traianus r. [ΑΥΤ ΚΑΙC ΝΕΡ ΤΡΑΙΑΝΟC CΕΒ ΓΕΡΜ]
R/Hygieia, wearing long chiton and peplos, seated r. on rock. [ΕΤ $\overline{\text{ΑΜ}}$]

1240	H, Field 3 Locus 8	10,25	24	↑	BMC. *Palestine*, p. 6, n. 10, SNG. ANS, *Palestine-South Arabia*, 1101; CHL, pl. 65, 5 and pl. 66, 6	*54

Elagabalus (218–222)
AE (218)
O/Draped bust of Elagabalus, laureate, r.; [---]
R/Asklepios l. and Hygieia r. [ΤΙΒΕ?]

1241	H, Field 3 Locus 8	13,45	28	↑	CHL, pl. 66, 19	*61

1237

1238

1239

1240

1241

Mint of Abila
Marcus Aurelius* and *Lucius Verus (161–169)
AE
O/Draped bust laureate of Lucius Verus; [---AYP OYHPOC]
R/Arch of tetrastyle temple with Tyche standing r.; exergue [CE ABIΛHNΩN]

1242	H, Field 3 Locus 8	11	28	↑	Spijkerman 1978, 1; CHL, pl. 124, 12	*51

Mint of Gadara
Marcus Aurelius and ***Lucius Verus*** (161–169)
AE
O/Draped bust laureate of Lucius Verus; [AYT KAICAP Λ AYP OYHPOC]
R/Laureate bust of Heracles, draped in lion skin; [ΓAΔAPEΩN EKC]

1243	H, Field 3 Locus 8	7,75	24	↑	Spijkerman 1978, p. 123, 37; SNG. ANS, *Palestine-South Arabia*, 1311; CHL, pl. 139, 53–56	*52

Mint of Hippos (Antiocheia ad Hippum)
Elagabalus (218–222)
AE
O/Draped bust of Elagabalus, laureate r.; [---]
R/Pegasus with spread wings standing l. with head reverted; [ANTIOX P ΙΠ IЄP ACYΛ]

1244	H, Field 3 Locus 8	12,1	25	↑	SNG. ANS, *Palestine-South Arabia*, 1148–1152; CHL, pl. 147, 33–34	*127

Mint of Nysa-Scythopolis
Commodus (180–192)
AE (182–183)
O/Laureate head of Commodus r.; [AVT KOMOΔ ANTΩNINOY]
R/Dionysus nude, standing l. holding thyrsus; [NYC CK IEP ACYϛMC]

1245	H, Field 3 Locus 8	7,05	24	↑	CHL, pl. 149, 26	*56

Septimius Severus (193–211) for ***Julia Domna***
AE (206/207)
O/Draped bust of Julia Domna r.; [IOYΛA ΔOMNAC]
R/Demeter on the r., and Kore-Persephone on the l. standing facing each other; NYC CKVΘ IEP ACY

1246	H, Field 3 Locus 8	8,05	25	↑	Barkay 2003, pp. 211–212,43, 43a; CHL, pl.149, 30 and pl. 150, 31	*55

1242

1243

1244

1245

1246

Elagabalus (218–222)
AE (218–219)
O/Laureate and draped bust of Elagabalus r.; [AVT K M AY ANTΩNINOY]
R/Tyche standing, holding scepter and cornucopia; resting foot on half figure of river god swimming; exergue [BΠC]

1247	H, Field 3 Locus 8	9,6	23	↑	Barkay 2003, p. 220, 69; CHL, pl. 151, 46–47	*57

AE (220/221)
O/Laureate and draped bust of Elagabalus r.; [AVT K MA AY ANTΩNINOC CE]
R/Greek legend in four lines within wreath; [NYKA/CKVΘ/OπOΛ/IC]

1248	H, Field 3 Locus 8	8,35	23	↙	Barkay 2003, pp. 220–221, 76; CHL, pl. 151, 53	*126

Mint of Petra
Elagabalus (218–222)
AE
O/Laureate bust of Elagabalus with incompletely legend not preserved; [IMP C M AV ANTΩN]
R/Founder ploughing r. with bull and cow; in exergue: COLON [I]

1249	H, Field 3 Locus 8	4,65	19	↑	SNG. ANS, *Palestine-South Arabia*, 1373–1377; CHL, pl. 158, 53–55	*65

Uncertain Mint
Elagabalus (218–222)
AE
O/Laureate head of emperor r.; [---]
R/Traces not distinctly identifiable

1250	H, Field 3 Locus 8	11,15	24		same	*50
1251	H, Field 3 Locus 8	8,85	27		same	*59

1247

1248

1249

1250

1251

Roman provincial coins or provincial city coins of Syria and Palestine or of the Decapolis and Provincia Arabia (Second – second half of Third Century CE)

AE

O/Laureate bust of rulers or princes sometimes incompletely preserved; traces of Greek or Latin inscriptions

R/Traces of iconography not always identifiable

1252	H, Field 3 Locus 8	11,15	24		Corroded	*49
1253	H, Field 3 Locus 8	10,75	25		same	*53

AE O/ and R/Traces of inscriptions, imperial head and other images, but corroded by rust

1254	H, Field 3 Locus 8	5,9	23		same	*66
1255	H, Field 3 Locus 8	4,25	17		same	*60

Countermark types

Male head facing r.: oval, circular punches

Mints of Provincial Cities of Palestine and South Arabia?

1256	H, Field 3 Locus 8	8,55	33	↑	Howgego 1985, 111iv–114i	*128
1257	H, Field 3 Locus 8	9,18	26		same	*64

1252

1253

1254

1255

1256

1257

Roman imperial coins

Mint of Roma
Titus (79–81)
AR. Denarius (79, after July)
O/Head of Titus, laureate, r.; IMP TITVS CAES VESPASIAN AVG P M
R/Capricorn l., below globe; TR P VIIII IMP XIIII COS VII P P

1259	C, Field 29 Locus 667	2,7	18	↓	RIC II, 13	*988

Titus for ***Domitianus***
AR. Denarius (80)
O/Head of Domitianus, laureate, r.; CAESAR DIVI DOMITIANVS COS VII
R/Altar, garlanded and lighted; PRINCEPS IVVENTVTIS

1260	H, Field 3 Locus 7	3,05	18	↑	RIC II, 50	*828

Traianus (98–117)
AE, quadrans
O/Bust of Hercules, r., with lion's skin; IMP CAES TRAIAN AVG GERM
R/Boar walking r.; exergue; SC

1261	E, Field 7 Locus 815	3,1	15	↓	RIC II, 702	*30
1262	H, Field 2 Locus 10	3,1	16	↓	same	*107
1263	G, Field 9 Locus 1051	2,50	14	↓	same	*1251
1264	C, Field 16 Locus 589	2,05	14	↑	same	*1736
1265	E, Field 11 Locus 302	1,25	15	↓	same	*287

Hadrianus (117–138)
AR. Denarius (118)
O/Laureate head r., with drapery on l. shoulder; IMP CAESAR TRAIAN HADRIANVS AVG
R/Pax standing l.; PM TR P COS II; in exergue: PAX

1266	H, Field 3 Locus 7	3,2	19	↑	RIC II, 44(a)	*137

AR. Denarius (119–122)
O/Laureate head r; IMP CAESAR TRAIAN HADRIANVS AVG
R/Pax seated l. holding Victory and branch; P M TR P COS III

1267	H, Field 2 Locus 10	3,1	19	↓	RIC II, 95 (a)	*98

1259

1260

1261

1262

1263

1264

1265

1266

1267

Antoninus Pius for ***Marcus Aurelius***
AR. Denarius (154–155)
O/Head r. AVRELIVS CAESAR AVG PII FIL
R/Minerva helmeted, standing l. TR POT VIIII COS II

1268	H, Field 1	3,05	20	↑	RIC III, 463 (a)		*201

Volusianus (251–253)
AE. Sestertius
O/Draped bust, laureate, of Gordianus; IMP [---] C VIB [---]
R/Pax standing, holding branch and transverse sceptre; [PAX AVGVSTI] SC

1269	E, Field 10	15,52	27	↑	RIC IV.3, 256 (a)		*307L

Gallienus and ***Valerianus*** (253–260)
Asia Mint
AR. Antoninianus (255–257)
O/Radiate and draped bust of Gallienus r.; IMP C P LIC GALLIENVS P F AVG
R/Emperor standing r. receiving Victory on glob from Victory standing l.; VICTORIA AVG

1270	F, Field 25 Locus 351	3,65	20	↑	RIC V.1, 450	*	*438

Gallienus (260–268)
Asia Mint
AR. Antoninianus
O/Radiate and draped bust of Gallienus, r.; GALLIENVS AVG
R/Jupiter standing, holding scepter and thunderbolt; IOVI STATORI

1271	D, Field 1	3,65	20	↓	RIC V.1, 644	-/*	*253L

Indeterminate mint
AR. Antoninianus
O/Radiate and draped bust of Gallienus r.; [---] LIC [--]
R/Unreadable

1272	E, Field 11 Locus 301/302	1,5	19		RIC V.1?		*310

Gallienus (and ***Valerianus)*** for ***Salonina***
Asia Mint
AR. Antoninianus (255–258)
O/Diademed, draped bust r. without crescent; [CORN SALONINA AVG]
R/Emperor and empress clasping hands; CONCORDIA AVGG

1273	C, Field 22 Locus 614	3	20	↑	RIC V.1, p. 114, n. 63		*947

1268

1269

1270

1271

1272

1273

Aurelianus (270–275)
Mint of Antiochia
AR. Antoninianus
O/Radiate and draped bust of emperor r; [IMP C AVRE] LIANVS [AVG]
R/Female standing r. presenting wreath to emperor standing l holding spear; RESTITVT ORBIS

1274	D, Field 1	2,1	19	↓	RIC V.1, 347		*231L

AR. Antoninianus
O/Radiate and draped bust of emperor r; [IMP C AVRE] LIANVS [AVG]
R/Female standing r. presenting wreath to emperor standing l holding spear; RESTITVT ORBIS

1275	C, Field 15 ~~14~~ Locus 897	2,35	22	↑	RIC V.1, 386	?	*863

Aurelianus for ***Severina*** (274–275)
Mint of Roma
AR. Antoninianus
O/Diademed bust of Severina on crescent r.; SEVERINA AVG
R/Concordia standing l., holding two ensigns; CONCORDIAE MILITVM

1276	C, Field 3	2,51	22	↑	RIC V.1, 4	xx?/-	*171L

Probus (276–282)
Mint of Antiochia
AR. Antoninianus
O/Radiate, cuirassed and draped bust r.; IMP C M AVR PROBVS P F AVG
R/Female standing r. presenting wreath to emperor standing l., holding globe and spear; RESTITVTOR ORBIS

1277	H, Field 3 Locus 11	3,15	21	↓	RIC, V.2, 925	XXI/S	*76

Indeterminate authority and mint (second half of third century)
AR. Antoninianus
O/Radiate and cuirassed bust of emperor; [---]
R/Emperor standing r. holding sceptre, receiving Victory from Jupiter l. [*concordia militum* type?]

1278	C, Field 33 Locus 714	1,76	20	↓	RIC V.1–2?		1054

AR. Antoninianus
O/Radiate, draped and cuirassed bust r.; [---]
R/Unreadable

1279	E, Field 11 Locus 301/302	1,25	21		RIC V.1–2?		*342

1274

1275

1276

1277

1279

Diocletianus (before the reform 294)
Mint of Antiochia
MI. Antoninianus (293–295)
O/Radiate and draped head of Diocletianus; IMP C C VAL DIOCLETIANVS P F AVG
R/Emperor standing l. receiving Victory on globe from Jupiter l.; CONCORDIA MILITVM

1280	B, Field 5	2,45	21	↓	RIC V.2, 322	XXI•/B	*117L

Maximianus Herculius (before the reform 294)
Mint of Antiochia
MI. Antoninianus (ca. 293)
O/Radiate head of Maximianus Herculius; IMP C MA MAXIMIANVS P F A
R/Emperor standing r. holding sceptre and receiving Victory on globe from Jupiter l.; CONCORDIA MILITVM

1281	E, Field 8	2,98	20	↓	RIC V.2, 621	XXI/EΔ	*303L

MI. Antoninianus (ca. 285–295)
O/Radiate head of Maximianus Herculius; IMP C MA MAXIMIANVS P F A
R/Jupiter and Hercules standing face to face; IOV ET HERCV CONSER AVGG CONCORDIA MILITVM

1282	A, Field 5 Locus 269	2,6	20	↓	RIC V.2, 622	XXI/Γ	*437

Indeterminate mint
MI. Antoninianus
O/Radiate head of Maximianus Herculius; [---] MAXIMIANVS P F A
R/Emperor standing r. holding sceptre and receiving Victory on globe from Jupiter l.; CONCORDIA MILITVM

1283	E, Field 11 Locus 301/302	2,15	20	↓	RIC V.2?	?/-	*348

Diocletianus (after reform 294)
Mint of Antiochia
AE. Follis (296)
O/Radiate and draped bust of Diocletianus r.; IMP C C VAL DIOCLETIANVS P F AVG
R/Emperor standing r. in military dress, receiving small Victory on globe from Jupiter standing l.; CONCORDIA MILITVM

1284	E, Field 3	2,28	21	↓	RIC VI, 60(a)	ANT/B*	*283L

Indeterminate mint
AE. Radiate fraction
O/Radiate and draped bust of Diocletianus r.; [---] DIOCLETIANVS P F AVG
R/Emperor standing r. in military dress, receiving small Victory on globe from Jupiter standing l.; CONCORDIA MILITVM

1285	C, Field 7	2,89	19	↑	RIC VI?	-/B or Q?*	*185L

1280

1281

1282

1283

1284

1285

Maximianus Herculius (after the reform 294)
Mint of Alexandria
AE. Laureate fraction (305–306)
O/Laureate and draped bust of Maximianus r.; IMP C MAXIMIANVS P F AVG
R/Prince standing r. in military dress, receiving small Victory on globe from Jupiter standing l. leaning scepter; COMCORDIA MILITVM

1286	E, Field 3	2,22	18	↓	RIC VI, 59 (b) but laureate bust	ALE/Δ?	*282L

***Costantius* I**
Mint of Alexandria
AE. Radiate fraction (305–306)
O/Radiate and draped bust of Constantius r.; IMP C CONSTAN TIVS P F AVG
R/Emperor standing r. in military dress, receiving small Victory on globe from Jupiter standing l.; CONCORDIA MILITVM

1287	M, Field 2	2,2	21	↓	RIC VI, 59 (a)	ALE/Δ	*759

***Licinius* I**
Mint of Siscia
AE. Follis (320)
O/Helmeted and cuirassed bust r.; IMP LI CINIVS AVG
R/VIRTVS EXERCIT Standard inscribed VOT/XX; captive standing on ground on either side

1288	E, Field 3	1,95	18	↑	RIC VII, 128	BSISb/S/FHL	*281L

Mint of Heraclea
AE. Follis (318–320)
O/Bust with spear pointed forward; IMP LICI NIVS AVG
R/Camp gate with three turrets; PROVIDENTIAE AVGG

1289	D, Field 1	1,93	19	↑	RIC VII, 39 or 48	SMHB/-	*230L

Mint of Antiochia
AE. Follis (321–323)
O/Radiate, draped and cuirassed bust r.; IMP C VAL LICIN LICINIVS P F AVG
R/Jupiter standing l. holding Victory on globe; on ground to l. eagle with wreath; to r. captive; IOVI CONSERVATORI

1290	C, Field 6	2,21	18	↑	RIC VII, 35	SMNT/XIIΓ	*180L

***Constantinus* I**
Mint of Trier
AE. Follis (316)
O/Laureate and cuirassed head r.; CONSTANTINVS P F AVG
R/Sol standing l.; SOLI INVICTO COMITI

1291	C, Field 5	3,11	19	↑	RIC VII, 103, 105	ATR/T/F	*173L

1286

1287

1288

1289

1290

1291

AE. Follis (319)
O/Helmeted bust, laureate and cuirassed l.; IMP CONSTANTINVS MAX AVG
R/Two Victories standing, facing one another, together holding shield inscribed VOT/PR VICTORIAE LAETAE PRINC PERP

1292	G 101	2,05	18	↓	RIC VII, 214	STR/*	*774L

Mint of Roma
AE. Follis (317–318)
O/Laureate head, draped and cuirassed; IMP CONSTANTINVS P F AVG
R/Sol standing l.; SOLI INVICTO COMITI

1293	H, Field 2 Locus 4	2,2	21	↓	RIC VII, 97	RT/8	*70

Mint of Antiochia
AE. Follis (325–326)
O/Laureate head r.; CONSTANTINVS AVG
R/Camp gate, two turrets; PROVIDENTIAE AVGG

1294	E, Field 3	1,57	18	↑	RIC VII, 63	SMANT(Z)/-/-	*280L

Constantinus I for ***Crispus***
Arelate
AE. Follis (316–317)
O/Laureate head r.; CRISPVS [---]
R/Prince helmeted in military dress; PRINCIPIA IVVENTVTIS

1295	C, Field 7	2,54	18	↑	RIC VII, 106	ARL?/?	*182L

Indeterminate mint
AE. Follis (316–326)
O/Laureate and cuirassed bust r. [---] RISPVS NOB
R/Prince helmeted in military dress; PRINCIPIA IVVENTVTIS

1296	F, Field 27	2,58	18	↓	RIC VII?	?/B	*1772

Constantinus I for ***Constantius II***
Mint of Antiochia
AE. Follis (330–333, 335)
O/Laureate head, cuirassed r.; [FL I] VL CONSTANTIVS NOB C
R/Two soldiers standing, facing one another; between them, two standards; GLORIA EXERCITVS

1297	V, Field 2 Locus 278	1,3	17	↑	RIC VII, 88	SMANT(?)/-/-	*483

1292

1293

1294

1295

1296

1297

Constantinus I for ***Constantinus II***
Mint of Cyzicus
AE. Follis (331–333–334)
O/Laureate head, draped and cuirassed r.; CONSTANTINVS IVN NOB C
R/Two soldiers standing, facing one another; between them, two standards; GLORIA EXERCITVS

1298	F, Field 30 Locus 1102	1,75	17	↑	RIC VII, 80	SMKA(?)/-/-	*1570

Constantinus I
Indeterminate mint
MI. Follis (313–318)
O/Radiate, draped and cuirassed bust r.; [---]NVS PF AVG
R/Sol radiate l. Type: *soli invicto comiti*

1299	V, Field 3	1,05	17	↓	RIC VII?	?	*154L

Constantinus I or ***Licinius I***
Indeterminate mint
MI. Follis (313–318)
O/Radiate, draped and cuirassed bust r.; [---]
R/Sol radiate l. Type: *soli invicto comiti* or *iovi conservatori*

1300	D, Field 1	2,2	18	↓	RIC VII?	?	222L
1301	G, Field 1 Locus 268	2,15	18	↓	RIC VII?	?	*534
1302	C, Field 7	2,14	19	↑	RIC VII?	?	183L

Constantinus I and ***family*** for ***Urbs Roma***
Indeterminate mint
AE. Follis (330–337)
O/Bust, draped: VRBS ROMA
R/Wolf and Twins l.; above, two stars

1303	V, Field 3 Locus 677	1,3	17	↓	as LRBC 65	?	992

Constantinus I and ***family***
Indeterminate mint
AE. Follis (330–335)
O/Bust cuirassed; [---]
R/Two soldiers standing l.; each holding spear and leaning on shield; between them, two standards; [---]
Type: *gloria exercitus* two standards

1304	M, Field 22	1,65	18	↓	as LRBC 60	?	760

1298

1299

1301

AE. Follis (335–340, 347)
O/Bust cuirassed; [---]
R/Two soldiers standing l.; each holding spear and leaning on shield; between them, one standard; [---]
Type: *gloria exercitus* one standard

1305	H, Field 1 Locus 1	0,75	13	↑	as LRBC 1028	?	*67
1306	E, Field 3	0,73	14	↓	same	?	274L
1307	E, Field 3	0,63	15	↓	same	?	*275L

***Constantius* II**
Mint of Constantinopolis
AE3 (355–361)
O/Diademed, draped and cuirassed bust r.; D N CONSTANTIVS P F AVG
R/Falling horseman; [FEL TEMP REPARATIO]

1308	F, Field 33 Locus 1173	1,95	16	↓	as RIC VIII, 118 ss.	CON[-]/?	*1693

AE4 (355–361)
O/Diademed, draped and cuirassed bust r.; D N CONSTANTIVS P F AVG
R/Emperor, helmeted and in military dress, standing l. holding globe and spear; SPES REIPVBLICE

1309	F, Field 18 Locus 329	2	15	↓	RIC VIII, 149	CONS[-]/?	*175

Mint of Antochia
AE. Follis (347–348)
O/Diademed, draped and cuirassed bust of emperor r. [---] DN CONSTA [---] AVG
R/VOT XV MVLT XX in wreath

1310	F, Field 5, under stone pavement II	1,6	16	↑	RIC VIII, 114	SMAN(A)/-	*643L

AE3 (355–361)
O/Diademed, draped and cuirassed bust r.; D N CONSTANTIVS P F AVG
R/Falling horseman; FEL TEMP REPARATIO

1311	F, Field B Locus 281	2,20	17	↑	RIC VIII, 187A–188	ANΓ/-	1610
1312	F, Field 18 Locus 329	1,75	14	↓	RIC VIII, 187A–188	ANB/-	*1390

1305

1307

1308

1309

1310

1312

Indeterminate mint
AE3/4 (350–361)
O/Diademed, draped and cuirassed bust of emperor r. [---]
R/Falling horseman [--] Type: *fel temp reparatio*

1313	F, Field 18 Locus 329	2,15	17		as LRBC 2625, 2295	?	*180
1314	F (2013)	2,15	18		same	?	No nr.
1315	F, Field 18 Locus 351	1,5	16		same	?	*475
1316	F, Field 18 Locus 325	1,25	14		same	?	463
1317	F, Field 27 Locus 616	0,55	13		same	?	*927
1318	Cardo	0,5	14		same	?	726L

AE4 (355–361)
O/Diademed, draped cuirassed bust of emperor r.; D N CONTANTIVS PF AVG
R/Virtus helmeted r. holding globe and spear; SPES REIPVBLICE

1319	C, Field 33 Locus 712	2,45	14	↑	as LRBC 2504	?	1093
1320	V, Field 3	2,22	18	↓	same, exergue: ST (?)	?	153L
1321	F, Field 1	1,84	15	↑	same	?	*410L
1322	F, Field 27 Locus 615	1,7	13	↑	same	?	931
1323	F, Field 25 Locus 1101	1,05	13	↓	same	?	1535
1324	F, Field 33 Locus 1173	1	10	↓	same	?	1694
1325	F, Field 1	0,79	16	↑	same	?	*400L

Constantius* II** for ***Constantius Gallus
Mint of Heraclea
AE3 (351–355)
O/Diademed, draped and cuirassed bust r.; D N CONSTANTIVS NOB C
R/Falling horseman; FEL TEMP REPARATIO

1326	H, Field 3 Locus 7	1,75	18	↑	RIC VIII, 91	SMH?/-	*90

Contantius II, Constantius II for ***Gallus Caesar***
Indeterminate mint
AE4 (351–3354)
O/Draped and cuirassed bust of emperor r. [---] ANTI/VS [---]
R/Falling horseman [---]; type: *fel temp reparatio*

1327	F, Field 27 Locus 622	2	19	↓	as LRBC 2625, 2295	?	*925

1313

1315

1317

1321

1325

1326

1327

Contantius II, Constantius II for ***Gallus Caesar*** and ***Julianus Caesar***
Indeterminate mint
AE4 (355–361)
O/Diademed, draped and cuirassed bust of emperor r. [---]
R/Falling horseman [--]; type: *fel temp reparatio*

1328	F, Field 5, under stone pavement II	1,65	13	↓	as LRBC 2625, 2295	?	*673L
1329	F, Field 1	1,58	16	↓	same	?	403L
1330	F, Field 1, trench A	1,51	15	↑	same	?	*635L

AE4 (355–361)
O/Draped cuirassed bust of emperor r. [---]
R/Virtus helmeted r. holding globe and spear [---]; type: *salus reipublicae*

1331	F, Field 27 Locus 615	1,7	13	↑	as LRBC 2504	?	931

Valens
Constantinopolis
AE (464–367)
O/Pearl diademed, draped and cuirassed bust r.; DN VALENS PF AVG
R/Victory advancing l., holding wreath and palm; SECVRITAS REIPVBLICAE

1332	F, Field 30 Locus 1107	0,65	15	↑	RIC IX, 21 (b-c)	CONSP(Γ?)/-	*1518

Valentinianus I, Valens
Indeterminate mint
AE3 (364–367)
O/Diademed, draped and cuirassed bust of emperor r. [---]
R/Emperor facing, holding Victory on globe [---]; type: *restitutor reip*

1333	F, Field 25 Locus 351	1,15	15	↑	as RIC IX, 20 (a-b) or LRBC 1702	?	697

Gratianus
Indeterminate mint
AE 3 (378–383)
O/Diademed, draped and cuirassed bust of emperor r. [---]
R/Roma seated facing, holding globe with cross; type: *virtus romanorum*

1334	F, Field 20 Locus 298	1,11	15	↑	as LRBC 2673	?	619

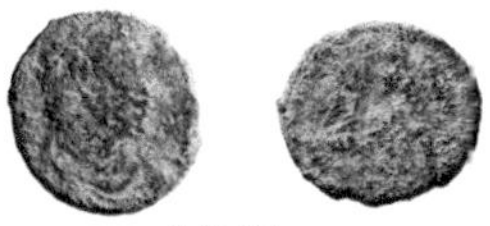
1328

1330

1332

***Valentinianus* II**
Mint of Antiochia
AE4 (383–388)
O/Diademed, draped and cuirassed bust of emperor r. [---]
R/VOT X MVLT XX in wreath

1335	F, Field 30 Locus 1117	1,4	17	↑	RIC IX, 65(a) 1	AN(A)/-	*1561

AE4 (383–392)
O/Diademed, draped and cuirassed bust of emperor r. [---]
R/Victory advancing l., holding trophy and dragging captive with l.; type: *salus reipublicae.*2

1336	F, Field 20 Locus 327	0,7	12	↑	as LRBC 1105 or RIC IX, 67(b)	?/₽	*428

Valentinianus I, Valens, Gratianus and Valentinianus II
Indeterminate mint
AE3 (364–383)
O/Diademed, draped and cuirassed bust of emperor r. [---]
R/Victory advancing l., holding wreath and palm [--]; type: *securitas reipublicae*

1337	F, Field 1	1,42	14	↑	as LRBC 527	?	*412L
1338	F, Field 31 Locus 1158	1	15	↑	as LRBC 527	?	1627

Theodosius I
Mint of Antiochia
AE4 (392–395)
O/Diademed, draped and cuirassed bust of emperor r.; DN THEODOSIVS PF AVG
R/Victory advancing l., holding trophy and dragging captive with l.; SALVS REIPVBLICAE

1339	H, Field 3 Locus 84	0,84	13	↓	RIC IX, 70 (a)	ANTA/₽	*1777

Arcadius
Mint of Antiochia
AE4 (383)
O/Diademed, draped and cuirassed bust of emperor r.; DNARCA [---]
R/VOT XX MVLT XXX in wreath

1340	H, Field 1 Locus 0	1,1	15	↓	RIC IX, 58 (c)	AN?/-	761

1335

1336

1337

1339

AE4 (392–395)
O/Diademed, draped and cuirassed bust of emperor r. [---] DIVS PF AVG
R/Victory advancing l., holding trophy and dragging captive with l.; type: *salus reipublicae*.2

1341	F, Field 1, trench A, BB	0,75	12	↑	RIC IX, 70 (a) or as LRBC 1105	ANT?/₽	*612L
1342	F, Field 1	0,52	11	↓	RIC IX, 70 (a) or as LRBC 1105	ANT?/₽	*420L

Indeterminate mint
AE4 (392–403)
O/Diademed, draped and cuirassed bust of emperor r. [---] DIVS PF AVG
R/Victory advancing l., holding trophy and dragging captive with l.; type: *salus reipublicae*.2

1343	F, Field 25 Locus 351	1,1	13	↓	as LRBC 1105	?/₽	*1540

Valentinianusus I, Valens, Gratianus, Valentinianusus II, Theodosius I and Arcadius
Indeterminate mint
AE3 (364–388)
O/Diademed, draped and cuirassed bust of emperor r. [---]
R/Emperor advancing r., with r. hand dragging captive and holding labarum in l. [--]; type: *gloria romanorum*.8

1344	F, Field C Locus 317	1,45	14	↑	as LRBC 338	?	*188
1345	F, Field 2	1,36	13	↑	same	?	*546L
1346	F, Field 7 Locus 282	1,05	18	↑	same	?	169
1347	F, Field 20 Locus 298	0,5	15	↑	same	?	618
1348	F, Field 25 Locus 1100	1,2	14	↑	same	?	1521

Arcadius
Mint of Antiochia
AE4 (383)
O/Diademed, draped and cuirassed bust of emperor r.; DN ARCADIVS PF AVF
R/VOT X MVLT XX in wreath; exergue: ANT[-]

1349	H, Field 2 Locus 4	1,05	13	↑	RIC IX, 56 (d)	ANS[?]/-	*71

Oriental Mint
AE4 (378–383)
O/Diademed, draped and cuirassed bust of emperor r. [---]
R/VOT X MVLT XX in wreath

1350	F, Field 1	1,12	11	↑	as RIC IX, 56 (a-d)	?	*407L

1341

1342

1343

1344

1345

1349

1350

AE4 (378–383)
O/Diademed, draped and cuirassed bust of emperor r. [---]
R/VOT XX MVLT XX in wreath

1351	F, Field 25 Locus 1101	1,05	14	↑	as RIC IX, 58 (a-c) (for Antiochia)	?	1546
1352	E, Field 3	1,02	13	↓	same	?	*279L
1353	Without context	1	12	↓	same	?	752
1354	M, Field 4 Locus 999	0,95	12	↓	same	?	668
1355	F, Field 2	0,74	13	↓	same	?	548L
1356	F, Field 25 Locus 351	0,72	13	↑	same	?	*1541

AE4 (second half of fourth century)
O/Diademed, draped and cuirassed bust of emperor r. [---]
R/Victory l. [---]

1357	F, Field 25 Locus 1100	1,3	12		RIC IX?	?	1522
1358	F, Field 25 Locus 1109	0,6	11		same	?	1647[11]

Valentinianusus II, Theodosius I and Arcadius
Mint of Alexandria
AE4 (388–392)
O/Diademed, draped and cuirassed bust of emperor r. [---]
R/Victory advancing l., holding trophy and dragging captive with l., SALVS REIPVBLICAE

1359	F, Field 2 West	1,02	14	↑	RIC IX, 20 (a-c)	ALE [?]/₽	*793L

Honorius
Mint of Rome or *Aquileia*
AE3 (408–423)
O/Diademed, draped and cuirassed bust of emperor, r.; DN HONORIVS PF AVG
R/Emperor standing r., head l., his r. hand on the head of a captive, his l. hand extended over a suppliant; GLORIA ROMANORVM

1360	F, Field 25 Locus 1101	2	18	↓	RIC X, 1355, 1358	?/-	*1529

11 R/Victory; [-]VGGG?

1352

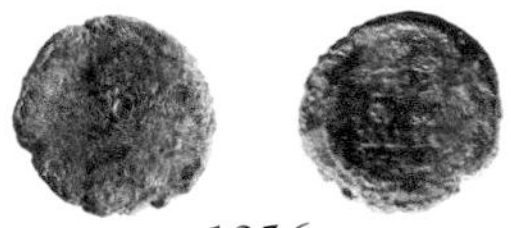
1356

1359

1360

Valentinianusus II, Theodosius I, Arcadius and Honorius
Mint of Antiochia
AE4 (383–395)
O/Diademed, draped and cuirassed bust of emperor r. [---]
R/Victory advancing l., holding trophy and dragging captive with l.; type *salus reipublicae*.2

1361	F, Field 1	0,59	11	↓	RIC IX, 67(a-d), 70 (a-c)	?/₽	*439L

Arcadius and Honorius
Indeterminate mint
AE4 (383–403)
O/Diademed, draped and cuirassed bust of emperor r. [---]
R/Victory advancing l., holding trophy and dragging captive with l.; type: *salus reipublicae.2*

1362	F, Field 25 Locus 351	0,95	13	↓	as LRBC 1105	?/₽	354

Theodosius II
Oriental mint
AE4 (425–435)
O/Diademed, draped and cuirassed bust of emperor r. [---]
R/No legend. Cross within wreath

1363	F, Field 27 Locus 624	0,75	10		as RIC X, 440–455		*926
1364	F, Field 25 Locus 1101	0,50	11		as RIC X, 442–455		*1643

Arcadius, Honorius and Theodosius II
Mint of Constantinopolis
AE3 (401–403)
O/Diademed, draped and cuirassed bust of emperor r. [---]
R/Constantinopolis enthroned facing, holding sceptre and Victory on globe; CONCORDIA AVGG

1365	F, Field 1	1,01	15	↑	RIC X, 85–90	CON [---]/-	*419L

Oriental mint
AE3 (395–401)
O/Diademed, draped and cuirassed bust of emperor r. [---]
R/Emperor standing l., holding spear. Victory, holding palm-branch in l., crowns him; VIRTVS EXERCITI

1366	E 22	1,18	16	↓	as RIC X, 56–76	?	*352L

1361

1363

1364

1365

1366

AE4 (404–406)
O/Diademed, draped and cuirassed bust of emperor r. [---]
R/CONCORDIA AVGGG, cross

1367	E, Field 20	0,85	14	↑	as RIC X, 123–138	?	*348L
1368	F, Field 1, trench A	0,68	9	↑	same	?	*619L
1369	F, Field 1, trench A	0,58	10	↑	same	?	*622L

Valentinianus II, Theodosius I, Arcadius, Honorius and Johannes
Indeterminate mint

AE4 (383–425)
R/Victoria l., type *salus reipublicae*.2

1370	F, Field 25 Locus 317	1,65	13	↓	as LRBC 1105	?/₽	1512
1371	F, Field 28 Locus 329	1,55	14	↑	same	?/₽	653
1372	F, Field 7	1,55	13	↑	same	?/₽	1709
1373	F, Field 25 US 1101	1,45	11	↑	same	?/₽	1531
1374	F 100:1	1,44	12	↑	same	?/₽	471L
1375	F, Field 32 Locus 1103	1,35	11	↓	same	?/₽	1618
1376	F 110	1,19	12	↑	same	?/₽	752L
1377	F, Field 32 Locus 1152	1,15	14	↑	same	?/₽	1617
1378	E, Field 35 Locus 320	1,11	12	↑	same	?/₽	1078
1379	F, Field 25 Locus 1100	1,10	12	↑	same	?/₽	1523
1380	F, Field 18 Locus 329	1,10	13	↑	same	?/₽	1667
1381	C, Field 22 Locus 595	1,05	12	↑	same	?/₽	918
1382	F, Field 25 US 1109	1,05	12	↑	same	?/₽	1646
1383	F, Field 1, trench A	0,98	15	↓	same	?/₽	631L
1384	F, Field 25 Locus 1101	0,95	12	↑	same	?/₽	1536
1385	F, Field 1	0,94	11	↓	same	?/₽	426L
1386	F, Field E Locus 291	0,90	12	↑	same	?/₽	470
1387	M	0,8	12	↓	same	?/₽	1191

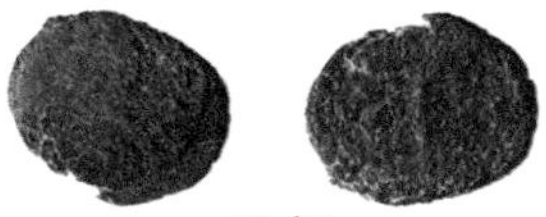
1367

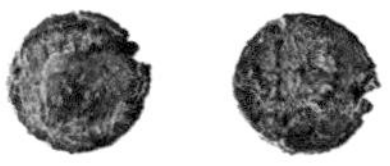
1368

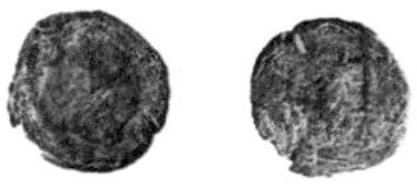
1369

1388	F, Field 1	0,68	12	↑	as LRBC 1105	?/₱	409L
1389	V, Field 1	0,62	11	↑	same	?/₱	*135L
1390	F, Field 25 Locus 1101	0,6	11	↓	same	?/₱	1533
1391	M	0,56	10	↑	same	?/₱	1191a
1392	E, Field 20	0,42	14	↑	same	?/₱	349L
1393	F 100:3	0,18	10	↑	same	?/₱	537L

***Valentinianus* III**
Mint of Rome
AE3 (425–ca. 435)
O/Diademed, draped and cuirassed bust of emperor r. [---]
R/Gateway surmounted by turrets, by star between pellets; VOT PVB

1394	E, Field 20	0,9	13	↓	RIC X, 2123–2128	[-]/S	*345L

Leo I
Oriental mint
AE4
O/Diademed, draped and cuirassed bust of emperor r.; [---]
R/Monogram within a wreath

1395	F, Field 30 Locus 1118	0,65	8		RIC X, 681–693 (monogram 2)		*1566

Imitations
As (fifth century)
O/Bust r.
R/Greek cross, sometime in within, without legend

1396	C, Field 13 Locus 596	1,3	10		as RIC X, 3819		911
1397	E, Field 20	0,68	10	↑	same		*346L
1398	F, Field 25 Locus 351	0,65	9	↑	same		*710
1399	F, Field 25 Locus 552	0,35	10		same		909
1400	F, Field 25 Locus 1101	0,50	8		No parallel		*1644

1389

1394

1395

1397

1398

1400

Indeterminate authority and mint

AE4 (fourth–fifth century)
O/Diademed, draped and cuirassed bust r.
R/Illegible or garbled

1401	F, Field 25 Locus 351	1,1	13	LRBC?	355
1402	V, Field 2 Locus 279	1,05	10	same	480
1403	D, Field 1	1	11	same	188L
1404	F, Field 1	0,86	13	same	411L
1405	F, Field 1	0,74	11	same	421L
1406	F, Field 1	0,39	11	same	423L

Late Roman period (fourth–fifth century)

AE3/AE4 or *minimi*
O/Traces of imperial head r.
R/Images, but corroded by rust

1407	E, Field 5 Locus 342	3,4	18	LRBC?	*571
1408	F 110	3,29	13	same	748L
1409	F, Field 5, under stone pavement II	2,74	14	same	647L
1410	E, Field 11	2,43	19	same	442L
1411	F, Field 3, East	2,1	16	same	786L
1412	E, Field 8 Locus 1067	1,65	14	same	1356
1413	F, Field 18 Locus 330	1,5	14	same	1557[5]
1414	F, Field 1	1,24	12	same	428L
1415	F, Field 1	1,21	12	same	437L
1416	F, Field 25 Locus 553	1,18	13	same	1779
1417	Without context	1,1	12	same	757
1418	F, Field 25 Locus 1100	1,10	15	same	1562[6]
1419	F, Field 25 Locus 351	1,05	8	same	*467
1420	F, Field 25 Locus 552	1,05	13	same	1577[7]
1421	F, Field 5, under stone pavement II	1,03	13	same	679L
1422	F, Field 1	1,01	12	same	430L
1423	A, Field 7 Locus 1197	1,01	14	same	1789
1424	F, Field 1	0,86	13	same	411L
1425	F, Field 20 Locus 375	0,8	10	same	675
1426	F, Field 25 Locus 351	0,8	11	same	*359
1427	F, Field 25 Locus 1109	0,80	11	same	1649[8]

5 O/Laureate head?
6 O/Head r.; R/Wreath?
7 O/Laureate head?
8 O/Laureate and draped head?

1407

1426

1428	F, Field 25 Locus 552	0,80	12	LRBC?	1578[9]
1429	F, Field 1	0,76	11	same	434L
1430	D, Field 1	0,76	13	same	190L
1431	F, Field 25 Locus 351	0,75	8	same	360
1432	F, Field 1	0,75	12	same	425L
1433	F 110	0,75	12	same	753L
1434	F 100:1	0,73	10	same	517L
1435	Without context	0,7	14	same	758
1436	F100: 3	0,69	10	same	529L
1437	F, Field 1	0,67	12	same	432L
1438	C, Field 6 Locus 589	0,65	14	same	1722
1439	F, Field 1	0,63	9	same	438L
1440	G 101	0,62	11	same	781L
1441	F 100:1	0,61	8	same	501L
1442	F, Field 1	0,6	9	same	413L
1443	Without context	0,6	9	same	664
1444	M (2013)	0,60	9	same	No nr
1445	F, Field 30 Locus 1117	0,55	7	same	1514[10]
1446	Whitout context	0,55	10	same	663
1447	M (2013)	0,55	10	same	No nr.
1448	F, Field 1	0,53	9	same	436L
1449	F, Field 1	0,51	11	same	429L
1450	F, Field 25 Locus 351	0,5	7	same	709
1451	F, Field 25 Locus 351	0,5	7	same	711
1452	F, Field 25 Locus 351	0,5	8	same	713
1453	F, Field 1	0,5	10	same	416L
1454	F, Field 1	0,49	10	same	418L
1455	F, Field 1	0,47	11	same	424L
1456	F 110	0,44	8	same	759L
1457	E, Field 11	0,44	9	same	462L
1458	F, Field 1	0,42	11	same	422L

9 O/Laureate head?; R/Wreath and *vota*?
10 O/Head r.?

1459	F, Field 1	0,42	11	LRBC?	435L
1460	C, Field 15 Locus 589	0,40	12	same	1740[11]
1461	F, Field 1	0,37	10	same	440L
1462	F, Field 1	0,37	11	same	433L
1463	F, Field 25 Locus 1099	0,30	8	same	1564
1464	F, Field 1	0,29	10	same	431L
1465	F, Field 1	0,27	10	same	441L
1466	F, Field 1	0,24	9	same	427L
1467	F, Field 25 Locus 351	0,15	10	same	*466
1468	F, Field 25 Locus 351	0,05	6	same	468

AE

Unstruck flan?

1469	H, Field 2 Locus 4	2,3	19		No nr.

AE

Corroded flan

1470	C, Field 31 Locus 698	10,9	23		1034
1471	H, Field 2 Locus 62	8,35	21		*140
1472	E, Field 11 Locus 301/302	7,95	24		*346
1473	C, Field 26 Locus 684	7,05	20		1023[12]
1474	E, Field 11 Locus 301/302	6,4	25		*329
1475	C, Field 26 Locus 637	6,25	20		961
1476	E, Field 11 Locus 303	5,65	21		*272
1477	D, Field 2	5,48	23		256L
1478	C, Field 28 Locus 639	5,47	15		970

11 Garbled.
12 Flan with limestone.

1467

1471

1472

1474

1476

1479	E, Field 11 Locus 303	5,15	21		*282
1480	C, Field 27 Locus 652	5	19		963
1481	E, Field 11 Locus 301/302	4,9	22		*308
1482	C, Field 27 Locus 636	4,9	22		964
1483	C, Field 22 Locus 607	4,9	18		972
1484	F, Field 4	4,78	18		365L
1485	E, Field 23	4,45	15		358L
1486	H, Field 2 Locus 62	4,4	20		*122
1487	E, Field 11 Locus 301/302	4,3	25		*319
1488	D, Field 1	3,9	20		194L
1489	C, Field 27 Locus 615	3,75	15		952
1490	V, Field 3	3,69	20		161L
1491	C, Field 31 Locus 253	3,45	18		975
1492	E, Field 11 Locus 300	3,45	18		*291
1493	D, Field 2	3,44	18		245L
1494	D, Field 2	3,39	21		244L
1495	F 100:3	3,23	19		521
1496	D, Field 1	3,17	19		191L
1497	V, Field 3 Locus 270	3,1	16		977
1498	E, Field 36 Locus 376	3,03	20		A16
1499	E, Field 11 Locus 301/302	2,95	19		*306
1500	F 101 North, disturbed stratigraphic context	2,89	15		839L
1501	E, Field 4	2,84	14		287L
1502	D, Field 6 Locus 863	2,81	14		A25.3
1503	F, Field 20 Locus 375	2,8	14		846

1479

1481

1486

1487

1492

1499

1504	F, Field 3 North	2,74	15		603L
1505	F, Field 1	2,66	17		1786
1506	C, Field 13 Locus 367	2,65	17		826
1507	C, Field 26 Locus 704	2,65	15		1050
1508	V, Field 2 Locus 932	2,65	16		1176
1509	V, Field 2 Locus 279	2,55	15		*481
1510	D, Field 1	2,53	16		248L
1511	C, Field 26 Locus 684	2,5	15		1024
1512	V, Field 2 Locus 279	2,45	14		*18
1513	F, Field 3 Locus 284	2,45	13		847
1514	E, Field 41 Locus 833	2,41	18		A33
1515	V, Field 3 Locus 767	2,4	15		979
1516	C, Field 31 Locus 664	2,35	17		976
1517	D, Field 1	2,33	15		221L
1518	F, Field 5, under stone pavement II	2,32	13		690L
1519	B, Field 1	2,28	16		108L
1520	E, Field 4	2,27	17		294L
1521	D, Field 1	2,27	20		189L
1522	V, Field 2 Locus 278	2,2	15		*524
1523	B, Field 5 Locus 296	2,2	13		632
1524	F, Field 25 Locus 118	2,2	20		670
1525	F, Field 25 Locus 552	2,2	20		905
1526	F, Field 7 North	2,13	16		811L
1527	D, Field 2 Locus 254	2,1	18		859
1528	E, Field 5 Locus 342	2,05	18		*32

1509

1512

1522

1528

1529	E, Field 11	2,04	18		*446L
1530	F, Field 20 Locus 298	2	22		620
1531	H, Field 1 Locus 3	2	15		*120
1532	West, in a fissure of the stone pavement	1,97	14		849L
1533	F, Field 28 Locus 329	1,95	13		*425
1534	D, Field 2	1,92	16		238L
1535	C, Field 26 Locus 684	1,9	13		1039
1536	E, Field 11 Locus 301/302	1,9	21		*313
1537	F, Field 3, East	1,9	13		788L
1538	E, Field 11	1,87	18		309L
1539	D, Field 1	1,86	15		249L
1540	F, Field 30 Locus 1115	1,86	15		1781
1541	C, Field 26 Locus 639	1,85	18		957
1542	C, Field 18 Locus 658	1,8	17		1084
1543	C, Field 15 Locus 879	1,8	13		*513
1544	C, Field 15 Locus 749	1,8	15		834
1545	F, Field 2	1,77	15		547L
1546	F, Field 25 Locus 552	1,75	11		907
1547	D, Field 1	1,71	15		209L
1548	F, Field 3, East	1,71	12		789L
1549	H, Field 1 Locus 94	1,7	13		*231
1550	F, Field 27 Locus 615	1,7	15		930
1551	M, Field 18 Locus 999	1,7	20		24
1552	F, Field 3 North	1,69	15		600L
1553	F 100:3	1,68	13		526L
1554	B S On the pavement A	1,67	15		891L

1529

1531

1533

1536

1543

1549

1555	E, Field 34 Locus 320	1,65	15		*455
1556	C, Field 15 Locus 754	1,65	13		839[13]
1557	F, Field 27 Locus 615	1,65	14		1658
1558	E, Field 11	1,64	16		459L
1559	Without context	1,64	14		A6.2
1560	E, Field 11 Locus 301/302	1,6	21		*311
1561	E, Field 14 Locus 383	1,6	17		1082
1562	C, Field 25 Locus 595	1,6	14		955[14]
1563	F, Field 18 Locus 325	1,6	13		875
1564	E, Field 20	1,56	13		344L
1565	H, Field 2 Locus 4	1,55	15		589
1566	C, Field 22 Locus 607	1,55	17		948
1567	C, Field 30 Locus 672	1,55	10		981
1568	E, Field 11 Locus 305	1,55	14		*302
1569	C, Field 20 Locus 617	1,55	12		940
1570	F, Field 31	1,55	10		1638
1571	C, Field 16 Locus 572	1,55	10		835
1572	F, Field 20 Locus 299	1,55	14		772
1573	V, Field 3 Locus 676	1,55	27		1011
1574	F, Field 2	1,54	11		544L
1575	F, Field 1	1,54	12		406L
1576	D, Field 1	1,54	18		220L
1577	G 100, North	1,51	10		852L
1578	F, Field 28 Locus 329	1,5	16		654
1579	C, Field 26 Locus 639	1,5	14		958

13 Perhaps Roman procurators (palm tree?)?
14 R/Perhaps two cornucopiae?

1555

1560

1568

1580	F, Field 18 Locus 325	1,5	13		*462
1581	H, Field 2 Locus 4	1,5	15		851
1582	F, Field 7	1,48	12		557L
1583	F 101, up to the pavement	1,45	12		859L
1584	F, Field 20 Locus 298	1,45	14		617
1585	C, Field 20 Locus 601	1,45	14		937
1586	E, Field 5	1,45	15		301L
1587	E, Field 7 Locus 815	1,45	15		1059
1588	V, Field 3 Locus 676	1,45	15		1012
1589	E, Field 11 Locus 302	1,45	20		*265
1590	G, Field 5 Locus 457	1,45	13		595
1591	D, Field 1	1,43	13		223L
1592	F 102, up to the stone pavement	1,42	12		870L
1593	E, Field 20	1,42	14		347L
1594	D, Field 9 Locus 716	1,4	14		1010
1595	E, Field 34 Locus 320	1,4	17		457
1596	F 110	1,36	14		754L
1597	E, Field 11 Locus 303	1,35	14		279
1598	D, Field 1 Locus 1202	1,35	16		635
1599	V, Field 2 Locus 278	1,35	15		487
1600	E, Field 38 Locus 794	1,35	16		A8
1601	V, Field 2 Locus 258	1,35	12		1175
1602	C, Field 28 Locus 639	1,3	15		969
1603	E, Field 33 Locus 320	1,3	13		1066
1604	F 100:1	1,27	11		494L
1605	F 100:1	1,26	15		465L

1580

1589

1606	H, Field 1 Locus 103	1,25	12		247
1607	F, Field 2, trench 1	1,25	14		711L
1608	F, Field 20 Locus 502	1,25	16		802
1609	E, Field 26 Locus 919	1,25	15		1147
1610	F, Field 3 Locus 901	1,25	14		1695
1611	F, Field 1, trench A, near BB	1,24	13		615L
1612	F, Field 6, on the stone pavement	1,24	14		882L
1613	E, Field 20	1,2	14		342L
1614	E	1,2	14		645
1615	F 25, Locus 351	1,2	13		699
1616	C 24, Locus 808	1,2	11		951
1617	C 36 Locus 822	1,2	13		A36
1618	V, Field 3 US 270	1,2	15		508
1619	F, Field 1	1,19	11		391L
1620	F, Field 2, trench 1	1,19	13		712L
1621	E, Field 39 Locus 812	1,19	14		A44.3
1622	F, Field 5, under stone pavement II	1,18	9		688L
1623	F, Field 27 Locus 624	1,16	13		1768
1624	F, Field 28 Locus 329	1,15	12		624
1625	F, Field 30 Locus 1115	1,15	14		1782
1626	C, Field 1 Locus 267	1,15	9		10
1627	C, Field 15 Locus 636	1,15	14		591
1628	E, Field 20 Locus 327	1,15	15		819

1629	F, Field 1, trench A, near BB	1,15	14			609L
1630	F, Field 22 Locus 514	1,15	13			807
1631	F, Field 25 Locus 552	1,15	16			904
1632	H, Field 2 Locus 4	1,15	12			1593
1633	G, Field 8	1,14	14			1183
1634	F, Field 5, under stone pavement II	1,13	13			642L
1635	F, Field 7	1,11	13			585L
1636	F 101, up to the pavement	1,1	12			864L
1637	E, Field 32 Locus 355	1,1	13			439
1638	D, Field 2	1,1	13			262L
1639	E, Field 5 Locus 342	1,1	14			572
1640	E, Field 11 Locus 301/302	1,1	15			314
1641	H, Field 1 Locus 94	1,1	15			207
1642	F, Field 25 Locus 351	1,1	12			364
1643	E, Field 13 Locus 357	1,1	17			552
1644	F, Field 20 Locus 502	1,1	14			805
1645	V, Field 1	1,1	11			136L
1646	F, Field 4	1,09	15			362L
1647	F, Field 3, under stone pavement	1,09	12			877L
1648	F, Field 1	1,09	11			396L
1649	F, Field 2, be-neath the mosaic	1,08	11			880L
1650	F 101, up to the pavement	1,07	11			860L
1651	F, Field 2, trench 1	1,07	12			722L

1652	F, Field 5, under stone pavement II	1,06	13	650L
1653	E, Field 39 Locus 814	1,06	10	A28
1654	C, Field 31 Locus 663	1,05	13	989
1655	H, Field 1 Locus 94	1,05	16	233
1656	F, Field 8 Locus 356	1,05	12	412
1657	H, Field 1 Locus 0	1,05	12	117
1658	C, Field 32 Locus 669	1,05	12	1048
1659	F, Field 5, under stone pavement II	1,03	12	644L
1660	F, Field 7	1,03	15	568L
1661	V, Field 2	1,02	12	146L
1662	F, Field 27 Locus 624	1,02	14	1769
1663	D, Field 6 Locus 863	1,02	13	A25.4
1664	F, Field 3 North	1,01	12	596L
1665	E, Field 20	1,01	11	343L
1666	D, Field 1	1,01	11	228L
1667	C, Field 20 Locus 601	1	14	938
1668	F, Field 3 Locus 284	1	13	141
1669	H, Field 1 Locus 0	1	13	211
1670	F, Field 10 Locus 286	1	13	633
1671	E, Field 29 Locus 804	1	15	893
1672	E, Field 36 Locus 321	1	14	732
1673	C, Field 12 Locus 636	1	14	622
1674	E, Field 20	0,99	11	338L
1675	F, Field 27 Locus 624	0,99	14	1767

1676	F 102, up to stone pavement	0,98	12	866L
1677	F, Field 1	0,97	13	388L
1678	F 101, North on stone pavement	0,96	12	875L
1679	E, Field 11	0,95	12	458L
1680	F, Field 25 Locus 351	0,95	13	352
1681	E, Field 13 Locus 357	0,95	16	548
1682	E, Field 11 Locus 301/302	0,95	15	318
1683	V, Field 2 Locus 279	0,95	11	202
1684	D, Field 6 Locus 865	0,95	12	A32
1685	F, Field 25 Locus 351	0,95	12	692
1686	F, Field 25 Locus 351	0,95	14	728
1687	F, Field 1, trench A filling	0,94	12	617L
1688	G 100, North	0,94	14	853L
1689	E, Field 20	0,93	12	335L
1690	D, Field 1	0,92	12	210L
1691	F 110	0,92	12	749L
1692	F, Field 7	0,92	11	576L
1693	F, Field 4	0,92	11	366L
1694	E, Field 22	0,91	12	353L
1695	F, Field 22 Locus 299	0,91	13	1784
1696	F, Field 25 Locus 351	0,9	13	698
1697	E, Field 11 Locus 301/302	0,9	14	341
1698	V, Field 1 Locus 755	0,9	14	511
1699	F, Field 7 Locus 282	0,9	14	166
1700	F, Field 25 Locus 351	0,9	11	356

1701	F, Field 25 Locus 351	0,9	10	363
1702	Without context	0,90	11	1761
1703	C, Field 22 Locus 607	0,9	13	973
1704	F, Field 20 Locus 500	0,9	13	766
1705	F, Field 23 Locus 507	0,9	12	795
1706	H, Field 2 Locus 10	0,9	17	106
1707	F 100:1	0,89	11	478L
1708	F, Field 1, trench A filling	0,89	11	630L
1709	F, Field 7	0,87	13	578L
1710	F, Field 5, under stone pavement II	0,87	14	639L
1711	F, Field 7	0,87	14	572L
1712	F, Field 18 Locus 329	0,85	15	176
1713	H, Field 1 Locus 86	0,85	13	148
1714	C, Field 31 Locus 698	0,85	12	1037
1715	E, Field 13 Locus 357	0,85	14	558
1716	F, Field 23 Locus 507	0,85	12	794
1717	F, Field 25	0,85	12	865
1718	H, Field 2 Locus 4	0,85	12	849
1719	Cardo	0,84	12	733L
1720	F, Field 7	0,84	12	579L
1721	E, Field 4	0,84	11	285L
1722	F 100:1	0,84	13	484L
1723	F 100:3	0,84	13	536L
1724	F, Field 3 East	0,84	13	787L
1725	F, Field 1	0,81	13	385L
1726	F, Field 1	0,81	14	384L
1727	C, Field 30 Locus 828	0,81	11	A41.2

1728	E, Field 11 Locus 302	0,8	13		288
1729	A, Field 5 Locus 269	0,8	11		527
1730	E, Field 9	0,8	11		305L
1731	C, Field 20 Locus 617	0,8	11		942
1732	H, Field 1 Locus 0	0,8	13		212
1733	F, Field 28 Locus 329	0,8	13		652
1734	F, Field 18 Locus 325	0,8	15		416
1735	F, Field 7, North East	0,8	12		834L
1736	C, Field 20 Locus 617	0,8	12		941
1737	D, Field 6 Locus 784	0,8	14		627
1738	F, Field 25	0,8	9		866
1739	Cardo	0,79	11		728L
1740	D, Field 2	0,79	11		263L
1741	E, Field 20	0,78	12		329L
1742	F, Field 1, trench A, near BB	0,78	9		608L
1743	F 100:3	0,77	12		534L
1744	F 100:3	0,77	10		533L
1745	F 110:4	0,76	14		772L
1746	E, Field 20	0,76	13		337L
1747	F 110:4	0,76	13		762L
1748	F, Field 22 Locus 299	0,76	14		1785
1749	D, Field 6 Locus 865	0,76	12		A37.3
1750	F 101, on the pavement	0,76	12		865L
1751	F, Field 7 North	0,76	11		821L
1752	Whitout context	0,75	12		646
1753	C, Field 26 Locus 684	0,75	13		1038
1754	C, Field 20 Locus 618	0,75	13		932

1755	E, Field 27 Locus 620	0,75	10		531
1756	E, Field 4	0,75	10		284L
1757	F, Field 25 Locus 552	0,75	10		908
1758	F, Field 25 Locus 552	0,75	14		897
1759	F, Field 25 Locus 351	0,75	15		353
1760	F, Field 28 Locus 329	0,75	14		651
1761	F, Field E Locus 291	0,75	11		469
1762	F 100:1	0,75	11		500L
1763	Without context	0,75	16		754
1764	D, Field 2	0,74	11		257L
1765	F, Field 2 West	0,73	11		802L
1766	F, Field 1, trench A, filling	0,73	12		626L
1767	F 100:3	0,72	14		531L
1768	F, Field 1, trench A, filling	0,71	12		616L
1769	E, Field 20	0,71	14		332L
1770	V, Field 2 Locus 276	0,7	15		516
1771	F 100:3	0,7	11		538L
1772	E, Field 34 Locus 320	0,7	13		671
1773	E, Field 3	0,7	14		273L
1774	D, Field 11 Locus 816	0,70	9		A43.2
1775	C, Field 15 Locus 752	0,7	12		836
1776	F, Field 25 Locus 351	0,7	10		720
1777	F, Field 2, trench 1	0,69	9		721L
1778	F, Field 1	0,69	12		408L
1779	E, Field 29 Locus 832	0,69	11		A42.2
1780	Cardo	0,68	12		724L

1781	F 101, North, on stone pavement	0,68	14		874L
1782	F 102, up to the stone pavement	0,68	13		871L
1783	F, Field 1	0,68	12		376L
1784	F 100:1	0,67	11		507L
1785	F 110	0,67	10		756L
1786	F, Field 5, under stone pavement II	0,67	10		692L
1787	F, Field 25 Locus 1101	0,67	12		1783
1788	E, Field 23	0,66	11		359L
1789	F 102, up to stone pavement	0,66	11		867L
1790	F, Field 7	0,66	12		559L
1791	H, Field 2 US 36	0,65	14		102
1792	E, Field 3	0,65	14		271L
1793	M, Field 20	0,65	14		603
1794	F 102, up to stone pavement	0,65	11		868L
1795	E, Field 34 Locus 320	0,65	11		611
1796	F, Field 25 Locus 351	0,65	14		693
1797	C, Field 27 Locus 639	0,65	14		966
1798	F 100:1	0,65	12		469L
1799	D, Field 4 Locus 770	0,65	12		738
1800	V, Field 30 Locus 676	0,65	11		1007
1801	F, Field 25 Locus 351	0,65	10		715
1802	F, Field 1	0,64	14		387L
1803	F 100:2	0,64	15		743L
1804	F 100:1	0,64	11		496L
1805	F, Field 7	0,64	11		558L
1806	F 101, up to the pavement	0,64	10		861L

1807	F 110:4	0,64	13		770L
1808	F, Field 7	0,63	10		573L
1809	F, Field 7	0,63	11		570L
1810	G 101	0,62	11		706L
1811	F, Field 1	0,62	12		386L
1812	D, Field 2	0,62	14		255L
1813	A, Field 4	0,62	11		105L
1814	D, Field 2	0,62	16		264L
1815	F, Field 2, trench 1	0,61	14		716L
1816	E, Field 20	0,61	14		350L
1817	E, Field 20	0,6	10		331L
1818	A, Field 4	0,6	10		104L
1819	E, Field 22	0,6	11		355L
1820	F, Field 7	0,6	11		590L
1821	C, Field 31 Locus 700	0,6	11		1033
1822	D, Field 2 Locus 254	0,6	14		525
1823	F, Field 18 Locus 329	0,6	14		419
1824	F, Field 7	0,6	14		575L
1825	V, Field 2	0,6	14		147L
1826	E, Field 11 Locus 302	0,6	12		289
1827	F, Field 25 Locus 351	0,6	12		704
1828	F, Field 21 Locus 297	0,6	12		769
1829	F, Field 25 Locus 351	0,6	11		691
1830	F, Field 25 Locus 351	0,6	9		707
1831	E, Field 20	0,59	12		340L
1832	F 100:1	0,59	11		516L
1833	E, Field 37	0,59	11		A38.3
1834	F 1, trench A, filling	0,58	10		628L
1835	V, Field 3 Locus 767	0,58	11		A3
1836	F, Field 1	0,57	12		415L
1837	F 1, trench A, filling	0,57	12		625L

1838	Without context	0,57	8		1759
1839	H, Field 3 Locus 1130	0,56	11		1787
1840	F, Field 2 West	0,56	8		798L
1841	F, Field 3 North	0,56	14		604L
1842	E, Field 13 Locus 357	0,55	12		445
1843	E, Field 34 Locus 318	0,55	12		423
1844	F, Field E Locus 291	0,55	12		471
1845	H, Field 1 Locus 94	0,55	12		239
1846	Cardo	0,55	11		731L
1847	F 101, up to the pavement	0,55	11		863L
1848	F 110:4	0,55	11		766L
1849	V, Field 3 Locus 677	0,55	11		1061
1850	V, Field 2 Locus 276	0,55	12		517
1851	E, Field 30 Locus 260	0,55	13		538
1852	E, Field 11 Locus 301/302	0,55	13		323
1853	M Locus 999	0,55	13		625
1854	F, Field 1	0,55	10		414L
1855	F, Field 1, trench A, filling	0,55	10		618L
1856	F, Field 7	0,55	9		554L
1857	E	0,55	11		823
1858	E, Field 26 Locus 919	0,55	13		642
1859	F, Field 2 West	0,55	14		794L
1860	F, Field 5, under stone pavement II	0,55	12		687L
1861	F, Field 23 Locus 509	0,55	13		764
1862	F, Field 23 Locus 509	0,55	12		806

1863	F, Field 25 Locus 558	0,55	10	878
1864	F, Field 25 Locus 351	0,55	11	705
1865	F, Field 25 Locus 351	0,55	13	729
1866	F, Field 25 Locus 351	0,55	10	690
1867	F, Field 25 Locus 522	0,55	12	906
1868	F, Field 25 Locus 351	0,55	9	682[15]
1869	F 100:3	0,54	12	525L
1870	E, Field 20	0,54	15	351L
1871	Cardo	0,53	10	729L
1872	F 102, up to the stone pavement	0,53	10	872L
1873	E, Field 22	0,52	11	354L
1874	F 100:3	0,52	11	520L
1875	F 110	0,52	11	758L
1876	F, Field 5, under stone pavement II	0,51	10	651L
1877	G 100:2, on the wall	0,51	11	844L
1878	F, Field 1	0,51	12	394L
1879	E, Field 34 Locus 318	0,5	11	424
1880	F, Field 7 Locus 282	0,5	11	162
1881	F, Field 25 Locus 351	0,5	11	361
1882	F, Field 25 Locus 351	0,5	11	366
1883	F, Field 7 Locus 282	0,5	9	163
1884	C, Field 20 Locus 601	0,5	11	939
1885	F, Field 19 Locus 353	0,5	13	397
1886	H, Field 1 Locus 94	0,5	13	193

15 Ptolemaic bronze coin as flan.

1887	F, Field 18 Locus 329	0,5	13		408
1888	F, Field 25 Locus 351	0,5	12		465
1889	C, Field 20 Locus 617	0,5	13		943
1890	F, Field 25 Locus 351	0,5	10		365
1891	F, Field 25 Locus 351	0,5	10		706
1892	F, Field 25 Locus 552	0,5	10		899
1893	C, Field 15 Locus 897	0,5	11		845[16]
1894	Without context	0,5	10		822
1895	F, Field 25 Locus 550	0,5	8		874
1896	F 100:2	0,49	21		744L
1897	F 100:1	0,48	12		487L
1898	F, Field 4	0,48	12		370L
1899	F 110:4	0,48	11		769L
1900	F, Field 6, on the stone pavement	0,48	11		886L
1901	F, Field 2 West	0,48	10		795L
1902	F, Field 7	0,48	10		580L
1903	G 100:2, on the wall	0,48	10		845L
1904	F, Field 1, trench A, near BB	0,47	10		607L
1905	F, Field 7	0,47	11		553L
1906	V, Field 1	0,47	11		130L
1907	F 100:1	0,47	9		489L
1908	F 100:1, up to the pavement	0,47	9		862L
1909	E, Field 37	0,47	12		A38.4
1910	G 101	0,47	11		698L
1911	F, Field 1, trench A, filling	0,46	10		627L
1912	E, Field 13 Locus 357	0,45	11		446

16 R/Perhaps palm or galley?

1913	F, Field 25 Locus 351	0,45	9		383
1914	E, Field 13 Locus 357	0,45	13		556
1915	C, Field 18 Locus 608	0,45	13		921
1916	F, Field 25 Locus 351	0,45	11		357
1917	F, Field 1, trench A, filling	0,45	11		621L
1918	M, Field 9 Locus 999	0,45	11		666
1919	F, Field 25 Locus 351	0,45	11		700
1920	E, Field 19 Locus 800	0,45	10		17
1921	F, Field 2	0,45	10		545L
1922	F, Field 7	0,45	10		555L
1923	Without context	0,45	9		1765
1924	C, Field 26 Locus 704	0,45	12		1051
1925	D, Field 4 Locus 770	0,45	11		742
1926	F, Field 25 Locus 351	0,45	9		683
1927	F, Field 7, North	0,45	10		820L
1928	F, Field 20 Locus 299	0,45	12		775
1929	F, Field 20 Locus 299	0,45	10		777
1930	F, Field 21 Locus 297	0,45	10		770
1931	F, Field 1, trench A, filling	0,44	8		629L
1932	F 110:4	0,44	11		764L
1933	E, Field 20	0,43	11		330L
1934	F, Field 6, on the stone pavement	0,43	10		887L
1935	F, Field 27 Locus 625	0,43	12		1770

1936	F, Field 27 Locus 624	0,43	11	1771
1937	F, Field 2 West	0,43	11	805L
1938	F 101 North, disturbed stratigraphic context	0,41	10	840L
1939	F, Field 4	0,41	10	363L
1940	G 101	0,41	11	780L
1941	F, Field 1	0,4	10	392L
1942	M, Field 59 Locus 999	0,4	10	661
1943	F, Field 25 Locus 351	0,4	10	712
1944	H, Field 1 Locus 94	0,4	11	238
1945	F, Field 25 Locus 552	0,4	11	902
1946	H, Field 2 Locus 5	0,4	12	173
1947	H, Field 3 Locus 67	0,4	12	498
1948	H, Field 1 Locus 94	0,4	12	237
1949	F, Field 20 Locus 298	0,4	12	613
1950	V, Field 1 Locus 267	0,4	12	629
1951	V, Field 2 Locus 277	0,4	13	495
1952	C, Field 26 Locus 704	0,4	12	1017
1953	Without context	0,4	12	824
1954	E, Field 33 Locus 320	0,4	12	1074
1955	E, Field 29 Locus 804	0,4	14	894
1956	F, Field 20 Locus 299	0,4	11	778
1957	F, Field 25 Locus 351	0,4	9	717
1958	F, Field 25 Locus 351	0,4	8	718
1959	F, Field 25 Locus 351	0,4	13	702

1960	F, Field 25 Locus 351	0,4	8	716
1961	V, Field 1 Locus 267	0,4		1099
1962	E, Field 20	0,39	12	339L
1963	F, Field 1, trench A, filling	0,39	11	624L
1964	F, Field 5, under stone pavement	0,39	10	645L
1965	F 110	0,39	9	757L
1966	F 100:3	0,38	10	522L
1967	G 101	0,38	11	704L
1968	F, Field 2 West	0,38	12	807L
1969	F 100:1	0,37	11	497L
1970	F, Field 5, under stone pavement II	0,37	9	682L
1971	B, Field 5	0,36	9	126L
1972	F 100:3	0,36	9	535L
1973	F 102, up to the stone pavement	0,36	10	869L
1974	F, Field 2, beneath the mosaic	0,36	10	879L
1975	F, Field 3 East	0,36	11	787L
1976	F, Field 1, filling	0,36	10	620L
1977	F, Field 3, East	0,36	10	792L
1978	F, Field 7	0,36	9	560L
1979	F, Field 25 Locus 351	0,35	10	379
1980	F, Field 5, under stone pavement II	0,35	10	657L
1981	E, Field 32 Locus 355	0,35	13	473
1982	F, Field 25 Locus 351	0,35	9	362
1983	C, Field 20 Locus 617	0,35	9	945
1984	F, Field 25 Locus 351	0,35	12	378

1985	C, Field 30 Locus 672	0,35	12	980
1986	B, Field 5 Locus 296	0,35	11	435
1987	E, Field 13 Locus 357	0,35	11	564
1988	V, Field 2 Locus 276	0,35	11	518
1989	F, Field 1	0,35	11	393L
1990	F, Field 25 Locus 351	0,35	8	372
1991	E, Field 10 Locus 453	0,35	12	503
1992	F, Field 23 Locus 507	0,35	10	796
1993	F, Field 25 Locus 558	0,35	11	871
1994	F, Field 25 Locus 351	0,35	10	869
1995	F, Field 25 Locus 351	0,35	9	688
1996	V, Field 2 Locus 258	0,35	13	599
1997	H, Field 1 Locus 91/94	0,35	11	224
1998	F 100:2	0,34	11	738L
1999	F 100:2	0,34	10	746L
2000	F 101 North, disturbed stratigraphic context	0,34	10	842L
2001	F 100:2	0,33	8	481L
2002	Cardo	0,33	12	732L
2003	F 101, North on stone pavement	0,33	11	876L
2004	F, Field 7 North	0,33	10	816L
2005	F 100:2	0,33	9	741L
2006	F, Field 3 East	0,33	11	791L
2007	F, Field 5, under stone pavement II	0,33	11	684L
2008	F 100:1	0,32	9	499L
2009	F, Field 2, trench 1	0,32	10	720L

2010	F, Field 7 North	0,32	10		830L
2011	F, Field 1, trench A, near BB	0,31	11		610L
2012	F, Field 7 North	0,31	11		822L
2013	H, Field 1 Locus 94	0,3	13		248
2014	F, Field 25 Locus 351	0,3	9		384
2015	C, Field 20 Locus 617	0,3	9		944
2016	F, Field H Locus 290	0,3	10		460
2017	D, Field 6 Locus 806	0,3	10		1065
2018	C, Field 21 Locus 610	0,3	10		946
2019	H, Field 1 Locus 1	0,3	11		119
2020	H, Field 1 Locus 39/98	0,3	11		196
2021	V, Field 2 Locus 278	0,3	11		490
2022	E, Field 11 Locus 301/302	0,3	12		322
2023	F, Field 25 Locus 351	0,3	8		371
2024	B, Field 5 Locus 296	0,3	11		604
2025	C, Field 15 Locus 754	0,3	11		840
2026	E, Field 13 Locus 357	0,3	11		566
2027	F, Field 7 North	0,3	11		827L
2028	F, Field 23 Locus 509	0,3	10		780
2029	F, Field 23 Locus 509	0,3	11		801
2030	F, Field 25 Locus 351	0,3	8		722
2031	F, Fied 25 Locus 351	0,3	10		723

2032	V, Field 3 Locus 676	0,3	11		1014
2033	F 100:3	0,29	10		543L
2034	E, Field 20	0,29	9		341L
2035	D, Field 11 Locus 816	0,29	9		A43.3
2036	F, Field 5, under stone pavement II	0,29	7		649L
2037	F, Field 2 West	0,29	11		804L
2038	F 102, up to the stone pavement	0,27	8		873L
2039	E, Field 19 Locus 527	0,27	10		A12.1
2040	D, Field 6 Locus 864	0,27	10		A2
2041	D, Field 39/41 Locus 814	0,27	9		A4.2
2042	F, Field 5, under stone pavement II	0,27	8		680L
2043	F 100:3	0,26	10		527L
2044	F, Field 1	0,26	11		389L
2045	E, Field 37	0,26	9		A38.1
2046	Without context	0,26	8		1764
2047	V, Field 2 Locus 277	0,25	11		496
2048	E, Field 13 Locus 357	0,25	10		555
2049	F, Field 19 Locus 353	0,25	10		399
2050	F, Field 18 Locus 324	0,25	10		414
2051	F, Field 25 Locus 351	0,25	10		374
2052	E, Field 13 Locus 357	0,25	9		448
2053	E, Field 34 Locus 320	0,25	9		450
2054	E, Field 32 US 355	0,25	9		440
2055	F, Field 7, North	0,25	9		826L

2056	F, Field 25 Locus 351	0,25	8	370
2057	D, Field 11 Locus 816	0,25	7	A43.4
2058	D, Field 39/41 Locus 814	0,25	8	A4.3
2059	C, Field 30 Locus 672	0,25	10	1091
2060	E, Field 13 Locus 357	0,25	11	567
2061	E, Field 20 Locus 327	0,25	11	820
2062	F, Field 18 Locus 317	0,25	9	644
2063	F, Field 20 Locus 299	0,25	10	779
2064	F, Field 25 Locus 552	0,25	10	880
2065	F, Field 25 Locus 351	0,25	11	381
2066	F, Field 25 Locus 351	0,25	7	724
2067	F, Field 25 Locus 351	0,25	8	721
2068	F, Field 25 Locus 351	0,25	8	725
2069	F, Field 18 Locus 331	0,25	11	669
2070	V, Field 2 Locus 276	0,25	9	521
2071	V, Field 2 Locus 279	0,25	9	636
2072	V, Field 2 Locus 1210	0,25	9	1255
2073	V, Field 3 Locus 767	0,25	14	996
2074	V, Field 3 Locus 767	0,25	9	994
2075	F, Field 2, West	0,24	8	797L
2076	F 110	0,24	9	750L
2077	E, Field 39 Locus 812	0,24	8	A44.5
2078	D, Field 6 Locus 874	0,24	9	A9

2079	Without context	0,24	6		1762
2080	F 100:2	0,24	9		745L
2081	F 101 North, disturbed stratigraphic context	0,24	10		841L
2082	F, Field 2 West	0,24	10		803L
2083	E, Field 39 Locus 812	0,23	8		A44.8
2084	F, Field 7 North	0,23	10		823L
2085	F, Field 7 North	0,22	9		831L
2086	F, Field 3 North	0,22	6		597L
2087	Cardo	0,21	8		734L
2088	F, Field 1	0,21	9		395L
2089	F 100:3	0,21	9		532L
2090	E, Field 29 Locus 832	0,21	8		A39.5
2091	E, Field 31 Locus 790	0,21	6		A14
2092	Without context	0,21	7		1763
2093	F, Field 2 West	0,21	10		806L
2094	F, Field 5, under stone pavement II	0,21	7		654L
2095	F, Field 25 Locus 351	0,2	8		385
2096	F, Field 25 Locus 351	0,2	8		377
2097	F, Field 25 Locus 351	0,2	8		380
2098	A, Field 1 Locus 296	0,2	9		580
2099	E, Field 13 Locus 357	0,2	9		449
2100	F, Field 7 Locus 282	0,2	9		161
2101	F, Field 25 Locus 351	0,2	9		708
2102	F, Field 2 West	0,2	10		800L
2103	E, Field 13 Locus 357	0,2	10		447

2104	F, Field 25 Locus 351	0,2	10		382
2105	G 101	0,2	10		705L
2106	F, Field 19 Locus 353	0,2	12		400
2107	H, Field 1 Locus 94	0,2	12		240
2108	F, Field 25 Locus 351	0,2	11		367
2109	F, Field 25 Locus 351	0,2	7		373
2110	F 100:3	0,2	7		542L
2111	F, Field 27 Locus 616	0,2	7		929
2112	Without context	0,2	8		1760
2113	C, Field 26 Locus 684	0,2	8		1044
2114	E, Field 13 Locus 357	0,2	11		568
2115	E, Field 32 Locus 355	0,2	10		474
2116	F, Field 25 Locus 351	0,2	8		687
2117	F, Field 5, under stone pavement II	0,2	9		665L
2118	F, Field 20 Locus 503	0,2	8		809
2119	F, Field 23 Locus 507	0,2	9		797
2120	V, Field 2 Locus 278	0,2	10		491
2121	H, Field 1 Locus 94	0,2	12		151
2122	H, Field 1 Locus 91/94	0,2	10		223
2123	F, Field 5, under stone pavement II	0,19	8		658L
2124	E, Field 36 Locus 321	0,19	7		1776
2125	F 100:1	0,18	8		482L
2126	E, Field 37	0,18	7		A38.2

2127	F, Field 5, under stone pavement II	0,18	8	691L
2128	F, Field 2 West	0,16	10	799L
2129	F, Field 25 Locus 351	0,15	8	369
2130	F, Field 1	0,15	8	381L
2131	C, Field 20 Locus 618	0,15	8	933
2132	V, Field 279 Locus 279	0,15	11	486
2133	F 100:1	0,15	11	498L
2134	C, Field 27 Locus 639	0,15	10	967
2135	F, Field 19 Locus 362	0,15	9	388
2136	F, Field 25 Locus 351	0,15	9	386
2137	F, Field 19 Locus 353	0,15	9	401
2138	V, Field 2 Locus 277	0,15	9	497
2139	C, Field 26 Locus 684	0,15	8	1043
2140	C, Field 33 Locus 713	0,15	8	1056
2141	E, Field 22a Locus 307	0,15	8	658
2142	E, Field 24 Locus 924	0,15	10	539
2143	F 110:4	0,15	8	767L
2144	F, Field 20 Locus 375	0,15	11	674
2145	F, Field 20/22 Locus 298	0,15	9	784
2146	F, Field 25 Locus 351	0,15	10	476
2147	F, Field 25 Locus 351	0,15	8	727
2148	F, Field 25 Locus 351	0,15	10	689
2149	F, Field 25 Locus 351	0,15	10	714
2150	F, Field 25 Locus 351	0,15	9	719

2151	H, Field 1 Locus 94	0,15	10	154
2152	V, Field 3 Locus 676	0,15	10	1013
2153	V, Field 3 Locus 767	0,15	11	995
2154	E, Field 29 Locus 832	0,14	6	A39.2
2155	F 100:3	0,14	9	541L
2156	F, Field 7, North	0,13	8	815L
2157	E, Field 42 Locus 873	0,13	6	A27.1
2158	E, Field 29 Locus 832	0,12	5	A42.3
2159	C, Field 16 Locus 588	0,12	9	A24
2160	F, Field 7 North	0,12	8	829L
2161	F, Field 2 West	0,11	6	808L
2162	F, Field 25 Locus 351	0,1	8	368
2163	F, Field 25 Locus 351	0,1	8	375
2164	B, Field 5 Locus 296	0,1	21	581
2165	C, Field 15 Locus 897	0,1	9	864
2166	C, Field 16 Locus 744	0,1	5	841
2167	C, Field 30 Locus 672	0,1	8	1090
2168	C, Field 8 Locus 729	0,1	8	1057
2169	E, Field 22 Locus 511	0,1	8	812
2170	F, Field 25 Locus 558	0,1	4	881
2171	F, Field 23 Locus 509	0,1	7	799
2172	V, Field 3 Locus 677	0,1	8	1004
2173	C, Field 30 Locus 828	0,08	6	A41.1
2174	H, Field 1 Locus 94	0,05	9	249

2175	F, Field 25 Locus 351	0,05	8	376
2176	E, Field 26 Locus 919	0,05	8	640
2177	F, Field 7 North-East	0,05	5	837L
2178	F, Field 25 Locus 351	0,05	7	726
2179	F, Field 19 Locus 353	0,05	7	402
2180	H, Field 1 Locus 94	0,05	7	149
2181	C, Field 10 Locus 727	0,01	6	9

AE

Fragment or fragments of coin

2182	F, Field 13 Locus 963	3,55	1205
2183	A, Field 8 Locus 1208	3,45	1184
2184	E, Field 26 Locus 920	2,65	1145
2185	C, Field 6 Locus 589	2,55	1719
2186	C, Field 6 Locus 589	2,55	1723
2187	F, Field 18 Locus 325	2,55	1551
2188	E, Field 6 Locus 1076	2,3	1375
2189	E, Field 46 Locus 917	2,1	1134
2190	V, Field 2 Locus 934	1,9	1159
2191	F, Field 13 Locus 963	1,85	1207
2192	E, Field 5 Locus 955	1,7	1190
2193	F, Field 13 Locus 963	1,65	1209
2194	C, Field 6 Locus 589	1,55	1720
2195	C, Field 6 Locus 589	1,55	1725

2196	F, Field 25 Locus 1100	1,55	1520
2197	G, Field 8 Locus 1043	1,55	1285
2198	F, Field 31 Locus 1158	1,4	1673
2199	F, Field 13 Locus 963	1,35	1210
2200	F, Field 31 Locus 1158	1,35	1670
2201	C, Field 15 Locus 589	1,3	1741
2202	D, Field 2 Locus 255	1,3	1604
2203	E, Field 26 Locus 919/920	1,3	1148
2204	G, Field 9 Locus 1211	1,3	1279
2205	E, Field 6 Locus 1076	1,2	1376
2206	E, Field 6 Locus 1076	1,2	1498
2207	E, Field 6 Locus 1083	1,2	1480
2208	F, Field 25 Locus 1101	1,2	1530
2209	F, Field 25 Locus 1109	1,2	1645
2210	F, Field 32 Locus 1152	1,2	1585
2211	A, Field 4 Locus 1209	1,16	1185
2212	E, Field 8 Locus 1063	1,15	1102
2213	C, Field 15 Locus 589	1,10	1751
2214	E, Field 26 Locus 919/920	1,1	1149
2215	F, Field 25 Locus 552	1,1	1576
2216	E, Field 7 Locus 1071	1,05	1415
2217	G, Field 9 Locus 1051	1,05	1261
2218	C, Field 6 Locus 589	1,01	1727

2219	E, Field 7 Locus 1068	1,01	1364
2220	F, Field 32 Locus 1152	1,01	1678
2221	G, Locus 455	1,01	1280
2222	E, Field 26 Locus 920	1	1146
2223	G, Field 8 Locus 1044	1	1284
2224	F, Field 7	0,97	583L
2225	E, Field 6 Locus 1076	0,95	1497
2226	F, Field 12 Locus 902	0,95	1130
2227	F, Field 14 Locus 921	0,95	1140
2228	F, Field 25 Locus 552	0,95	1579
2229	F, Field 31 Locus 1158	0,95	1628
2230	G, Field 8 Locus 1039	0,95	1252
2231	E, Field 8 Locus 1064	0,95	1293
2232	E, Field 6 Locus 1079	0,9	1499
2233	E, Field 8 Locus 1067	0,9	1357
2234	F, Field 31 Locus 1158	0,9	1626
2235	F, Field 7	0,9	1710
2236	D, Field 2 Locus 255	0,85	1609
2237	F, Field 25 Locus 351	0,85	1542
2238	C, Field 6 Locus 589	0,8	1728
2239	E, Field 2 Locus 982	0,8	1403
2240	F, Field 13 Locus 266	0,8	1195
2241	F, Field 13 Locus 964	0,8	1200

2242	F, Field 7 Locus 1071	0,8	1414[17]
2243	F, Field 25 Locus 351	0,75	1543
2244	E, Field 6 Locus 1076	0,75	1483
2245	E, Field 7 Locus 1071	0,75	1419
2246	E, Field 8 Locus 1065	0,75	1353
2247	F, Field 25 Locus 1101	0,75	1532
2248	F, Field 25 Locus 1101	0,75	1534
2249	F, Field 25 Locus 1109	0,75	1652
2250	E Field 7 Locus 1071	0,75	1413
2251	F, Field 18 Locus 553	0,7	1549
2252	F, Field 25 Locus 1109	0,70	1653
2253	F, Field 25 Locus 552	0,7	1538
2254	F, Field 31 Locus 1158	0,7	1629
2255	F, Field 32	0,7	1616
2256	F, Field 7 Locus 282	0,7	1186
2257	C, Field 15 Locus 589	0,65	1738
2258	C, Field 15 Locus 589	0,65	1750
2259	C, Field 15 Locus 589	0,65	1726
2260	E, Field 7 Locus 1071	0,65	1420
2261	E, Field 7 Locus 1071	0,65	1416
2262	F, Field 25 Locus 1109	0,65	1648
2263	E, Field 8 Locus 1064	0,65	1310
2264	E, Field 24 Locus 925	0,63	1155

17 Perhaps SNG. ANS, *Palestine-South Arabia*, 206–218? R/Two cornucopiae?

2265	C, Field 15 Locus 589	0,6		1743
2266	F, Field 30 Locus 1118	0,6		1756
2267	E, Field 6 Locus 1079	0,6		1501
2268	E, Field 7 Locus 1071	0,6		1443
2269	V, Field 2 Locus 932	0,6		1178
2270	F, Field 18 Locus 329	0,55		1393
2271	E, Field 7 Locus 1071	0,55		1445
2272	F, Field 13 Locus 266	0,55		1196
2273	F, Field 13 Locus 963	0,55		1213
2274	F, Field 25 Locus 557	0,55		1692
2275	F, Field 25 Locus 552	0,55		1580
2276	F, Field 36 Locus 377	0,55		1126
2277	F, Field 25 Locus 552	0,55		1582
2278	M, Field 20	0,55		1700
2279	D, Field 11 Locus 816	0,55		1701
2280	F, Field 31 Locus 1161	0,54		1666[18]
2281	F, Field 3 North	0,52		595L
2282	D, Field 2 Locus 255	0,5		1608
2283	F, Field 25 Locus 1101	0,5		1405
2284	E, Field 3 Locus 1092	0,5		1507
2285	E, Field 3 Locus 1092	0,5		1508
2286	E, Field 6 Locus 1079	0,5		1470
2287	E, Field 7 Locus 1071	0,5		1425

18 Perhaps fifth century CE?

2288	F, Field 25 Locus 325	0,5	1394
2289	F, Field 25 Locus 1100	0,5	1525
2290	F, Field 25 Locus 1109	0,50	1651
2291	F, Field 25 Locus 552	0,5	1581
2292	F, Field 25 Locus 1100	0,5	1544
2293	G, Field 10 Locus 1054	0,5	1256
2294	E, Field 8 Locus 1064	0,5	1298
2295	V, Field 2 Locus 931	0,5	1172
2296	V, Field 2 Locus 967	0,5	1225
2297	E, Field 6 Locus 1076	0,45	1485
2298	E, Field 6 Locus 1076	0,45	1486
2299	E, Field 6 Locus 1076	0,45	1377
2300	E, Field 6 Locus 1079	0,45	1472
2301	E, Field 8 Locus 1064	0,45	1340
2302	F, Field 7	0,45	593L
2303	F, Field 16 Locus 1103	0,45	1683
2304	F, Field 25 Locus 1100	0,45	1524
2305	F, Field 25 Locus 1110	0,45	1527
2306	F, Field 31 Locus 1158	0,45	1630
2307	G, Field 8 Locus 1046	0,45	1246
2308	E, Field 8 Locus 1064	0,45	1296
2309	E, Field 8 Locus 1064	0,45	1299
2310	G, Field 8 Locus 940	0,45	1244

2311	G, Field 9 Locus 1051	0,45		1267
2312	H, Field 3 Locus 7	0,45		1592
2313	V, Field 2 Locus 930	0,45		1174
2314	V, Field 2 Locus 967	0,45		1226
2315	C, Field 6 Locus 589	0,4		1729
2316	E, Field 18 Locus 325/329	0,4		1398
2317	F, Field 30 Locus 1102	0,4		1572
2318	F, Field 30 Locus 1104	0,4		1513
2319	E, Field 7 Locus 1071	0,4		1428
2320	E, Field 7 Locus 1074	0,4		1455
2321	E, Field 8 Locus 1064	0,4		1320
2322	E, Field 8 Locus 1064	0,4		1321
2323	E, Field 8 Locus 1090	0,4		1386
2324	F, Field 14 Locus 921	0,4		1143
2325	F, Field 18 Locus 1111	0,4		1688
2326	F, Field 25 Locus 1101	0,40		1537
2327	F, Field 31 Locus 1158	0,4		1674
2328	F, Field 31 Locus 1163	0,4		1681
2329	F, Field 32 US 1104	0,4		1614
2330	E, Field 7 Locus 1071	0,4		1431
2331	G, Field 9 Locus 1047	0,4		1253
2332	H, Field 2 Locus 1121	0,4		1589
2333	V, Field 2 Locus 967	0,4		1224

2334	C, Field 6 Locus 589	0,35	1731
2335	E, Field 6 Locus 1076	0,35	1488
2336	E, Field 6 Locus 1079	0,35	1460
2337	E, Field 7 Locus 1073	0,35	1369
2338	E, Field 8 Locus 1064	0,35	1323
2339	F, Field 18 Locus 325/329	0,35	1401
2340	F, Field 25 Locus 351	0,35	1559
2341	F, Field 3 Locus 902	0,35	1119
2342	C, Field 6 Locus 589	0,30	1733
2343	F, Field 25 Locus 552	0,3	1583
2344	E, Field 26 Locus 919/920	0,3	1152
2345	E, Field 6 Locus 1079	0,3	1459
2346	E, Field 6 Locus 1079	0,3	1474
2347	E, Field 6 Locus 1079	0,3	1461
2348	E, Field 7 Locus 1071	0,3	1433
2349	E, Field 7 Locus 1071	0,3	1448
2350	E, Field 8 Locus 1063	0,3	1350
2351	E, Field 8 Locus 1063	0,3	1351
2352	F, Field 7	0,3	586L
2353	F, Field 3 North	0,3	597L
2354	F, Field 18 Locus 1111	0,3	1689
2355	F, Field 30 Locus 1100	0,3	1545
2356	E, Field 7 Locus 1071	0,3	1444

2357	F, Field 3 Locus 284	0,3		1123
2358	G, Field 9 Locus 1051	0,3		1275
2359	F, Field 3 North	0,26		594L
2360	C, Field 15 Locus 589	0,25		1752
2361	C, Field 15 Locus 589	0,25		1755
2362	C, Field 15 Locus 589	0,25		1734
2363	E, Field 3 Locus 1092	0,25		1509
2364	E, Field 34 Locus 321	0,25		1705
2365	E, Field 6 Locus 1079	0,25		1458
2366	E, Field 6 Locus 1079	0,25		1504
2367	E, Field 7 Locus 1071	0,25		1424
2368	E, Field 7 Locus 1071	0,25		1429
2369	E, Field 7 Locus 1071	0,25		1446
2370	E, Field 7 Locus 1071	0,25		1449
2371	E, Field 8 Locus 1064	0,25		1319
2372	E, Field 8 Locus 1064	0,25		1301
2373	E, Field 8 Locus 1064	0,25		1302
2374	E, Field 8 Locus 1067	0,25		1359
2375	E, Field 8 Locus 1090	0,25		1388
2376	E, Field 11 Locus 305	0,25		303
2377	F, Field 18 Locus 1110	0,25		1685
2378	F, Field 18 Locus 325/329	0,25		1400
2379	F, Field 25 Locus 1101	0,25		1406

2380	F, Field 31 Locus 1158	0,25	1631
2381	F, Field 3 Locus 265	0,25	1132
2382	F, Field 19 Locus 362	0,25	1660
2383	F, Field 31	0,25	1640
2384	F, Field 31 Locus 1158	0,25	1632
2385	F, Field 31 Locus 1161	0,25	1661.1[19]
2386	E, Field 7 Locus 1071	0,25	1432
2387	E, Field 8 Locus 1064	0,25	1300
2388	G, Field 9 Locus 1048	0,25	1277
2389	H, Field 3 Locus 1133	0,25	1596
2390	H, Field 3 Locus 21	0,25	1590
2391	C, Field 15 Locus 589	0,20	1739
2392	F, Field 25 Locus 552	0,2	1584
2393	E, Field 36 Locus 376	0,2	1128
2394	E, Field 6 Locus 1079	0,2	1380
2395	E, Field 6 Locus 1079	0,2	1475
2396	E, Field 6 Locus 1079	0,2	1462
2397	E, Field 6 Locus 1079	0,2	1463
2398	E, Field 6 Locus 1079	0,2	1503
2399	E, Field 7 Locus 1071	0,2	1447
2400	E, Field 7 Locus 1073	0,2	1454
2401	E, Field 8 Locus 1064	0,2	1344
2402	E, Field 8 Locus 1064	0,2	1343

19 Perhaps fifth century CE?

2403	E, Field 8 Locus 1064	0,2	1333
2404	E, Field 8 Locus 1064	0,2	1337
2405	E, Field 8 Locus 1065	0,2	1354
2406	F, Field 3 Locus 902	0,2	1120
2407	F, Field 11 Locus 970	0,2	1229
2408	F, Field 13 Locus 266	0,2	1197
2409	F, Field 13 Locus 963	0,2	1219
2410	F, Field 25 Locus 1109	0,20	1654
2411	F, Field 25 Locus 1109	0,20	1655
2412	F, Field 25 Locus 552	0,2	1539
2413	F, Field 25 Locus 554	0,2	1547
2414	F, Field 30 Locus 1102	0,2	1573
2415	F, Field 30 Locus 1107	0,2	1565
2416	F, Field 31 Locus 1158	0,2	1633
2417	F, Field 32 Locus 1103	0,2	1619
2418	F, Field 5 Locus 956	0,2	1189
2419	E, Field 7 Locus 1071	0,2	1434
2420	E, Field 8 Locus 1064	0,2	1328
2421	G, Field 8 Locus 1044	0,2	1247
2422	G, Field 9 Locus 1048	0,2	1266
2423	C, Field 15 Locus 589	0,15	1742
2424	V, Field 2 Locus 258	0,15	1169
2425	E, Field 25 Locus 929	0,15	1157

2426	E, Field 26 Locus 919/920	0,15	1153
2427	E, Field 6 Locus 1076	0,15	1489
2428	E, Field 8 Locus 1067	0,15	1361
2429	E, Field 7 Locus 1074	0,15	1456
2430	E, Field 7 Locus 1073	0,15	1370
2431	E, Field 8 Locus 1064	0,15	1342
2432	E, Field 8 Locus 1064	0,15	1304
2433	E, Field 8 Locus 1064	0,15	1305
2434	E, Field 8 Locus 1064	0,15	1307
2435	E, Field 8 Locus 1064	0,15	1334
2436	E, Field 7 Locus 1073	0,15	1371
2437	E, Field 6 Locus 1079	0,15	1381
2438	F, Field 13 Locus 963	0,15	1222
2439	F, Field 16 Locus 1103	0,15	1684
2440	F, Field 16 Locus 1157	0,15	1615
2441	F, Field 25 Locus 325	0,15	1554
2442	F, Field 25 Locus 1101	0,15	1659
2443	F, Field 30 Locus 1100	0,15	1528
2444	F, Field 31 Locus 1158	0,15	1634
2445	E, Field 7 Locus 1071	0,15	1436
2446	E, Field 7 Locus 1071	0,15	1451
2447	G, Field 10 Locus 1054	0,15	1257
2448	G, Field 9 Locus 1051	0,15	1263

2449	V, Field 2 Locus 931	0,15	1165
2450	V, Field 2 Locus 932	0,15	1179
2451	V, Field 2 Locus 932	0,15	1180
2452	F, Field 7	0,14	582L
2453	E, Field 8 Locus 1063	0,10	1104
2454	E, Field 25 Locus 929	0,1	1158
2455	E, Field 3 Locus 1092	0,1	1510
2456	F, Field 30 Locus 1114	0,1	1519
2457	E, Field 34 Locus 321	0,1	1706
2458	E, Field 6 Locus 1076	0,1	1487
2459	E, Field 6 Locus 1076	0,1	1490
2460	E, Field 6 Locus 1079	0,1	1476
2461	E, Field 6 Locus 1079	0,1	1477
2462	E, Field 6 Locus 1079	0,1	1465
2463	E, Field 6 Locus 1079	0,1	1505
2464	E, Field 6 Locus 1080	0,1	1569
2465	E, Field 8 Locus 1063	0,1	1105
2466	E, Field 8 Locus 1064	0,10	1338
2467	E, Field 8 Locus 1064	0,1	1345
2468	E, Field 8 Locus 1064	0,1	1303
2469	E, Field 8 Locus 1064	0,1	1306
2470	E, Field 8 Locus 1064	0,1	1308
2471	E, Field 8 Locus 1064	0,1	1327

2472	E, Field 8 Locus 1064	0,1	1335
2473	E, Field 8 Locus 1064	0,1	1336
2474	E, Field 8 Locus 1067	0,1	1360
2475	F, Field 1 Locus 992	0,1	1230
2476	F, Field 12 Locus 265	0,1	1124
2477	F, Field 13 Locus 963	0,1	1223
2478	F, Field 18 Locus 1110	0,1	1686
2479	F, Field 18 Locus 325/329	0,1	1402
2480	F, Field 18 Locus 329	0,1	1668
2481	E, Field 22a Locus 316	0,1	1703
2482	F, Field 25 Locus 1101	0,10	1407
2483	F, Field 3 Locus 265	0,1	1133
2484	E, Field 7 Locus 1071	0,1	1435
2485	E, Field 7 Locus 1071	0,1	1450
2486	G, Field 10 Locus 1054	0,1	1258
2487	G, Field 9 Locus 1211	0,1	1274
2488	G, Field 9 Locus 1051	0,1	1268
2489	F, Field B Locus 281	0,1	1611
2490	V, Field 2 Locus 935	0,1	1163
2491	V, Field 2 Locus 937	0,1	1173
2492	C, Field 15 Locus 589	0,05	1744
2493	E, Field 26 Locus 919/920	0,05	1154
2494	E, Field 6 Locus 1076	0,05	1491

2495	E, Field 6 Locus 1079	0,05		1464
2496	E, Field 6 Locus 1079	0,05		1478
2497	E, Field 6 Locus 1079	0,05		1479
2498	E, Field 8 Locus 1063	0,05		1352
2499	E, Field 8 Locus 1063	0,05		1106
2500	E, Field 8 Locus 1065	0,05		1355
2501	E, Field 6 Locus 1079	0,05		1382
2502	E, Field 11 Locus 301/302	0,05		315
2503	F, Field 33 Locus 298	0,05		1138
2504	F, Field 25 Locus 551	0,05		1687
2505	F, Field 25 Locus 1100	0,05		1389
2506	F, Field 25 Locus 1109	0,05		1656
2507	F, Field 25 Locus 1109	0,05		1657
2508	F, Field 29 Locus 1021	0,05		1240
2509	F, Field 3 Locus 901	0,05		1696
2510	F, Field 3 Locus 902	0,05		1121
2511	F, Field 31 Locus 1158	0,05		1635
2512	F, Field 31 Locus 1163	0,05		1682
2513	E, Field 7 Locus 1071	0,05		1437
2514	E, Field 7 Locus 1071	0,03		1440
2515	F, Field 31 Locus 1161	0,02		1663
2516	F, Field 31 Locus 1161	0,02		1664
2517	F, Field 25 Locus 1100	0,02		1526

No coin, metal fragment?

2518	E, Field 8 Locus 1064	1339
2519	E, Field 8 Locus 1067	1362
2520	E, Field 7 Locus 1073	1372
2521	F, Field 18 Locus 329	1392
2522	E, Field 7 Locus 1071	1438
2523	E, Field 7 Locus 1071	1439
2524	E, Field 7 Locus 1071	1452
2525	E, Field 7 Locus 1071	1453
2526	E, Field 6 Locus 1076	1492
2527	E, Field 3 Locus 1092	1511
2528	F, Field 16 Locus 1157	1677
2529	C, Field 6 Locus 589	1735

Exagia

AE (fourth–fifth century)

2530	F, Field 25 Locus 317	13,55	19	Wreath
2531	E, Field 36 Locus 376	2,25	17	corroded

Byzantine coins

Iustinianus I
Mint of Salona

AE. ½ follis (552–553?)
O/Bust facing; in field r., cross
R/K, plain border

2532	Locus 15A	4,1	16	↑	MIBE, 250; DOC I, 360	*892L

Iustinus II
Mint of Constantinopolis

AE. Follis (568–569)
O/Justin on l., Sophia on r., seated, nimbate, on double throne; D N IVSTINVS P P AVC
R/M above cross, to l. ANNO, in exergue: CON/Δ, to r. IIII

2533	E, Field 11	10,18	29	↓	MIBEC 43a; DOC I, 25d	*323L

Mint of Nicomedia

AE. Follis (566–578)
O/Justin on l., Sophia on r., seated, nimbate, on double throne; D N IVSTINVS P P AVC
R/M above cross, to l. ANNO [---], in exergue: NIKO/Δ, to r. Γ

2534	E, Field 11	10,25	28	↓	MIBEC 46a; DOC I, 96	*324L

AE. Follis (575–576)
O/Justin on l., Sophia on r., seated, nimbate, on double throne; D N IVSTINVS P P AVC
R/M above cross, to l. ANNO, in exergue: NIK/B, to r. XI

2535	E, Field 11 Locus 300	11,25	30	↓	MIBEC, 47b	*290

AE. Follis (576–577)
O/Justin on l., Sophia on r., seated, nimbate, on double throne; D N IVSTINVS P P AVC
R/M above cross, to l. ANNO, in exergue: NIK/A, to r. XII

2536	E, Field 11	11,25	29	↓	MIBEC 47a	*313L

Mint of Antiochia

AE. Follis (569–570)
O/Justin on l., Sophia on r., seated, nimbate, on double throne; D N IVSTINVS P P AVC
R/M above cross, to l. ANNO, in exergue: THEЏP′, to r. II III

2537	Survey	13,57	33	↓	MIBEC 56a	*890L

2532

2533

2534

2535

2536

2537

Mauritius Tiberius
Mint of Cyzicus

AE. Follis (584–585)
O/Bust facing, wearing cuirass and crown with cross and pendilia: DN MAVRIC TIbER PP A
R/M above cross, to l. ANNO, in exergue: KYZ/A? to r. II I

2538	E, Field 11	8,74	29	↓	MIBEC, 84D; DOC I, 120.a	*312L

Indeterminate mint

AE. ½ follis (582–602)
O/Bust facing, wearing cuirass and crown with cross and pendilia: DN MAVRIC TIbER PP A
R/K above cross, to l. ANNO; in exergue: A?

2539	F, Field 19 Locus 353	4,85	24	↓	MIBEC?	*887

Heraclius
Mint of Constantinopolis

AE. ½ follis (620–621)
O/Bust bearded, facing, wearing cuirass with shield and crown with pendilia; δNEhRACLI PERP AVG
R/K, above cross, to l. ANNO, to r. XI

2540	F, Field 25 Locus 351	7,5	27	↙	MIB III, 169	*351

AE. Follis (629–630)
O/To l. Heraclius standing; he holds in r. hand long cross. To r. Heraclius Constantine standing, with short beard and crown with cross
R/M, above cross, to l. ANNO, to r. XX; under M: e

2541	E, Field 36 Locus 321	5,05	29	↓	DOC II.1, 105	*825

AE. ½ follis (620–621)
O/Bust bearded, facing, wearing cuirass with shield and crown with pendilia; δNEhRACLI PERP AVG
R/K, above cross, to l. ANNO, to r. XI

Mint of Alexandria

AE. Dodecanummus (632–641)
O/Three figures standing wearing chlamys and holding globus in r. hand
R/Cross above M between IB

2542	D, Field 1	8,25	18	↗	DOC II.1, 105	*252L

2538

2539

2540

2541

2542

Constans II
Mint of Constantinopolis
AE. Follis (659–664)
O/Emperor standing, facing, long cross and globus
R/Three emperors standing, facing, wearing chlamys

2543	Without context	6,4	14	↑	MIB III, 175		*453

Imitative coin
AE. Follis (ca. 642)
O/Corroded [but, perhaps emperor standing, facing, long cross and globus]
R/m

2544	F 100:1	4,24	16	↑	MIB III, X29	CON	*470L

2543

2544

Arab-Byzantine coins

Hoard ***Under the Umayyads, pre-reform***

Mint of Tiberias

AE (ca. 660–680)

O/Three standing figure, each holding a globus cruciger, + on crowns, no legend

R/M, above ₽, A below; TIBEPIAΔOI; exergue (Arabic legend): *ṭabaryya* r.

2545	E, Field 11	3,79	28	↑	SICA 587–591; Foss 2008, 81; CHL, pl. 68, 40–43	*317L
2546	E, Field 11	2,37	26	↙	*same*	*322L
2547	E, Field 11	3,45	26	↓	*same*	*321L
2548	E, Field 11	2,07	27	↓	*same*	*320L
2549	E, Field 11	3,84	26	↓	*same*	*319L
2550	E, Field 11	3,48	26	↙	*same*	*318L
2551	E, Field 11	2,35	20	←	*same*	*316L
2552	E, Field 11	2,95	28	↓	*same*	*315L
2553	E, Field 11	3,68	27	↓	*same*	*314L

Single finds ***Under the Umayyads, pre-reform***

The Earliest Arab-Byzantine Coins

Cyprus Imitations

AE. Fulus (638–ca. 645)

O/Three standing emperors facing, wearing chlamys and crown with cross, holding globus cruciger in r. hand

R/M, Γ below (?); uncertain legend r.

2554	E, Field 11	3,45	23	↑	Foss 2008, pp. 22–23, p. 123, 3–4	*445L

Imitative coins (647–ca. 670)

AE. Fulus

O/Standing imperial figure [EN T8TO NIKA]

R/m, above * (?); unclear letters in exergue

2555	F 101, on the pavement	4,29	13	↑	Foss 2008, p. 125, 8–13, p. 126, 16–18	*858L

AE. Fulus

O/Standing imperial figure [EN T8TO NIKA]

R/m, above + (?); ANA l., unclear letters r. and in exergue

2556	E, Field 11 Locus 301/302	1,8	19	↑	Foss 2008, p. 125, 9	*317
2557	F 100:2	1,8	19	↑	same	*736L

AE. Fulus

O/Standing imperial figure [EN T8TO NIKA]

R/m, above + (?); unclear letters r. and in exergue

2558	D, Field 1	4,1	18	↑	Foss 2008, p. 124–125 8–22: 22	*192L

2545

2546

2547

2548

2549

2550

2551

2552

2553

2554

2555

2556

2557

2558

The Caliphate of Mu'awiya
First Bilingual Series (Standing Imperial Figure)
Mint of Damascus

AE. Fulus (660–680)
O/Standing imperial figure, bird on T l.; field X АИ and traces of other letters
R/M, above ⳨ (?), below *; *dimashq wafiya jāza hadhā*

2559	F, Field 20 Locus 298	3,25	21	↑	Foss 2008, pp. 130–131, 35–38	*781
2560	D, Field 1	2,89	21	↑	same	*235L
2561	E, Field 11	2,35	21	↓	same	*326L

The Main Bilingual Series (Standing Imperial Figure)
Mint of Damascus

AE. Fulus (660–680)
O/Standing imperial figure, field [ΛEO] and traces of other letters
R/M, above ⳨ (?), below; exergue: [ΔAM]

2562	E, Field 11	2,68	19	↙	Foss 2008, p. 132, 46–55	*328L

Mint of Tiberias

AE. Fulus (660–680)
O/Three standing figure, each holding a globus cruciger, + on crowns, no legend
R/M, above ⳨, A below; TIBEPIAΔOI; in exergue: *ṭabaryya* r.

2563	E, Field 11 Locus 300	3,8	25	↑	SICA 587–591; Foss 2008, 81; CHL, p. 68, 40–43	*331
2564	E, Field 11 Locus 300	3,95	24	↓	same	*347
2565	E, Field 11	2,97	24	↑	same	443L
2566	E, Field 11	1,57	15	↑	same	454L

Caliph Standing Type
Jund of Quinnasrin? Mint of Halab?

AE. Fulus
O/Standing bearded figure of the caliph, wearing on Arab headdress and long robe, his right hand on the hilt of his sword, which diagonally to his left; (li) *'abd allah 'abd al-malik amīr al-mu'minīn*
R/Φ on four steps and around the inscription; *lā ilaha illāallah waḥdahu muḥammad rasūl allah*

2567	E, Field 11 Locus 300	2,25	20	↑	Foss 2008, p. 146, 115–119	*336

Indeterminate Mint

AE. Fulus
O/Standing bearded figure of the caliph, wearing on Arab headdress and long robe, his right hand on the hilt of his sword, which diagonally to his left; (li) *'abd allah 'abd al-malik amīr al-mu'minīn*
R/Φ on four steps and around the inscription; *lā ilaha illāallah waḥdahu muḥammad rasūl allah*

2568	C, Field 7 Locus 748	1,9	17		Foss 2008, pp. 146–147	*861

2559

2560

2561

2562

2563

2564

2567

2568

Arabic Coins

Arianna D'Ottone

Arab-Byzantine and transitional issues

1.Arab	D1A	AE	1,92	14	Ḥimṣ (?)/ʿAmmān	1st c. AH/ AD 7th c.

Umayyad: Post-reform

2.Arab	F 101, on the ground	AE	1,89	14	ʿAbd Allāh al-Walīd (86–96 AH/ AD705–714) (?)	1st c. AH/ AD 7th c.
3.Arab	E, Field 30 US 1093	AE	2,20	16	al-Urdunn	Undated [c.a 1st c. AH/AD 7th c.]
4.Arab	D 1	AE	5,19	17	Ṭabariyya with the district name of al-Urdunn	c.a 100 AH/AD 718
5.Arab	E 11	AE	1,44	24	Dimashq (?)	1st–2nd c. AH/ AD 7th–8th c.
6.Arab	F Field 30 US 1093	AE	1,95	16	No Mint [Filasṭīn or al-Urdunn]	1st–2nd c. AH/ AD 7th–8th c.
7.Arab		AE			Dimashq	1st–2nd c. AH/ AD 7th–8th c.
8.Arab	F Fiel 30 US 1097	AE	4,8	16		1st–2nd c. AH/ AD 7th–8th c.
9.Arab	Survey	AE	4,42	16	ʿAbd al-Malik b. Yazīd (131–132 AH/AD 749–750)	No date [second quarter 2nd c. AHAD/mid-8th c.]
10.Arab	F, Field A US 280	AE	2,4	15		ca. first half 2nd c. AH/ AD second quarter 8th c.
11.Arab	F, Field 20 US 375	AE	1,85	15	No mint [al-Urdunn (?)]	ca. 2nd c. AH/ AD 8th c.
12.Arab		AE	0,77	13	No Mint [Filasṭīn or al-Urdunn]	2nd c. AH/ AD 8th c.

Ḥimṣ: cfr. Walker 1956, pp. 9–10: 27–34; ʿAmmān: cfr. SNAT 1993, p. 42: 492 and pl. 16.	*250L
Mint no longer readable – a palm branch on the right of the Rev. [Ṭabariyya (?)/al-Ramla (?)] Ṭabariyya: cfr. SNAT 1993, p. 32: 313 and pl. 11. CHL, vol. I, p. 74: 61–62 and vol. II, pl. 69; al-Ramla: cfr. Walker 1956, p. 257: 846; CHL, vol. I, p. 128: 1 and vol. II, pl. 119	*857L
SNAT 1993, p. 44: 531 and pl. 17.	*1515
Shamma 1400/1980, p. 82: 24 and pl. 2. SNAT 1993, p. 32: 331 and pl. 11; CHL, I, p. 74: 63 and II, pl. 69.	*225L
Walker 1956, p. 252: 835 and pl. XXVII.	*308L
SNAT 1993, p. 46: 571 and pl. 18.	*479
Walker 1956, p. 249: 817; Lavoix 1887, pp. 375–376: 1442–4; Nützel 1898, p. 306 : 1973	783
Fahmī 1965, p. 449: 1388 and pl. 31.	*1517
Miles 1958, p. 480: 7 and pl. XXVII.	*889L
SNAT 1993, p. 46: 560 and pl. 18.	478
cfr. SNAT 1993, p. 46: 547–550 and pl. 18.	*676
cfr. SNAT 1993, p. 46: 570 and pl. 18.	461

1.Arab

2.Arab

3.Arab

4.Arab

5.Arab

6.Arab

8.Arab

9.Arab

11.Arab

Umayyad – Undetermined

13.Arab	D 1	AE	2,52	29	Post-reform	1st–2nd c. AH/ AD 7th–8th c.	SICA?; SNAT?	*206L
14.Arab	D1	AE	1,38	13	Post-reform	1st–2nd c. AH/ AD 7th–8th c.	SICA?; SNAT?	*224L
15.Arab	D 1	AE	2,95	15	Post-reform	1st–2nd c. AH/ AD 7th–8th c.	SICA?; SNAT?	*226L
16.Arab	E 11	AE	2,51	24	Post-reform	1st–2nd c. AH/ AD 7th–8th c.	SICA?; SNAT?	*310L
17.Arab	E 11	AE	2,01	21	Post-reform	1st–2nd c. AH/ AD 7th–8th c.	SICA?; SNAT?	*311L
18.Arab	E, Field 11 US 300	AE	1,6	21	Post-reform	1st–2nd c. AH/ AD 7th–8th c.	SICA?; SNAT?	*312
19.Arab		AE			Post-reform	1st–2nd c. AH/ AD 7th–8th c.	SICA?; SNAT?	317
20.Arab	E22	AE	2,34	18	Post-reform	1st–2nd c. AH/ AD 7th–8th c.	SICA?; SNAT?	*357L
21.Arab	E11	AE	2,26	19	Post-reform	1st–2nd c. AH/ AD 7th–8th c.	SICA?; SNAT?	*447L
22.Arab	E 11	AE	2,76	21	Post-reform	1st–2nd c. AH/ AD 7th–8th c.	SICA?; SNAT?	*449L
23.Arab	E 11	AE	2,54	16	Post-reform	1st–2nd c. AH/ AD 7th–8th c.	SICA?; SNAT?	*450L
24.Arab	F Field 3 US 265	AE	1,65	17	Post-reform	1st–2nd c. AH/ AD 7th–8th c.	SICA?; SNAT?	*451
25.Arab	E 11	AE	1,33	14	Post-reform	1st–2nd c. AH/ AD 7th–8th c.	SICA?; SNAT?	*460L
26.Arab	C, Field 15 US 879	AE	2,15	15	Post-reform	1st–2nd c. AH/ AD 7th–8th c.	SICA?; SNAT?	*512
27.Arab		AE	3,25	23	Post-reform	1st–2nd c. AH/ AD 7th–8th c.	SICA?; SNAT?	*734a/b
28.Arab	F, Field 27 US 620	AE	2,5	23	Post-reform	1st–2nd c. AH/ AD 7th–8th c.	SICA?; SNAT?	*529
29.Arab	F3, under stone	AE	1,69	14	Post-reform (?)	1st–2nd c. AH/ AD 7th–8th c.	SICA?; SNAT?	*885L
30.Arab	C, Field US 270	AE	3,15	16	Post-reform (?)	1st–2nd c. AH/ AD 7th–8th c.	SICA?; SNAT?	*971
31.Arab	F, Field 30 US 1097	AE	2,6	13	Post-reform (?)	1st–2nd c. AH/ AD 7th–8th c.	SICA?; SNAT?	*1560

13.Arab

14.Arab

15.Arab

16.Arab

17.Arab

18.Arab

20.Arab

21.Arab

22.Arab

23.Arab

24.Arab

25.Arab

26.Arab

27.Arab

28.Arab

29.Arab

30.Arab

31.Arab

Abbasid – Undetermined

32.Arab	Road 4	AE	1,58	19	Abbasid	2nd–3rd c. AH/ AD 9th–10th c.		*167L
33.Arab	D 1	AE	3,03	19	Abbasid	2nd–3rd c. AH/ AD 9th–10th c.		*236L
34.Arab	E, Field 11 US 300	AE	2,4	22	Abbasid	2nd–3rd c. AH/ AD 9th–10th c.		*309
35.Arab	F, Field A US 280	AE	2,4	15	Abbasid	2nd–3rd c. AH/ AD 9th–10th c.		*478
36.Arab	F 1	AE	1,19	17	Abbasid	2nd–3rd c. AH/ AD 9th–10th c.		*634L

Mamluk

37.Arab	Survey	AE	17	16	Dimashq Al-Manṣūr Ḥusām al-Dīn Lājīn – 3rd reign (696–698 AH/AD 1296–1299)	Undated	Balog 1964, p. 131: 166 and pl. VII.	*639
38.Arab		AE	3,10	17	[Dimashq] Al-Nāṣir Muḥammad b. Qalāʿūn – 3rd reign (709–741 AH/AD 1310–1341)	[735–739 AH/ AD 1334–1339]	Cfr. Balog 1964, p. 150: 222–225 and pl. IX; Mitchiner 1977, p. 197: 1171.	*454
39.Arab	M Field 5A	AE		17	[Dimashq] Al-Ṣāliḥ Ṣalāḥ al-Dīn Hājj II – first reign (783–784 AH/ AD 1381–1384)	[783 AH/ AD 1381–82]	Balog 1964, p. 243: 524 and pl. XXI (524a-b).	*662

Ottoman

40.Arab	Field 3 US 11	AE-Bakir	5,65	21	Mişr Abdülaziz (1277–1293 AH/ AD 1861–1876)	1277 (?) AH/ AD 1861 (?)	Pere 1968, p. 269: 954 and pl. 62.	*92
41.Arab	M, Us 999	AE-Bakir	2,5	22	Qusṭanṭiniyya Abdülhamid II (1293–1327 AH/AD 1876–1909)	1293 AH/AD 1877	Pere 1968, p. 281: 996 and pl. 66.	*924

PS. Further 27 coins were found in the excavations, possibly all dating back to Islamic times, but they were worn and corroded and impossible to classify.

32.Arab

33.Arab

34.Arab

35.Arab

36.Arab

37.Arab

38.Arab

39.Arab

40.Arab

41.Arab

The Latin kingdom of Jerusalem

Amaury (1163–1174)
AR. Denier
O/Cross; AMALRICVS REX
R/Church of the Resurrection + DE IERVSALEM

LC1	A, Field 7 US1197	0,75	17	↑	Metcalf 1995, 169–194	*1788
LC2	Road 2	0,55	18	↑	Metcalf 1995, 169–194	*145L

LC1

LC2

Modern Coins

British Palestine Administration

AR. 100 Mils (1935)
O/Olive branch, vertical; PALESTINE (also in Arabic and Hebrew); in the l. and r. side: 1935
R/In the field: 100; around ONE HUNDRED MILS (also in Arabic and Hebrew)

1MC	H, Field 1 US 0	11,6	29	↑	Krause, Mishler 1990, p. 1058	*83

AE. 1 Mil (1927)
O/In the field: 1; around ONE MIL (also in Arabic and Hebrew)
R/Olive branch, vertical; PALESTINE (also in Arabic and Hebrew); under the legend 1927

2MC	H, Field 1 US 0	3	21	↑	Krause, Mishler 1990, p. 1057	*206

AE. 1 Mil (1940 ca.)
O/In the field: 1; around ONE MIL (also in Arabic and Hebrew)
R/Olive branch, vertical; PALESTINE (also in Arabic and Hebrew); under the legend 1940(?)

3MC	H, Field 2 US 13	2,25	21	↑	Krause, Mishler 1990, p. 1057	*94

United States of America

Nickel Five Cent Piece. 5 cent. (1923)
O/Indian Head; at the l. side: 1923; around, at r. side: LIBERTY
R/Buffalo l.; around: UNITES STATES OF AMERICA; in the field: E PLURIBUS UNUM; exergue: FIVE CENTS

4MC	H, Field 3 US 7	4,46	21	↓	Krause, Mishler 1990, p. 1731	*109

Corroded flan of modern coin

5MC	H, Field 3 US 7	3,4	21	763
6MC	Without context	1,85	19	753[20]

20 R/Eagle on the field?

1MC

2MC

3MC

4MC

Bibliography

Abdy R., "The Severans", in Metcalf W. (ed.), *The Oxford Handbook of Greek and Roman Coinage*, New York 2012, pp. 499–513.

Abou Diwan G., *Sarepta V: The Coin Finds of Areas I and II (X, Y). Persian, Hellenistic, Roman, Byzantine and Medieval Periods*, Beirut 2016 (*BAAL. Hors-Série* 14), pp. 17–18.

Abu-'Uqsa H., "The Finding from Two Excavations at Migdal", *'Atiqot* 42 (2001), pp. 9–25 (Hebr.) and pp. 321–322 (English summary).

Abu-'Uqsa H., "Migdal. Final Report", *Hadashot Arkheologiyot* 2001, p. 117 (https://atiqot.org.il).

Ahipaz N., "Floor Foundation Coin Deposit in Byzantine-Period Synagogue", in Guri-Rimon O. (ed.), *Hoards and Genizot as Chapters in History*, Haifa 2013, pp. 63–69.

Al-Akra H., *L'histoire de Baalbek à l'époque médiévale d'après les monnaies (636–1516)*, Beirut/Damascus 2016 (Études arabes, médiévales et modernes 287).

Al-Bakrī A.'U., *al-Masālik wa-l-mamālik*. 2 vols J. Ṭalba (ed.), Bayrut 2003.

Album, Goodwin 2002 Album S., Goodwin T., *Sylloge of Islamic Coins in the Ashmolean. Vol. 1: The pre-reform coinage of the early Islamic period*, London 2002.

Al-'Ush M., *Kanz Dimashq al-fiḍḍī/ The Silver Hoard of Damascus*, Damascus 1972.

Amitai-Preiss N., "The Coins", in Mazar A. (ed.), *Excavations at Tel Beth-Shean 1989–1996. Vol. 1: From the Late Bronze Age IIB to the Medieval Period*, Jerusalem 1999, pp. 607–615.

Amitai-Preiss N., "Byzantine and Medieval Coins from the Synagogue of Hammath Tiberias", in Dothan M. (ed.), *Hammath Tiberias. Vol. 2: Late Synagogues*, Jerusalem 2000, pp. 95–101.

Ariel D. T., "Coins from the Synagogue at Horvat Kanef", *INJ* 4 (1980), pp. 59–62.

Ariel D. T., "A Survey of Coin Finds in Jerusalem (Until the End of the Byzantine Period)", *LA* 32 (1982), pp. 273–326.

Ariel D. T., "The Coins", in Levine L. I., Netzer E. (eds.), *Excavations at Caesarea Maritima. 1975, 1976, 1979. Final Report*, Jerusalem 1986 (Qedem 21), pp. 137–148.

Ariel D. T., "Coins from the Synagogue at 'En Nashut", *IEJ* 37 (1987), pp. 147–157.

Ariel D. T., "Coins, Flans and Flan Moulds", in Idem, *Excavations at the City of David 1978–1985*. Vol. II, Jerusalem 1990 (Qedem 30), pp. 99–118.

Ariel D. T., "Coins from Excavations at Tel Nahariya, 1982", *'Atiqot* 22 (1993), pp. 125–131.

Ariel D. T., "Coins from the Synagogue at Korazim", in Yeivin Z. (ed.), *The Synagogue at Korazim. The 1962–1964, 1980–1987 Excavations*, Jerusalem 2000 (IAA Reports 10), pp. 33–49.

Ariel D. T., "Judean Perspectives of Ancient Mints and Minting Technology", *INR* 7 (2012), pp. 43–80.

Ariel D. T., "The Coins", in Ben-Ami D. (ed.), *Jerusalem: Excavations in the Tyropoeon Valley (Giv'ati Parking Lot) I*, Jerusalem 2013 (IAA Reports 52), pp. 237–264.

Ariel D. T., "A Mini-Hoard of Tiberias. Coins from Excavations at et-Tell (Bethsaida)", in Strickert F., Freund R. (eds.), *"And They Came to Bethsaida ...". A Festschrift in Honor of Rami Arav*, Newcastle on Tyne 2019, pp. 61–76.

Ariel D. T., "Jerusalem Ha-Nev'im Street: The Coins", *Hadashot Arkheologiyot* 132 (2020a), pp. 1–8 (https://www.hadashot-esi.org.il/default_eng.aspx).

Ariel D. T., "The Byzantine Coins", in Ben-Ami D., Tchekhanovets Y. (eds.), *Jerusalem. Excavations in the Tyropoeon Valley (Giv'ati Parking Lot) II. The Byzantine and Early Islamic Periods*, Jerusalem 2020b (IAA Reports 66), pp. 159–182.

Ariel D. T., "The Coins of the City of David ('Ir David), Siloam Road", *'Atiqot* 101 (2020c), pp. 89–91 (https://atiqot.org.il).

Ariel D. T., "Coins of Alexander Yanai (Jannaeus): A Battle over Identity", INR 17 (2022), pp. 95–127.

Ariel D.T., Berman A., "The Coins from Strata III–II", in Ben-Ami D., Tchekhanovets Y. (eds.), *Jerusalem. Excavations in the Tyropoeon Valley (Giv'ati Parking Lot) II. The Byzantine and Early Islamic Periods*, Jerusalem 2020 (IAA Reports 66), pp. 524–529.

Ariel D.T., Bijovsky G., "The Numismatic Evidence and the History of Sepphoris", in Meyers E., Meyers C. L., Gordon B. D. (eds.), *The Architecture, Stratigraphy, and Artifacts of the Western Summit of Sepphoris* 2, University Park 2018 (Duke Sepphoris Excavation Reports III), pp. 485–587.

Ariel D.T., Fontanille J.-Ph., *The Coins of Herod. A Modern Analysis and Die Classification*, Leiden/Boston 2012.

Ariel D.T., Sokolov H., "The Kafr Bara Hoard", *INR* 13 (2018), pp. 151–193.

Arslan E., "Il deposito di 20.323 Nummi tardo romani della Sinagoga di Cafarnao: come procedere a un campionamento scientifico", *International Numismatic Newsletter* 29 (1996), pp. 6–7.

Arslan E., "Monete axumite di imitazione nel deposito del cortile della Sinagoga", *LA* 46 (1996), pp. 307–316.

Arslan E., "Il deposito monetale della trincea XII nel cortile della Sinagoga di Cafarnao", *LA* 47 (1997), pp. 245–328.

Arslan E., "Dall'Italia a Magdala in Terra Santa. Un pellegrino del V secolo e le sue monete", in Bottini G. C., Di Segni L., Chrupcała L. D. (eds.), *One Land – Many Cultures. Archaeological Studies in Honour of Stanislao Loffreda ofm*, Jerusalem 2003, pp. 33–40.

Arslan E., "Le emissioni monetarie "Isiache" di IV secolo a Roma e Alessandria", in Bonacasa N. *et alii* (eds.), *Faraoni come dei, Tolomei come faraoni. Atti del V Congresso Internazionale Italo-Egiziano. Torino, Archivio di Stato – 8–12 dicembre 2001*, Torino-Palermo 2003b, pp. 171–178.

Arslan E., "Problemi ponderali di V secolo. Verso la riforma del Nummus. Il deposito di Cafarnao", *RN* 159 (2003c), pp. 27–39.

Arslan E., "The L 812 Trench Deposit inside the Synagogue and the Isolated Finds of the Coins in Capernaum, Israel: A Comparison of the Two Groups", *INR* 6 (2011), pp. 148–162.

Arslan E., "'Abraxas' a Cafarnao. Anticipazioni sugli amuleti nel deposito sotto la pavimentazione della sinagoga", *VAMZ* III/54 (2021), pp. 123–138.

Arundell Burton I., *The inner life of Syria, Palestine, and the Holy Land. From my private journal*, London 1875.

Asolati M., *Il tesoro di Falerii Novi. Nuovi contributi sulla monetazione italica in bronzo degli anni di Ricimero (457–472)*, Padova 2004 (Numismatica Patavina 4).

Asolati M., "Il ripostiglio di Camporegio (Grosseto). Note sulle imitazioni bronzee di V secolo d.C. e sulla questione della cosiddetta moneta in rame dell'Italia longobarda", *RIN* 106 (2006), pp. 113–161.

Asolati M., "Nota aggiuntiva all'edizione del ripostiglio di Camporegio (Grosseto). Quale metodo?", *RIN* 109 (2008), pp. 537–557.

Asolati M., *Praestantia nummorum. Temi e note di numismatica tardo antica e alto medievale*, Padova 2012 (Numismatica Patavina 11).

Asolati M., "Questioni di fiduciari età: la tesaurizzazione del nummo e le riforma monetarie da Anastasio a Giustiniano I", in Asolati M., Gorini G. (eds.), *I ritrovamenti monetali e i processi storico-economici nel mondo*, Padova 2012 (Numismatica Patavina 12), pp. 283–325.

Avaliani E., "The cult of Tanit in the context of the Punic cultural model of North Africa", *NAC* 28 (1999), pp. 25–38.

Avshalom-Gorni D., "Migdal. Preliminary Report", *Hadashot Arkheologiyot* 2009a (https://www.hadashot-esi.org.il/default_eng.aspx).

Avshalom-Gorni D., *One of the Oldest Synagogues in the World was Exposed in the IAA Excavation at Magdala*, 2009b https://www.antiquities.org.il/article_eng.aspx?sec_id=25&subj_id=240&id=1601.

Avshalom-Gorni D., Najar A., "Migdal. Preliminary Report", Excavations and Surveys in Israel 125 (2013) (https://www.hadashot-esi.org.il/default_eng.aspx).

Bagatti B., *Antichi villaggi cristiani di Galilea*, Jerusalem 1971 (Collectio Maior 13).

Balog P., *The Coinage of the Mamlūk Sultans of Egypt and Syria*, New York 1964 (Numismatic Studies 12).

Barag D., "The Countermarks of the Legio Decima Fretensis" in Kindler A., *The International Numismatic Convention, Jerusalem/Tel Aviv 1967*, Jerusalem 1967, pp. 117–125.

Barag D., "Tyrian Currency in Galilee", *INJ* 6–7 (1982–1983), pp. 7–13.

Barag D., Qedar S., "A Lead Weight of Malichus II", *INJ* 15 (2003–2006), pp. 62–63.

Barkay R., "Roman Byzantine Coins", in Hirschfeld Y. (ed.), *The Roman Baths of Hammat Gader*, Jerusalem 1997, pp. 279–318.

Barkay R., "The Coins of Horvat 'Eleq", in Hirschfeld Y. (ed.), *Ramat Hanadiv Excavations. Final Report of the 1984–1998 Seasons*, Jerusalem 2000, pp. 377–419.

Barkay R., *The Coinage of Nysa-Scythopolis (Beth-She'an)*, Jerusalem 2003.

Barkay R., "Roman Influence on Jewish Coins", in Jacobson, Kokkinos 2012, pp. 19–26.

Bauckham R., "Magdala in Rabbinic Traditions", in Bauckham R. (ed.), *Magdala of Galilee. A Jewish City in the Hellenistic and Roman Period*, Waco 2018, pp. 307–344.

Belloni G. G., "Le monete di Cesarea", in *Scavi di Cesarea Marittima*, Cariplo - Istituto Lombardo, Accademia di Scienze e Lettere, Milano, pp. 229–234.

Berlin H., *The coins and banknotes of Palestine under the British mandate 1927–1947*, Jefferson 2001.

Berman A., "The coins", in Stacey D. (ed.), *Excavations at Tiberias, 1973–1974. The Early Islamic Period* Jerusalem 2004 (IAA Reports 21), pp. 221–245.

Berman A., "List of Coins", in Mazor G., Najjar A. (eds.), *Nysa-Scythopolis. The Caesareum and the Odeum*, Jerusalem 2007 (IAA Reports 33), pp. 273–275.

Berman A., "The Coins", in Bar-Nathan R., Atrash W. (eds.), *Baysan. The Theater Pottery workshop (Bet She'an 2)*, Jerusalem 2011 (IAA Reports 48), pp. 87–115.

Berman A., "The Coins", in Mazor G., Atrash W. (eds.), *Bet She'an* III. *Nysa Scythopolis. The Southern and Severan Theaters, Part 1: The Stratigraphic Finds*, Jerusalem 2015 (IAA Reports 58/1), pp. 229–272.

Berman A., Bijovsky G., "The Coins from Nevé-Ur", *'Atiqot* 43 (2002), pp. 177–184.

Berman A., Bjiovsky G., "*The Coins*", in Tzaferis V., Israeli Sh. (eds.), *Paneas. Vol. 2: Small Finds and Other Studies*, Jerusalem 2008 (IAA Reports 38), pp. 11–99.

Bijovsky G., "The Gush Halav Hoard Reconsidered", *'Atiqot* 35 (1998), pp. 77–106.

Bijovsky G., "The Currency of the Fifth Century CE in Palestine. Some Reflections in Light of Numismatic Evidence", *INJ* 14 (2000–2002), pp. 196–210.

Bijovsky G., "A Hoard of Byzantine solidi from Bet She'an in the Umayyad Period", *RN* 158 (2002), pp. 161–227.

Bjiovsky G., "Coins", in Hirschfeld Y. (ed.), *Excavations at Tiberias, 1989–1994*, Jerusalem 2004a (IAA Report 22), pp. 169–175.

Bijovsky G., "The Coins from Khirbet Badd 'Isa-Qiryat Sefer. Isolated Coins and two Hoards Dated to the Bar-Kokhba Revolt", in Magen Y. *et alii* (eds.), *The Land of Benjamin*, Jersualem 2004b, pp. 243–300.

Bijovsky G., "The Coins", in Hirschfeld Y., Gutfeld O. (eds.), *Tiberias: Excavations in the House of the Bronze. Final Report I*, Jerusalem 2008 (*Qedem* 48), pp. 63–105.

Bijovsky G., "Numismatic Report", in Meyers E. M., Meyers C. L. (eds.), *Excavations at Ancient Nabratein. Synagogue and Environs*, Winona Lake 2009, pp. 374–395.

Bijovsky G., "A Byzantine Gold Hoard from Rehob (H. Parwa)", *INR* 7 (2012a), pp. 147–158.

Bijovsky G., *Gold Coin and Small Change: Monetary Circulation in Fifth-Seventh Century Byzantine Palestine*, Trieste 2012b.

Bijovsky G., "Arab-Byzantine Coins from Excavations in Israle: An Update", in Oddy A., Schulze I., Schulze W. (eds.), Coinage and History in the Seventh Century Near East, IV: Proceedings of the 14th Seventh Century Syrian Numismatic Round Table Held at the Hive, Worcester, on 28th September 2013, London 2015, pp. 85–114.

Bijovsky G., "The Coins", in Greenberg R., Tal O., Da'adli T. (eds.), *Bet Yerash* III. *Hellenistic Philoteria and Islamic al-Sinnabra*, Jerusalem 2017 (IAA Reports 61), pp. 179–188.

Bijovsky G., "The Coins from Kirbet Wadi Hamam", in Leibner U. (ed.), *Khirbet Wadi Hamam. A Roman-Period Village and Synagogue in The Lower Galilee*, Jerusalem 2018 (Qedem Reports 13), pp. 518–582.

Bijovsky G., "The Coins", in Magen Y., Bijovsky G., Tzionit Y., *Mount Garizim Excavations* III, Jerusalem 2021.

Bijovsky G., Kool R., "Crusader Period Finds from the Temple Mount Excavations in Jerusalem", *'Atiqot* 26 (1995), pp. 87–104.

Bijovsky G., Leibner U., "Two Hoards from Khirbat Wadi Hamam and the Scope of the Bar Kokhba Revolt", *INR* 8 (2013), pp. 109–134.

Blackburn M., "What factors govern the number of coins found on an archaeological site?" in Clarke H., Schia E. (eds.), *Medieval Archaeology Research Group. Proceedings of the first meeting at Isegran, Norway 1988*, Oxford 1989 (BAR.I 556), pp. 15–24.

Brockelmann C., *Geschichte der Arabischen Litteratur. 1. Band*, Weimar 1898.

Brusin G., *Gli scavi di Aquileia. Un quadriennio di attività dell'Associazione nazionale per Aquileia (1929–1933)*, Udine 1934.

Bunnell Ch., "Catalogue of the Coins", in Waterman L. (ed.), *Preliminary Report of the University of Michigan Excavations at Sepphoris, Palestine, in 1931*, Ann Arbor 1937a, pp. 37–83.

Bunnell Ch., "Catalogue of the Coins", in Waterman L. (ed.), *Preliminary Report of the University of Michigan. Excavation at Sepphoris, Palestine, in 1932*, Ann Arbor 1937b, pp. 303–337.

Butcher K., "Coinage and Currency in Syria and Palestine to the Reign of Gallienus", in King C. E., Wigg D. G. (eds.), *Coin finds and coin use in the Roman world. The thirteenth Oxford Symposium on Coinage and Monetary History, 25.–27.3.1993*, Berlin 1996, pp. 101–112.

Butcher K., "Small Change in Ancient Beirut. Coins from BEY 006 and BEY 045", *Berytus* 45–46 (2001–2002), Beirut 2003.

Butcher K., *Coinage in Roman Syria. Northern Syria, 64 BC – AD 253*, London 2004.

Callegher B., "Un ripostiglio di monete d'oro bizantine dalla Sinagoga di Cafarnao", *LA* 47 (1997), pp. 329–339.

Callegher B., "Trento-Teatro Sociale. Scavi 1990–1992. Le monete repubblicane, imperiali e medievali. Analisi critica e catalogo del complesso numismatico", in Cavada E., Gorini G. (eds.), *Materiali per la storia urbana di* Tridentum, Vol. II: *Ritrovamenti monetali*, Trento 1998, pp. 7–341.

Callegher B., *Cafarnao IX. Monete dall'area urbana di Cafarnao (1968–2003)*, Jerusalem 2007 (Collectio Maior 47).

Callegher B., "Cafarnao IX. Addenda. Monete dalle ricognizioni di superficie (2004–2007)", *LA* 57 (2007), pp. 493–502.

Callegher B., "Note su un peso fenicio in piombo da Magdala", *NAC* 37 (2008), pp. 321–329.

Callegher B., "Cafarnao IX. Addenda: monete dalle ricognizioni di superficie (2007–2009)", *LA* 60 (2010), pp. 393–394.

Callegher B., "Emissioni in rame d'epoca giustinianea in area adriatica. Il ruolo di Salona", *Atti e Memorie Deputazione di Storia Patria per le Marche* 109 (2013), pp. 81–123.

Callegher B., "Un tesoro ritrovato: aurei romani imperiali (ca. 70–160) dall'Alta Galilea o dal Golan", *RIN* 116 (2015), pp. 103–120.

Callegher B., "Imitations and proto-vandalic *nummi* in the circulating stock in Upper Galilee between the end of the 5th and early 6th century. The Capernaum deposit (Locus 812)", in Chameroy J., Guihard P.-M. (eds.), *Produktion und Recyceln von Münzen in der Spätantike. Produire et recycler la monnaie au Bas-Empire,* Mainz 2016, pp. 155–196.

Callegher B., "Trieste. Scavi nell'area di Piazzetta Santa Lucia: rinvenimenti monetali", *AqN* 89 (2018a), pp. 111–123.

Callegher B., "Un ripostiglio di solidi di Eraclio (632–641) da Gerusalemme", *RN* 2018b, pp. 331–353.

Callegher B., "Nummi nordafricani e occidentali (V-inizi VI secolo) in Palestina: Nuovi dati", in Krmnicek S., Chameroy J. (eds.), *Money Matters. Coin Finds and Ancient Coin Use*, Bonn/Mainz 2019, pp. 101–115.

Callegher B., "Un ripostiglio di solidi di VII secolo (603–681) dalla costa mediterranea palestinese (Gaza?)", *RN* 178 (2021), pp. 251–272.

Callegher B., D'Ottone Rambach A., "Coins from the Excavations at St. John Prodromos Church– Jerusalem", *RB* 123 (2016), pp. 418–437.

Callu J.-P., *Fouilles d'Apamée de Syrie* VIII.I: *Les monnaies romaines*, Brussels 1979.

Callu J.-P., "Rôle et distribution des espèces de bronze de 348 à 392", in *Imperial Revenue, Expenditure and Monetary Policy in the Fourth Century A.D.*, Oxford 1980 (BAR.I 76), pp. 41–93, 173–212.

Carlà F., "Il sistema monetario in età tardo antica. Spunti per una revisione", *AIIN* 53 (2007), pp. 155–218.

Carlà F., *L'oro nella tarda antichità. Aspetti economici e sociali*, Torino 2009.

Carlà F., Marcone A., *Economia e finanza a Roma*, Bologna 2011.

Casey P. J., *Understanding ancient coins. An introduction for archaeologists and historians,* London 1986.

Casey P. J., "Justinian, the *limitanei* and Arab-Byzantine relations in the 6th c.", *JRA* 9 (1996), pp. 214–222.

Chameroy J., "La monnaie comme source historique de l'armée romaine du Bas-Empire", in Le Bohec Y., Wolff C. (eds.), *L'Armée romaine de Dioclétien à Valentinien. Ier. Actes du Congrès de Lyon (12–14 septembre 2002),* Lyon 2004 (Collection du Center d'Études Romaines et Gallo-Romaines. Nouvelle Série 26), pp. 139–155.

Clamer Ch., *Fouilles archéologique de 'Aïn ez-Zâra/Callirrohë*, Beirut 1997.

Cobb P. M., "al-Urdunn: 2. History", *Encyclopaedia of Islam*, Vol. 2: *T-U*, Leiden 2000, pp. 882–884.

Corbo V., "Scavi archeologici a Magdala (1971–1973)", *LA* 24 (1974), pp. 5–37.

Corbo V. "La città romana di Magdala. Rapporto preliminare della IV campagna di scavo: 1 ottobre-8 dicembre 1975", in Testa E., Mancini I., Piccirillo M. (eds.), *Studia Hierosolymitana in onore del P. Bellarmino Bagatti, I. Studi archeologici,* Jerusalem 1976 (Collectio Maior 22), pp. 355–378.

Corbo V., "Piazza e villa urbana a Magdala", *LA* 28 (1978), pp. 232–240.

Corbo V., "La mini-synagogue de Magdala", *Le monde de la Bible* 51 (1989), p. 15.

Cotton H.M, "The Legio VI Ferrata", in Le Bohec Y., Wolff C. (eds.), *Les Légions de Rome sous le Haut Empire. Actes du Congrès de Lyon (17–19 septembre 1998),* Lyon 2000 (Collection du Centre d'Études Romaines et Gallo-Romaines. Nouvelle Série 20), pp. 351–357.

Crawford M., *Coinage and Money under the Roman Republic. Italy and the Mediterranean Economy,* London 1985.

Crawford P., "Flora of Tell Hesban and Area, Jordan", in LaBianca Ø. S. (ed.), *Hesban Vol. 2: Environmental Foundations. Studies of Climatical, Geological, Hydrologicala and Phytological Conditions in Hesban and Vicinity*, Berrien Springs 1986, pp. 77–98.

D'Ottone A., *Monnaies islamiques* (in press).

Dabrowa E., "Legio X Fretensis", in Le Bohec Y., Wolff C. (eds.), *Les Légions de Rome sous le Haut Empire. Actes du Congrès de Lyon (17–19 septembre 1998),* (Collection du Center d'Études Romaines et Gallo-Romaines. Nouvelle Série 20), Lyon 2000, pp. 317–325.

De Callataÿ F., "Statistique et numismatique. Les limites d'un apport", *Revue des Archéologues et Historiens d'Art de Louvain* 20 (1987), pp. 76–95.

De Luca S., "Magdala Project 2007", *Notiziario Studium Biblicum Franciscanum, Jerusalem: Anno Accademico 2006–2007,* Jerusalem 2008, pp. 12–17.

De Luca S., "La città ellenistico-romana di Magdala/Taricheae. Gli scavi del Magdala Project 2007 e 2008: Relazione preliminare e prospettive di indagine", *LA* 49 (2009), pp. 343–562.

De Luca S., "Magdala Project 2008–2010", in *Notiziario Studium Biblicum Franciscanum, Jerusalem: Anno Accademico 2009–2010,* Jerusalem 2011, pp. 13–18.

De Luca S., Leibner U., "A Monastery in Magdala (Taricheae)?," *JRA* 32 (2019), pp. 391–414.

De Luca S., Lena A. "The Harbor of the City of Magdala/Taricheae on the Shores of the Sea of Galilee, from the Hellenistic to the Byzantine Times: New Discoveries and Preliminary Results", in Ladstätter S., Pirson F., Schmidts Th. (eds.), *Häfen und Hafenstädte im östlichen Mittelmeerraum von der Antike bis in byzantinische Zeit. Neue Entdeckungen und aktuelle Forschungsansätze,* Vol. 1, Istanbul 2014a (*Byzas* 19), pp. 113–163.

De Luca S., Lena A., "The mosaic of the thermal bath complex of Magdala reconsidered: archaeological context, epigraphy and iconography", in Bottini G.C, Chrupcała L. D., Patrich J. (eds.), *Archaeological and Historical Essays in Honour of Leah Di Segni*, Milano 2014b, pp. 1–33.

Depeyrot G., "La silique à la fin du IVe siècle", in Gorini G. (ed.), *La zecca di Milano. Atti del Convegno internazionale di studio, 9–10 maggio 1983*, Milano 1984, pp. 199–216.

Depeyrot G., "Le système monétaire de Dioclétien à la fin de l'Empire Romain", *RBN* 138 (1992), pp. 33–106.

Derose Evans J., *Caesarea Maritima. Excavation Reports Vol 6: The Coins and the Hellenistic, Roman and Byzantine Economy of Palestine*, Boston 2006.

Di Segni L., "The Beersheba Tax Edict Reconsidered in the Light of a Newly Discovered Fragment", *Scripta Classica Israelica* 23 (2004), pp. 131–158.

Dothan M., "A Sign of Tanit from Tel 'Akko", *IEJ* 24 (1974), pp. 44–49.

Duyrat F., *Arados hellénistique. Étude historique et monétaire*, Beirut 2005.

Eadie J., "One hundred years of rebellion. The eastern army in politics, A.D. 175–272", in Kennedy D. L. (ed.), *The Roman Army in the East*, Portsmouth 1996 (JRA.S 18), pp. 135–151.

El Cheikh N. M., *Byzantium Viewed by the Arabs*, Cambridge/London 2004.

Elayi J., "Une novelle grotte à Ibiza?", *Transeuphratène* 15 (1998), pp. 55–67.

Elayi J., Elayi A. G., "Trésors de monnaies phéniciennes et circulation monétaire (Ve-IVe siècles avant J.-C.)", *Transeuphratène Supplement* 1, Paris 1993.

Elayi J., Elayi A. G., "Recherches sur les poids Phéniciens", *Transeuphratène Supplement* 5, Paris 1997, pp. 43–46.

Elayi J., Elayi A. G., "Nouveaux poids phéniciens (I)", *Transeuphratène* 17 (1999a), pp. 35–43.

Elayi J., Elayi A. G., "Quelques particularités de la culture matérielle d'Arwad au Fer III/Perse", *Transeuphratène* 18 (1999b), pp. 9–27.

Elisséef N., *Dimashḳ, Encyclopaedia of Islam*, Vol. 2: *C-G*, Leiden 1991, pp. 277–291.

Elliott C. P., "The Acceptance and Value of Roman Silver Coinage in the Second and Third Centuries AD", *NC* 174 (2014), pp. 129–152.

Fahmī 'A., *Mawsū'at al-nuqūd al-'arabiyya wa-'ilm al-nummiyāt* – 1: *Fajr al-sikka al-'arabiyya, s.l.* [al-Qāhira] 1965.

Farhi Y., "Coins and Weight from Mount Nitai", in Leibner U. (ed.), *Khirbet Wadi Ḥamam. A Roman-period village and synagogue in the lower Galilee*, Jerusalem 2018 (Qedem Reports 13), pp. 582–592.

Farhi Y., Leibner U., "Coins from the Rock Shelters and Fortified Enclosure of Mt. Nitai, Eastern Lower Galilee", *INJ* 18 (2011–2014), pp. 184–197.

Fiensy D. A., Strange J. R., *Galilee in the Late Second Temple and Mishnaic Periods. Vol.* 2: *The Archeological Record from Cities, Towns and Villages*, Minneapolis 2015.

Fiensy D. A., Strange J. R., *Galilee in the Late Second Temple and Mishnaic Periods. Vol.* 1: *Life, Culture, and Society*, Minneapolis 2014.

Findlater C., "Limes Arabicus, via militaris and resource control in southern Jordan", *Limes XVIII*, pp. 137–152.

Finkielsztejn G., "Poids de plomb inscrits du Levant. Une réforme d'Antiochos IV?", *Τοποι Supplement* 8 (2007), pp. 35–60.

Finkielsztejn G., "The Weight Standards of the Hellenistic Levant. Part One: The Evidence of the Syrian Scale Weights", *INR* 9 (2014), pp. 61–94.

Finley I. M., *The Ancient Economy*, Berkeley/Los Angeles 1973.

Fitzgerald G., *Beth-Shean Excavations 1921–1923. The Arab and Byzantine Levels*, Philadelphia 1931.

Flavius Josephus, The Jewish War, Cambridge/London 1927 (LCL 203).

Foss C., "The Coinage of the first century of Islam", *JRA* 16 (2003), pp. 748–760.

Foss C., *Arab-Byzantine Coins. An Introduction with a Catalogue of the Dumbarton Oaks Collection*, Washington 2008.

Garza-Díaz Barriga A., "Las cuatro monedas de Magdala. El dinero que circuló en Galilea. Las monedas que coincidieron en Magdala y Gamla", *El Pensador. Monográficos* 5 (2013), pp. 76–83.

Garza-Díaz Barriga A., "Understanding the Continuous Chronology of Magdala in the Various Periods through its Ancient Coins, and the Spatial Distribution of the Jannaeus Coins at the Site", *Abstract of the paper given at the American Schools of Oriental Research Congress (San Diego, California (USA), November 22, 2019)* available online: https://scholar.google.com.mx/citations?user=DlKqK-5MAAAAJ&hl=es (last accessed: August 2021).

Gatier P.-L., Weights and civic life in the Hellenistic and Roman Near East, "Dialogues d'histoire ancienne", Supplément n°12, pp. 125–162

Gilliland D. R., "Palaeoethnobotany and Palaeoenvironment", in LaBianca Ø. S. (ed.), *Hesban Vol.* 2: *Environmental Foundations. Studies of Climatical, Geological, Hydrologicala and Phytological Conditions in Hesban and Vicinity*, Berrien Springs 1986, pp. 123–142.

Gichon M., "45 years of research on the limes Palaestinae. The findings and their assessment in the light of the criticisms raised (c. 1st-c. 4th)", in *Limes XVIII*, pp. 185–206.

Gitler H., "The Coins", in Wachsman S. (ed.), *The Excavations of an Ancient Boat in the Sea of Galilee (Lake Kinneret)*, Jerusalem 1990, pp. 101–106.

Gitler H., "A Comparative Study of Numismatic Evidence from Excavations in Jerusalem", *LA* 46 (1996), pp. 317–362.

Gitler H., "The Coins", in Geva H. (ed.), *Jewish Quarter Excavations in the Old City of Jerusalem conducted by Nahman Avigad 1969–1982*, Jerusalem 2003, pp. 453–492.

Gitler H., Weisburd D., "Coin Finds from Villages in Palestine during the Late Roman and Byzantine Periods (A.D. 383–696/7). A Quantitative Examination of Monetary Distributions", in Lefort J., Morrisson C., Sodini J.-P. (eds.), *Les Villages dans l'Empire byzantin (IVe-Xve siècle)*, Paris 2005 (Réalités Byzantines 11), pp. 539–552.

Goodwin T., *Arab-Byzantine Coinage*, London 2005.

Goodwin T., *The Standing Caliph Coinage*, London 2018.

Gorini G., "Zum Münzumlauf in nachrömischer Zeit in Oberitalien", in *Litterae numismaticae Vindobonenses* 4 (1992), pp. 77–84.

Gyselen R., Kalus L., *Deux trésor monétaires des premiers temps de l'Islam*, Paris 1983.

Hackens T., Moucharte G. (eds.), "Numismatique et histoire économique phéniciennes et puniques", *Studia Phoenicia* 9 (1993), pp. 51–58.

Hamburger H., "Minute Coins from Caesarea", *'Atiqot* 1 (1955), pp. 115–138.

Hamburger H., "A Hoard of Syrian Tetradrachms from Tiberias", *'Atiqot* 2 (1959), pp. 133–145.

Hanson R. S., *Tyrian Influence in Upper Galilee*, Cambridge 1980 (Meiron Excavation Project 2).

Hanson R. S., Bates M., "Numismatic Report", in Meyers E. M., Kraabel A. T., Strange J. F. (eds.), *Ancient Synagogue Excavations at Khirbet Shema', Upper Galilee, Israel 1970–1972*, Durham 1976 (*AASOR* 42), pp. 146–169.

Hart H. StJ., "The coins of "Render unto Caesar ..." (A note on some aspects of Mark 12:13–17; Matt. 22:15–22; Luke 20:20–26)", in Bammel E., Moule C. F. D. (eds.), *Jesus and the Politics of his Day*, Cambridge/New York 1984, pp. 241–248 DOI: https://doi.org/10.1017/CBO9780511554834.015

Heidemann S., "The merger of two currency zones in Early Islam. The Byzantine and Sasanian impact on the circulation in former Byzantine Syria and Northern Mesopotamia", *Iran* 36 (1998), pp. 95–112.

Hendy M., *Studies in the Byzantine Monetary Economy c.300–c.1450*, Cambridge 1985.

Hennequin G., Al-'Ush A., *Les monnaies de Bālis, Damas*. Damas 1978 (Publications de Institut Français de Damas 107).

Hohlfelder R. H., "Crusader Coin Finds from Caesarea Maritima. The Joint Expedition's Excavations, 1971–1979", in Edbury P. W., Metcalf D. M. (eds.), *Coinage in the Latin East. The Fourth Oxford Symposium on Coinage and Monetary History*, Oxford 1980 (BAR.I 77), pp. 127–131.

Hohlfelder R. L., "The Coins", in Oleson J. P. (ed.), *The Harbours of Caesarea Maritima. Results of the Caesarea Ancient Harbour. Excavation Project 1980–1985*, Oxford 1994 (*BAR.I* 594), pp. 77–82.

Howgego Ch., "The Relationship of the Issar to de Denar in Rabbinic Literature", *INJ* 5 (1984–1985), pp. 59–64.

Howgego Ch., *Greek Imperial Countermarks. Studies in the Provincial Coinage of the Roman Empire,* London 2005.

Ilisch L., "'Abd al-Malik's Monetary Reform in Copper and the Failure of Centralization", in Haldon J. (ed.). *Money, Power and Politics in Early Islamic Syria. A Review of Current Debates*, Ashgate 2010, pp. 125–146.

Jacobson D., Kokkinos N. (eds.), *Judaea and Rome in Coins 65 BCE–135 CE*, London 2012.

Kadman L., *The Coins of Caesarea Maritima*, Jerusalem 1957.

Kadman L., "Hoard of Tyrian Shekels Found on Mount Carmel", *Numismatist* 73 (1960a), pp. 851–852.

Kadman L., "A large hoard of Tyrian shekels discovered on Mount Carmel", *Seaby's Coins and Medal Bulletin* 507 (1960b), pp. 309–310.

Kadman L., *The Coins of Akko Ptolemais*, Jerusalem 1961 (Corpus Nummorum Palaestinensium 4).

Kadman L., "Temple Dues and Currency in Ancient Palestine in the Light of Recent Discovered Coins Hoards", *Israel Numismatic Bulletin* 1 (1962), pp. 9–11.

Kadman L., "Temple Dues and Currency in Ancient Palestine in the Light of Recently Discovered Coins Hoards", in Instituto Italiano di Numismatica (eds.), *Congresso Internazionale di Numismatica 2*, Roma 1965, pp. 69–77.

Kaegi W. E., *Byzantium and the early Islamic conquest*, Cambridge 1992.

Kark R., Goren H., "Pioneering British exploration and scriptural geography: The Syrian Society/The Palestine Association", *The Geographical Journal* 177 (2011), pp. 264–274.

Katsari C., *The Roman Monetary System. The Eastern Provinces from the First to the Third Century AD*, Cambridge 2011.

Kindler A., *The Coins of Tiberias*, Tiberias 1961.

Kindler A., "The Monetary Pattern and Function of the Jewish Coins", in Kindler A. (ed.), *International Numismatic Convention. Jerusalem 27–31 December 1963*, Tel Aviv 1967, pp. 180–203.

Kindler A., *Coins of the Land of Israel*, Jerusalem 1974.

Kindler A., "Was there a Detachment of the Third Legion Cyrenaica at Neapolis in A.D. 251–253?", *INJ* 4 (1980), pp. 56–58.

Kindler A., "The Coin Finds at the Excavations of Bethsaida", in Arav R., Freund A. R. (eds.) *Bethsaida. A City by the North Shore of the Sea of Galilee*. Vol. II, Kirksville 1999a, pp. 251–268.

Kindler A., "Summary of Twelve Years of Numismatic Finds in the Excavations at Sumaqa (1983–1995)", in Dar S. (ed.), *Sumaqa. A Roman and Byzantine Jewish Village on Mount Carmel*, Israel, Oxford 1999b (BAR.I 815), pp. 347–390.

Kokkinos N., "The Location of Tarichaea. North or South of Tiberias", *PEQ* 142 (2010), pp. 7–23.

Kokkinos N., "The Prefects of Judaea 6–48 CE and the Coins of Misty Period 6–36", in Jacobson, Kokkinos 2012, pp. 85–112.

Kool R., "Coins at Vadum Jacob. New Evidence on Circulation of Money in the Latin Kingdom of Jerusalem during the Second Half of the Twelfth Century", *Crusades. The Journal of the Society for the Study of the Crusades and the Latin East* 1 (2002) pp. 73–88.

Kool R., "Coin circulation in the villeneuves of the Latin Kingdom of Jerusalem. The Cases of Parva Mahumeria and Bethgibelin", in Edbury P., Kalopissi-Verti S. (eds.), *Archaeology and the Crusaders*, Athens 2007, pp. 133–156.

Kool R., *The Circulation and Use of Coins in the Latin Kingdom of Jerusalem 1099–1291 CE*, PhD diss. Hebrew University, Jerusalem 2013.

Kool R., Uzi'ad U., "A Late Twelfth-Century Silver Purse Hoard from Ibelim", *INR* 11 (2016), pp. 163–180.

Krause C. L., Mishler C., *Standard Catalogue of World Coins*, Iola 1990.

Kushnir-Stein A., "On the Chronology of Some Inscribed Lead Weights from Palestine", *ZDPV* 113 (1997), pp. 88–91.

Kushnir-Stein A., "Two Inscribed Lead Weights of Agrippa II", *ZPE* 141 (2002), pp. 295–297.

Kushnir-Stein A., "The City-Goddess on the Weight of Ascalon", *INR* 1 (2006), pp. 117–122.

Kushnir-Stein A., Gitler H., "On some inscribed lead weights from Palestine", *NAC* 28 (1999), pp. 221–234.

Lampinen P., "The Coins, Preliminary Report 1990", in Vann R. L. (ed.), *Caesarea Papers*, Ann Arbor/Chicago 1994 (JRA.S 5), pp. 169–172.

Lassen M. (van), "The Coinage Pattern of Palestine in the First and Second Centuries A.D.", *Numismatic Circular* 79 (1971), pp. 240–241.

Lavoix H., *Catalogue des monnaies musulmanes de la bibliothèque nationale. Khalifes orientaux*, Paris 1887.

Le Rider G., Seyrig H., "Objets de la collection Louis De Clercq", *RN* 10 (1968), pp. 30–40.

Leadbetter B., "Galerius and the eastern frontier", *Limes XVIII*, pp. 85–90.

Lena A., "Magdala 2007. Preliminary Report", *Hadashot Arkheologiot/Excavations and Surveys in Israel* 125 (2013) (http://www.hadashot-esi.org.il/report_dtail_eng.aspx?id=4342&mag_id=120).

Lena A., Rossi V., Palmieri M., Marchesini M., "A glimpse under the water-table. The Magdala Harbour bio-archive: An integrated analysis of carpological and faunal data", *West and East. Rivista della Scuola di Specializzazione in Beni Archeologici* 2 (2017), pp. 42–62.

Levy B., "Tyrian Shekels. The Myth of the Jerusalem Mint", *Journal of the Society for Ancient Numismatics* 19 (1995), pp. 33–35.

Lewin G., "Diocletianus. Politics and *limites* in the Near East", *Limes XVIII*, pp. 91–101.

Lewin A., "*Limitanei* and *comitatenses* in the Near East from Diocletianus to Valens", in Le Bohec Y., Wolff C. (eds.), *Les Légions de Rome sous le Haut Empire. Actes du Congrès de Lyon (17–19 septembre 1998)*, Lyon 2004 (Collection du Center d'Études Romaines et Gallo-Romaines. Nouvelle Série 26), pp. 227–236.

Lichtenberger A., Raja R., "Roman City Coins of Gerasa. Contextualizing Currency and Circulation from the Hellenistic to the Late Roman Period", in Lichtenberger A., Raja R. (eds.), *Hellenistic and Roman Gerasa. The Archaeology and History of a Decapolis,* Turnhout 2020, pp. 369–381.

Liebeschuetz J. H. W. G., "Late Antiquity (6th–7th centuries) in the cities of the Roman Near East", *Mediterraneo Antico* 3 (2000), pp. 43–75.

Liebeschuetz J. H., Wolfgang G., *The Decline and Fall of the Roman City*, Oxford 2001.

Freeman I. P., Bennett J., Fiema Z. T., Hoffmann B. (eds.), *Limes XVIII. Proceedings of the XVIIIth International Congress of Roman Frontier Studies held in Amman, Jordan (September 2000)*, Oxford 2002 (BAR.I 1084).

Loffreda S., *Scavi di Et-Tabgha,* Jerusalem 1970.

Loffreda S., "Alcune osservazioni sulla ceramica di Magdala", in Testa E., Mancini I., Piccirillo M. (eds.), *Studia Hierosolymitana in onore del P. Bellarmino Bagatti, I. Studi archeologici,* Jerusalem 1976 (Collectio Maior 22), pp. 338–354.

Loffreda S., "Magdala-Tarichea", *Bibbia e Oriente* 18 (1976b), pp. 133–135.

Loffreda S., *Cafarnao VI. Tipologie e contesti stratigrafici della ceramica (1968–2003)*; *Cafarnao VII. Documentazione grafica della ceramica (1968–2003)*; *Cafarnao VIII. 8: Documentazione fotografica degli oggetti (1968–2003)*, Milano 2008.

Lönnqvist K., *The Report of the Amman Lots of the Qumran Silver Coin Hoards*, Amman 2007.

Lynch W. F., *Narrative of the United States' Expedition to the River Jordan and the Dead Sea*, Philadelphia 1849.

Magness J., "The Pottery from Area V/4 at Caesarea", in Dever, W. (ed.), *Preliminary Excavation Reports*, Atlanta 1994 (*AASOR* 52), pp. 133–145.

Malan A. N., Solomon C., *Memorials of His Life and Writings*, Whitefish 2012 (1st ed. London 1897).

Malingue G., *The Coinage of Domitius Alexander (308–310 AD)*, Barcelona 2018 (Numismatica Antigua 9).

Manns F., "Magdala dans les sources littéraires", in Testa E., Mancini I., Piccirillo M. (eds.), *Studia Hierosolymitana in onore del P. Bellarmino Bagatti, I. Studi archeologici,* Jerusalem 1976 (Collectio Maior 22), pp. 307–337.

Manns F., "Quelques poids et pesons du Musée de la Flagellation", in Testa E., Mancini I., Piccirillo M. (eds.), *Studia Hierosolymitana in onore del P. Bellarmino Bagatti, I. Studi archeologici,* Jerusalem 1976 (Collectio Maior 22), pp. 6–110.

Marot T., "Monedas omeyas halladas en el mercado romano de Gerasa (Jordania)", in Alfaro Asíns C., Sáenz-Díez J. I. (eds.), *III Jarique de Numismática Hispano-Árabe*, Madrid 1992, pp. 291–298.

Marot T., *Las monedas del Macellum de Gerasa*, Madrid 1998.

Mattila S. L., "Revisiting Jesus' Capernaum. A Village of Only Subsistence-Level Fishers and Farmers?" in Fiensy D. A., Hawkins R. K. (eds.), *The Galilean Economy in the Time of Jesus*, Atlanta 2013, pp. 75–138.

Mattila S. L., "Capernaum. Village of Naḥum from Hellenistic to Byzantine Times", in Fiensy D. A., Strange J. R. (eds.), *Galilee in the Late Second Temple and Mishnaic Periods. The Archaeological Record from Cities, Towns, and Villages*, Minneapolis 2015, pp. 217–257.

Mazor G., "The Coins", in Mazor G., Najjar A. (eds.), *Bet-Sh'ean I: Nysa-Scythopolis. The Caesareum and the Odeon*, Jerusalem 2007 (IAA Reports 33), pp. 123, 273–275.

McAlee R., *The Coins of Roman Antioch*, Lancaster/London 2007.

Meier J. P., *A Marginal Jew. Rethinking the Historical Jesus. Vol. 1: The Roots of the Problem and the Person*, London 1991.

Meier C., "Appendix", in Arav R., Freund A. R. (eds.) *Bethsaida. A City by the North Shore of the Sea of Galilee. Vol. I*, Kirksville 1995, pp. 53–63.

Meir C., "Tyrian Sheqels and Half Sheqels with Unpublished Dates from the 'Isfiya Hoard in the Kadman Numismatic Pavillon", *INJ* 3 (2008), pp. 117–123.

Meir C., "Tyrian Sheqels from the 'Isfiya Hoard, Part One", *INJ* 4 (2009), pp. 63–71.

Meir C., "Tyrian Sheqels from the 'Isfiya Hoard, Part Two", *INJ* 5 (2010), pp. 143–149.

Meistermann B., *Guida di Terra Santa*, Florence 1925.

Meshorer Y., "A Hoard of Coins from Migdal", *'Atiqot* 11 (1976), pp. 54–71.

Meshorer Y., "Note on Migdal Hoard", *'Atiqot* 14 (1980), p. 95.

Meshorer Y., *Ancient Jewish Coinage*, I–II, Nyack/New York 1982.

Meshorer Y., "The Coins of Masada", in Yadin Y., Naveh J. (eds.), *Masada I: The Yigael Yadin Excavations 1963–1965*, Jerusalem 1989.

Meshorer Y., "The 'Black Silver' Coins in the Babatha Papyri: A Revaluation", *INJ* 10 (1992), pp. 67–74.

Meshorer Y., "Coins 1968–1986", in Sharon C. H. (ed.), *Tel Anafa I,i: Final Report on Ten Years of Excavation at Hellenistic and Roman Settlement in Northern Israel*, Ann Arbor 1994 (JRA.S 10), pp. 241–260.

Meshorer Y., "Coins from Areas A and C", in Stern E. (ed.), *Excavations at Dor, Final Report Vol. I B: Areas A and C. the Finds*, Jerusalem 1995 (Qedem Reports 2), pp. 461–472.

Meshorer Y., *A Treasury of Jewish Coins from the Persian Period to Bar Kokhba*, Jerusalem 2001.

Meshorer Y., "The Coins", in Netzer E. (ed.), *Hasmonean and Herodian Palaces at Jericho. Final Reports of the 1973–1987 Excavations, Vol. II: Stratigraphy and Architecture*, Jerusalem 2004, pp. 289–316.

Meshorer Y., "Coin Hoard from a Third-Century CE Shipwreck of the Carmel Coast", *'Atiqot* 63 (2010), pp. 111–135.

Metcalf D. M., *Coinage of the Crusades and the Latin East in the Ashmolean Museum Oxford*, 2nd edition, London 1995.

Metcalf D. M., "The Metrology of the Amalricus Denier of Jerusalem in the Early Thirteenth Century", *INJ* 14 (2002), pp. 239–244.

Metcalf D. M., "The Jaffa Hoard of 1954: Crusader Coinage of the Late 12th Century", *INJ* 15 (2003–2006), pp. 138–139.

Metcalf D. M., Holland L., "Crusader Coins from Caesarea Maritima", *INJ* 13 (1994–1999), pp. 156–162.

Meyers E. M., Strange J. F., Meyers C. L., *Excavations at Ancient Meiron, Upper Galilee, Israel 1971–72, 1974–75, 1977*, Cambridge 1981 (Meiron Excavation Project 3), pp. 260–272.

Meyers E. M., Netzer E., Meyers C. L., "Sepphoris 'Ornament of All Galilee", *Biblical Archaeologist* 49 (1986), pp. 4–18.

Migeotte L., "Le pouvoirs des agoranomes dans les cités greques", in Wallace R. W., Gagarin M. (eds.), *Symposion 2001. Vorträge zur griechischen und hellenistischen Rechtsgeschichte (Evanston, Illinois, 5.–8. September 2001)*, Wien 2005, pp. 287–300.

Miles G. C., "The Early Islamic Bronze Coinage of Egypt", in Ingholt H. (ed.), *Centennial Publication of the American Numismatic Society*, New York 1958, pp. 471–502.

Milik J. T., Seyrig H., "Trésor monétaire de Murabba'ât", *RN* 6e série (1958), pp. 11–26.

Mitchiner M., *Oriental Coins and their Values. The World of Islam*, London 1977.

Morris B., *The Birth of the Palestinian Refugee Problem Revisited*, Cambridge 2004.

Morrisson C., "Le trésor byzantin de Nikertai", *RBN* 118 (1972), pp. 31–91.

Morrisson C., "La diffusion de la monnaie de Carthage hors d'Afrique", in Lancel S. (ed.), *Afrique du Nord antique et médievale. Numismatique, langues, écritures at arts du livre, spécificités des arts figurés. Actes du VIIe Colloque international sur l'Afrique du Nord*, Paris 1999, pp. 109–118.

Morrisson C., "L'atelier de Carthage et la diffusion de la monnaie frappe dans l'Afrique Vandale et Byzantine (439–695)", *ATar* 11 (2003a), pp. 65–84.

Morrisson C., "Byzance", in Alfaro C., Burnett A. (eds.), *A Survey of Numismatic Research 1996–2001*, Madrid 2003b, pp. 347–374.

Morrisson C., "La monétarisation en Egypte et en Syrie-Palestine du IVe à la fin du VIIe siècle. Le témoignage de l'archéologie", *ATar* 12 (2004), pp. 405–413.

Morrisson C., "La monnaie sur les routes fluviales et maritimes des échanges dans le monde méditerranéen (VIe-IXe siècle)", in *Atti CISAM*, Spoleto 2008, pp. 631–670.

Morrisson C., "Tra Vandali e Bizantini: la prosperità dell'Africa (V–VII secolo) attraverso le fonti e la documentazione monetale", *Incontri di Filologia Classica* 10 (2010–2011), pp. 145–169.

Morrisson C., Prigent V., "L'empereur et le calife (690–695). Réflexions à propos des monnayages de Justinien II et d'Abd al-Malik", in Charpentier G., Puech V. (eds.), *Hommages à Georges Tate*, Lyon 2013 (Topoi. Supplement 12), pp. 571–592.

Newell E. T., "The Coins", in Lamon R., Shipton S. (eds.), *Megiddo I. Seasons of 1924–1934: Strata I–V*, Chicago 1938, pp. 196–212.

Newell E.T, Witschonke R., "Coins from the excavations at Beisan (Nysa-Scythopolis, Tel Beth Shean): 1929–1935", *AJN* 20 (2008), pp. 1–52.

Noell E. S., "Marktless World'? An Examination of Wealth and Exchange in the Gospels and First Century Palestine", *Journal of Markets and Morality* 10 (2007), pp. 85–114.

Noy I., "Head Decoration Representation on Hasmonean and Herodian Coins", *INJ* 8 (2013), pp. 39–53.

Nützel H., *Königliche Museen zu Berlin. Katalog der orientalischen Münzen, Vol. I: Die Münzen der östlichen Chalifen*, Berlin 1898.

Oddy A., "Whither Arab-Byzantine Numismatics? A Review of Fifty Years' Research", *BMGS* 28 (2004), pp. 121–152.

Olavarri Goicoechea E., *Excavaciones en el Agora de Gerasa en 1983*, Madrid 1986.

Bottini G. C., Di Segni L., Chrupcała L. D. (eds.), *One Land – Many Cultures. Archaeological Studies in Honour of Stanislao Loffreda ofm*, Jerusalem 2003.

Panella C., "Merci e scambi nel Mediterraneo tardo antico", in *Storia di Roma. III-2*, Torino 1993, pp. 613–697.

Parise N., "Unità ponderali e rapporti di cambio nella Siria del Nord", in Archi A. (ed.), *Circulation of Goods in non-palatial Context in the Ancient Near East*, Roma 1984, pp. 125–138.

Parise N., "Unità ponderali e circolazione metallica nell'Oriente mediterraneo", in Hachens T. *et alii* (eds.), *A Survey of Numismatic Research 1985–1990*, Brussels 1991, pp. 28–34.

Parker S. T., "The Roman frontier in Jordan: An overview", in *Limes XVIII*, pp. 77–84.

Sheedy K., Carson R., Walmsley A. (eds.), *Pella in Jordan 1979–1990. The Coins*, Adapa/Sydney 2001.

Pere N., *Osmanlılarda Madenî Paralar – Coins of the Ottoman Empire*, Istanbul 1968.

Petersen A., *A Gazetteer of Buildings in Muslim Palestine*, Vol. I, Oxford 2001 (*British Academy Monographs in Archaeology*).

Philipps M., "Currency in seventh-century Syria as historical source", *BMGS* 28 (2004), pp. 13–31.

Piccirillo M., *Un uomo di pace. Padre Bellarmino Bagatti (1905–1990)*, Gorle 2001.

Picozzi V., "Le monete nei Vangeli", *NAC* 1 (1972), pp. 79–87.

Polanyi K., *The Great Transformation,* New York 1944 (ital. transl. *La grande trasformazione*, Torino 2000).

Prigent V., "Le rôle des provinces d'Occident dans l'approvisionnement de Constantinopolis. Témoignages numismatiques et sigillographique", *MEFREM* 118 (2006), pp. 269–299.

Prigent V., "Notes on the Production and Circulation of the Byzantine Ravennate Coinage", in Cosentino S. (ed), *Ravenna and the Traditions of Late Antique and Early Byzantine Craftsmanship. Labour, Culture and the Economy*, Berlin/New York 2021 (Millennium-Studien/Millennium Studies 85), pp. 293–310.

Qedar S., "Two Lead Weights of Herod Antipas and Agrippa II and Early History of Tiberias", *INJ* 9 (1986–1987), pp. 29–35.

Rahmani L. Y., "Two Hoards of 'Moneta Regis' Coins Found in Northern Israel", *INJ* 4 (1980), pp. 72–76.

Rahmani L. Y., "Two Hoards of 'Moneta Regis' Coins Found in Northern Israel. Addendum", *INJ* 5 (1981), p. 89.

Rahmani L. Y., Sharabani M., "Catalogue of coins", in Dothan M. (ed.), *Hammath Tiberias. Early Synagogues and the Hellenistic and Roman Remains*, Jerusalem 1983, pp. 71–74.

Raschke M., "New Studies in Roman Commerce with the East", in Temporini H., Haase W., (eds.), *Aufstieg und Niedergang der Römischen Welt* II: *Principat*, Vol. 9.2, Berlin/New York 1978, pp. 604–1378.

Ravegnani G., "Le unità dell'esercito bizantino nel VI secolo tra continuità e innovazione", in Gasparri S. (ed.), *Alto medioevo mediterraneo*, Firenze 2005, pp. 185–205.

Ravetz A., "The Fourth-century Inflation and Romano British Coin Finds, I: Patterns of Fourth-century Coinage on Romano British Sites", *NC* 4 (1964), pp. 201–231.

Raynor J., Meshorer Y., *The Coins of Ancient Meiron*, Winona Lake 1988.

Reden S. von, *Exchange in Ancient Greece*, London 1995.

Reece R., *Roman Coins and Archaeology. Collected Papers*, Wetteren 2003 (Moneta 23).

Reisner G. H., Fisher C. S., Lyon D. G. (eds.), *Harvard Excavations at Samaria 1908–1910*, Vol. I, Cambridge 1924.

Robinson E., Smith E., *Biblical Researches in Palestine, Mount Sinai and Arabia Petraea. A Journal of Travels in the year 1838*, Vol. III, Boston 1841.

Roll I., "Imperial Roads Across and Trade Routes Beyond the Roman Provinces of Judaea-Palaestina and Arabia: The State of Research", *Tel Aviv* 32 (2005), pp. 107–118.

Rosenberger M., *The Coinage of Eastern Palestine and Legionary Overstrucks, Bar-Kokhba*, Jerusalem 1978.

Roth C., "The Historical Implications of the Jewish Coinage in the First Revolt", *IEJ* 12 (1962), pp. 33–46.

Roth J., "The Army and the Economy in Judaea and Palestine", in Erdkamp P. (ed.), *The Roman Army and the Economy*, Amsterdam 2002, pp. 375–397.

Rouvier J., "Numismatique des villes de la Phénicie", *Journal International d'Archéologie Numismatique 3–7* (1900–1904).

Russell K. W., "The Earthquake Chronology of Palestine and Northwest Arabia from the 2nd through the Mid-8th Century AD", *BASOR* 260 (1985), pp. 37–58.

Safrai Z., *The Missing Century. Palestine in the Fifth Century, Growth and Decline,* Leuven 1998.

Saller S., *Excavations at Bethany (1949–1953)*, Jerusalem 1957.

Sawaya Z., *Histoire de Bérytos et d'Héliopolis d'après leurs monnaies (Ier siècle av. J-C. – IIIe siècle apr. J.-C.),* Beirut 2009 (BAH 185).

Sawaya Z., "The Coin Finds from Hellenistic and Roman Berytos (Fourth Century BC – Third Century AD", in Holmes N. (ed.), *Proceedings of the XIVth International Numismatic Congress, Glasgow 2009*, Glasgow 2011a, pp. 376–381.

Sawaya Z., "Tyr à l'époque hellénistique de la conquête macédonienne à l'autonomie (332–126/5 av. J.-C.): Histoire et monnaie", *BAAL Hors-Série* 8 (2011b), pp. 269–284.

Sawaya Z., "Production et circulation monétaire en Phénicie de l'époque perse à l'époque byzantine (Ve siècle av. J.-C.-VIIe siècle ap. J.-C.)", in Martiniani-Reber M., Maïla Afeiche A.-M., Haldimann M.-A. (eds.), *Fascination du Liban. Soixante siècles d'histoire de religion, d'art et d'archéologie*, Genève 2012, pp. 245–248.

Sawaya Z., "Les monnaies de JEM 002, JEM 003 et JEM 004 à Jemmayzeh-Beirut", *BAAL Hors-Série* 13 (2016), pp. 21–234.

Sawaya Z., "Catalogue des monnaies", in Frangié-Joly D. (ed.), *Le site de Beirut-144, Fouilles et étude de la céramique (période hellénistique – début de l'ère romaine),* Oxford 2017 (*BAR.I* 2881), pp. 117–126.

Schaberg J., *The Resurrection of Mary Magdalene. Legends, Apocrypha and the Christian Testament*, London/New York 2004.

Schindel N., "The End of Umayyad Coinage in Southern Bilad al-Sham", *INR* 1 (2006a), p. 137–150.

Schindel N., "A Hoard of Umayyad Copper Coins from Baysān", *NC* 166 (2006b), pp. 385–392.

Schulze I., Schulze W., "The Coins of the Jerash Northwest Quarter Project and the Umayyad Money Circulation in Jund al-Urdunn", in Lichtenberger A., Raja R. (eds.), *Metal Finds and Coins. Final Publications from the Danish-German Jerash Northwest Quarter Project II*, Turnhout 2020 (Jerash Papers 7), pp. 131–178.

Seetzen U. J., *A brief account of the Countries adjoining the Lake of Tiberias, the Jordan, and the Dead Sea*, London 1810.

Segal A., Mlynarczyk J., Burdajewicz M., *Hippos (Sussita). Third Season of Excavations. July 2002,* Haifa 2002.

Segal A., Mlynarczyk J., Burdajewicz M. *et alii*, *Hippos (Sussita). Fifth Season of Excavations (September-October 2004),* Haifa 2004.

Segal A., Mlynarczyk J., Burdajewicz M. *et alii*, *Hippos (Sussita). Seventh Season of Excavations (July 2006),* Haifa 2006.

Segal A., Mlynarczyk J., Burdajewicz M., *Hippos (Sussita). First Season of Excavations. July 2000,* Haifa 2000.

Segal A., Mlynarczyk J., Burdajewicz M., *Hippos (Sussita). Second Season of Excavations. July 2001,* Haifa 2001.

Segal A., Mlynarczyk J., Burdajewicz M. *et alii*, *Hippos (Sussita). Ninth Season of Excavations (June-July 2008),* Haifa 2008.

Shachar I. "The historical and numismatic significance of Alexander Jannaeus's later coinage as found in archaeological excavations", *PEQ* 136 (2004), pp. 5–33.

Shamma S., *al-Nuqūd al-islāmiyya allatī ḍuribat fī-l-Filasṭīn*, s.l., 1400/1980.

Shamma S., *A Catalogue of ʿAbbasid Copper Coins*, London 1998.

Sharabani M., "Coins", in Tzaferis V., "The Excavation of Kursi-Gergesa", *ʿAtiqot* 16 (1983), pp. 39–40.

Sharabani M., "Coins from the Late Roman-Byzantine Bathhouse at Bet She'an", *ʿAtiqot* 46 (2004), pp. 83–86.

Shneydor N. A., "The Inscriptions on Modern Palestinian and Israeli Currency", *INR* 4 (2009), pp. 159–172.

Sigismund M., "Small Change? Coins and Weights as a Mirror of Ethnic, Religious and Political Identity in 1st/2nd Century C. E. Tiberias", in *Religion and Ethnicity* 2007, pp. 315–336.

Solarewicz B., "Pieniądz pograniczu Trzech Kultur Monety z Kościola w Hippos, w Dekapolis (Izrael), in Pieniądz na pograniczah/Currency in borderlands", *Acta Archaeologica Lodziensia* 61 (2015), pp. 39–48.

Sole L., "Nuove considerazioni sull'unità ponderale della prima serie monetale di Biblo", *Transeuphratène* 20 (2000), pp. 61–72.

Soler R., *Edward Robinson (1794–1863) et l'émergence de l'archéologue biblique,* Paris 2014.

Sourdel D., *Filasṭīn*, *Encyclopaedia of Islam* II: *C-G*, Leiden 1991, pp. 910–913.

Spijkerman A., "A Hoard of Syrian Tetradrachms and Eastern Antoniniani", *LA* 9 (1958–1959), pp. 568–584.

Spijkerman A., *Cafarnao*, Vol. III: *Catalogo delle monete della città*, Jerusalem 1975.

Stella A., *Aquileia tardoantica. Moneta, storia ed economia*, Trieste 2019 (Polymnia. Numismatica antica e medievale. Studi 13).

Sutherland G. V., "The pattern of monetary development in Phoenicia and Palestine during the early empire", in Kindler A. (ed.), *Proceedings of the International Numismatic Convention. Jerusalem 27–31 December 1963*, Tel Aviv 1967, pp. 88–105.

Syon D., "Kisas", *Hadashot Arkheologiyot* 112 (2000), pp. 2–7.

Syon D., "A Hoard of Byzantine Solidi from Hurvat Kab", *INJ* 14 (2000–2002), pp. 211–223.

Syon D., "The Coins from Migdal", *ʿAtiqot* 42 (2002), pp. 33–36 (Hebr.).

Syon D., "Omrit. The Coins (1999–2001)", in Overman J. A., Schowalter D. N. (eds.), *The Roman Temple Complex at Horvat Omrit. An Interim Report*, Oxford 2011 (BAR.I 2205), pp. 105–122.

Syon D., "Galilean Mints in the Early Roman Period. Politics, Economy, and Ethnicity", in Jacobson, Kokkinos 2012, pp. 65–84.

Syon D., "The Coins", in Syon D. (ed.), *Gamla III. The Shmarya Gutmann Excavations 1976–1989 Finds and Studies. Part 1*, Jerusalem 2014 (IAA Reports 56), pp. 109–231.

Syon D., *Small Change in Hellenistic-Roman Galilee. The Evidence from Numismatic Site Finds as a Tool for Historical Reconstruction*, Jerusalem 2015.

Syon D., "The Hellenistic, Roman and Byzantine Coins", in Hartal M., Syon D., Stern E., Tatcher A. (eds.), *ʿAkko II. The 1991–1998 Excavations. The Early Periods*, Jerusalem 2016 (IAA Reports 60), pp. 203–226.

Syon D., "Coins", *ʿAtiqot* 90 (2018), pp. 117–119.

Syon D., "The Hasmonean Settlement in Galilee. A Numismatic Perspective", in Berlin M. A., Kosmin J. P. (eds.), *The Middle Maccabees. Archaeology, History and the Rise of the Hasmonean Kingdom*, Atlanta 2021, pp. 177–192.

Taylor J. E., "Missing Magdala and the Name of Mary 'Magdalene'", *PEQ* 146 (2014), pp. 205–223.

Testa E., Mancini I., Piccirillo M. (eds.), *Studia Hierosolymitana in onore del P. Bellarmino Bagatti, I. Studi archeologici,* Jerusalem 1976 (Collectio Maior 22).

Testaferri F., "Magdala. Una cittadina al tempo di Gesù. Breve storia delle fasi dell'esplorazione archeologica", *LA* 65 (2015), pp. 407–429.

Tzaferis V., *Excavations at Capernaum*, Vol. I: *1978–1982*, Winona Lake 1989.

Vaselá M., *Alois Musil (1868–1944): Archaeology of late antiquity and the beginning of Islamic archaeology in the Middle East*, PhD Thesis Západočeská univerzita v Plzni, Université de Paris I Panthéon – Sorbonne 2021.

Vorderstrasse T., "Byzantine and Early Islamic Coinage at Excavations in Jericho", in Oddy A., Schulze I., Schulze W. (eds.), *Coinage and History in the Seventh Century Near East 4 – Proceedings of the 14th Seventh Century Syrian Numismatic Round Table held at The Hive, Worcester, on 28th and 29th September 2013*, Exeter 2015, pp. 37–51.

Walker J., *A Catalogue of the Muḥammadan Coins in the British Museum, II: A Catalogue of the Arab-Byzantine and Post-Reform Umaiyad Coins*, London 1956.

Walker D. R., *The Metrology of the Roman Silver Coinage, from Pertinax to Uranius Antoninus*, Oxford 1978 (*BAR.S* 40).

Walmsley A., "Coinage and the Economy of Syria-Palestine in the Seventh and Eighth Centuries CE", in Haldon J. (ed.), *Money, Power and Politics in Early Islamic Syria. A review of current database*, Princeton 2010, pp. 21–44.

Walmsley A., "Coin Frequencies in Sixth and Seventh Century Palestine and Arabia: Social and Economic Implications", *Journal of the Economic and Social History of the Orient* 42 (1999), pp. 326–350.

Waner M., Safrai Z., "A Catalogue of Coin Hoards and the Shelf Life of Coins in Palestine Hoards During the Roman and Byzantine Periods", *LA* 51 (2001), pp. 305–336.

Wilson C. W., "The bronze and silver coins", in Tzaferis 1989, pp. 139–143.

Wilson C. W., "The gold hoard", in Tzaferis 1989, pp. 145–190.

Wolff S., Stern I., Erlich A., "A newly discovered Tanit pendant from Maresha", *Rivista di Studi Fenici* 46 (2018), pp. 29–42.

Zangenberg J.K, Attridge H. W., Martin D. B. (eds.), *Religion, Ethnicity, and Identity in Ancient Galilee. A Region in Transition*, Tübingen 2007.

Zangenberg J. K., "Archaeological News from the Galilee. Tiberias, Magdala und Rural Galilee", *Early Christianity* 1 (2010), pp. 471–484.

Zangenberg J. K., "Anchoring Ancient Galilee at the Lakeshore Towards Re-conceptualizing Ancient Galilee as a Mediterranean Environment", *Early Christianity* 10 (2019), pp. 265–291.

Zapata-Meza M., Garza-Diaz Barriga A., Sanz-Rincón R., "The Magdala Archaeological Project (2010–2012). A Preliminary Report of the Excavations at Migdal", *'Atiqot* 90 (2018), pp. 83–125.

Zayadine F., "Une tombe nabatéenne près de Dhat-Râs", *Syria* 47 (1970), pp. 117–135.

Zilli S., *Sir Richard F. Burton, Trieste e l'esplorazione. Gli itinerari nel mondo,* Trieste 2019.

Zissu B. *et alii*, "Coins from the Bar Kokhba Revolt Hidden in Me'arat Ha-Te'omim (Mŭghâret Umm et Tûeimîn), Western Jerusalem Hills", *INJ* 17 (2009–2010), pp. 113–147.

Zlotnik Y., *Alexander Jannaeus' coins and their dates*, www.ins.org.il/Publications.htm

Zuckerman C., *Du village à l'empire. Autour du registre fiscal d'Aphroditô (525/526)*, Paris 2004.